THE ROBE AND THE LEDGER

"In a world of Robes and Jabots, truth is the one thing nobody can afford."

Alex Matthews

The Mamashimi Trust - Brisbane Australia

This book analyzes recurring patterns in institutional crisis handling using publicly available records and materials. Many chapters are introduced as **"Composite"**. A Composite chapter is a dramatized, illustrative scenario that blends elements from multiple public matters and has been materially altered (including names, timelines, locations, roles, and other identifying details) to avoid depicting any specific individual, proceeding, or institution. Composite chapters are included for narrative clarity and thematic illustration and are **not** presented as a verbatim or definitive account of any particular case. Where the book discusses factual material drawn from public sources, those sources are identified in chapter introductions, notes, or references. Any errors are unintentional. All interpretations, opinions, and conclusions are the author's. Any resemblance to actual persons or specific matters is coincidental or arises from the generalized nature of the issues discussed.

The author and publisher acknowledge the Traditional Owners of Country throughout Australia and acknowledge their continuing connection to land, waters and community. We pay our respects to the people, the cultures and the Elders past and present. Aboriginal and Torres Strait Islander people should know that this book might include stories featuring deceased individuals, though these characters are fictional. Book cover by the author.

Illustrations by unknown artist/s

The Robe and The Ledger | First edition, Sydney, Australia | Amsterdam, Netherlands 2026 1-1,000

Online contact with author and book shop: www.robeledger.com or www.books.by/robes-ledgers
Online orders: ISBN: 978-1-7644567-0-8   Email author: alexmatthewsauthor@gmail.com

Contents

PRELIMINARY MATTER

THE MAMASHIMI TRUST - BRISBANE AUSTRALIA

HOW TO READ THIS BOOK - PRGR QUICK START

PERSONAL REASON-GIVING RECORD

The author organized the book into five Parts that move from lived experience to analysis and, finally, to practical tools. **Part I** introduces the core problem and its human stakes. **Part II** traces how the system works in practice and how failure becomes normalized. **Part III** sets out the book's central pattern-mechanism and shows how it reproduces itself across institutions. **Part IV** deepens the analysis through structured comparisons and recurring motifs, sharpening the reader's ability to recognize the same dynamics in different settings. **Part V** turns recognition into action, offering a clear framework and concrete pathways for response and reform. All may hold elements of a memoir, institutional critique, composite case files, and policy blueprint.

To reinforce and train pattern-recognition, the book includes **33** case files, added not as side-stories but as deliberate exercises-each one designed to deepen understanding and help readers *see the repeating structure* behind apparently unrelated events.

The back matter includes **five appendices** (expanded case file material, methodological and supporting resources, and practical reference tools), a **glossary** of key terms, and a navigational structure that lets readers either follow the main argument straight through or move between cases, concepts, PRGR-END CAPS and tools as needed.

PRGR stands for Personal Reason-Giving Record. In plain terms: whenever an institution takes (or permits) an action that can cause irreversible harm, someone must write the reasons and sign their name to the decision.

You will see a **PRGR END-CAP** at the end of certain cases (21 in total). Use it as a reader's instrument:

- Identify the primary mechanism (Money, Intimacy, or Procedure).
- Locate the decision-point that made harm easier to deny or diffuse.
- Ask what would have changed if that step required a signed reason and a remedy trigger.

If you want the full technical detail (triggers, countersignatures, module-by-module use), see Appendix B: THE LINE THAT CANNOT BE CROSSED. Readers who feel fatigued by the case files might benefit from jumping to Appendix B to re-engage with the mechanics of the solution before continuing.

PERSONAL REASON-GIVING RECORD (PRGR) AS TEST CONDITION

HARM MUST BE AUTHORED. THE FORECAST MUST BE WRITTEN. REPAIR MUST BE PRE-COMMITTED.

A test condition is only useful if it can be run. PRGR is not a slogan; it is a small procedural lock that forces an institution to stop speaking in fog.

PRGR in one sentence:

Foreseeable harm must have a named author, a written forecast, and a pre-committed repair trigger.

THE PRGR RECORD (one page, max)

A decision cannot proceed past the last reversible step until this record exists and is stored in a place that can be audited.

- Decision being taken (plain language).
- Decision-author (name, role) and reviewer (name, role).
- Facts relied on (what you believe to be true; what you have not checked).

• Foreseeable harm (what could happen to a person if you are wrong).

• Why you believe the act is justified despite that risk.

• Disclosure statement (what has been shared with the affected person; what has been withheld, and why).

• Remedy trigger (what automatically happens if later evidence shows you were wrong).

• Review date (when this must be reopened even if nobody complains).

WHEN PRGR IS REQUIRED

PRGR is required whenever an institution is about to do something that cannot be cleanly undone, or that will predictably silence challenge.

Use it before:

• Irreversible steps (dismissal, expulsion, custody transfer, conviction, sentencing, deportation, removal of credentials).

• Reputation locks (labels like "vexatious", "unreliable", "non-compliant" that become fate).

• Secrecy walls (redactions, sealed files, privilege claims, "handled internally").

• Concentrated access (one person controlling funds, files, keys, archives, schedules, or confessional knowledge).

• Any trade-off that buys quiet (donor pressure, informal settlements, "pastoral discretion", career threats).

WHAT PRGR CHANGES IN PRACTICE

It does not assume angels. It assumes ordinary humans in robes will drift toward convenience unless the drift has a cost.

PRGR removes four escape hatches:

1) Passive voice (it happened) → active authorship (I did it).

2) Time as a weapon (wait them out) → mandatory review dates.

3) Secrecy as virtue (discretion) → auditability and stated reasons.

4) 'Process' as alibi → process as a signed choice with consequences.

REMEDY TRIGGERS (the 'R' in PRGR)

A remedy trigger is not punishment; it is a pre-agreed repair path that activates without begging.

Choose one or more, appropriate to the case:

• Automatic reopen / rehearing when a defined doubt threshold is met.

• Independent review (external to the chain of command that benefited).

• Immediate preservation order (no disposal, no 'lost files').

• Temporary stay (pause irreversible steps until review is complete).

• Restitution pathway (financial return, reinstatement, correction of record).

• Referral trigger (mandatory reporting to a body with power to act).

MINI RERUN (how to use this book)

Pick any scene you have just read and rerun it in three questions:

1) Who is the author of the harm here-name, not title?

2) What harm was foreseeable at the time, not in hindsight?

3) What remedy would have triggered automatically if the author was wrong?

Now ask yourself:

If you had to sign the PRGR record, would you still proceed as you did-or would you slow down, disclose more, recuse, or refuse?

AUTHORED HARM - QUICK END-CAP

Where the book shows a failure, rerun the scene under one structural requirement:

Harm must be authored. The forecast must be written. Repair must be pre-committed.

A WARNING FROM THE ROBES

CONSTRAINING POWER - STRESS TEST

The robes speak, though they no longer watch. The jabots whisper still, though their threads are silent. What follows in these pages are glimpses-stories drawn from public records, shaped to reveal the machinery of authority and the human flaws it conceals. They are mirrors, not verdicts. The records that feed these accounts are never neutral. They arrive trimmed by procedure, filtered by discretion, and sometimes softened by settlement language or sealed files. Silence can be a deliberate instrument; so can formality. A signature, a stamp, a robe, a collar-each can steady standalone the public gaze while misdirection does its work. When the record is incomplete, the omission is part of the story: absence is often the loudest evidence.

Some stories stand alone-single cases drawn from public records. Others share the same core, the same patterns, the same merit. These are presented as composite stories: blends of facts, actions, and behaviors of multiple individuals, embodied in a single narrative. Their purpose is not accusation but illumination-showing how authority, ritual, and human weakness intersect repeatedly across time and place.

Many stories contain sensitive material, including sexual harassment, unwanted solicitation, abuse of power, and other forms of misconduct. Readers should proceed with caution.

No person is guilty of any act or misconduct unless proven so before a court of law. The garments may tremble with history, the halls may echo with judgment, but the law alone carries the ultimate word.

Read these as mirrors, not verdicts. Track the pattern, not the costume. Where judgment belongs, I leave it: to evidence, to testimony, to justice.

If you feel a verdict rising in you, pause. Ask first what the mechanism bought-and who paid for it. The law has always tried to bind power without making governance impossible. But safeguards often become a second costume: they make decisions look clean even when the human choice inside them is not.

What matters for this book is not the history lesson. It is the recurring trade: institutions exchange responsibility for procedure, then call the result legitimacy.

STRESS TEST (not theory):

- When something goes wrong, does the system name an author-or does it name a process?
- Does oversight create truth-or only paperwork?
- Does transparency reveal decisions-or merely distribute documents?

If you want one structural safeguard that doesn't become ritual, make harm ownable: no decision that foreseeably harms a person stands without a signed author and a remedy trigger.

THE ROBES AND THE LEDGER

ROBES, JABOTS AND HUMAN FAILURE; A SYSTEM MUST NAME AN AUTHOR.

"Ubi toga fulget, jabot superbit, umbra regnat."

"Where the robe shines, the jabot prides, the shadow rules."

"Wo der Talar glänzt, der Jabot sich brüstet, herrscht der Schatten."

"Là où la robe brille, le jabot s'enorgueillit, l'ombre règne."

"Waar de toga glanst, de bef pronkt, heerst de schaduw."

"Dove la toga splende, il jabot si inorgoglisce, governa l'ombra."

"Donde la toga brilla, el jabot se enorgullece, manda la sombra."

"Kung saan kumikinang ang toga, nagmamalaki ang jabot, ang anino ang naghahari."

"San áit a lonraíonn an róba, a dhéanann an jabóid mórtas, rialaíonn an scáth."

WHY THIS BOOK WAS NECESSARY

PREFACE

This book's purpose is not to accuse individuals or expose sensational wrongdoing. The author wrote it because certain forms of harm persist precisely where wrongdoing is least visible: in institutions that function correctly, follow procedure, and speak the language of legitimacy.

The cases gathered in "The Robe and The Ledger" share a disturbing feature. No single moment reveals clear malice. We cannot easily isolate any individual as "the villain."

Instead, harm emerges gradually, quietly, and lawfully-through decisions that are formally justified and professionally defensible. This is precisely what makes these cases difficult to confront and easy to dismiss. The central claim of this book is that justice can fail even when the system works as intended.

Modern institutions rely on specialisation, hierarchy, and procedural rationality. These features are indispensable to governance and law. Yet they also carry a moral cost by fragmenting responsibility, displacing ethical judgment, and encouraging individuals to act without fully owning the consequences of their actions.

Over time, this produces what the book names human failure-not as a moral insult, but as a predictable outcome of institutional life.

Here, the robe and the jabot do not symbolize corruption. They are symbols of authority stripped of responsibility. They represent roles so stabilised that the human being within them is no longer expected to answer the most basic ethical question: Should this be done?

This book adopts a unified approach to its cases because the harm described is not episodic. The harm occurs in a patterned way. To treat each case as an isolated failure would be to miss what connects them: a recurring architecture of obedience, fear, procedural loyalty, and moral silence.

The aim is not to dismantle institutions, but to remind them of a truth they often resist: without personal moral responsibility, legitimacy becomes a mask rather than a foundation.

This book therefore speaks to victims, critics, and institutional actors alike. It asks whether justice can survive when those entrusted with it no longer experience themselves as morally accountable agents.

Disclaimer: The stories are works of fiction. Characters are composites. Any resemblance is coincidental. Patterns seen across many documented events inspired stories.

INTRODUCTION

ONE MUST FIRST UNDERSTAND THE COSTUMES THAT ALLOW INSTITUTIONS TO SPEAK WITHOUT WORDS.

Throughout various institutions such as courts, parliaments, universities, and religious establishments, robes and jabots serve as a powerful visual representation of authority. These garments, while not designed for practicality, often hinder movement, obscure the wearer's physical form, and diminish personal identity. Despite their limitations, people have preserved and regulated them over centuries, reflecting a deep-seated reverence for tradition. The dress codes governing these items vary significantly across different jurisdictions and organisations, yet they share a common aim: to convey legitimacy, establish hierarchy, and create a sense of distance between the authority figures and the public.

In certain legal frameworks, the design of the robe is purposefully austere and uniform, aimed at suppressing individual expression in favor of a cohesive institutional identity. Conversely, other systems embrace more elaborate designs, featuring ornate jabots, vibrant colors, or intricate trims that openly signify rank and seniority. These minor distinctions in fabric and style often reveal profound cultural values-balancing humility against spectacle, transparency against mystique, and accountability against reverence. For instance, people in one nation may perceive a white jabot as a neutral accessory, while people in another nation see it as a symbol of heightened moral authority. Such variations transcend simple aesthetics; they are deeply rooted in ideological frameworks that shape societal perceptions of power and legitimacy.

The implications of dress codes extend beyond mere identification of roles; they also play a crucial role in shaping behavior. The robe acts as a barrier, separating the wearer from the everyday world, which can elevate their judgment or, conversely, shield them from accountability. People often interpret any deviation as a sign of disrespect towards the institution itself in environments where strict regulations govern attire. In contrast, customary practices maintain adherence to tradition where dress codes are more relaxed, rather than formal enforcement. In both scenarios, clothing functions as a silent yet potent language, guiding observers in their judgments about whom to trust, whom to fear, and whom to challenge.

This book seeks to explore robes and jabots not merely as historical artifacts or fashion statements, but as instruments of power that can uphold dignity and impartiality while simultaneously obscuring accountability and facilitating failure. The variations in dress codes across different systems reveal how power manifests itself and highlight the ease with which symbols intended to promote justice can overshadow the individuals they represent. The institution remains largely a flat antagonist: it resists change, defaults to concealment, and only reforms reactively after exposure. Its arc is steadiness rather than moral growth - it adopts reforms in ways that preserve continuity rather than accepting full authorship. That flat arc is accurate because institutional incentives push toward containment and veneer rather than full transformation. That is why they will be the biggest opponent. I will introduce the PRGR to you. PRGR stands for Personal Reason-Giving Record. In plain terms: whenever an institution takes (or permits) an action that can cause irreversible harm, someone must write the reasons and sign their name to the decision. We can feel the resistance starting - and I want to name it without escalating it.

If your first impulse is to dispute, discredit, or defend, I'd ask: **why begin with a fight before you've even tested whether this could reduce foreseeable harm?** A defensive posture may protect the institution's image in the short term, but it also signals that the primary goal is containment rather than learning.

My claim is not that "institutions are evil." My claim is structural: institutions protect **continuity** and treat accountability as a reputational risk, so reform arrives reactively after exposure. If you believe that characterization is unfair, here is a concrete way to prove it wrong:

Engage the PRGR as an empirical test. Don't argue intentions. Don't argue my tone.

Argue outcomes. To critique PRGR objectively, you would need to show one (or more) of the following with evidence:

1. **PRGR does not reduce preventable harm** in your context (measure harm indicators before/after).
2. **PRGR undermines procedural fairness** (show where it conflicts with due process and why mitigations can't work).
3. **PRGR creates perverse incentives** (e.g., risk dumping, scapegoating, over-caution) that outweigh benefits.
4. **Existing mechanisms already provide equivalent transparency and authorship** (show the documents, triggers, and signatory accountability you already use).
5. **PRGR is not implementable at a reasonable cost** compared with the cost of current failures (show the operational model and trade-offs).

If you can show-cleanly, with data and examples-that PRGR doesn't work for your institution, I will publish that critique as part of the record. But if the response is only denial, outrage, or a character argument, then it confirms the very dynamic under discussion: **defense first, learning later**.

So I'm offering a simple starting point:

Pick one high-stakes decision pathway where foreseeable harm occurs. Pilot PRGR for a defined period. Measure what changes. Then we can talk like adults about results rather than narratives.

To understand human failure within institutions, one must first understand the costumes that allow those institutions to speak without words.

PART I

SETUP, FIRST SHOCKS, LENS

THE MAMASHIMI TRUST - BRISBANE AUSTRALIA

PROLOGUE

JUSTICE IS NOT BLIND. SOMETIMES, IT SIMPLY PEEKS THE OTHER WAY.

I did not begin with a theory. I started with a loss: the moment you realize duty's language can form a curtain. Once you have watched that curtain descend-once you have paid the private cost of someone else's public composure-you stop mistaking calm for truth.

That is the change this book documents in me as much as in the institutions it describes. I used to read decisions as if they were primarily about facts. I used to think that if the evidence was clear, the outcome would follow.

My stance was epistemic trust: the assumption that procedures exist to discover reality.

Now I read the way the institution reads. I ask what a phrase buys. I ask what a delay buys. I ask what 'policy' protects and what it permits. I look for the human hand inside the glove. Not because cynicism is wiser than hope, but because hope without authorship becomes an accomplice. No one tells you, when you first step into the law, that tradition and illusion equally hold the profession together. The robes, the jabots, the solemn nods across polished timber benches-these are costumes in a theatre where every actor insists the script is sacred, even when they scribble their own lines in the margins. I believed in that script once. I believed in fairness, integrity, and the quiet dignity of service. I then learned how easily those with two faces can expertly twist those ideals.

I am a former lawyer-former, by choice and not by choice. Some of the very people who walk through the pages of this book disbarred me. They sit on the benches of justice, stand at the bar table, hover in chambers with an air of moral certainty. They speak of ethics, yet many cannot see their own reflections without flinching. Their public face beams with authority and righteousness; their private one whispers deals, grudges, indulgences, and secrets better left behind locked doors and closed curtains. I had the misfortune of meeting both faces. The first encounter with the system occurred on the very day and just minutes after I took my oath as a barrister and solicitor. Clad in my new fine wool toga and pristine jabot, I made my way on a cold, bright day in February to the court signage, which was along the road of about one hundred metres from the main entrance of the district court, separated by a pond with a huge fountain, splashing water, renewing oxygen levels in the water. A symbol of a refreshing start to a career I never thought possible. My employer asked me to capture some photos in that scene for his office website. Just two days later I received a letter from the staff holder issuing me a first warning, emphasising that my toga and jabot were not a carnival costume. I still have that letter, a blend of shock and amusement forever etched in my memory, and I now know exactly where to categorise it within my collection of experiences.I asked the National Bar of Advocates to end my registration as a lawyer effective 31 December 2013. By then, the robe no longer fit.

I made my decision months earlier. In October 2013, I changed course and informed the staff holder responsible for my file. I still believed that within the folds of the institution, candour had a place. I was mistaken.

The letter-writing staff holder's term ended. And another one appeared on the stage. The journey is smooth. Curtains closed for this staff holder and the person who later filed a complaint against me, appeared on the stage of the theatre. The presiding staff holder framed the charge using procedural language, as is customary for such matters: failure to comply with instructions to hand over private and office financial records. The refusal was real. The reason was simple. It was the fourth request within twelve months. The previous three inspections had produced nothing-no findings, no fault, no stain upon the cloth. Yet the hands kept returning to the same pocket, as if persistence itself might conjure guilt.

There was a reason.

Between 2009 and 2011, I sat on a committee that examined the financial statements of the local Supervisory Board before the local members of the Bar reviewed and approved them during the annual meeting, as the law required. In 2011, I wore the chairperson's robe. The role came with a script. The chair was expected to recite the same text at the annual meeting each year-words polished smooth by repetition, emptied of meaning but heavy with reassurance. The only thing that changed in the text were the names of the members of the committee and the change in the annual membership fee the lawyers have to pay.

That year, I refused to read the script. I did not tell anybody. Instead, I spoke plainly.

Behind the management table occupied by the Members of the Supervisory Board, the robes stiffened. Faces flushed red, not with shame, but with outrage. Among the members, indignation spread quickly, for I had disturbed the choreography in their favor. I had treated the ceremony as a forum rather than a performance. In institutions built on appearance, this is the unforgivable sin. But something remarkable happened: the members called for an independent committee to explore my findings. The Board intentionally did not record any of the previous points because time will pass and other things will become more important for the members, causing them to forget these points.

The cost was my position.

Not long after, I received a visit. The staff holder returned, accompanied by a member of the Supervisory Board. Their soft, almost compassionate message came across. I could, they said, become the lawyer with the most complaints on record. A prediction offered as advice. A threat wrapped in civility. The robe, they reminded me, protects those who obey - and bruises those who do not.

This is where my professional story is often said to end. It does not.

My fall from their graces was not spectacular. There was no scandal, no crime, no smoking gun-just a quiet, calculated erasure. A decision made by those who needed a cautionary tale, or perhaps simply someone to blame or to get rid of because I entered their world behind the curtains, they desperately wanted to be kept closed. I became a footnote in their minutes, a name crossed out with a flourish. But disbarment did something they did not expect: it freed me. It allowed me to speak. It allowed me to see behind the facades they guard so desperately. I became the stage manager while the theatre moved on. I could open and close the curtains whenever I wanted again.

Sustained glimpses-stories gathered across years from corridors and courtrooms, from robing rooms and offices, from publicly accessible sources and from the dim margins where truth is deliberately kept small-formed this book. The figures you will meet here, reduced to their essence, are real people. The writer veiled their identities. Their conduct is not.

Their habits, their vanities, their cowardice, and their cruelties remain intact. Some drink too much. Some believe too readily in their own virtue. Some know far less than the authority of their robes implies. Some bend rules until they break, then blame the fracture on procedure. Some smile as they push the knife. Some kneel in prayer while committing abuse behind closed doors. These are not exceptions. People tolerate them, enable them, and quietly protect them.

Each of them helped construct the system that shaped me-and ultimately destroyed my place within it. Not through conspiracy, but through compliance. Not through evil acts alone, but through routine indifference, selective blindness, and the disciplined refusal to intervene.

This book is not about me. I am a part of it. Some will accuse it of bitterness, of grievance, of revenge. They are wrong. I made my choices. I could have remained silent. Silence was available, encouraged, and rewarded. I chose instead to speak. For that, I accept full responsibility.

Others paid a price alongside me. Staff, my wife and children, my family, friends-drawn unwillingly into the fallout of my decision. That is the only regret I carry. Institutions recover quickly. People do not. Life continues, but it does not absolve.

If there is one lesson this book insists upon, it is this: facades work. They work frighteningly well. The robe does not merely conceal misconduct; it legitimises it. Two faces are not an anomaly in such systems-they are a survival strategy. No one is immune. Not clients. Not colleagues. Not officers of the court. Not even those who share offices, lunches, and laughter with the very people who will later deny knowing anything at all. If PRGR had existed when I was disbarred, someone would have had to do what the institution avoided most: **write to me as the harmed person and sign the harm in plain language**.

Not "the respondent is unsuitable." Not "the standards require." Not "confidence in the profession." Those are curtains.

A PRGR would have forced one responsible signatory-the smallest role with real stop-power-to write something like:

You are being removed from your profession. The foreseeable harms are permanent loss of livelihood, loss of status, reputational stain that will follow you into other work, financial collapse through reduced earning capacity, and long-term psychological impact. The sanction will also impair your ability to repay debts and maintain stability, which may later be used as evidence against you. We accept these harms.

We accept them because we believe your conduct makes you unfit to practise, and because lesser measures would not protect the public, the court, and the credibility of the Bar to the degree we consider necessary.

We considered less harmful alternatives: a time-limited suspension with strict conditions; supervised practice; restriction from certain case types; mandatory oversight and audits; a structured remediation plan with measurable benchmarks; staged return contingent on performance and compliance. We rejected these because [*the specific reasons must be stated here, tied to the facts, not to the language of fear*]. That is what PRGR would have demanded: not sympathy, but **authored causation**-a signed admission that the institution is choosing a human cost and believes the cost is justified.

And if they could not write it without hiding behind "process," they would have had to face the possibility that what they were doing was not ethics but theater.

Justice is not blind. Sometimes, it simply peeks the other way. What follows is a revelation.

My full account appears in "THE WARNING LETTER of THE QUIET ERASURE". The epilogue explains what happens after the robe is set aside.

Welcome to the world behind the ledgers, the robes and jabots, the cassocks and stoles, the mantles and ceremonial collars, where Justice is not blind. Sometimes, it simply peeks the other way.

Brisbane, February 2026
Alex Matthews

THE AUTHOR HAS TO EXIST

I NOTICE WHAT I'M DEFENDING: JUSTICE, OR THE COSTUME OF IT.

In my case there wasn't an author. I should correct myself: there was a clerk, dutifully copying the standard and attaching my particulars like labels on a file. The "judges" evaporated. One stepped back before the start and was replaced. One retired after the hearing-replaced by someone who never saw me, never heard my voice. In the verdict, my defense barely existed, as if it didn't matter enough to be named.

By the time you finish the first handful of chapters, the faces start to blur. The way my judges would not recognise me in the street. I was a case number. A magistrate, a bishop, a professor-different costumes, same motion: truth gets "heard" and then seated against the wall where it can't reach consequence. That sameness isn't a flaw. It's the clue. I built the book to make the repetition visible, because repetition is how systems confess without meaning to.

> So here is the one PRGR point you should carry forward: a system must name an author, not a process.

PRGR demands one responsible signatory-one human being who cannot hide behind "committee," "policy," or "the office." I've watched institutions survive by turning harm into weather-something that "happened," not something someone did. PRGR breaks that spell. If a decision can't survive a human signature, it shouldn't survive at all. And if I feel defensive reading that, I notice what I'm protecting: justice, or the costume of it.

1

"THE INVISIBLE HAND, THE ENKOLPION, AND THE MANTLE"

THREE THRESHOLDS. THREE DOORS. THREE VERSIONS OF AUTHORITY PUTTING ITSELF ON.

08:14 - THE CORRIDOR / THE SACRISTY / THE LAB

While Magistrate Giovanni Bellini walked into his courtroom, Professor Jonathan Reed entered the laboratory. While Reed's incubators hummed into warmth, Bishop Gregorios Kalogeris fastened his enkolpion to his chest and checked his reflection in a piece of polished metal that had once been a mirror and was now an instrument of composure.

Three thresholds. Three doors. Three versions of authority putting itself on.

Bellini's robe did what robes are designed to do: it made the person inside it less personal. It made his movements appear ordained rather than chosen. In the corridor outside Courtroom Two, portraits of predecessors watched him pass-oil-painted faces whose eyes said, without saying: We outlasted complaints. Reed's mantle was not fabric in the lab; it was reputation. It was the ceremonial stole he wore on conference stages, the polished language of innovation, the unspoken privilege that comes with being the one everyone calls a "leader in the field." He loved control the way certain men love silence: not for peace, but for ownership.

Gregorios' enkolpion, gold, icon, chain, rested over his heart like a visible vow. It gleamed. It reassured. It said: trust this chest, even if you cannot see inside it.

None of them woke up that morning thinking, Today I will cross the line. They woke up thinking, Today I must keep the institution stable.

Stewards who confuse survival with virtue cross the line everywhere, not monsters.

08:31 - THE FIRST CONSTRAINT

While Bellini placed his file on the bench and skimmed an agenda written in the antiseptic language of procedure, Reed opened a shared drive and saw a folder renamed overnight-cleaner, neater, less likely to frighten a sponsor. While Reed's cursor hovered, Gregorios listened to his finance officer whisper numbers like a confession: debt, repair costs, delayed salaries, the shelter budget that never stretched far enough.

The first constraint always arrives before the crisis. It arrives as a small narrowing:

In law, it is admissibility-what truth is "allowed" to be.

In Church, it is unity-what truth is "helpful."

In science, it is direction-what truth is "publishable," "fundable," "strategic."

Constraining power does not need to smash truth. It only needs to make truth expensive to speak.

Bellini had learned to love the clean logic of the law because it promised order. But he had also learned-slowly, safely, profitably-that editing order was possible. A case delayed is a case softened. A hearing postponed is a hearing that loses public heat. A procedural wrinkle becomes a rope: you can pull someone back by calling it a "technicality."

Reed had learned to love the clean logic of data because it promised certainty. Yet, he also discovered, slowly, safely, and professionally, that framing data was possible. A negative result becomes "inconclusive." A failed replication becomes "outlier contamination." A rough edge becomes a "limitations section." Language becomes the velvet rope around inconvenient numbers.

Gregorios had learned to love the clean logic of doctrine because it promised moral clarity.

But he had also learned-slowly, safely, pastorally-that he could deploy doctrine. We can turn forgiveness into a gag. Patience can become a leash. Framing "avoid scandal" as "protect the faithful" is an option.

The misuse is not new. What is new is how gracefully it now presents itself as governance.

08:52 - LUCIA / EMILY / ANDREAS

While Bellini's clerk called the court to order, Lucia Romano sat at her desk with the posture of someone trained to be invisible and therefore trained to notice everything. In her first year, she had believed invisibility was safety. After ten years, she knew it was also a kind of slow violence: you learn to watch your own reactions as if they are irrelevant evidence.

Lucia's father had been a man who respected uniforms. A meter reader for the city, he used to tell her that rules were what separated ordinary people from chaos. "Follow the process," he said, "and the process will follow you back." When she took her job as clerk, she repeated that sentence like prayer. She liked the work because it was clean. It had stamps and dates and the hard comfort of procedure. It gave her the illusion that if you did things properly, harm could be contained.

Then she began to see how harm wears proper clothes.

It started with something small, the kind of thing you can dismiss if you want to keep sleeping: a file that disappeared for two days and returned without a trace of who had handled it. A signature that appeared on a document that had not been signed in the room. A defendant asking-quietly, ashamedly-whether it was normal that the judge had spoken to his lawyer in chambers without him.

Lucia told herself she didn't know. Lucia told herself it wasn't her job. Lucia told herself she was lucky to have stability in a city where stability was rare.

And then one afternoon an intern-young, eager, still believing in the romance of courtrooms-came out of an office with her face rearranged. Not crying. Not dramatic. Just altered, like a person who has been instructed to distrust her own mind.

Lucia offered her water. The intern said, "It's nothing," and Lucia heard, in that nothing, a decade of trained minimization.

That was Lucia's first shift: she stopped thinking of her invisibility as protection and started noticing it as access. If you are overlooked, you can move through rooms collecting what powerful people forget to hide. She began to keep copies. Nothing dramatic. Just duplicates. An extra printout filed at home under old tax records. A diary that did not look like a diary: dates, case numbers, the time a file changed hands, the time a door closed.

Her desire was not heroism. Her desire was to never be blamed. In her office, blame moved downhill like water. She had watched other clerks become scapegoats for decisions they did not make. She had learned to survive by being impeccable.

Now impeccability became evidence.

But evidence is not action. Evidence can be a way of postponing action. Lucia told herself she was "preparing," which is a polite word for fear.

The moment that broke her was not an abuse she witnessed. It was the system doing what systems do: turning truth into administrative inconvenience.

A woman came to the desk-trembling, controlled-and asked whether she could report something that had happened in chambers. Lucia handed her the form, the official channel, the civilized path. The woman filled it out carefully, thanked Lucia, and left with the exhausted hope of someone who has done everything right.

Two weeks later, Lucia saw the form stamped "Received," then marked "Insufficient information," then quietly archived.

No call. No follow-up. No consequences. Procedure used as a sponge.

Lucia felt something in her chest that was not anger but betrayal of her own beliefs. She had handed the woman a ritual and watched it become nothing.

That was her point of no return: not outrage, but disillusionment. The loss of the old sentence-*Follow the process, and the process will follow you back.*

Lucia realized the process followed power, not people.

She did not become brave in a cinematic way. She became precise. She copied the archived form. She attached it to the timeline she had built. She sent it-quietly, carefully-to the oversight office, not under her name at first, but as an anonymous packet. She knew anonymity was cowardice. She also knew anonymity was survival. When oversight responded with a request for a "source," Lucia understood the trap: truth without a body attached cannot be disciplined into a person.

And then she did the hardest thing for an invisible worker: she made herself visible.

Her signature entered the record. Her name became "the complainant." The institution's eyes found her.

After that, she paid the ordinary price whistleblowers pay: colleagues stopped speaking freely around her. She became "difficult." She became "someone with opinions." Her supervisor reminded her-gently-that loyalty was a form of professionalism. Doors closed more firmly. A promotion that had been "likely" became "not the right time."

But Lucia's arc was not a victory march. It was a conversion: from believing in procedure as protection to understanding procedure as a weapon that can be handed either direction.

She didn't leave the courthouse. She stayed. Not because she trusted it again, but because she finally trusted herself more than she trusted the building.

While Reed adjusted his glove and moved a tray with the same careful precision he used when moving people's concerns off the agenda, Dr. Emily Saunders opened a spreadsheet that refused to behave.

Emily's colleagues often called her meticulous, which was their way of saying she was safe. Emily had built her career by being the person who never made noise. In meetings, she spoke last. She asked questions that sounded technical so nobody could accuse her of emotion. She had learned that for women in expert roles, certainty must be performed without arrogance, and doubt must be hidden without becoming deceit.

Her desire was not to expose Reed. Her desire was to be taken seriously without having to fight for it every day. The spreadsheet misbehaved in a way that triggered her oldest instinct: self-blame. She assumed she had made an error. She checked her formulas, her inputs, her version history. The numbers kept moving, quietly, as if edited by a hand that knew exactly how much change could be tolerated before suspicion would seem paranoid. Emily stayed late. Not because she was heroic, but because she could not bear the feeling that she was incompetent.

When she found the version log-timestamps that didn't align, edits under accounts that shouldn't have had access-she felt the first deep vertigo: the possibility that her doubt was not a flaw but an accurate signal.

Her arc began as a professional one: from internalizing institutional gaslighting to recognizing it as a technique. She started tracking not only what changed, but *how* changes were justified. Reed didn't delete numbers. He reframed them. He used "clarifications," "standardization," "rounding." He did to data what predators do to people: he made manipulation sound like care.

Emily's first attempt at action was safe. She raised the issue as a technical question in a meeting. Reed smiled and thanked her for her diligence. He suggested she might be "overfitting noise." The room laughed lightly. The laugh carried a message: don't be difficult.

Emily went home and cried-not because she was weak, but because she recognized the pattern: you bring a problem, and the institution returns you as the problem.

Her point of no return came when a junior analyst asked her privately, "Do you think I'm going crazy?" The analyst had noticed the same shifts and assumed she was at fault. Emily saw herself, ten years earlier, swallowing doubt until it became anxiety.

That was when Emily stopped trying to be harmless.

She wrote a report that did not plead. It documented. It mapped. It showed the pattern in the only language Reed could not charm away: reproducible evidence. She attached the version histories. She built a narrative out of timestamps the way a prosecutor builds one out of phone records.

And then she did something that changed her: she accepted that she would be disliked.

This is a character arc most whistleblowers are not given on the page. We make them pure. In life, they are rarely pure. They are people who reach a point where peace is no longer possible, and they choose conflict as a form of integrity.

Emily lost invitations. She lost informal mentoring. Her competence was reframed as "rigidity." But she gained something she hadn't had before: an internal alignment. Her work no longer required her to apologize for her own perception.

She didn't become fearless. She became unwilling.

While Gregorios rehearsed a sermon about humility, Father Andreas-reassigned, obedient, "difficult"-stood in a side chapel and prayed the prayer that is less request than warning.

Andreas's arc was the most painful because it required the betrayal of a vow.

He had entered the priesthood believing that obedience was a path to purity. He had been raised to admire men who did not question. His first rector used to say that doubt was a luxury for people without responsibility.

Andreas carried that too: *Don't make trouble. Don't scandalize the faithful. Don't confuse people who need certainty.*

His desire was not to expose Gregorios. His desire was to keep faith intact-his own and other people's.

He tried, at first, to correct quietly. A conversation in a corridor. A cautious suggestion that boundaries mattered. A reminder that donors should not determine appointments. Gregorios smiled like a man hearing a child explain weather.

"My dear Andreas," he said. "You must learn discernment." Discernment was the Church's word for hierarchy.

Andreas's first complicity beat was silence. He told himself that silence protected the community. He told himself that patience was spiritual maturity. He told himself that if he endured, the system would correct itself. Then an altar server came to him trembling. Not with a dramatic accusation, just with the look of a young person whose internal compass has been sabotaged. Andreas listened, and he felt the old theology crack: obedience is not holy when it protects harm.

His point of no return was not public scandal but private sacrilege: he watched Gregorios use confession-like intimacy as leverage. He watched faith become a currency. He realized that his silence was not humility; it was participation.

So Andreas did what felt, to him, like sin: he documented.

He wrote names. He wrote dates. He wrote patterns of reassignments, patterns of donations coinciding with promotions, patterns of "spiritual guidance" that slid into dependence. Every line felt like betrayal-of his bishop, of his institution, of the naive version of himself that believed holiness ensured safety.

When he finally spoke, he was not triumphant. He was grieving. His voice sounded, even to him, like a man giving up a childhood belief.

The consequences were predictable: he was called divisive. He was told he lacked charity. He was warned about scandal. People praised his "concern" while advising silence. He learned that institutions prefer quiet saints to loud truth-tellers.

And yet the arc completed: Andreas stopped confusing obedience with goodness.

He did not leave the Church. He stayed, but as a different kind of priest: one who understood that a robe can sanctify a man who does not deserve it, and that faith without accountability is not faith-it is vulnerability dressed as virtue.

09:07 - WHEN TECHNICAL TRUTH GETS A CHAIR AT THE TABLE

While Bellini listened to arguments with the calm face of inevitability, Reed attended a meeting where a university administrator smiled indulgently and said something that sounded like wisdom but functioned like permission: "Jonathan, our job isn't to police the world. It's leading it." While Gregorios accepted a call from Petros Anagnostou-shipping magnate, philanthropic reputation, tailored suit-whose generosity arrived with the quiet confidence of a man who knows what he has purchased.

A chair at the table is not power. It is often the opposite: a controlled position that allows the institution to say we listened while ensuring nothing changes.

In Bellini's courtroom, technical truth was the file itself: facts arranged into charges, charges arranged into procedure. Yet procedure can be a solvent. It can dissolve meaning without ever denying it. Bellini had long commanded respect for meticulous attention to detail-detail that, over time, became a tool: the power to elevate or bury a fact by deciding which detail mattered.

In Reed's world, technical truth was the raw dataset. Yet Reed had treated truth as something subordinate to "direction." Not accuracy-direction. He framed it as leadership. He spoke about strategy. He used the language of progress to justify smoothing away the very friction that makes science honest.

In Gregorios' world, technical truth was the financial reality of the diocese: debt, leaking roofs, salaries lagging. Petros' money arrived quickly. Repairs began quickly. Newspapers printed photos of the bishop's "leadership." The city praised. And then Petros requested something small: a priest reassigned because he was "difficult."

A small request is how dependency proves itself.

Gregorios complied. He told himself it was pastoral. He told himself it was governance. He told himself unity mattered.

Reed complied too, in his own way. He told himself the world needed results. He told himself sponsors needed confidence. He told himself an imperfect truth delivered quickly was better than a perfect truth delivered too late to matter.

Bellini complied most quietly of all. He told himself he was managing risk. He told himself he was preventing chaos. He told himself he could balance justice and self-interest without tipping into corruption.

Each of them, in that moment, offered truth a chair.

Not at the head of the table. Not at the center. A chair near the wall, from which they could reference truth but not permit it to steer.

09:24 - THE MECHANISMS BEHIND THE PORTRAITS

While Bellini's hand moved through routine-signature, stamp, nod-Lucia watched the choreography behind the choreography: a file that moved too smoothly for certain names, a request granted too quickly, a missing note that reappeared with a different timestamp. While Reed spoke in a meeting about "protecting the lab's mission," Emily checked the shared drive and found missing files. While Gregorios sat beneath icons and negotiated with numbers, Andreas listened for what the bishop did not say-the careful avoidance of moral language when money was present.

Portraits and icons and institutional histories do not merely decorate. They instruct. They produce an atmosphere in which questioning feels like vandalism.

Mechanisms maintained that atmosphere so common they are mistaken for normal life:

Framing. Bellini framed irregularities as "procedural." Reed framed anomalies as "limitations." Gregorios framed entanglement as "necessary compromise."

Vocabulary. Bellini spoke of "technicalities." Reed spoke of "outliers." Gregorios spoke of "unity." Each word was a valve.

Process as a shield. Bellini could delay without denying. Reed could "review" without correcting. Gregorios could convene a panel without ever surrendering control of the narrative.

Social penalties. Lucia would become "difficult" if she asked too much. Emily would become "junior" if she insisted on raw data. Andreas had already become "divisive" simply by worrying aloud.

Moral outsourcing. The court says: the judge decides. The Church says: God will judge. The university says: the data will speak. Each of these phrases can be true-and still be used to postpone responsibility until it evaporates.

This is constraining power: the ability to narrow reality while calling it professionalism.

09:41 - THE FIRST DIRECT QUESTION

While Bellini sat in his office after court, the private space where decisions become less visible, Lucia brought him a discrepancy. While Reed leaned over Emily's spreadsheet, he listened to her careful voice: "Professor, I can't reconcile these figures with the primary data." While Andreas requested a meeting with Gregorios, his tone respectful enough to be ignored politely.

Three people asked, in three dialects, the same question: What am I seeing?

Bellini did not respond with anger. He did not need to. He cultivated an environment of dual authority: public-facing documents and private influence from the hidden recesses of ceremonial power. That is the invisible hand-never seen, always felt.

Reed did not raise his voice either. He looked at Emily the way a senior scientist looks at a lab tech who has spilled buffer-disappointment wrapped in superiority. "You're thinking too small," he said. "The question isn't whether every data point is pretty. The question is whether the work is moving in the right direction."

Direction. Not truth. Not accuracy. Direction.

Gregorios' response to Andreas was gentler still. That made it worse. He did not deny the concern; he reframed it. "My son," he said, "you must understand the realities of shepherding. We do not live in a world of ideals." He spoke about roofs and salaries and the shelter. He made compassion into a trap: Would you prefer the cathedral leak so your conscience can remain dry?

In all three rooms, truth was not rejected. Truth was repositioned-given a chair, thanked for attending, and then prevented from touching the steering wheel.

10:08 - THE DOCUMENTATION PHASE

While Bellini walked a corridor where clerks lowered their eyes out of habit, Lucia began to remember with precision. While Reed returned to his lab bench and resumed control like a man tightening a lid, Emily began documenting quietly: version histories, file edits, sponsor requests, draft revisions. While Gregorios prepared for a public service and the city prepared to admire him, Andreas began asking questions in the careful way priests ask questions when they fear being labeled disloyal.

This is the phase institutions underestimate: the quiet gathering of proof by those without the authority to enforce it.

The powerful assume the less powerful will tire. And they often do, because the cost of persistence is something the less powerful bear privately and cumulatively.

Lucia understood that proof in law is not simply knowledge. It is admissible knowledge, properly obtained, properly handled, properly introduced. The system can punish the person who discovers truth if the discovery breaches protocol. This is the genius of institutional defense: it makes the method of uncovering wrongdoing itself a vulnerability.

Emily understood that proof in science is not simply data. It is publishable data, framed data, authorized data. The system can recast her concern as naivety: she is too junior to grasp "real-world constraints." It can interpret her accuracy as ideology.

Andreas understood that proof in Church is not simply pattern. It is a morally actionable pattern, recognized by people who benefit from not recognizing it. The system can recast his concern as spiritual immaturity: he is "critical," not "servant."

Three systems. One defensive reflex.

10:27 - ROBES, JABOTS, AND THE ARCHITECTURE OF HUMAN FAILURE

While Bellini's robe hung in his office like a second skin, Reed's mantle moved with him into every room-conference, committee, donor dinner-like a shield. While Gregorios' vestments and enkolpion caught candlelight, their symbolism did what symbolism always does: it made doubt feel indecent.

The failure here is not fabric. It is architecture.

People design courthouses as fortresses. They communicate inevitability. People designed cathedrals as heavens. They communicate sanctity.People conceived universities as temples of reason. They communicate authority.

And within these architectures, a human weakness becomes structurally powerful:

When you can speak from the robe, the jabot, the mantle, you can make your interests sound like principle. Bellini's office had ceremonial clutter-tokens of office, reminders of hierarchy. Hidden among respectability, influence can hide as easily as dust. Public-facing procedure becomes a curtain. The invisible hand operates behind it.

Reed's environment was modern, sleek, humming with machines. Yet the most powerful tool in his lab was not an instrument-it was prestige. Prestige allows ethical erosion to look like ambition. It allows compromise to be described as strategy. Arrogance becomes philosophy through its influence: we are educated; we are elite, therefore we are safe to trust.

Gregorios' cathedral was ancient, reverent. Yet the mechanism was the same: tradition allows dependency to look like providence. It allows a donor's leverage to look like "God's blessing."

In biology, a system under stress will sometimes choose survival over health. Institutions do the same.

10:54 - THE PIVOTAL MOMENT ARRIVES DIFFERENTLY IN EACH ROOM

While anti-mafia investigators scrutinized irregularities in Bellini's administrative choices, Reed's partner received a leak: a file of internal emails, sponsor requests, and edited drafts. An investigative journalist began tracing ties between Petros' donations and diocesan endorsements, and Gregorios received a call stating that funding would be withdrawn if the bishop did not "cooperate."

Here is the global pattern in its clearest form:

Truth does not arrive as pure moral revelation. It arrives as paperwork. It arrives as email trails. It arrives as ledgers. It arrives as bank compliance notices. It arrives as a journalist's spreadsheet. It arrives as the stubbornness of documents that will not pray, will not be persuaded, will not be soothed by ceremony.

Bellini's pivotal moment was not cinematic. It was procedural-warrants, interviews, scrutiny. Once the investigation started, his calm authority could no longer shape the frame. The invisible hand was exposed not by outrage but by traceability.

Reed's pivotal moment was similar: no lab fire, no explosion-just the dry inevitability of physics. Measuring friction prevents romanticizing motion. Arguments could not make the data trail innocent.

Gregorios' pivotal moment was the donor's confidence turning explicit. "Your shelter needs funding," Petros said softly. "Do you want it to close? The rich used the poor as hostages to secure themselves. Dependency revealing its true face.

Here, we can most clearly observe the line that must not be crossed: when a leader embraces hostage logic as governance.

11:18 - THE INSTITUTION'S FIRST SELF-DEFENSE

While the court system began preparing statements about "maintaining public confidence," the university prepared language about "academic misunderstanding," and the diocese prepared language about "repentance" and "review panels," Lucia, Emily, and Andreas each experienced the same subtle violence: the institution's instinct to minimize.

Minimization is not always an explicit lie. It is the strategic reduction of scale.

Bellini's misconduct would be framed as personal failure-isolated, individual, regrettable-rather than as a symptom of a system that allows a magistrate to cultivate dual authority in private.

Reed's ethical erosion would be framed as misunderstanding-complex, nuanced, "a disagreement about standards"-rather than as the predictable outcome of sponsors shaping truth through prestige.

Gregorios' entanglement would be framed as necessity-good intentions, difficult circumstances-rather than as dependency becoming leverage and doctrine becoming cover.

And since the public loves clean stories, institutions frequently encourage the public to believe them.

But if these are isolated incidents, why do they share identical stages? Why does every institution reach first for reputation, then for process, then for delay, then for reframing the dissenter?

Isolation does not reproduce itself with such mechanical regularity. A pattern does.

11:42 - ANTICIPATED COUNTER-ARGUMENTS (and Why They Fail)

While the three institutions assembled their defenses, I could already hear the familiar sentences-because I have heard them, in one form or another, behind every robe and jabot I have ever studied.

They claim, "This is isolated." Patterns do. The playbook is the same: constrain truth, then call the constraint professionalism.

"There is no proof." In systems where proof is controlled by the powerful, "no proof" often means "no access." Lucia cannot lawfully extract the ledger that would convict. Emily cannot achieve transparency if gatekeepers restrict data access. Andreas cannot audit the diocese when they hold the books as sacrosanct.

"We must follow due process / internal procedure / pastoral prudence." Yes. But procedure can become a substitute for moral clarity. Prudence can become an excuse to avoid consequences. "Internal" can become a synonym for "unaccountable."

"You are harming the institution." This is the most revealing defense. It treats the institution as the patient and truth as the disease. It asks victims and witnesses to keep bleeding quietly so the building looks clean.

"We acted for the greater good." The greater good becomes a blank check. It can justify delaying justice, polishing data, laundering influence through piety. Without accountability, "greater good" is simply power with perfume.

These defenses work because they sound reasonable. They are the language of a system protecting itself while claiming it is protecting everyone else.

12:09 - THE LINE THAT CANNOT BE CROSSED, CROSSED AGAIN

While Bellini sat composed and framed the investigation as political overreach, Reed implied Emily was too junior to grasp "real-world constraints," and Gregorios dismissed Andreas gently -smothering him with pastoral language-each man took the same step: he treated truth as something to be managed rather than obeyed.

This is the crossing.

Not the bribe. Not the donation. Not the edited spreadsheet. Those are symptoms.

At the crossing, an authority decides that truth will be permitted only as long as it does not endanger the institution's continuity.

A courtroom, a cathedral, or a lab can make that decision. Anyone can make that decision in any building that has a hierarchy and where consequences can be hidden by language.

And therefore the "isolated incident" argument must fail. If the pattern can occur in three unrelated sectors with three unrelated uniforms in three unrelated countries, then the driver is not the uniqueness of the men. It is the replicability of the mechanism.

12:37 - CONSEQUENCES WITHOUT CATHARSIS

While the public demanded clarity, institutions offered process.

Bellini faced suspension and potential criminal charges. The headlines were loud. Inside the system, the adjustments were quiet: colleagues repositioning, alliances shifting, the building trying to preserve the idea that it remained pure.

Reed was suspended from administrative roles. Funding was reviewed. Some projects halted. Not everything burned. Some prestige remained. Institutions are skilled at containing damage without dismantling the conditions that created it.

Gregorios was "advised" to reduce appearances. The diocese convened a review panel. Petros withdrew funding. The roof remained repaired. The shelter's future grew uncertain. The faithful were told to pray. The institution chose the kind of accountability that preserves itself.

No single event exploded. That is the modern form of scandal: ethical erosion disguised as normalcy.

Lucia did not become a hero. Clerks rarely do. She watched the system convulse and then attempt to return to posture.

Emily did not become triumphant. She watched colleagues who once laughed at Reed's jokes now avoid his name as if it carried contagion.

Andreas did not get vindication in sermons. He watched rain run down cathedral steps and into a gutter, carrying city dust and cigarette ends past the doors of holiness.

This is why I refuse to tell these as three neat stories with three neat endings. Real institutional misuse does not resolve; it migrates. It changes names. It shifts roles. It waits for fatigue.

EPILOGUE THREAD - WHAT THIS UNDERWRITES

While readers will later encounter many chapters-many costumes, many rooms-this braided chapter is meant to function like a spine beneath the book's final compilation: a single demonstration that the misuse is not local, not rare, not confined to one faith or one nation or one discipline.

The mechanism is global because hierarchy is global. The costumes differ because culture differs. The misuse repeats because incentives repeat.

And so, when someone tells you-later, at the end of the book-that this was just one bad magistrate, you will remember Bellini's invisible hand moving through procedure like a glove. When someone tells you the Church is being unfairly targeted, you will remember Gregorios touching the enkolpion like a reflex while compromise hardened into doctrine. When someone tells you science is self-correcting, you will remember Reed saying "direction" as if it were a substitute for truth, and Emily documenting quietly because the chair offered to truth was placed against the wall.

This is what I need you to see now, before the book assembles its final indictment:

The problem is not that people sometimes lie. The problem is that institutions have learned to seat truth-to grant it a chair, to thank it politely, and to keep it from touching consequence.

And the line that cannot be crossed is crossed each minute a steward decides stability matters more than reality. Because once truth can be rearranged without penalty, the robe becomes a mask, the enkolpion becomes jewelry, the mantle becomes theater-and the building remains beautiful while something inside it rots.

That rot is not isolated.

It is structural. It is exportable. It is happening, somewhere, while you read this-while a magistrate enters his courtroom, while a professor enters his lab, while a bishop fastens his enkolpion and steps into light that makes the gold look like certainty.

2

"THE PROSECUTOR'S SHADOW"

SUBTLE MANIPULATION CAN DEVASTATE TRUST EVEN WHEN IT LEAVES NO OVERT TRACE.

> Judicial misconduct and harassment investigations, Belgium, 2006-2014 (composite case), PRGR

The courthouse in Brussels held winter in its stone. Coats steamed on radiators. Umbrellas dripped into corners. On the morning Marie Lefèvre first realized she was being managed, the air outside was bright and deceptive-a pale sun behind thin cloud, clean light with hidden glare.

Prosecutor Alain Dupont liked that kind of light because it made people squint.

He entered Courtroom 4 without hurry, robe falling perfectly, white bands at his throat sharp as paper. He didn't raise his voice. He didn't have to. A pause before he spoke made clerks stop shuffling. A glance made a witness adjust their story. He didn't demand obedience; he made obedience feel like the sensible response to competence.

Dupont was not the loud kind of dangerous. He was the meticulous kind-the man who learned early that institutions reward those who never force the room to admit it is being forced.

He kept a small black notebook in the inside pocket of his robe, the kind of thing journalists imagine contains secrets. It contained something more banal and more lethal: lists. Names, dates, the stray phrase a junior had used that revealed insecurity. "Over-apologizes." "Needs to be chosen." "Will fold if corrected in public." It looked like professional diligence. It *was* professional diligence, just applied to humans the way one applies it to evidence.

In the hallway, juniors called him brilliant. In private, he called them fragile.

"You're clever," he told Marie when he offered mentorship, "but you don't yet understand how power behaves." He said it kindly, almost as if he were protecting her. The kindness carried superiority. Dupont spoke of working-class witnesses as "unsophisticated." He described emotional testimony as "noise." When a clerk asked for clarification, he replied, smiling, "We're not teaching a night class."

Marie told herself she could handle him. She was rising fast-sharp, disciplined, the kind of prosecutor leadership liked to showcase. Dupont's attention felt, at first, like oxygen: invitations to "strategy discussions," praise in front of senior staff, suggestions she had "the temperament for high-profile matters."

Praise from above is never just praise. It is a reagent. It changes what happens next.

Dupont's meetings had a structure he would have denied possessing. He did not think of it as manipulation. He thought of it as *training*. Affirmation, then destabilization, then rescue. He would compliment her brief, then point out a flaw in her tone, then offer to "help" her correct it. He would call her exceptional, then suggest that exceptional people attract enemies. He would describe the profession as ruthless, and himself as one of the few people who could teach her how not to be eaten.

He was always careful to frame dependency as realism.

"You'll hear a lot of nonsense about boundaries," he said once, as if boundaries were a fad. "People who need boundaries are people who can't handle ambiguity."

He made ambiguity sound adult.

The questions drifted. Work habits became exhaustion, exhaustion became personal life, personal life became fear. He didn't ask the questions like a predator. He asked them like a physician, like someone taking a history. "Are you lonely?" he asked once, as if loneliness were a procedural issue. "Who do you talk to when you're overwhelmed?" And he smiled like a man who already knew the answer, because he had already narrowed the room until the only obvious answer was him.

Nothing explicit. Nothing prosecutable. That was the point: he operated in the penumbra where complaint sounds irrational. Where the person who names the unease becomes the problem for "bringing emotion into work."

Women in the office began comparing notes in whispers-quiet enough to survive, not loud enough to be heard by the wrong people. They described the same experience: leaving Dupont's office "smaller," hungry for approval, ashamed for feeling uneasy. His mild disappointment could ruin an entire week.

The institution treated it as personality. Dupont delivered convictions. He made the office look effective. And effectiveness has a narcotic effect on administration: it numbs moral nerves.

When a clerk mentioned, cautiously, that Dupont's meetings with interns felt "too personal," a senior administrator shrugged.

"Dupont is intense," he said. "That's how excellence looks." That sentence was the complacency that kept the shadow intact.

The first crack came through casework. Marie noticed that Dupont's "guidance" sometimes aligned too neatly with outcomes that benefited certain relationships: an unusual concession after a private corridor conversation, a witness deprioritized for reasons that sounded procedural but felt strategic. An intern who resisted his attention found herself quietly excluded from meaningful assignments.

Power doesn't always punish through violence. It punishes through access. It reallocates oxygen.

Marie began documenting in the only language the institution respected: timestamps, emails, meeting invitations, patterns of assignment and exclusion. She wrote phrases Dupont used-his insistence that "only amateurs need boundaries," his habit of labeling discomfort as "insecurity," his casual remarks about "people who don't understand how grown-ups work."

A formal complaint finally landed when an intern-new enough to still trust her instincts-reported an after-hours meeting that left her shaking. She described how Dupont framed dependency as mentorship and implied her career would suffer if she "misread" his attention. She remembered the door closing and his voice lowering until the room felt like a sealed jar.

PRGR END-CAP - AUTHORED HARM TEST

(for "THE PROSECUTOR'S SHADOW")

This case doesn't pivot on a single obscene sentence. It pivots on a professional move that looks, from the outside, like management: **reallocating work.** That is why it persists. It uses the institution's ordinary tools-assignments, evaluations, access-as weapons that don't clang.

PRGR would attach authorship at the moment Prosecutor Dupont converts mentorship into career control. The authored harm is not "creepiness." It is the administrative throttling of someone's future while calling it "development."

The hinge-steps where PRGR would force the author to exist

The closed-door mentorship invitation

The first danger isn't romance; it's *private access framed as professional necessity.* When Dupont insists on one-on-one meetings in spaces without witnesses-"strategy discussions," "career development," "just a quick debrief"-PRGR would require him to file a short, reasoned record:

Why does this meeting need to be private? What work output is expected?

What safeguards exist (open door, calendar transparency, optional third party)? If he cannot write a legitimate reason that survives daylight, the "mentorship" is already functioning as leverage.

The moment he reframes boundaries as immaturity

The line "only amateurs need boundaries" (or its equivalents) is not just rhetoric. It is **a governance move**: it disqualifies discomfort before it can become reportable.

PRGR would force Dupont to author what he is doing:

I am treating a junior's boundary request as a competence issue. Here is the evidence that boundary-setting undermines work.

Here is the alternative I am rejecting (structured mentoring; documented feedback; third-party present). PRGR doesn't debate feelings. It demands the causal claim in writing.

The assignment reallocation - the career harm step

This is the concrete act your example points to, and it's the fulcrum:

Dupont's assignment of the intern away from meaningful cases

-or his quiet exclusion of a resistant junior from high-value work-is the step where PRGR forces him to author the harm to her career.

Because it is an irreversible fork. Access is the currency of prosecution offices: access to trials, to brief-writing, to high-profile files, to senior visibility. Losing it changes trajectories.

Under PRGR, Dupont would have to write:

What objective criteria justify this reassignment? What performance evidence supports it?

What alternatives were considered (co-supervision; structured feedback; rotating opportunities)?

What harm is foreseeable (stalled development, reputational signaling, chilling effect on reporting)? And he would have to sign it.

The point is simple: if he is retaliating, PRGR makes him admit the retaliation in the only language institutions respect-authored reasons tied to career consequences.

The "tone" evaluation move

Dupont's control works through interpretation: "too sensitive," "anxious," "misread," "not resilient."

PRGR would require that any negative evaluation tied to "professionalism" include:

specific work behaviors, not personality labels, concrete incidents, not impressions,

and an explicit statement that the evaluation is not punishment for raising concerns. This blocks the classic tactic: turning discomfort into a defect and defect into an official record.

The corridor concession / informal influence step

If the chapter includes case outcomes being nudged by private conversations, PRGR bites there too: any material concession, deprioritization of a witness, or strategic shift after an off-record exchange must be authored with:

what changed, why it changed, who benefits,

and what oversight review exists. Because this is where "I'm just being pragmatic" becomes untraceable influence.

What PRGR would force in this case (practical tool, not slogan)

1. **No career-impact decision without a signed reason**
   Assignments, removals from meaningful work, changes in supervision, and negative evaluations become PRGR-trigger events because they are *career-irreversible* and easily disguised as management.

2. **A boundary-safe default**
   PRGR would require the institution to set a default that removes the ambiguity Dupont feeds on:

   mentoring meetings are scheduled, agenda-noted, and optionally include a third party;

door policies are explicit;

juniors can decline private meetings without penalty. This doesn't criminalize mentorship. It prevents mentorship from being convertible into dependency.

3. **A retaliation tripwire** PRGR would establish a reversal trigger tied to patterns rather than "proof of intent": "If a complainant or boundary-setter experiences measurable access loss (case removal, fewer meaningful files, sudden negative evaluations) within X months, an automatic review occurs."
4. This matters because in this story, harm is administered through **access**, not assault.

The questions that keep the case sharp (specific to Dupont)

If you were Dupont: can you write, in plain language, why the intern was removed from meaningful work-without using personality terms, without "fit," without "tone"? Would you sign it knowing it will be read by oversight?

If you were Marie: what is the first decision you would force into authored form-the private meetings, the "tone" critique, or the assignment exclusion?

If you were the office leadership: what would you protect first-your conviction metrics, or the integrity of your pipeline of junior prosecutors?

PRGR doesn't ask whether Dupont intended harm. It asks where he **converted institutional tools into personal leverage**-and it forces him to **author the harm at the exact step where a career is quietly bent out of shape.**

3

"THE CLERIC'S SECRET"

WHAT STAYS HIDDEN DOESN'T STAY HARMLESS.

Clerical misconduct and concealed assets, Spain/France, 2000s (composite case)

The sacristy smelled of wax and damp fabric, the quiet scent of things used, folded, stored, and used again. Father Tomás Álvarez liked the sacristy because it was a room designed for secrecy-behind the altar, behind the public face of worship, behind the part people photographed. He was the cleric who seemed incapable of scandal. Mid-fifties, soft-spoken, educated, careful. He treated liturgy like a craft: vestments aligned, vessels polished, schedules precise. Parishioners called him "steady," which is another way of saying he didn't disturb anyone.

Tomás worked in diocesan administration as well-helping manage funds for restoration and charity. He spoke fluent procedure. He could make a questionable transfer sound routine. He could make an odd invoice sound like a necessity. His tone carried the calm superiority of someone who believed he was above ordinary temptation because he understood temptation's mechanics. That belief was his cover.

His secret wasn't a single act. It was a compartment-built. A private bank account under a foundation's name. Gifts received "for the parish" that never entered parish books. A discreet relationship maintained through travel schedules and plausible errands. None of it looked like a theft from a distance. It looked like administrative life. The way mold looks like shadow until you smell it.

A maintenance worker named Raúl discovered the first physical trace while repairing a leak behind the sacristy wall. The plaster was soft with moisture. A slow drip had been feeding rot for months. Raúl pulled away a panel and found, not pipes, but a small metal box tucked into the cavity, wrapped in plastic to protect it from damp.

Inside were documents: account details, receipts, and letters. The paperwork that doesn't belong behind a Church wall.

Raúl didn't understand all of it. He didn't have Tomás's vocabulary. But he recognized secrecy the way the body recognizes smoke: immediate, involuntary.

He told the parish administrator, who told the diocese. Tomás was called in "for clarification."

He arrived in perfect black, collar crisp, face calm. He listened to questions as if they were mildly embarrassing rather than dangerous. When shown the documents, he didn't panic. He did something more revealing: he corrected terminology.

"That account is not personal," he said. "It's held in trust." "That transfer is not irregular," he said. "It's an allocation." "That letter is not evidence," he said. "It's a misunderstanding."

He spoke as if words could change chemistry-rename poison as medicine and the body will accept it.

His superiority surfaced when he addressed Raúl indirectly. "These situations often arise," Tomás said, "when people without training misinterpret administrative material."

People without training. As if truth required credentials.

The diocese's first instinct was to minimize. A scandal would harm donations, parish stability, and the Church's public face. Committees met. Lawyers advised. Language softened. They framed the matter as "administrative complexity."

But the documents were stubborn. They showed a parallel financial system. Money routed around official accounts. Gifts recorded privately. Notes showing Tomás had used diocesan funds for travel that wasn't diocesan.

A second revelation arrived from a bank compliance officer, alerted by the inquiry. The foundation account had unusual flows-donations arriving from sources that didn't match declared charity work, withdrawals timed around Tomás's travel.

Now the secret was no longer architectural. It was financial. Unlike rumor, finance allows for tracing.

Tomás adjusted his story. He claimed he was protecting the parish from bureaucratic delay. He said the funds were "held safely" for future repairs. He implied that only someone naive would insist on rigid procedure when souls were at stake.

This is how arrogance operates in clerical form: morality used as a bypass lane.

The diocese faced a choice it hated. Criminal referral would mean public disgrace. Quiet reassignment would mean continued risk. They tried the compromise institutions prefer: containment with minimal admission. The Church took away Tomás's financial responsibilities. A retreat house became his destination "for discernment." The parish was told little.

Raúl, meanwhile, became the subject of whispered suspicion. Not because he had done wrong, but because he had disrupted the story the community wanted to keep telling. In hierarchical systems, truth-tellers often receive the shame that belongs to the powerful.

Tomás did not confess publicly. He did not apologize in plain language. He framed the outcome as misunderstanding, persecution, "spiritual warfare." Some parishioners believed him because believing him preserved the comfort of their faith.

A biblical image fits here, modestly: a prophet once described people entering holy spaces while keeping hidden idols in inner rooms-private chambers of loyalty that contradicted public worship. The warning wasn't about theatrics. It was about divided hearts, about secrets that reshape sacred life from the inside.

Tomás's secret had done exactly that. It turned the sacristy-a room meant for preparation-into a storage place for concealment. It used trust as camouflage. It used education as entitlement.

After they repaired the leak, they sealed the wall again. Fresh plaster. Fresh paint. From the outside, nothing remained. But Raúl never looked at the Church the same way. He had learned a lesson that doesn't require a degree:

Hidden things don't remain contained simply because someone declares them so. They stay contained only until moisture finds them - until pressure changes - until a crack opens. And cracks, in old buildings, are inevitable. The conflict didn't end with paint either.

When Tomás left for the retreat house, the parish bell still rang on schedule, bright as a spoon tapping a glass. The sound floated over roofs and washing lines, over morning traffic, over the bakery where caramel hung in the air like innocence-sweet, familiar, and manufactured. People kept buying it because the alternative was to admit what it cost.

Raúl walked home past the river and watched sunlight fracture on the surface, each ripple cutting the reflection into a thousand trembling shards. It looked like certainty until a gust rearranged it. That was the Church, he thought: a single image held together by distance. Up close-too close-you saw seams.

At night he dreamed of the wall cavity: the box wrapped in plastic, the damp eating stone, the slow drip that never asked permission. He understood, with a kind of bleak tenderness, that institutions don't collapse like towers. They spoil like fruit. First, a bruise you can hide under a thumb. Then the smell.

And somewhere behind the altar, behind the polished vessels and perfectly folded cloth, something else remained-unseen but active: not the money, not the papers, but the lesson. When authority learns it can be forgiven, it begins to confuse forgiveness with immunity.

4

"THE PROFESSOR WHO PLAYED WITH MINDS"

THE VERY TOOLS OF GUIDANCE HAD BECOME INSTRUMENTS OF COERCION.

Academic exploitation through psychological manipulation, Germany (composite case)

Professor Klaus Reinhardt had always been a master of perception, but not in the way his colleagues meant when they praised his "clarity."

In the lecture halls of Heidelberg, he wore his authority like a tailored instrument: a black academic robe falling with measured weight, a white jabot stiff at the throat, a small architectural certainty that told the room who was allowed to be unsure. He did not pace. He did not fumble. He stood still in a way that made other people rearrange themselves around him.

To colleagues, he was brilliant, incisive, exacting-an efficient mind with a taste for clean models. To students, he was awe with a voice: a man whose lectures folded complexity into elegant sentences, whose jokes arrived with the timing of practiced charm. He seemed, from a distance, like the best version of intellectual adulthood. Up close, he had a different gift. He could tell, within minutes, who would try too hard.

It began the way many abuses begin: with a story he could tell himself without flinching. He expanded office hours. He framed it as care. "I don't like wasted talent," he told the department secretary, loudly enough for people to hear. He cultivated the reputation of a hard mentor who rescued students from mediocrity. The university likes that story; it flatters its self-image.

Students came in with notebooks and gratitude, struggling through cognitive theory, desperate for a stable handle on difficult material. Klaus smiled and asked them to define the concept again, slower this time, and watched not their words but their breathing. He noticed the tremor before an exam. The way someone apologized for not understanding quickly enough. The small confession that always escaped when the mind was under pressure: *I'm afraid I don't belong here.*

He heard those confessions the way other people hear compliments. They made him feel necessary. Klaus did not think of himself as cruel. He thought of himself as **accurate**. In his mind, students were not children in need of protection; they were raw material in need of refinement. Weakness was not sacred. Weakness was data.

When a student began to relax in his office-when their shoulders dropped, when the defensive smile faded-he would do what he did best: he would reframe. "That's not a cognitive problem," he would say softly, as if offering a key. "That's a coping style."

His language was always clinical, always plausible. He could turn intimacy into pedagogy by naming it.

Soon, his "guidance" shifted-quietly, like a current changing direction. Students were called in to "discuss research opportunities," and the conversation drifted toward personal matters: family illness, relationship stress, depression, panic. Klaus listened with a concentrated calm that felt, to the student, like safety. He nodded. He did not interrupt. He asked questions with the neutral tenderness of a man gathering evidence.

Then, afterwards, he would summarize their vulnerabilities in the same tone he used to summarize papers. "So," he'd say, tapping a pen against the desk, "you respond to pressure by pleasing. You avoid conflict. You have a pattern of apologizing pre-emptively."

The student would sit stunned, hearing their private self turned into a diagnostic outline, and the stunned feeling would be mistaken for insight.

Klaus enjoyed that moment most of all: the second when someone's interior life became something he could hold.

The abuse was rarely overt at first. That was part of its design. A hand resting a fraction too long on a shoulder. A comment delivered as mentorship but planted like a hook. "You're special," he would say, and then-almost carelessly-"Don't make me regret investing in you."

He tested limits the way a good researcher tests hypotheses: incrementally, carefully, with attention to outcomes. If a student stiffened, he retreated and became purely academic for a week-enough to reset their doubt. If a student leaned in, hungry for approval, he increased the dosage: more meetings, more private language, more insinuation that their future depended on his guidance.

In seminars, he praised compliance as "maturity." He framed dissent as "defensiveness." Students who challenged his methods found themselves subtly isolated-not by overt punishment, but by tone. He would treat their questions as symptoms. "That resistance is interesting," he'd say with a smile, as if the student had just revealed something embarrassing in public.

The room would laugh lightly, relieved it wasn't them.

The robe and jabot-symbols meant to signal scholarship-became, for Klaus, tools of atmosphere. He knew precisely what they did to a young person's nervous system. They produced the old spell: *he is serious; I am lucky to be here.* He did not need to shout. He only needed to let the uniform do its ancient work.

For years the pattern persisted, protected by the university's favorite narcotic: productivity. Klaus published. Klaus won grants. Klaus made the department look impressive. Administration does not like to disturb impressive things; it fears the embarrassment of finding rot inside its trophies.

Students who worried about grades or their future came alone, trusting his judgment like a compass. Some found themselves pulled into ethically ambiguous arrangements:

pressured to reveal personal information "for research validity," nudged to bend rules "for the sake of the project," taught that boundaries were a bourgeois distraction from real science. He justified all of it as mentorship, as necessary correction, as the cultivation of talent.

In Klaus's private doctrine, **consent was simply another cognitive bias**.

The whistleblower was a graduate student named Mara, and what made her dangerous was not her anger but her method. She did not begin with outrage. She began with timestamps.

She documented irregularities: emails that summoned students late, patterns of grade shifts after private meetings, repeated requests for "confidential disclosures" framed as research, the same phrases Klaus used to make discomfort feel childish. She collected the small, repeatable things-the things institutions can recognize without having to admit they ignored the big ones.

When Mara finally spoke, she did so in the only language the university respects: corroboration. Accounts from several students converged. Calendar entries aligned. Phrases repeated. What emerged was not a single scandalous incident but a system: a carefully maintained network of influence and dependency, with Klaus at its center like a quietly spinning blade.

The dean summoned him to the office. The confrontation was formal, methodical, and devastating-not theatrical, not loud. The dean laid out statements, documents, evidence of boundary violations, and coercive mentorship practices. Klaus had always relied on atmosphere; in the dean's office, atmosphere did not belong to him.

For the first time, the robe was not present to do its work. The jabot was not there to declare authority before he spoke.

He tried to reword the accusations into his familiar language. "These students are anxious," he said. "They misinterpret intensity. They confuse guidance with-" he paused, searching for the right word, the word that made other people the problem-"with intimacy."

He heard himself. He realized, too late, that he had stated the hierarchy plainly: he was the interpreter; they were unreliable material. He resigned.

The university announced reforms with the careful tone of an institution protecting itself: mandatory ethics workshops, independent oversight of faculty-student interactions, a formalized complaint channel for confidential reporting. It all sounded clean, like aftercare written by lawyers.

The students affected struggled in the aftermath. Some began their careers with compromised confidence; others carried long-term psychological scars: the peculiar injury of trust being used as leverage. Counseling programs helped, but the deeper damage was epistemic. They had learned that insight can be a weapon when held by someone who is not accountable.

The university faced scrutiny for what it had been willing not to notice.

Even in solitude, Klaus framed his consequences as theory. He told himself he had been misunderstood, that the faculty had panicked, that "mediocre people" always resent the demands of excellence. But underneath the story, another realization pressed harder, less narratable: authority without accountability is not only dangerous-it is **addictive**.

And symbols-robes, jabots, titles-are the perfect delivery system for addiction. They let a person feel elevated without having to become good.

In the echoing halls where he once enthralled students, he walked differently now: not tragic, not enlightened, simply stripped of the costume that had made his hunger look like pedagogy.

THE MECHANISMS BEHIND THE PORTRAITS

PORTRAITS BLUR; MECHANISMS DO NOT.

The day of my trial, the tribunal had a stack of "complaint" cases to clear. Each allotted thirty minutes. Twenty minutes for the hearing. Ten minutes to deliberate. No more-preferably less. Five counsel members, consolidated into one expression: attentive neutrality, practiced speed. Next case. Same ritual. Same cadence. There is a point in any collection of case-stories where the faces begin to merge. Judge. Bishop. Professor. In ceremonial dress, each speaks the language of merit and duty and makes a quiet discovery: they can take much without seeming to take anything. It happens in a blink-one procedural shortcut, one euphemism, one "standard practice" that trims a human life down to what fits the allotted time.

That sameness is not a failure of imagination. It is the clue. When authority repeats itself, it is usually because it has found a reliable mechanism.

Across the academy, the court, and the Church, three mechanisms recur so often they start to look like personality. They are not. They are systems of leverage.

First: financial concealment.

Not always theft-often simply the comfort of complexity. Money becomes a fog: donations "allocated", grants "re-profiled", fees "administrative", expenses "reimbursed". The paperwork grows thicker than the conscience. The actor relies on three shields: plausible deniability, institutional fatigue, and the public's boredom with numbers.

Second: sexual coercion and intimate capture.

Rarely a dramatic assault. More often a slow exchange-rate: access for compliance. A recommendation letter that someone can withhold. A scholarship's delay is possible. A confession that someone can reframe as a private bond. Here, dependence is the weapon-and crossing the boundary a millimetre at a time until the victim's world narrows to one gatekeeper is often the crime.

Third: procedural manipulation.

The rulebook serves not to uphold fairness but to ration it. Complaints vanish into process. Postponing hearings until witnesses tire is a common tactic. A single decision determines the entire outcome: who is appointed, who is heard, and what is deemed "out of scope." It is corruption that can be defended with a citation.

These mechanisms produce the illusion of variety. Different countries. Different institutions. Different titles stitched on different gowns. Yet the pattern remains recognisable: control access, control narrative, control consequence.

From here on, let the scenes do what arguments cannot: show how money turns to fog, how intimacy becomes leverage, how procedure becomes cover. The robe is rarely the cause-but it is often the hiding place.

5

"THE PROSECUTOR WHO CROSSED THE LINE"

IF JUSTICE IS TO BE MORE THAN COSTUME, IT MUST BE WATCHED.

Prosecutorial misconduct and procedural abuse (composite case)

Prosecutor Jonathan Keller moved through the marble hallways of the federal courthouse the way a man moves through a house he believes he owns. Not loudly-never loudly.

Ownership, in institutions, manifests through smaller gestures: a nod that prompts a clerk to hurry, a pause that silences a junior attorney mid-sentence, and a glance that transforms a hallway into a corridor of permission.

In court he wore the black robe and stark white jabot, the uniform that tells the public: this man is not a man; he is a function.

The robe erases personality. The jabot suggests cleanliness-moral linen, pressed, without wrinkle. People do not only listen to a prosecutor; they listen to the costume. They want to believe the fabric has been laundered in principle.

At first, Keller gave them what they wanted. He was meticulous. He could build a case the way an engineer builds a bridge: load-bearing facts, reinforced timelines, witnesses arranged like beams. Jurors admired him. Judges trusted him. Colleagues copied his habits. If you were a prosecutor, you learned quickly that you could measure your own seriousness against Keller's restraint.

It is always easier to admire someone than to audit them.

And that is the first prompt to the reader-whether you like it or not-because you already know the temptation: you want institutions to be true. You want the courthouse to be cleaner than the street. You want the Church to be holier than the market. You want the university to be wiser than the bar. Your mind prefers the comforting geometry of symbols. It prefers the idea that authority is evidence.

Keller understood that preference. He fed it.

His manipulations began in the realm where misconduct is almost indistinguishable from strategy. A witness placed first rather than last. A phrase chosen in an affidavit that made uncertainty sound like certainty. A line of cross-examination that suggested guilt without stating it. He told himself-truthfully at first-that this was not corruption, but craft.

Trials are not seminars. They are contests. Every prosecutor learns to shape narrative. But narrative is a drug. It does not stop at the dose you intended.

Soon Keller was doing something else: not shaping narrative, but shaping reality. He learned the power of omission-the most seductive kind of wrongdoing because it feels like restraint. Evidence that complicated the story stayed in a folder longer than it should. A note from a detective about an alternative suspect was dismissed as "noise."

A defense request that deserved a response was answered late, just late enough to matter.

He never had to invent facts. That would have felt criminal. He simply learned how to starve the court of oxygen until the only thing left to breathe was his version of events.

If you are reading this near the end of the book, you can feel the pattern. The stories have been warning you, quietly, that evil rarely arrives with horns. It arrives with procedures.

Keller began cultivating relationships that were not illegal on paper, only poisonous in effect. He gave detectives small professional favors-introductions, speaking slots at conferences, commendations whispered into the right ears. In return, he received what prosecutors crave: the best information first.

The cleanest reports. The narratives polished before they reached defense counsel.

Then came the perks. They did not come as cash in an envelope; Keller was too clever, too disciplined. They came as "honoraria" for lectures.

Consulting stipends. Travel paid by organizations that enjoyed his public image. A private dinner hosted by a forensic vendor who wanted the office to renew a contract. Each benefit was small enough to be defended, large enough to change his appetite.

He told himself the same lie every institution teaches its high performers: You deserve this. You are carrying the burden. You are holding the line.

That lie is the engine of gradual ethical collapse. It turns virtue into entitlement.

The damage, of course, traveled outward. Defendants who should have had trials were pressed into plea bargains because the deck was stacked. A shaky case became "strong" because contradictions were quietly hidden.

People on the margins-the poor, the addicted, the mentally ill-were the easiest to move through the system like cattle. Even some who were not innocent exactly, but not what Keller claimed them to be, were crushed by the convenience of his certainty.

And here the book's tone must harden, because you asked it to.

We can stop pretending that institutions merely "fail." Institutions choose. They choose who is protected by ambiguity and who is punished by precision. They choose which errors are treated as learning and which become exile. They choose whether truth is a goal or a tool.

Keller thrived because the system rewarded him for winning, not for being right.

The first cracks emerged because someone closer to the ground had less to lose by noticing-and more to lose by remaining silent.

Maria Lopez was a junior paralegal, the kind of person courthouses depend on and barely see.

She was not celebrated. She did not have a robe or a jabot. Her authority was not symbolic; it was clerical, which means it was invisible until something broke. Her desk was where paper became fate. Her job was to move files, not question them.

But she had a habit that institutions fear: she read.

She noticed that certain exhibits listed in discovery never appeared in trial binders. She noticed "corrected" reports that carried the faint ghost of an earlier version. She noticed witness statements that had been summarized too cleanly, as if uncertainty were being shaved away. She began to compare outcomes with inputs, the way you compare a recipe with the cake it produces.

The cake was too perfect. Too sweet. Too consistent.

Maria documented anomalies quietly-dates, file numbers, versions. She did not dramatize. She did not accuse. She assembled pattern the way an archeologist assembles bone fragments into a skeleton. The more she assembled, the more she realized: Keller's brilliance was not just talent. It was control.

When her compilation reached an oversight committee, it did not explode like a scandal at first. It behaved like a slow chemical reaction: mild heat, then visible change, then something that could not be reversed.

Federal investigators traced financial records and communications. They cross-checked witness preparation against policy. They interviewed detectives who, at first, defended Keller with almost religious devotion-he's tough but fair, he's the best we have-until the questions became specific enough to puncture loyalty.

Evidence revealed a calculated pattern: strategic withholding, procedural manipulation, and gifts accepted in ways that compromised impartiality. Keller's robe and jabot, once props for public trust, became a grotesque frame: the uniform of a man who had learned how to weaponize belief.

The public reaction was swift once the story reached daylight, and the reaction was not just anger at Keller. It was anger at the system for being so predictable.

Media coverage did what institutions hate: it connected individual wrongdoing to structural incentives. Wrongful convictions were reviewed. Plea deals were reopened. Families spoke of the humiliation of discovering that the state's "truth" was curated.

And now, as the book closes in on its own conclusion, you-the reader-cannot remain neutral. You must decide what you believe about institutions, because institutions demand belief in exchange for belonging. Maybe you want to believe the courthouse is fundamentally good, and Keller was an aberration.

That is the optimistic reading, and it offers comfort: remove the bad actor, restore the system.

Maybe you want to believe the courthouse is fundamentally neutral: a machine that reflects human inputs, no more moral than a blade.

That is the pragmatic reading, and it offers resignation: fix the incentives, improve the oversight, accept imperfection.

Or maybe you want to believe the courthouse is, by nature, vulnerable to becoming predatory-because it concentrates power, cloaks it in ritual, and calls obedience "respect."

That is the darker reading, and it offers responsibility: vigilance forever, not as a phase after scandal, but as the price of authority.

The reforms came-mandatory disclosures, enhanced audits, rotation in sensitive cases, oversight with real teeth.

Keller faced criminal charges: obstruction, misconduct in office, conflicts of interest. Stripped of title, barred from practice, sentenced.

The system staged what it often stages: a public sacrifice to reassure the crowd that the altar still works.

But the deeper question remained-one you can't escape in the final pages of a book like this: Was Keller the disease, or was he a symptom?

In solitary moments, Keller reportedly reflected on the allure of power, but that reflection is not the point. Everyone reflects when the lights go out. The point is what the rest of us do while the lights are still on.

The courthouse endured because buildings always do. The robe and jabot endured because symbols are stubborn.

But the reader's trust-your trust-is the fragile thing. Once cracked, it does not heal with ceremony.

And that is the undisguised conclusion this story insists on delivering:

The robes permit omission. Jabots do not press ethics into shape. The institution can bless itself all day with procedure and still be sick.

If justice is to be more than costume, it must be watched-not with reverence, but with clear eyes that refuse to confuse dignity with innocence.

6

"THE GABBAI'S KITTEL"

WHITE CLOTH DOES NOT MAKE CLEAN HANDS.

Documented patterns of charity-fund misuse and governance failures in religious nonprofits/communities (composite), Israel, PRGR

The investigation was not dramatic at first. It was meetings in back rooms. It was emails that asked for clarification. It was Gavriel Stein growing suddenly defensive, then suddenly conciliatory. He offered to "repay." He offered to "explain." He insisted he had meant well. "I was protecting the fund," he told them, palms open. "Sometimes you have to move things around to keep it safe." Miriam answered, "Safe for whom?" On the eve of Yom Kippur, the synagogue appeared as though snow had dusted it. Men in white kittel moved through the aisles in a hush that felt older than the building itself. The air held candle wax, wool, and the faint sweetness of polished wood. Outside, an icy wind combed the street, lifting dry leaves and setting them down again as if trying to rewrite the same sentence.

Gavriel Stein, the gabbai, stood at the front with a clipboard tucked against his ribs. He wore his own kittel beneath a dark jacket, as though he wanted the purity close but not too visible. He liked things orderly-who sat where, who received honors, who got which prayer. Order was his liturgy, his private form of devotion.

A man named Ari approached him near the bimah. "Gavriel," Ari whispered, "my father-he can't afford the appeal this year. You said the fund could help."

Gavriel's expression softened. "Of course. We'll see what we can do." "Tonight?" Ari pressed. "He's... he's ashamed." Gavriel laid a hand on Ari's shoulder. "This is Yom Kippur. No one is beyond mercy."

He said it warmly, and Ari believed him because warm words are easy to believe when the world is cold. Gavriel turned away and made a note on the clipboard that looked like care: Ari's father-review. Then he slid the clipboard under his arm and moved toward the office that kept the charity envelopes.

The tzedakah fund was the synagogue's quiet heart. There were receipts and records-enough to satisfy trustees, enough to comfort donors. But there was also discretion, and discretion is a door that can swing either way.

Gavriel controlled that door. In meetings he was called "reliable," "devoted," "the man you can trust with keys." He had the keys, literally: to the office cabinet, to the safe, to the back entrance.

The first time he dipped into the fund, it wasn't theft in his mind. It was a correction.

A major donor had promised money for repairs, then delayed. A plumber demanded payment. Gavriel advanced cash from the charity funds and told himself he'd replace it when the donor came through. The donor did.

Gavriel replaced the money. The system returned to balance. The story ended neatly. Neat endings are addictive. When his daughter needed braces, he borrowed again-"just for a month." When his wife's business faltered, he took "a temporary loan." Each time, he left a trail of small notes to himself and moved money between categories the way a skilled hand moves cards: gently, without noise.

In the ledger he wrote the words that tranquilize conscience-reimbursement pending, bridge, timing issue. He prayed longer on those nights, as if prayer would cover a withdrawal the way snow covers dirt.

Outside, autumn rain fell. It tapped the synagogue windows in careful rhythms, like a soft interrogation. Water ran down the glass in thin lines, as though the building were trying to weep without being seen.

One Tuesday evening, Miriam Kalt arrived early to volunteer. She was a school administrator, practical, numbers-literate, and unusually unimpressed by titles. As she stacked prayer books, she noticed Gavriel in the office, the cabinet open, envelopes fanned across the desk like a magician's trick. He looked up too quickly. "Miriam," he said, smiling, "you're early." "I forgot my scarf," she replied, then nodded at the envelopes. "Big donations?"

Gavriel's smile held. "High holy days. People are generous." Miriam hesitated. "Do we log them right away?" "Of course," he said, and the word of course sounded like a door closing. He slid the envelopes into the safe with a deliberate click, a sound that made privacy physical.

Later that week, Miriam sat with the fund's spreadsheet-simple columns, simple totals-and felt something tighten in her chest. Withdrawals clustered strangely. The "emergency disbursements" increased, but the list of recipients didn't. The cash-on-hand line moved like a tide with no moon to explain it.

She printed the records and compared them to the bank statements. The numbers didn't reconcile. Not by a lot. By enough.

She approached Gavriel after mincha, when the sanctuary was emptier and the light slanted through the windows like pale blades.

"Gavriel," she said quietly, "I'm looking at the tzedakah account. There are gaps." He blinked once. "Gaps?" "Transfers," she corrected. "Cash withdrawals that aren't matched to distributions."

Gavriel laughed softly, as if she had made a charming mistake. "Miriam, you know how it is. People need help quickly. The paperwork follows."

"The paperwork doesn't follow," she said. "It disappears." His smile did not drop, but it hardened at the edges. "Be careful," he said, still gently. "You don't want to fall into lashon hara."

The phrase landed like a warning disguised as piety. Miriam stared at him. She realized that holiness could serve as a shield to protect the powerful from scrutiny, rather than to protect the poor.

That night, wind pushed through the street trees, stripping leaves and hurling them across the pavement in spirals. Miriam watched from her kitchen window and thought of how easily systems become weather: inevitable, impersonal, excused. The synagogue's fund was mercy made concrete. Instead, it had become a private reservoir.

On Erev Yom Kippur, the kittel returned-the sanctuary again full of white. The congregation struck their chests in the confessional prayers, voices rising together like surf. Gavriel stood near the front, his kittel bright under the lights, looking like purity personified.

Miriam watched him and felt the bitterness of contradiction: he could recite repentance while still refusing accountability. She remembered a teaching her grandfather quoted whenever a leader tried to silence critique with reverence: It is not the garment that atones; it is the heart. She wished the synagogue believed that.

After services, Ari found Gavriel again. "Did you check? About my father?"

Gavriel's eyes flickered-fatigue, annoyance, something like shame. "Not yet," he said. "After the fast." "But you promised," Ari whispered, voice cracking. "It's... it's urgent."

Gavriel leaned closer, lowering his voice. "Ari, don't make demands on holy days."

Ari stepped back as if slapped. The quiet exchange revealed the scandal's full moral geometry: the administrator's comfort required the poor to wait.

Miriam decided then. She did not argue publicly. She documented. She photocopied receipts, captured timestamps, and saved bank notifications. She brought the file to the trustees-two older men who had known Gavriel for decades.

One of them stared at the pages and said, "This can't be right." Miriam's voice stayed steady. "It is."

The other trustee rubbed his forehead. "If this becomes public, it will shame the community." Miriam replied, "The shame already happened. We just haven't admitted it."

When the trustees finally removed his access, it felt anticlimactic. No police arrived. No headlines flashed. The synagogue did not burn. But the wound spread quietly. People stopped giving as readily. The poor hesitated to ask for help. Trust, once cracked, does not reseal easily.

On the night after Yom Kippur, the first real rain came-hard, cleansing, relentless. It hammered the roof and flooded the gutters, dragging dirt and leaves toward the drains.

Miriam stood under the awning and watched water carve paths through the dust. It made her think of consequences: they do not always arrive as lightning. Often they arrive as runoff, exposing what has been building unseen.

Gavriel returned once, weeks later, to attend a weekday service. He wore a dark coat now, no kittel, no visible whiteness. He stayed near the back.

A few people nodded stiffly. Others looked away.

The synagogue continued-the prayers, the calendar, the routine. But something had shifted.

The community had learned, the hard way, that systems rescue after harm because rescue is visible, while prevention requires suspicion, and suspicion feels impolite.

The kittel had looked like innocence. It had been a curtain.

PRGR END-CAP - AUTHORED HARM TEST

(for "THE GABBAI'S KITTEL")

The harm in this case does not begin with theft in the cinematic sense. It begins with a softer move: **the gabbai's ability to make money feel holy and administration feel like faith.** The kittel is the perfect camouflage because it signals purity at the exact moment the institution needs fewer questions.

PRGR would attach authorship at the moment sacred trust becomes a discretionary wallet. In this story, the hinge-steps are specific and repeatable-small decisions that look like "community care" until you realize they are also the mechanism of untraceable control.

The hinge-steps where PRGR would force the author to exist

The first off-ledger disbursement framed as "urgent tzedakah" When the gabbai authorizes cash assistance or a transfer without the ordinary record-because the need is "too sensitive" or "too urgent"-that is the first authored-harm moment. PRGR would require him to write, even briefly:

Who is receiving it (or, if anonymity is essential, who is verifying identity)? What criteria justify urgency?

Why can this not follow the normal ledger route?

What prevents repeat discretionary payments to the same network? The harm forecast is not only financial. It is structural: *a parallel system of giving that cannot be audited becomes a parallel system of power.*

The "purity shield" move: invoking sanctity to block questions

In this chapter, the kittel matters because it **discourages scrutiny**. The moment the gabbai answers a ledger question with moral pressure-"Do you really want receipts for charity?" "Are you doubting someone's mitzvah?"-PRGR would force authorship of the tactic:

I am using religious framing to discourage oversight. Here is why the question is illegitimate (if it is).

Here is the alternative that preserves dignity without erasing accountability (two-person verification, anonymized coding, independent review). PRGR treats "holiness" as an environment, not an exemption.

The gatekeeping of dignity: deciding who deserves help and who deserves exposure

The gabbai's leverage is not just money; it is **the power to grant or deny privacy**. If recipients know that assistance depends on staying "good" with him-obedient, grateful, quiet-then charity becomes coercion.

PRGR would attach at the moment he:

conditions help on access to personal information, requests private meetings for "assessment," or signals that someone's reputation could be harmed if they complain. He would have to author: *what information is necessary, what is optional, what safeguards prevent coercion, and what recourse exists for recipients.*

The ledger manipulation step: classification and concealment

If the story includes "miscellaneous" categories, split transactions, delayed entries, or donor money being redirected, PRGR bites precisely where classification becomes concealment:

re-labeling restricted donations as general funds,

paying favored vendors/relatives through the charity channel,

or moving money through accounts "for convenience." PRGR would require a written reason for any deviation from donor intent and any payment that bypasses normal review-signed by the gabbai and countersigned by a second authority.

The retaliation-by-access step

In synagogue life, punishment often arrives as exclusion: fewer honors, fewer invitations, less standing in the community. When someone raises questions and then quietly loses access-committee removal, social demotion, sudden coldness from leadership-that is not "community dynamics." It is governance.

PRGR would force the author to exist at the moment leadership makes that access decision:

Why is this person being removed?

What is the documented basis?

What harm is foreseeable (reputation damage, chilling effect on reporting)? What appeal mechanism exists?

What PRGR would force in this case (practical, not preachy)

1. **Charity is not a discretionary zone**
   PRGR would treat *tzedakah disbursement* as a high-risk decision type because it combines: money + vulnerability + shame. So PRGR requires a **minimum auditable trail** even when privacy is essential: coded entries, two-person verification, periodic independent audit.

2. **Sanctity cannot be used as an oversight shield**
   Any time holiness is invoked to stop a question, PRGR requires a counter-move:
   "If the work is holy, it is worth protecting with transparency-because holiness without accountability becomes permission."

3. **A donor-intent lock**
   If donations are restricted (for families, schools, medical aid), PRGR requires explicit authorship for any redirection-no "everyone understands," no "urgent needs." Donor intent is a boundary, not a mood.

4. **A recipient-safe complaint path**

PRGR demands a reporting channel that does not route through the gabbai's social network. Because in this case, the harm is not only financial; it is **community captivity**.

The questions that keep this End-Cap tied to the kittel (not generic)

If you were the gabbai: which specific disbursement would you be willing to sign your name under, with criteria and verification, knowing it could be reviewed later? If you won't sign it, why should others accept it?

If you were a recipient: at what moment does help become leverage-when you are asked for personal details, when you are told to be grateful, or when you see others punished for questioning?

If you were the board or rabbi: which step would you force into authored form first-the off-ledger cash, the reclassification of donor funds, or the quiet social demotion of a questioner?

PRGR doesn't accuse the gabbai of evil. It isolates the moment he **converted sacred trust into discretionary power**-and it forces him to **author the harm at the exact step where a community's vulnerability becomes an unofficial budget line.**

THE TRIAD MAP

WHAT MOVES, WHAT BREAKS.

A map is not an argument. It is a way of seeing the same pattern without mistaking it for repetition. The triad is not three themes. It is three ways institutions turn harm into something that feels normal.

Money - what it buys

- Access (to decisions, rooms, files)
- Silence (non-complaints, non-questions)
- Speed (a shortcut around scrutiny)
- Immunity (exceptions made to look routine)

Intimacy - what it buys

- Confession (information you wouldn't say in daylight)
- Dependence (care that becomes leverage)
- Shame (a muzzle)
- Loyalty (a private bond used as public shield)

Procedure - what it buys

- Delay (until people tire)
- Disappearance (files, minutes, memory)
- Deference (the spell of 'process')
- Distance (harm without a hand)

HOW INSTITUTIONS HIDE EACH MECHANISM

They conceal money under stewardship, reimbursement, 'donor relations', and 'budget reality'.

They conceal intimacy behind care, mentorship, spiritual guidance, discretion, and 'private matters'.

They conceal the procedure under neutrality with statements like: 'we followed policy', 'the file progressed', 'nothing further can be done'.

Reader checkpoint:

When a decision feels inevitable, ask which lever is doing the work-Money, Intimacy, or Procedure-and who benefits from it feeling inevitable

Who does the blur protect?

Who is paying for it?

PERSONAL REASON-GIVING RECORD (PRGR) AS TEST CONDITION

Harm must be authored. The forecast must be written. Repair must be pre-committed.

A test condition is only useful if it can be run. PRGR is not a slogan; it is a small procedural lock that forces an institution to stop speaking in fog.

PRGR in one sentence:

Foreseeable harm must have a named author, a written forecast, and a pre-committed repair trigger.

THE PRGR RECORD (one page, max)

A decision cannot advance past the last reversible step until this record exists and a responsible party stores it in a place that can be audited.

- Decision being taken (plain language).
- Decision-author (name, role) and reviewer (name, role).
- Facts relied on (what you believe to be true; what you have not checked).
- Foreseeable harm (what could happen to a person if you are wrong).
- Why you believe the act is justified despite that risk.
- Disclosure statement (what has been shared with the affected person; what has been withheld, and why).
- Remedy trigger (what automatically happens if later evidence shows you were wrong).
- Review date (when someone must reopen this even if no complaints arise).

When PRGR becomes necessary.

An institution needs to implement PRGR whenever it plans to do something that cannot be cleanly undone or will predictably silence challenge.

Use it before:

- Irreversible steps (dismissal, expulsion, custody transfer, conviction, sentencing, deportation, removal of credentials).
- Reputation locks (labels like "vexatious", "unreliable", "non-compliant" that become fate).
- Secrecy walls (redactions, sealed files, privilege claims, "handled internally").
- Concentrated access (one person controlling funds, files, keys, archives, schedules, or confessional knowledge).
- Any trade-off that buys quiet (donor pressure, informal settlements, "pastoral discretion", career threats).

WHAT PRGR CHANGES IN PRACTICE

It does not assume angels. It assumes ordinary humans in robes will drift toward convenience unless the drift has a cost.

PRGR removes four escape hatches:

1. Passive voice (it happened) → active authorship (I did it).
2. Time as a weapon (wait them out) → mandatory review dates.
3. Secrecy as virtue (discretion) → auditability and stated reasons.
4. 'Process' as alibi → process as a signed choice with consequences.

REMEDY TRIGGERS (the 'R' in PRGR)

A remedy trigger is not punishment; it is a pre-agreed repair path that activates without begging.

Choose one or more, appropriate to the case:

- Automatic reopen / rehearing when a defined doubt threshold is met.
- Independent review (external to the chain of command that benefited).
- Immediate preservation order (no disposal, no 'lost files').
- Temporary stay (pause irreversible steps until review is complete).
- Restitution pathway (financial return, reinstatement, correction of record).
- Referral trigger (mandatory reporting to a body with the power to act).

MINI RERUN (How to use this book)

Pick any scene you have just read and rerun it in three questions:

1. Who is the author of the harm here-name, not title?
2. What harm was foreseeable, not in hindsight?
3. What remedy would have triggered automatically if the author was wrong?

Now ask yourself:
If you had to sign the PRGR record, would you still proceed as you did-or would you slow down, disclose more, recuse, or refuse?

AUTHORED HARM - QUICK END-CAP

Where the book shows a failure, rerun the scene under one structural requirement: Someone must author the harm. Someone must write the forecast. Repair must be pre-committed.

7

"THE RABBI'S FROZEN ACCOUNTS"

TRUST CAN SIT IN A PERSONAL BANK LIKE A STONE IN A STOMACH.

> UK charity funds held in personal accounts by a prominent rabbi; funds later agreed to be returned after an investigation; governance scrutiny followed.

In the London winter, rain comes sideways-small, persistent needles that make the city look freshly accused. The streets shine like black glass. Buses hiss at stops. Pigeons huddle under ledges as if they, too, are waiting for a verdict. The synagogue doors are heavy, varnished, warm to the touch, as if wood can remember the hands that have pushed them open in hope. Inside, the air carries wool coats and old prayer books, that clean-paper scent that promises order even when the world is messy.

Rabbi Elior Ben-Ami wears the tallit like a familiar horizon. When he steps to the front, the fringes at his sides move with him, soft punctuation that makes people listen before he speaks. He is not a man who demands trust. He wears it. His voice is careful-mercy without sentiment, duty without cruelty.

When he says tzedakah, the word lands like something solid, a coin you can hold. So when an overseas foundation sends a large sum for "education and relief," it feels natural-almost inevitable-that it passes through his hands.

At first, it is practical. He will "hold it briefly" while the recipients are confirmed. He will "avoid delays." He will "protect the gift from administrative friction." The community nods because friction is what bureaucrats create, and rabbis-so the story goes-remove obstacles. A transfer into his personal account serves as a temporary harbor, a safer shore. People accept the metaphor because they want to believe the sea is kinder when a holy man points to it.

The money stays longer than expected.

It is not a mask and a weapon that steal it. Because it is kept with language. "Waiting on documentation." "A complexity with the transfer." "A matter of timing." Each sentence is smooth enough to be believed. Each explanation is plausible enough to be forgiven. And each week that passes makes the return feel less like a simple act and more like an admission.

Ben-Ami tells himself he is safeguarding the funds. He tells himself the people asking for distribution are impatient, emotional, possibly irresponsible. He tells himself that control is stewardship. It is a common conversion: caution becomes ownership without ever announcing the change. The longer he holds it, the more his mind treats it as part of his domain-an extension of his pastoral authority, like keys on his ring.

A bookkeeper named Rivka notices because she still trusts arithmetic more than status. Rivka's upbringing taught her to respect rabbis, but ledgers make a different demand: the totals must reconcile, or they must confess. She watches the entries slide into "temporary holding," then watches "temporary" become a season, then watches it become a habit. She sees transfers that look like detours. She sees amounts that don't match the committee minutes. She feels a strange physical response-heat in the chest, a tightening in the throat-because she realizes she has made something sacred private.

She tries the gentle path first. She asks the treasurer if they distributed the funds. The treasurer smiles too quickly and says, "The rabbi is handling it." She asks for a timeline. "Soon," he says, as if soon is a policy. At home, Rivka hears the rain striking her window like fingertips. She thinks about the families whose names appear in the requests: a widow behind on rent, a man who can't afford his insulin, a student's tuition balance that has become a cliff edge. The money is not abstract. It is food and heat and breath. The rabbi's delay is not a pause in paperwork; it is a pause in living.

When she asks Ben-Ami directly, the answer arrives wrapped in gentleness.

"Do not worry," he says, voice low, paternal. "These matters are sensitive. Better the funds remain safe than scattered. Trust."

Trust. The word falls like a curtain.

Rivka leaves his office with the sensation of being chastised for caring. In the corridor she sees a framed quote from the sages-decorative Hebrew curling like vines around the letters. She remembers a line her grandfather repeated when he wanted to end an argument without ending the truth: "The seal of the Holy One... is truth." The phrase is old, almost worn smooth by repetition, but now it feels sharp. If truth is the seal, then what is being stamped here-holiness or fear?

She tries to speak to the fundraising committee, but the room tightens. One member warns against lashon hara-evil speech-using the prohibition as a fence against scrutiny. Another whispers hillul Hashem, desecration of God's name, as if the sin is exposure rather than the act. Rivka feels the trap close: reverence becomes a tool to protect reputation, and reputation becomes a tool to protect power.

Outside, wind pushes wet leaves along the pavement in little spirals that look like pages torn from a book. The Thames-grey, swollen, indifferent-moves under bridges with a slow confidence. Rivka understands then that the community's greatest vulnerability is not greed. It is reverence. A tallit can make a man look like an argument you may not challenge.

Still, she documents. She prints the bank statements. She saves the emails that repeat the same soothing phrases. She writes dates beside withdrawals and notes the moments the rabbi's explanations change slightly, like a story being revised in real time. She does not feel brave; she feels nauseated. Bravery, she learns, is often just the refusal to stop being uncomfortable.

The turning point comes when a donor asks for verification-quietly, politely-because accountants have their own commandments. The committee panics, not for the poor, but for the optics. The committee brought in an external compliance officer. Questions arrive in writing. Writing has a way of hardening what people prefer to keep soft.

When regulators finally freeze the accounts, the synagogue doesn't explode. There are no sirens. No flames. Only the slow, humiliating drip of public knowledge. People read about it on their phones between meetings and train stops. A few stare at the headline as if it is in the wrong language. Donors feel betrayed. Recipients feel mocked. And the community learns a bitter lesson: people withheld money, and this withholding caused harm. Powerful people demanded that the poor wait to ensure their own safety.

Ben-Ami returns the funds in the end. He says the right words. He looks appropriately tired.

He speaks about "misunderstandings" and "the burden of leadership." Some people accept the explanation because acceptance is easier than re-evaluating a beloved figure. Others don't. They have heard a different rhythm beneath the sermons: the steady beat of accountability.

But the arithmetic has already preached its own sermon: a person can keep charity in a personal account and still speak beautifully about righteousness-until the numbers, like witnesses, refuse to be silenced.

The congregation will remember, not as scandal alone, but as a fracture in the logic they wanted to live by: that holiness automatically protects.

The tallit remains white.

The stain? Elsewhere.

8

"THE STOLE AND THE LEDGER"

TWO SCENES. ONE MECHANISM. DIFFERENT SCALES OF SANCTITY, THE SAME CONVERSION OF MORAL OFFICE INTO INSTITUTIONAL PROTECTION.

Part I: The Epitrachelion

> Recurring real-world patterns of opaque parish real-estate leasing, patronage, and "restoration" schemes in historic religious sites (composite), Greece, 1990-1995

We meet the first story where the sacred garment is close enough to smell candlewax-where authority is personal and therefore deniable.

When blessing becomes leverage, the altar becomes a desk.

The Church owned land. Not much, but enough-an olive grove above the village, two storefronts near the quay, a crumbling house whose view mattered more than its walls. The deeds were old, written in a legal Greek that looked like scripture. "For the poor," the margins promised. "For the liturgy." Language pure enough to make greed feel like sacrilege.

Then came Nikos Vrellis, a business executive from the city, with a plan for "restoration."

He arrived with rolled drawings and expensive shoes and spoke of heritage the way financiers speak of "assets." He offered to repair the church roof "at no cost," renovate the parish hall, even fund new vestments. Theophanes listened and told himself he was being prudent. Epictetus had warned that things do not disturb us, but the views we take of them; Theophanes took Nikos as providence.

"The village deserves dignity," Nikos said, smoothing his papers. "And you, Father, deserve a partner who can make things happen."

The first agreement was small: a short-term lease of the quay storefront "for a community cafe." The rent was modest but "reliable," Nikos promised. Theophanes signed, telling the council that reliability was righteousness. A second storefront followed. Then the olive grove-"only for an event space," Nikos said, "weddings, baptisms, beautiful things." Theophanes repeated the word beautiful the way a man repeats a charm.

It was not theft done in darkness. It was theft done in daylight, under the clean mask of paperwork.

A cantor named Eleni noticed first because she noticed everything that affected the poor. Food parcels began shrinking. They announced repairs, but the delay hindered the work. The parish's "restoration" fund grew in speeches but not in receipts. She asked for the books and was told, gently, that she was "not to worry." "Father," she said one evening as rain tapped the windows like impatient fingernails, "the olive grove-who approved the sublease?"

Theophanes looked up from his desk. "Sublease?"

Eleni held a printed page. "Nikos's company leased it to another company. For triple." Theophanes's mouth tightened. "These are business details."

"They are moral details," Eleni replied.

Theophanes smiled with controlled patience. "You sing the services, Eleni. Let those appointed handle administration."

It sounded like an order. It was dismissal dressed as piety.

The next Sunday, wearing the epitrachelion, Theophanes preached on obedience-how sheep scatter when they distrust the shepherd. Eleni listened and thought of Musonius Rufus, the Stoic teacher few remembered by name; the philosopher insisted people must practice virtue, not admire it. Theophanes admired goodness publicly. He practiced a different craft privately: managing appearances.

The unraveling began as weather does-slowly, then all at once.

A winter storm split a section of the church roof. Water poured into the nave and pooled beneath the icons like tears. Parishioners arrived with buckets, furious. Nikos's promised repairs had been "scheduled," always scheduled, like mercy postponed. Under pressure, the parish council demanded documents. Theophanes stalled. Stalling, too, is a kind of power.

Then the metropolitan's office sent auditors. They came with polite faces and hard questions. They traced rent payments that moved through Nikos's subsidiaries like currents around a reef, returning thinner each time. They asked why the parish had waived penalties, why the lease terms were so favorable, and why council votes were missing minutes. Theophanes answered with calm phrases about complexity and "protecting the Church."

In his mind, he was defending the institution's survival-an argument Marcus Aurelius might have recognized and rejected: "What is not right, do not do; what is not true, do not say." Theophanes, however, had learned to do and say what kept the machine quiet.

When the auditors questioned Nikos's donations, the archpriest's composure cracked. "Do you want the roof fixed or not?" he snapped. "Do you want the poor fed or not?"

One auditor replied evenly, "We want them fed without being used as a shield."

Outside, the sea roared. Wind whipped olive branches until they struck each other like clapping hands. Nature, indifferent, performed its own judgment: erosion does not care for motives, only outcomes.

Reviewers are suspending Theophanes pending a review. Ecclesiastical softness accompanied the Church's announcement of-"for the moral order of the Church"-but the village understood the word removal. Some parishioners defended him: "He meant well." Others said bitterly, "Meaning well is not an accounting method." On his last evening in the rectory, Theophanes folded the epitrachelion carefully and stared at the gold thread. He remembered a line attributed to Cleanthes, the Stoic who wrote hymns to Zeus: Cleanthes said that the willing are led, and the unwilling dragged. Theophanes had insisted he was leading, but he realized admiration had dragged him -, by comfort, by the thrill of being the gate through which money entered holiness.

The parish rebuilt slowly, this time with transparent controls and shared keys. The roof was repaired, late. The poor were helped, late. The village learned, late, that rescue after harm is not protection before it. A stole can bless. It can also hide a handshake.

The epitrachelion remained a symbol. The question was: symbol of what?

Comparison

In the village, the instrument is a sublease and a smile. In the cathedral, it is a foundation name, a quarterly report, a ledger that looks complete. The difference is scale; the similarity is moral laundering.

Ask yourself: when an institution speaks in the language of 'survival' or 'stewardship', do you feel relief-or do you feel the weight of a choice being hidden inside a word?

Part II: The Secret Ledger

Catholic Church Financial Scandals, (Italy & Vatican Banking systems), 1980s–2010s (composite case)

Here the sacred is no longer local. They administer it-perform it at a distance, protected by impeccable paperwork.

Numbers, like souls, are sometimes messy.

Donations arrived through foundations with names that suggested transparency-Fondazione Santa Misericordia and similar entities that sounded as if they could only exist for good. The paperwork was immaculate. Foundations issued receipts. They filed reports. Budgets appeared with careful language: education, hospitals, outreach, renovation.

But the accounting did not end where it appeared to end.

A portion of the money traveled outward in a way that never looked like theft on a single page. Small transfers divided the funds. The team routed these funds through consulting fees, administrative costs, and "special project" disbursements. They reappeared in jurisdictions that specialized in discretion-Switzerland, Luxembourg, and island accounts that existed primarily to be difficult to examine. The shell companies above them were like decorative windows, using religious terms, believable mission statements, and ownership structures that made it hard to prove what they intended to do.

Marchetti called it prudence when he explained it to himself. The Church, he believed, had to survive the world as it was, not as it wished it to be. If influence required financial leverage, then financial leverage became a form of pastoral strategy. He did not feel like a criminal. He felt like a realist operating inside an institution that rewarded realism when it remained quiet.

Only a few people had access to enough detail to notice the pattern. Fewer still had the nerve to name it. Carla Benedetti was his private secretary-efficient, methodical, the person who kept the archbishop's life smooth enough that no one thought about the effort required. Her work included preparing quarterly financial summaries that were meant, in theory, to show good governance. She had handled numbers long enough to recognize the difference between complexity and disguise.

Late one evening, while assembling a report, she saw discrepancies that resisted ordinary explanations. The committee allocated renovation funds and then "reclassified" them. Interest payments did not align with the balances they were supposed to reflect. None of it was blatantly absurd. That was what made it credible-and what made it dangerous.

She reviewed the entries again, then again, searching for the reassuring error that would let her close the file and go home.

She didn't find it.

When she finally spoke to Marchetti, she chose her words carefully.

"Your Excellency," she said, "some of these figures don't reconcile. I'm not sure how to present them."

He looked at her as though he were weighing her-not only her competence but her temperament. Then his expression softened into something paternal, gentle enough to be disarming.

"Carla," he said, "numbers, like souls, are sometimes messy. Be patient. The truth of things comes in time."

He briefly placed his hand over hers, an act that people could interpret as kindness or control. It did what it did: it redirected the emotional burden back onto her. If she pressed further, she would be the impatient one, the anxious one, the person who did not understand the world as deeply as he did.

She left the office unsettled, and then-almost involuntarily-ashamed of being unsettled. That was one of Marchetti's gifts. He could make doubt feel like a personal failing rather than an institutional warning.

Outwardly, nothing changed. Marchetti attended events, hosted donors, and delivered speeches on poverty and compassion. He greeted dignitaries with practiced warmth. He wore the robe as if it were proof.

Privately, the ledger continued.

A discreet call to a banker. An instruction passed through an intermediary. The scribe signed the document where no one would ever read it aloud. The pleasure, for him, was not only the money. It was the sense of operating above ordinary scrutiny-of holding an institution's moral language in one hand and its hidden transactions in the other.

The first public disturbance came the way such disturbances often do: not through internal oversight, but through an external reader who didn't share the institution's incentives.

A journalist named Lorenzo Ricci received an anonymous tip. Ricci had covered corruption long enough to recognize a familiar structure: foundations, layered transfers, and the slow migration of money into places where accountability became a technical problem rather than a moral one. He spent months following the routes, checking registries, tracing corporate ownership, and waiting to publish the story once it could not be dismissed as rumor.

When it broke, the headlines were blunt and humiliating. Some framed it as betrayal. Others framed it as hypocrisy. The public reaction came in predictable waves: outrage, disbelief, rationalization, and then a quieter, more corrosive cynicism.

Marchetti responded with the discipline of someone who had rehearsed crisis without expecting to need it.

He called a press conference inside the cathedral. He arrived in full ceremonial presentation, allowing the setting to suggest innocence before he said a word. He spoke in the language institutions prefer when the facts are inconvenient: complexity, misunderstandings, administrative errors, modern financial systems. He admitted "mistakes" without admitting intent. He promised an audit without conceding why an audit was necessary. He gave the crowd repentance without confession.

It was not a legal defense. It was a narrative defense.

An internal Vatican review followed. The review examined transactions. An internal Vatican review compared accounts. The Vatican requested documents in a manner that demonstrates concern while maintaining control. The financial architecture, designed to be technically lawful, worked as intended. Prosecutors could not cleanly prosecute much of what Marchetti had done. Marchetti built it to exist in the gap between wrongdoing and proof.

The review produced consequences, but not the kind the public imagines when it imagines accountability. The Church reassigned Marchetti to a smaller diocese in central Italy. Commentators described the move as administrative-an "opportunity for renewed focus," a "reorientation of pastoral leadership." It removed him from the direct center of the scandal while preserving the dignity of the office. It prevented a trial of the institution by allowing the individual to carry the burden quietly elsewhere. The system remained intact.

Carla Benedetti resigned. Not in protest, not with a statement, but with the slow exhaustion of someone who realized that clarity was unwelcome. She did not become a whistleblower. She did not become a heroine. She simply stepped away, carrying with her the knowledge that an institution can absorb almost anything as long as it controls the surrounding language.

Marchetti continued to preach. In photographs, his vestments remained crisp. In public, his voice remained steady. Marchetti's authority persisted not from a widespread belief in his words, but from institutions' capacity to outlast such belief. They rely on structure, ceremony, and the careful management of consequences.

The ledger did not need to be destroyed. It only needed to be made harder to see. And so it was.

His jabot stayed perfectly arranged. The stain was elsewhere.

How do you feel reading these in parallel-angry, resigned, familiar?

What would you do if you were inside the system: comply, report, leave, or rationalize?

Is there a smaller version of this in daily life-where procedure or 'good intentions' becomes a shelter for harm? Who signed the first paper?

Who will own the outcome?

9

"THE COUNSEL'S DOUBLE GAME"

TWO LEGAL ROLES. ONE EXPLOITATION-OF-TRUST MECHANISM: CONFIDENCE HARVESTED AS LEVERAGE, PROCEDURE USED AS COVER.

Legal misconduct and client exploitation, France, 2000s-2010s (composite case)

1. ADVOCATE

Yet beneath the surface of elegance lay ambition entwined with moral compromise. Pierre's clients trusted him completely, often with their most sensitive secrets, their fortunes, and sometimes their freedom. He had learned early that legal expertise alone was not enough; ascendancy, subtle manipulation, and careful orchestration of human behaviour were the true tools of mastery.

Pierre's misconduct was not overtly criminal, but it was ethically corrosive. He selectively withheld information from clients, delayed cases strategically, and cultivated dependencies that ensured loyalty and obedience. A corporate client's CFO, Sophie Dubois, discovered this truth gradually. Initially captivated by Pierre's intellect and charisma, she deferred entirely to his judgment, believing that his brilliance guaranteed the best outcome.

Their professional relationship soon deepened into something more insidious. Late-night strategy sessions in his office - ostensibly for legal consultation - became emotionally charged. Pierre subtly intertwined flattery, psychological pressure, and emotional dependency. Sophie found herself torn between admiration, trust, and an unease she could not articulate.

Pierre's motivations were a mixture of intellectual satisfaction and personal gratification. He enjoyed the thrill of shaping outcomes - not only in court but in human lives. Sophie, talented and ambitious, became the focus of his subtle manipulations. He strategically gave her praise, measured his criticism to maintain her dependence, and offered opportunities in ways that increased her loyalty to him. He even calibrated his silences: a delayed reply could make her doubt herself more efficiently than any insult.

The turning point arrived when Sophie, after months of subtle manipulation, realized the ethical breach. She had begun cross-checking his advice with independent legal counsel and discovered discrepancies in case strategies, financial disclosures, and risk assessments. Pierre's careful orchestration had diverted resources, influenced decisions, and manipulated outcomes to enhance his control, not necessarily her benefit. She noticed, too, how he positioned himself as the sole interpreter of complexity-turning every question into an implied accusation of her incompetence.

Despite the shock, Sophie found the courage to confront the situation. She documented the discrepancies, consulted ethics bodies, and eventually filed a complaint with the Paris Bar Association. The investigation revealed a consistent pattern of client exploitation: selective disclosure, emotional manipulation, and unethical influence over outcomes. Witness statements described an identical sensation: clients felt reassured after consultations, but later discovered the doctor had used anesthesia as reassurance.

Pierre's public persona remained unshaken throughout the investigation. In court, he used measured gestures, spoke with a steady voice, wore impeccable robes, and perfectly framed his jabot. Colleagues and clients still admired his intellect. Yet behind the scenes, the legal authorities examined every case he had touched, investigating his strategies, advice, and interactions. The inquiry did not revolve around a single dramatic offense but around accumulation-the way small, defensible choices can form a larger pattern of betrayal.

The tribunal concluded that Pierre had breached ethical standards, exploiting client trust for personal satisfaction and influence. The authorities did not pursue criminal charges because most actions technically stayed within legal limits, but the professional consequences were severe. Formal reprimands, a twelve-month restriction from high-profile client cases, and supervision by the Bar Association were the consequences imposed on him. Legal peers and informed clients irreparably damaged his reputation, which had once been untouchable.

Sophie, though initially shaken, emerged empowered. She had witnessed firsthand the seductive power of charisma, intellect, and authority - and the way trust, when exploited, could distort judgment and manipulate outcomes. Her courage in documenting and confronting Pierre's behaviour ensured accountability and served as a warning to other lawyers and clients about the subtle perils of misplaced trust.

Pierre continued his practice, but with restrictions. He remained a figure of prestige; robes and white necktie intact, he continued to appear in court with confidence. Behind the doors of his home, the thrill of covert influence, the quiet satisfaction of shaping outcomes unseen, had vanished. Every decision now carried oversight; every action was accountable. A paper trail replaced the freedom he had prized-the ability to steer without being seen steering-, by required disclosures, by the watchful presence of compliance.

In cafes near the Palais, his name became shorthand: not for scandal in the tabloid sense, but for a particular danger-polished, plausible, difficult to prove until someone compares notes. The recital of Pierre Leclair became a cautionary tale in Parisian legal circles. Lawyers, interns, and clients alike learned from the recital of Pierre Leclair about the dangers of unchecked influence and the ethical responsibility that accompanies intellect and authority. The narrative endured not only because of misconduct, but because it highlighted the psychological nuance of manipulation: charm and brilliance, when untempered by accountability, could be as dangerous as overt criminality.

Even after the reprimand, Pierre maintained appearances: flawless robes, a perfectly positioned jabot, and measured gestures. Yet those who knew the story understood that true mastery of influence comes with a price. Ethics, once breached, leaves traces that persist beyond the courtroom, beyond reputations, and into the delicate balance of trust between advocate and client. In the evenings, when rain slicked the streets and the city's lights smeared across the pavement, Paris still looked beautiful-but beauty, Sophie now knew, can be a surface that hides the direction of the flow underneath.

People discussed Pierre's case in a language older than Paris, as they reached for ancient metaphors to describe what they sensed but struggled to name whenever modern rules feel too thin. In the corridors, a senior avocat compared him to a Roman Scriba who knows where to press the wax tablets without leaving obvious marks.

Roman law, for all its marble confidence, depended on records-on the Acta, on the careful custody of documents, on the assumption that procedure was a scaffold for fairness rather than a costume for power. Pierre had treated the procedure like a praetor's edict written in pencil: adjustable, strategic, crafted to favor the patron who stood closest to him. He never shattered the Twelve Tables; he simply learned to stand in their shadow and interpret them in ways that kept his hands technically clean.

2. BARRISTER

She was brilliant, and in public her brilliance looked like a forte. She wore her robes with controlled ease. Always crisp, centered, and immaculate, her white neckbands were uniform details that persuaded people of her discipline before she had to prove anything. Judges trusted her. Clients trusted her. Even opposing counsel respected her because she made her work look clean.

But Charlotte didn't merely argue cases. She collected them.

In her practice, information wasn't just evidence. She treated information as a substance with weight and reactivity-a chemical that could be diluted, concentrated, transferred. Confidentiality, which protects clients, became her favorite element to handle. She learned how to keep secrets the way a lab keeps volatile compounds: sealed, labeled, and ready for use when conditions were right.

Over time, she cultivated relationships that were difficult to describe without sounding paranoid: friendly conversations with prosecutors that seemed too familiar, casual connections with investigators that ran too warm, informal rapport with court staff that opened doors other people didn't know existed. None of it was overt. Overt misconduct creates heat. Charlotte preferred the cool approach: minor adjustments, plausible deniability, the influence that moves like air pressure-present everywhere, visible nowhere.

Her first significant slide happened in a mid-level property fraud matter.

Her client, an emerging entrepreneur-Simon P.-was facing charges that could have ended his career before it began. The evidence wasn't trivial. The paper trail was thick. The narrative was ugly. The case needed more than advocacy; it needed a reshaping of what the court would pay attention to.

Charlotte represented him with outward precision. She also maintained discreet contact with the other side-just enough to "help" the matter proceed efficiently, just enough to guide emphasis away from the most damaging details. No direct betrayal. Nothing crude. More like a subtle reframing: if the prosecution looked here, it wouldn't look there; if a witness was pressed on this inconsistency, the larger story would blur.

It resembled an optical illusion: you don't change the object; you change the viewer's focus.

Simon won. The court noted Charlotte's skill. People congratulated her in corridors with smiles that carried professional envy. Simon thanked her with genuine warmth, unaware that she had used him as much as she had defended him. Charlotte returned to chambers and filed her notes with practiced care, managing two storylines at once without leaving any obvious trace.

She told herself it was artistry. She also told herself it was harmless. Then came the grimmer case: a local council bribery scandal.

The client was a senior official accused of awarding contracts in exchange for favors. The evidence, again, was not nothing-circumstantial but sufficient to ruin a career and stain a public office. Charlotte dismantled witnesses with controlled charm, introduced small contradictions that left jurors uncertain, and played the courtroom like a calibrated instrument.

Outside court, she contacted a prosecution investigator-someone flattered by her attention, impressed by her intellect, eager to be seen as close to brilliance. Charlotte didn't need to give instructions. She guided by suggestion: a question posed as curiosity, a remark offered as helpful context, an idea placed lightly into someone else's mind like a reagent dropped into solution.

Over time, the investigator's line of questioning shifted in ways that benefited Charlotte's narrative. Not because he was bribed. Not because he was threatened. Because he believed he was participating in sophistication.

That was Charlotte's gift: she could make people feel intelligent while they were being used.

For a while, she operated as if she could hold both sides in balance indefinitely-the way a particle in a thought experiment seems to occupy two states until measurement forces a choice. In her world, "measurement" was scrutiny. Scrutiny could be delayed. Scrutiny could be redirected. Scrutiny could be managed.

But systems don't stay stable forever. Entropy is patient.

The turning point wasn't a dramatic exposure. It was a quiet human fact Charlotte had underestimated: some people watch without wanting anything in return.

An intern-bright, observant, still untrained in institutional loyalty-noticed the pattern. Not one conversation, not one email, but the shape of Charlotte's connections. Meetings that didn't belong on calendars. Familiarity that seemed misplaced. A strange overlap between what Charlotte knew and what she should not have known at that stage.

The intern reported concerns to the professional regulator.

An inquiry began, slow and procedural. Charlotte responded exactly as someone like her would: with calm, poise, and impeccable presentation. No panic. No confession. She understood that the system, like any apparatus, responds differently to different inputs. She gave it the input it prefers-professionalism.

The investigators struggled to pin down a single illegal act. That was also by design. Charlotte's conduct lived in the gray zones where ethical boundaries exist but criminal codes hesitate. Yet when they reviewed patterns-dual communications, conflicts of interest, strategic overlaps-what emerged was not one incident, but a method.

And methods are harder to excuse.

The inquiry took months. It didn't explode her reputation overnight; it corroded it. Colleagues began to keep distance. Junior barristers who once tried to impress her stopped asking for advice. Senior clients, who can smell reputational risk the way animals smell smoke, quietly withdrew. The courtroom-her preferred stage-began to feel less like a home and more like a place where everyone had learned to look twice.

At the hearing, Charlotte adjusted her neckband in the mirror with the reflex of habit. She told herself it was theatre-another performance to survive. She spoke in the language of interpretation: misunderstandings, professional courtesy, ordinary contact, coincidence.

The tribunal's findings were not cinematic. They rarely are.

Charlotte's superiors formally reprimanded her. She kept her license, but her career stalled. Her career stalled like a body stalls when circulation is restricted: technically alive, functionally limited. Major briefs slowed. Invitations stopped. Careful politeness replaced the easy warmth of professional respect. And that, for her, was a different punishment: the loss of the room's oxygen.

She moved into consultancy work, where she drafted, advised, and operated behind closed doors to control her visibility. She remained clever. She remained meticulous. But her preferred drug had always been the public arena: the moment a jury turns, the moment a judge signals, the moment the room agrees you're the most competent person in it.

Now the room was gone.

In her office, late at night, she sometimes stared at her robes draped over a chair-heavy cloth without a body inside it-and understood what she had refused to admit for years: power borrowed from trust is always on loan. It can feel permanent until the moment it isn't. She had played both sides because she believed she could keep the system in superposition-two realities held at once, neither collapsing into consequence.

But eventually, observation arrives. And when manipulation becomes visible, isolation follows-quietly, inexorably-like the moment a sealed chamber loses pressure and the air that once held everything together thins.

Comparison

One seduces with proximity; the other exploits distance. Both rely on the same quiet miracle: raw material is the client's trust.

How do you feel when you see it laid bare-betrayed, unsurprised, complicit?

What would you do if you were the client and the file was already moving without you: fight, freeze, leave, submit?

Do you recognise smaller versions of this-places where you hand over trust because 'that's how it works'? Who used trust as a tool?

Who will own the outcome?

PART II

MONEY / DONOR LEVERAGE / HIDDEN LEDGERS

THE MAMASHIMI TRUST - BRISBANE AUSTRALIA

WRITE TO THE PERSON, NOT THE ARCHIVE

THE POINT WHERE REPETITION STOPS BEING LITERATURE AND STARTS BEING A MIRROR.

Reading the verdict, I felt as if it were about someone else. My name appeared at the top. Then, through the body of the document, I became "he," or "the defendant." That is how institutions remove emotion-and worse, personality. A name becomes a case number. Done. Archived.

Around this point, the stories began to feel like déjà vu: the calm voice, the careful minutes, the soft delay that calls itself prudence. What changes is the building. What doesn't change is the mechanism.

The PRGR detail that bites hardest here is simple: the audience is the harmed person. Not counsel. Not supervisors. Not an internal file "for record." It is written to the one who will carry the harm. I know what institutions do when they write for themselves: they launder. They choose language that stays clean under the gaze of people who already want to be reassured. But when you have to write to the person you're injuring, the distance collapses. The prose can't live on abstractions for long.

So I'm asking you-quietly, as you read-what would change if decision-makers had to address you directly. Not "the public." Not "stakeholders." You.

That is the point where repetition stops being literature and becomes a mirror.

10

"THE IMAM AND THE DONATION LIST"

WHEN GIVING BECOMES SPECTACLE, HEARTS BECOME ACCOUNTS.

> Composite patterns of donor favoritism, coerced "public virtue," and misuse of zakat/sadaqah signaling (fictionalized), United Arab Emiretas, PRGR.

The coast city lived by tides. Sea wind swept salt through the streets, and fishers mended nets in doorways, patient as prayer.

Masjid An-Nur sat two blocks from the harbor. Its courtyard was modest, but its imam, Sheikh Adil Farouq, carried a presence that filled space. On Fridays he wore a clean thawb and a simple cloak, and his voice rose and fell with a rhythm that made even distracted men look up. He preached often about ikhlas-sincerity-about giving for God, not for praise.

Then he created a donation list.

It began as administration. The mosque's roof needed repairs, the school needed books, and the zakat committee needed reliable funds before Ramadan. Adil proposed a board in the entrance hall: names and amounts, updated weekly. "Transparency," he called it. "Encouragement," he called it. People nodded because transparency sounds like morality, and encouragement sounds like care.

The first week, the board worked. Donations rose. Wealthier families competed quietly, the way the sea competes with the shore-by returning again and again. Men paused at the entrance to scan the names. Some smiled with pride. Some frowned at their own absence.

A fisherman named Nabil stood in front of the board after Maghrib and stared at the numbers until they blurred. His hands smelled of salt and rope. He had given what he could-small, folded bills-but next to corporate donors his gift looked like a raindrop in the ocean.

A volunteer approached and whispered, "Your name isn't there." Nabil said, "I gave."

The volunteer shrugged. The minimum is posted. Otherwise it's... clutter."

Clutter. The word stung more than the omission. Outside, wind pushed sea spray down the lane, leaving a white crust on metal shutters. Nature left salt on everything; the mosque was leaving shame.

Adil noticed the effect and told himself it was temporary discomfort for long-term benefit. He told himself a little competition would fund the poor. He told himself that public lists prevented suspicion. Yet he also felt, privately, the satisfaction of seeing the mosque's income rise under his management, as if money were proof of divine approval.

Soon donors requested favors with their giving. A business owner asked for front-row seating during Eid. A shipping agent wanted his son chosen for a prestigious recitation slot. A developer suggested the khutbah emphasize "gratitude for enterprise." None of the requests were written. They arrived like mist: deniable, everywhere.

Adil rarely said yes explicitly. He simply arranged outcomes so that the requesters felt heard. He told himself he was maintaining harmony. He told himself he was protecting the mosque from losing support. Slowly, the donation list stopped being a record and became a ladder.

The zakat committee felt the shift first. Their work required discretion-quiet transfers to widows, rent support, medical costs. But donors now asked, "Where does my money go?" and demanded public proof. Some wanted recipients' names "for accountability." Adil, trying to satisfy both sides, proposed a compromise: categories posted on the board-"food aid," "medical," "education"-and occasional "success stories" in the newsletter. The poor became a narrative tool.

One afternoon, Adil filmed a brief "success story" with a widow named Samira. A neighbor later mocked her for it, and Samira stopped accepting aid for months. Shame had cost her food.

A storm rolled in off the sea. Wind bent palm trees; waves slammed the breakwater; the city's power flickered. In the mosque, water leaked into a bucket-drip, drip-like a quiet accusation.

An accountant on the board, Layla Hussain, asked for a full audit. She had noticed donor-restricted funds drifting into general accounts and general funds being used to cover "event expenses" that benefited prestige donors. The numbers weren't catastrophic; they were worse-systematic.

Adil resisted. He spoke of trust, of unity, of not "airing doubts." But Layla had grown up by the sea; she understood undertow. The surface can look calm while the current pulls steadily.

The audit revealed no dramatic embezzlement. It revealed something more corrosive: the donation list had reshaped governance. The audit revealed donor influence increased; they compromised zakat discretion, and spending choices tracked prestige more than need. Transparency had become theater.

When the board removed the public list, some donors protested. "People will suspect misuse," they said. Others, quietly relieved, began giving again without asking for credit. Nabil returned one evening with a small envelope and slipped it into the box instead of asking for recognition. He felt lighter, as if he had stopped bargaining with his own conscience.

Adil delivered a khutbah on sincerity the following Friday. He spoke about giving in secret, about the danger of showing off, and about guarding the heart from vanity. His voice was steady. Yet he felt the irony like salt on the tongue: he had built a system that trained people to perform uprightness, then tried to preach them out of it. After prayer, he walked alone to the harbor. The tide was going out, pulling seaweed and small debris away from the stones. The water did not request permission; it simply revealed what had been left behind. Adil watched gulls circle and thought of the moral the city had taught him every day: what you display attracts attention, and attention changes behavior.

The community did not need rescue from scandal; it needed protection from incentives that turn worship into status. A list meant to encourage giving had turned giving into a scoreboard. And scoreboards do not measure sincerity. They only measure who can afford to be seen.

That evening, sea wind moved through the streets, leaving salt on windows and metal rails. Salt preserves and stings. Adil understood both. He returned to the mosque and took the empty board down from the wall. The nails remained, small dark points in plaster-proof that even good intentions can leave holes.

PRGR END-CAP - AUTHORED HARM TEST

(for "THE IMAM AND THE DONATION LIST")

The harm in this case doesn't begin with missing cash. It begins with a quieter conversion: **a donation list turning from record-keeping into a lever.** When names and amounts become a way to allocate standing, access, forgiveness, or fear, money stops being support and becomes governance.

PRGR would attach authorship at the first step where the Imam (or his office) converts generosity into pressure. In this story, the hinge-steps are specific, social, and repeatable.

The hinge-steps where PRGR would force the author to exist

The creation and control of the list - who gets to see it

The first authored-harm moment is not a theft; it's **centralizing the donor ledger under one person's discretion**. When the Imam (or a trusted aide) decides that the list is private "for unity," PRGR requires a written record:

Who has access, and why?

What separation exists between spiritual authority and financial control?

What safeguards prevent selective disclosure or manipulation? Because in this case, the list is not just accounting. It is *social power*.

The public recognition mechanism - when giving becomes status

When donations are read aloud, hinted at in sermons, posted on boards, or used in "thank you" rituals that clearly differentiate donors, PRGR triggers at the decision to use names and amounts. The Imam must author:

what is the purpose (transparency, encouragement, fundraising)?

what harms are foreseeable (coercion, shame, retaliation, exclusion of the poor)?

what alternatives exist (anonymous totals, opt-in recognition, capped ranges rather than exact amounts)? The key is that "transparency" can be weaponized when it is selective.

The pastoral leverage step - forgiveness or access tied to giving

If the Imam implies, directly or indirectly, that donations affect:

access to him, committee roles, marriage introductions, community inclusion,

or moral standing, then the authored harm is the linkage itself.

PRGR would force him to write a reasoned record for any formal privilege tied to giving:

what objective criteria justify the decision,

what safeguards ensure non-donors are not punished,

and how conflicts are handled. PRGR is blunt here: *spiritual authority cannot trade grace for money without naming the trade.*

The "discreet request" step - targeting vulnerable congregants

The most corrosive harm often sits in private: the "quiet appeal" to a family with a sick child, the suggestion that "Allah sees who supports," the implication that refusal will be remembered. PRGR would attach at the moment the Imam authorizes or conducts targeted solicitation based on private knowledge of vulnerability. He must author:

why the person was approached, what information was used, and what consent boundaries exist. Because in this case, the misuse is not only financial; it is informational.

The retaliation-by-community step - exclusion after refusal or questioning

If someone refuses to donate, questions the list, or asks for accounting-and then loses access (committee removal, coldness, informal shaming), PRGR triggers at the *governance decision* that changes their standing. Someone must author:

why the person's role/access changed, what evidence supports it,

what harm is foreseeable (reputation damage, chilling effect, polarization), and what appeal path exists.

What PRGR would force in this case (practical measures matched to the story)

1. **A firewall between spiritual authority and financial discretion**
   PRGR would require that the Imam cannot be the sole controller of:
   the donation list,
   the distribution of funds, or
   recognition decisions.
   A separate finance committee with independent oversight must make decisions, preventing spirituality from serving as the unchallengeable seal on financial power.

2. **Opt-in recognition and non-coercive fundraising defaults** If recognition is used, PRGR forces it to be: opt-in, non-specific (ranges or anonymous totals), and explicitly non-linked to access or privileges. The institution must write: *donation is voluntary and does not affect pastoral care, services, or community participation.*

3. **A "vulnerability clause"**
   PRGR requires a rule: private knowledge gained through pastoral relationships cannot be used for targeted fundraising without explicit consent and a documented process. Because otherwise "care" becomes a pipeline to pressure.

4. **A reversal trigger tied to pattern, not proof of intent**
   PRGR would set an automatic review if any of these appear:

repeated complaints about pressure, donor privilege clustering,

unexplained exceptions in disbursement,

or role removals after questions. The trigger matters because this case is built on **soft coercion**-hard to "prove," easy to normalize.

The questions that keep this End-Cap case-specific (not generic)

If you were the Imam: can you write, and sign, a statement explaining why certain names/amounts were disclosed or used-knowing it will be read by those who felt pressured?

If you were a congregant: what is the first hinge-step that tells you giving has become governance-the public list, the private "appeal," or the sudden loss of access after refusal?

If you were the board/committee: which step would you force into authored form first-the control of the list, the recognition policy, or the retaliation-by-community decisions?

PRGR doesn't argue about whether fundraising is necessary. It isolates the precise moment the institution **turns generosity into leverage**-and forces a named author to exist at the step where spiritual authority becomes a financial instrument.

11

"THE MUTAWALLI'S LEASE"

PROPERTY BECOMES A HYMN WHEN THE PAPERWORK SINGS IN UNISON.

Alleged misuse/irregularities involving waqf properties and lease manipulation; investigations and raids; broader reporting on waqf land disputes and plunder.

In the first heat before the monsoon, the city's dust tastes metallic, as if it stored the air too long. It coats tongues and window ledges, settles into the folds of clothing, turns every breath into something you feel you've borrowed. The mosque stood calm in the shimmer-its courtyard tiles pale, its shade deep, its calligraphy patient. The lines on the walls spoke of mercy and order, of a world governed by meaning. Around it, however, land had become a fever. Every wall was a boundary. Every boundary was a temptation.

Mutawalli Farid Qureshi wore a cream robe that caught sunlight softly, and over it, on festival days, a dark Bisht edged with gold-a garment that turned him into a symbol. People greeted him as "trustee" with the same respect they reserved for elders and judges. In the neighborhood imagination, he was not merely a manager; he was a custodian of the sacred. A role meant to be a weight, not leverage.

The waqf properties under his oversight were modest on paper and enormous in reality:

old shops in a crowded market lane, a strip of land behind the mosque, a decaying building whose location mattered more than its bricks. "For the community," the documents said. "For charitable use." The language looked pure enough to be printed on a plaque. It echoed the moral architecture people want to live inside: that people remove certain things from appetite and dedicate them to God.

Then the "renovation" began.

A developer arrived with a smile and a plan. The plan came with diagrams, promises, and a phrase Farid learned to love: no cost to the community. He could almost hear the applause in advance. Repairs without fundraising. Upgrades without pain. Progress without argument. The developer spoke about dignity for worshippers, safer wiring, and better drainage before the monsoon season. He spoke as if the only thing standing between the community and relief was Farid's signature.

The landlord presented the lease as a formality.

It was not a theft done in darkness. It was a theft done in daylight with signatures.

First, a "temporary" lease to enable construction staging. Then an extension "to recover costs." Then a sublease to a cousin's company "for operational efficiency." The rent amounts were just plausible enough to escape scandal and just low enough to guarantee profit elsewhere. Receipts came on letterhead. Stamps appeared. Files thickened. The system looked legitimate simply because it looked busy.

Farid told himself he was being shrewd. That he was protecting the waqf from bureaucratic delay, from municipal predation, from the endless grind of permits. He told himself that outcomes mattered more than procedural purity. When he spoke to the committee, he used the vocabulary of necessity-maslahah, public interest-without naming it as such. And when anyone hesitated, he performed calm the way skilled men perform piety: gently, as if caution itself were an insult.

A committee member named Sameer-quiet, detail-oriented-noticed that the minutes never matched the deeds. He noticed that the trustee's explanations always traveled faster than the questions. He noticed that Farid's robe seemed to do half the arguing for him. When Sameer asked why rent was being collected by a private entity instead of the waqf, Farid answered with the calm disdain of someone accustomed to deference: "You want charity to survive? Then you must understand reality."

Reality, in Farid's mouth, meant control.

Sameer went home that night under a sky the color of brass. The air was thick, waiting. In the alley behind his building, a stray cat nosed through trash, searching for something edible, and Sameer felt an old anger stir: the endowment existed for the vulnerable, not for the comfortable. He thought of a verse he had learned as a boy and never needed to test until now-"Do not consume one another's wealth unjustly." He repeated it like a small resistance in his chest, because injustice, when it wears polite paper, is easy to mistake for governance. Shops appeared on waqf land without prior approval. Temporary scaffolding became permanent partitions. A kiosk selling phone accessories sprouted beside the courtyard wall like a weed in a crack. Officials collected rent in cash. Delays answered the complaints.

And whenever someone pushed too hard, Farid spoke about unity-about avoiding fitnah, discord-as if transparency were the genuine danger. He quoted the value of harmony the way a man quotes scripture to close a conversation. In the committee room, the word fitnah became a curtain, and once they spoke it, they made questions feel like sins.

Sameer documented. He photographed the new shops. He pulled the property maps. He copied the lease drafts and compared them to the committee resolutions. The discrepancies were not subtle. The slow confidence of authority simply enveloped the discrepancies. Farid's supporters dismissed Sameer as difficult, "too rigid," "not practical." The insult was always the same: that ethics were naive.

But the Qur'an has a harsh clarity about trusteeship. "Allah commands you to render trusts to whom they are due." Sameer wrote the phrase at the top of his notes, not as decoration but as an indictment. A waqf is not a private inheritance; it is a trust held on behalf of those who will never sit at the table. To treat it as personal leverage is not cleverness. It is betrayal.

The pre-monsoon heat pressed harder. Dust gathered in the corners of the mosque courtyard like secrets. In the market lane, the smell of frying oil mixed with exhaust, and the sky looked swollen, as if clouds were accumulating grievances. People continued to pray. They continued to donate. The rhythms of faith endured because faith must. Yet beneath the rhythm, mistrust spread-softly at first, like mildew in a shaded room.

The trigger for intervention did not arrive as moral outrage. It arrived as paperwork-an outside bank refusing to process a transfer without verification, a municipal clerk noticing irregular registrations, a rival developer filing a complaint. Investigations often begin not because people suddenly become righteous, but because someone's interests collide.

When investigators finally arrived, they came like weather: not personal, not moral, just force. Doors opened. The investigators took the files. The investigators made copies of the phones. The neighborhood watched from balconies and shopfronts, the way people watch a storm approach-fascinated, fearful, secretly relieved that something larger had finally interrupted the local arrangements. The official vehicles looked out of place in narrow lanes, their tires grinding grit into the road.

Farid protested innocence. He spoke of misunderstanding. He spoke of enemies. He spoke, as administrators always speak when the ground gives way, about process. But the process was the very tool that had allowed the harm to wear a clean face. He claimed the leases were "temporary" and the cash collections were "for convenience." He spoke as if intent mattered more than outcome, as if the poor could live on explanations.

Sameer listened and recognized the bitter truth of another warning: "Woe to those who give less." Farid had short-changed the community-reducing what was meant for public benefit into private gain, shaving off integrity in small increments until the whole thing became a different substance. He had not emptied the endowment in one dramatic theft. He had thinned it quietly, like watering down milk and calling it mercy. When the monsoon finally broke, it did not arrive delicately. Rain slammed the city with impatient force.

Gutters overflowed. Water ran brown along the streets, carrying wrappers, leaves, and the small debris of daily life-everything people had dropped when no one was watching. In the mosque courtyard, rivulets formed along the grout lines between tiles, tracing paths that had always been there. It looked like a parable: water finds the channels already carved. So does corruption. So does consequence.

Afterward, the mosque remained. The prayers continued. The faithful kept arriving with bare hands and honest intent. But the community had learned the same old lesson in a new costume: endowments are only as holy as their oversight. If the system fails to prevent exploitation, it will eventually stage a rescue-raids, audits, public statements-after the damage has already metabolized into poverty and cynicism. Rescue is loud. Prevention is quiet. Institutions often prefer naive loudness because it looks like action.

Farid's bisht still shimmered on special occasions, gold edging catching light as if nothing had happened. Yet the garment could no longer do its old work. Something broke the spell. People had learned that cloth and title do not sanctify a trustee; only accountability does.

And on the days when the air cooled after rain, when the city briefly smelled clean, Sameer would remember the simplest underlining of the case: trust is not a symbol. It is a duty. When it is sold, the community pays twice-once in money, and once in the slow corrosion of belief.

The Bisht still shimmered. The land did not forget.

12

"THE ARCHBISHOP'S SILENT DEAL"

THE CURTAIN IS PULLED BACK AND EVERYONE REALIZES THE SANCTUM WAS NEVER AS SEALED AS THEY IMAGINED.

Church corruption and organised crime, Italy, 2009 (composite case), PRGR

It began with real estate. Parish properties-old buildings with thick walls, basement rooms, and excellent locations-were desirable to syndicates for laundering and logistics. Mancini controlled the administrative levers: transfers, leases, approvals, the polite paperwork that turns appetite into legality. He sanctioned discreet agreements under the language of "community development" and "restoration." The words were clean. The tenants were not. In exchange, the archbishop received political protection, discreet financial advantages, and something more intoxicating than money: the sensation of being untouchable.

A commanding figure in Rome, Archbishop Vittorio Mancini presided over one of the city's oldest archdioceses. His ceremonial cassock and intricately embroidered stole carried centuries of accumulated meaning-authority made visible, tradition stitched into cloth. The faithful revered him; clergy deferred; international visitors treated his office as spiritual gravity. In public, he moved with measured solemnity, as if history had rehearsed every gesture.

Yet behind that veneer of sanctity, Mancini negotiated with criminal syndicates behind closed curtains, entangling the Church in a web of secrecy and compromise. He didn't look like a man making deals. He looked like a man blessing the world. That was part of the utility.

The arrangements grew more complex. Donations appeared at the right moment. Sponsorships funded charitable events that looked radiant on posters. Certain contractors always won bids. Promotions went to certain priests who were compliant, quiet, and pliable. The Church moved others aside "for pastoral reasons." Clergy learned quickly which questions led to closed doors and which led to invitations.

He told himself it was pragmatic. Italy's political and social environment, he insisted inwardly, required negotiation with powerful actors to preserve the Church's resources and influence. He framed it as governance, not corruption-an argument that sounds sophisticated until you notice it always ends in the same place: protection of the institution's image over protection of people.

And he enjoyed it.

Not the crude pleasure of cash, but the controlled pleasure of secrecy-the private thrill of navigating arrangements without exposure. Psychologically, it followed a familiar pattern: *moral licensing* and *incrementalism*. The first compromise felt like an exception justified by the good he would do later. The second felt smaller because the first had already stretched the boundary. Soon, he wasn't crossing lines-he was living beyond them.

The stole and cassock didn't restrain him; they magnified him, turning every "request" into an implied command.

Father Lorenzo Rossi, an idealistic priest in the archdiocese, noticed "mistakes" in property transfers and the flow of funds to the notary tied to those transactions. Donations seemed misdirected, while construction projects benefited shadowy intermediaries rather than parish needs. Meetings appeared on calendars with vague titles, always behind closed doors in the archbishop's office. Lorenzo began documenting dates, amounts, names, and patterns. His notes were not dramatic. They were worse-precise.

What unsettled him most was Mancini's demeanor. In public, the archbishop spoke about humility; in private, his impatience surfaced as contempt. He described concerned parishioners as "simple," priests as "overwrought," and critics as "people who want purity because they can't manage reality." He didn't deny wrongdoing; he denied the *right* of others to judge it. That is the psychology of superiority: the belief that rank changes morality.

The turning point came when an investigative journalist from Rome's daily press received anonymous tips about ecclesiastical complicity in underworld property deals. Lorenzo supplied corroborating documents: ledgers, correspondence, notes on clandestine meetings. The reporting did what internal committees often refuse to do: it connected fragments into a single pattern and placed it in daylight.

Public reaction was immediate and intense. Parishioners felt betrayed; clergy were scandalized; Vatican oversight committees opened formal inquiries. The Vatican removed Mancini from administrative responsibilities pending an investigation. Canon law and institutional caution blurred the edges of accountability, but civil authorities reviewed transactions and uncovered financial and ethical mismanagement. The same garments that had once signaled moral authority now looked like camouflage-beautiful cloth draped over decay.

A biblical comparison fits here with uncomfortable clarity: *the thirty pieces of silver*. Not because Mancini betrayed one man with a kiss, but because he treated sacred trust as negotiable currency. Like Judas, he didn't begin as a cartoon villain; he began with proximity to holiness and the quiet belief that he could manage darkness without being changed by it. The tragedy in that story is not the coin-it's the self-deception that makes betrayal feel practical until the consequences arrive.

Rome, indifferent and ancient, kept moving around him. The Tiber slid past the embankments with its silted patience, carrying leaves and scraps like unjudging testimony. Rain varnished the cobblestones outside the chancery, and the city's bells sounded different in wet air-less triumphant, more like a warning. In courtyards, cypress trees stood dark despite that, as if listening.

Mancini had always loved the theater of sanctity: incense rising like mist, candlelight tremoring against marble, vestments flowing like banners in a controlled wind. But nature does not flatter. It erodes. It exposes. It returns every polished facade to stone and dust.

He reached for the familiar defenses-necessity, governance, stability-when they finally confronted him, but the words tasted stale, like bread left too long in the sacristy. A single line from Scripture surfaced with unwanted force: "For what shall it profit a man, if he shall gain the universe, and lose his own soul?"

In the quiet after headlines, after committees, after lawyers, that question hung over him like a winter sky. The city's lights kept changing-gold at sunrise, iron at dusk-while his certainty thinned, flaking away in layers, like old paint under salt wind.

The scandal forced reforms: stricter oversight, transparency in property dealings, clearer accountability mechanisms for high-ranking clergy. Institutions find it easiest to praise whistleblowers after the damage has become public.

In the end, Mancini kept his title, but his authority diminished, his legacy stained by the tension between ceremonial grandeur and ethical lapse. The faithful learned what they should never have had to learn: symbols do not guarantee virtue. When power is unchecked, the trappings of holiness can become instruments of concealment-until the curtain is pulled back and everyone realizes the sanctum was never as sealed as they imagined.

PRGR END-CAP - AUTHORED HARM TEST

(for "THE ARCHBISHOP'S SILENT DEAL")

The harm in this case doesn't begin when the headline breaks. It begins earlier, at the moment **Archbishop Mancini uses ordinary administration as a covert gate**-when a signature converts criminal access into "community development," and sacred property into a logistics node.

PRGR would not wait for scandal. It would attach authorship at the first institutional hinge-step.

In this story, the hinge-steps are concrete:

The first "restoration" lease approval

The point of authored harm is not "corruption in general." It is **Mancini approving a parish property lease / transfer to a syndicate-linked tenant under clean language** ("restoration," "development").

PRGR trigger: the moment he signs or instructs staff to process it, he must write: *Why this counterparty? What due diligence exists? What foreseeable harms follow if we are wrong?*

The contractor pipeline

The pattern becomes structural when **the same contractors repeatedly win bids** and "sponsorship" money appears at convenient times. *PRGR trigger:* the moment procurement is steered-formally or informally-PRGR forces Mancini to author the harm: *I am overriding neutrality; I am trading integrity of process for speed/loyalty/quiet; here is who benefits and who bears risk.*

The personnel silencing move

Mancini doesn't only launder money; he launders dissent-**priests are moved aside "for pastoral reasons," while compliant clergy are promoted.**

PRGR trigger: the reassignment memo. That is where PRGR would require him to state plainly: *This transfer will reduce a critic's visibility/authority; what is the legitimate basis;*

what alternative exists; what is the predicted damage to truth-finding and trust?

The "reality" defense as governance

His psychological move-calling critics "simple," priests "overwrought," and insisting purity is for those who "can't manage reality"-isn't just attitude. It is **an operational tactic that pre-emptively disqualifies testimony.**

PRGR trigger: the first time he uses this framing to block inquiry or discredit a report, PRGR forces a written record: *I am treating discomfort as immaturity; what evidence supports that? What safeguards prevent retaliation?*

What PRGR would force in this case (not as slogan, as tool)

1. **Named author at each hinge**
   Every lease approval, contractor decision, donation-routing choice, and reassignment tied to these transactions must carry,
   the **name of the author** (not "the Chancery," not "administration"), the **reason**, and the **harm forecast**.

2. **A "sacred-asset conflict" declaration**
   Because the harm pathway is specifically "holy symbols + property power," PRGR would require Mancini to explicitly state:
   whether the counterparty has criminal exposure, what independence checks exist, and what would happen to parishioners if the Church is later revealed as complicit.

3. **A pre-committed reversal trigger**
   PRGR would require a sentence like:
   "If X indicator appears (journalistic tip, unexplained donation timing, repeated contractor concentration, notary irregularities), then Y must occur automatically (external audit + suspension of approvals), without needing a whistleblower to beg."

In this case, that trigger would have activated **when Father Lorenzo first documented irregular transfers and the notary-linked flow of funds**-not after the press connected fragments.

The questions the reader cannot dodge (specific to Mancini's deal)

If you were Mancini: at the moment you approved the first syndicate-friendly lease under "restoration" language, what would you write as the reason-and would you sign it if it had to be read aloud to parishioners?

If you were Father Lorenzo: what is the first *documentable hinge* you would force into a record-the lease approval, the contractor concentration, or the "pastoral transfer" of critics?

If you were Vatican/archdiocesan oversight: which is more dangerous to protect-reputation today, or the institution's ability to tell the truth tomorrow?

PRGR isn't asking whether Mancini "meant well." It asks where he **converted sanctity into leverage**-and makes him **author the harm at the exact administrative step where concealment becomes policy.**

13

"THE BISHOP WHO BROKE SACRED TRUST"

SOME FIRES KEEP BURNING IN THE BODY LONG AFTER THE ROOF IS REPAIRED

Abuse of authority in religious institutions (composite case)

Some churches burn in a single night, and people rebuild them with astonishing speed-scaffolding rising like ribs, cranes hovering like mechanical saints, and workers return stone and timber to shape before grief has even learned its own language. Other churches burn, leaving only a hollow outline. This blackened shell becomes a cautionary monument, but people eventually dismantle the monument, and they pave over the place. Fire is not only destruction. Fire is a test of what a community restores and what it quietly lets vanish.

Bishop Laurent Dubois moved with deliberate grace through the vaulted halls of his cathedral, his black robe and finely pleated jabot flowing with each step.

To the faithful, he looked like continuity made flesh: a man whose posture seemed to sanctify the surrounding space. He spoke in measured tones, blessed infants with practiced tenderness, and gave homilies that made people feel-briefly, gratefully-that the world's disorder could be arranged into meaning.

But the cathedral's calm represented an architecture of belief, and people can use belief.

It began, as most betrayals begin, with the smallest gestures that no one thinks to challenge. Seminarians came to him with questions they were too ashamed to ask their peers. Parents sought counsel for marriages tightening into resentment. Parishioners offered their secrets the way people offer candles-small flames of hope meant to be protected.

Laurent listened with devotion on his face and patience in his hands. He learned quickly the strange power of being the person others confess to: you become a mirror in which their fear looks manageable. And then he discovered the thrill.

Not crude lust at first, not overt predation. Something subtler and more corrosive: the pleasure of influence. The sensation that a slight tilt of his approval could lift a man's confidence or crush it; that a gentle reprimand could reorder a family's internal politics; that a soft phrase-God asks much of you-could make a person surrender more than they intended. Laurent hungered for that sensation the way some men hunger for applause: not because they need noise, but because they need confirmation that they are real.

In the cathedral's side rooms, trust gathered like dry wood.

Over time, people's trust in him allowed him to manipulate them. Confessions offered in trembling honesty served as leverage. Private meetings framed as spiritual guidance became opportunities to test boundaries. A hand resting lightly on a shoulder. A lingering touch as he adjusted a stole. A "fatherly" embrace that lasted one second too long and left a question in the body.

Pastoral care could explain everything. The language of care is broad enough to cover almost any gesture if the person watching wants to believe.

Laurent rationalised it as mentorship, as preparation, as intimacy demanded by a life of faith. He told himself that narrating the intention as noble meant no harm was done. That is the inner trick of moral drift: you don't change the act; you change the surrounding story until the act feels permissible.

But the effects were not stories. The effects lived in people.

Seminarians avoided private encounters. They found reasons to bring companions to meetings. They requested reassignment for "study" or "health," or for any reason that could be documented on a form without exposing the real motive. Parishioners experienced a new guilt-one that did not feel like repentance but like contamination.

Some stopped confessing altogether, as if the sacrament itself had become unsafe.

Others blamed themselves, because victims often do when the abuser wears a holy costume: If he is holy, the discomfort must be my sin.

Whispers circulated the way smoke does-thin at first, dismissible, then persistent, then impossible to pretend you don't smell. A staff member noticed the pattern of closed-door meetings. A parent remarked carefully that their son returned from counsel "different." A journal entry surfaced. A letter appeared with phrasing too precise to be mere misunderstanding.

At first, the hierarchy dismissed concerns as misinterpretation, the common institutional reflex: interpret harm as confusion, and you never have to admit it is harm.

Yet complaints accumulated like soot in a bell tower.

Eventually, a formal inquiry began. Investigators documented testimonies, cross-referenced accounts, and reviewed communications.

The process was delicate because Laurent's influence extended beyond the cathedral into the diocese's social fabric-donors, parish councils, old friendships forged in committee rooms where people often treat loyalty as uprightness. Still, patterns emerged with the grim clarity of fire damage: where the heat had been greatest, the structure had failed.

The evidence revealed a consistent pattern of emotional and sexual exploitation orchestrated under the guise of mentorship and pastoral authority.

The robe and jabot, once symbols of sanctity, now sharpened the sense of betrayal. Clothing does not commit misconduct, but it can intensify the wound: the same garments that inspired trust, the perpetrator used as camouflage for harm.

Authorities suspended Laurent from ministerial duties and barred him from contact with seminarians and parishioners pending review. The institution introduced supervised-meeting policies. Oversight committees formed. They made reporting structures clear and publicised them. In statements, the diocese spoke of safeguarding and renewal.

It looked, to the outside, like reconstruction.

But reconstruction is not resurrection. Rebuilding a church in stone and timber is possible; a sense of safety is slower. For some of those harmed, the cathedral would never again feel like shelter.

Once a sanctuary becomes associated with coercion, the mind treats arches and incense differently. The bells still ring, but their sound now carries a second meaning: a reminder of how easily holiness can be imitated. While alone, Laurent wrestled with the outcomes, but others couldn't trust even his struggles. Remorse is difficult to measure. It can be genuine. It can also be another performance. That ambiguity causes damage: when trust is broken, even sorrow looks like strategy.

He walked the cathedral halls-now familiar yet emptied of warmth-and felt what power feels like when it evaporates. Not merely loss, but exposure. The influence he had enjoyed was not his by right; it was borrowed from belief. Once belief withdrew, he was simply a man in a building, stripped of the invisible armor that ceremony provides.

And the diocese faced its own contradiction. The cathedral endured; its walls still held, its rituals continued. Yet endurance can become denial if it is used to imply that nothing truly collapsed. Communities often want the comfort of swift rebuilding: scaffolding, new policies, public assurances. They want to say the fire is over.

But some fires continue to burn in the body long after the roof has been repaired.

The community's intolerance for a space means they rebuild some churches with lightning speed, as the metaphor requires. Others vanish forever-not because people cannot replace the stones, but because people cannot reclaim the meaning. In Laurent Dubois's case, the building remained, yet for some, the cathedral as sanctuary had burned.

What returned afterward was an altered structure: outwardly intact, inwardly changed, carrying the faint smell of smoke that only the harmed can detect.

In the end, the robe and jabot remained as objects, but their meaning shifted. They were no longer simple emblems of virtue. They became reminders that tradition without accountability is combustible-that even in the most venerable spaces, human weakness can behave like fire: quiet at first, almost invisible, then suddenly consuming, leaving behind the question every community must answer when the flames go out:

What will we rebuild-and what will we finally admit is gone?

14

"THE SHAMASH AND THE SILVER BOX"

QUIET FEELS LIKE CONTROL.

Documented patterns of donation-box theft, fund diversion, and trust abuse in places of worship (composite).

The synagogue's silver pushke sat near the entrance where light from the street caught its polished surface. It wasn't large-just a dignified metal box with a narrow slot-but it had the gravity of an altar. People dropped coins into it the way they dropped prayers: quietly, expecting the sound to travel somewhere good.

On Friday afternoons, the neighborhood smelled of challah and damp pavement. In winter, wind tunneled down the street and rattled the windows, as if the cold were trying to get inside and listen.

Yitzhak Peretz, the shamash, arrived early to set the chairs and lay out the siddurim. His keys jingled at his belt. He was familiar with every creaky door, every flickering lightbulb, and every senior member of the congregation who preferred the aisle seat. He wore no robe, no public authority, just a plain coat, and a knitted kippah. Yet he held the building's secret arteries: locks, schedules, access.

Rabbi Sussman trusted him completely. "Yitzhak," he said often, "you keep the house running." Yitzhak would smile. "Someone has to sweep the floors."

He swept the floors. He also began, quietly, to sweep the pushke.

It started in a week when his son's asthma worsened and the pharmacy bill arrived like a punch. Yitzhak stood in the kitchen counting coins in his palm, feeling the humiliation of small numbers. Outside, rain streaked the window, and he felt the old bitterness: the world asked too much, and mercy always came in small doses.

That evening, alone in the sanctuary, he opened the cabinet to store the Torah covers and glanced at the silver box. He told himself a story before he acted-people always do. He told himself he would borrow a little. He told himself he would repay it on payday. He told himself that charity belonged to the community, and he was part of the community, and the need was urgent.

He slid a thin wire into the slot and jiggled it with careful patience. Coins clinked softly, obediently. He caught them in his palm and felt heat bloom in his chest-not relief exactly, but the sudden intoxicating sensation of getting away with it.

He repaid some of it. He also did it again.

Soon he learned the rhythm: which days the box was fuller, which holidays brought heavier coins. The theft stayed small enough to be invisible, but steady enough to become meaningful. The pushke, meant to be a conduit of mercy, became his private ATM.

Miriam Adler, who coordinated the food pantry, noticed first-not through the box, but through the pantry shelves.

"We're short," she told Rabbi Sussman in the office, flipping a clipboard. "We've been short three weeks in a row."

The rabbi frowned. "Donations were strong last month." Miriam's eyes narrowed. "That's what you said last month."

The rabbi called Yitzhak in after mincha. Outside, wind shoved leaves against the door like impatient fingers. "Yitzhak," Sussman began gently, "how often do you empty the pushke?"

Yitzhak's smile stayed steady. "Every Wednesday. Sometimes Friday." "And you count it with the treasurer?"

"Of course," Yitzhak said, too quickly.

The rabbi watched him. "You seem offended." Yitzhak shrugged. "I just don't like being questioned." Sussman sighed. "Questioning isn't an accusation."

Yitzhak's eyes flicked toward the door. "Sometimes it feels like it."

That night, Miriam stayed late, pretending to organize canned goods. In truth, she watched. The sanctuary was dim; the lamps casting long shadows across the floor. She saw Yitzhak pause by the silver box, glance around, then move his hand in a small, practiced motion-too quick, too familiar.

Her stomach dropped. Betrayal is often a quiet thing. She confronted him in the hallway. "Yitzhak."

He froze. "What?" "I saw you."

He laughed once, sharply. "You saw me what?" "Touching the pushke."

His face reddened. "I was moving it." "Don't," Miriam said. "Not with me."

Yitzhak's shoulders slumped. For a moment he looked less like a thief and more like a tired man carrying too much. "I needed it," he whispered.

Miriam's voice stayed hard. "So did the families who came here hungry." He swallowed. "I was going to repay it."

"When?" she demanded.

He stared at the floor, and the silence answered.

The board met the next day. The rabbi's hands shook as he read the report, not from anger but from grief. The synagogue issued no public statement at first. They wanted it quiet. They always want it quiet. Quiet feels like control.

But the pantry shelves remained bare, and the families kept coming. Prevention had failed; now they had to do rescue-emergency fundraising, appeals, replacement funds.

The community's generosity returned, but its trust did not.

Weeks later, on a bright, frosty morning, sunlight glittered off puddles like broken glass. The pushke sat back in its place. People continued to drop coins in, but now the clink sounded different-louder, more deliberate, like a question.

The rabbi stood near the door and watched congregants hesitate before giving. He understood the moral without needing to preach it: the rabbi believed charity is sacred and must therefore be protected. A system that relies on reverence without oversight is an unlocked door on a windy street.

The silver box still shone.

But everyone knew now that it was possible to open it.

15

"THE LEDGER TRILOGY"

AS LONG AS THEY CAN ROUTE IT SOMEWHERE IT WON'T REACH CONSEQUENCES.

A consolidation of three cases on financial misuse, France, Netherlands, Austria, 2020-2023

THE PERPETRATOR

How the mind justifies the hand.

Armand Vermeer liked clean paper.

He liked the way a stapled bundle looks inevitable once it's bound. He liked how a signature can turn uncertainty into "next steps." He liked the clerical magic of accounting: columns that turn appetite into administration. In his world, money was not a thing. Money was a method.

Armand wore no robe. He didn't need one. His uniform was competence: a tailored coat, a calm voice, and an ability to make urgency sound like stewardship. He was the finance director of a legal charity with a public reputation for mercy-appeals funded, families kept intact, errors challenged when the state insisted on certainty. People wanted to believe it was clean. He helped them keep believing.

Armand did not wake up thinking, *I will steal.* He woke up thinking, *I will prevent collapse.*

That was his first strategy: **to frame himself as infrastructure.** If he were infrastructure, questioning him would threaten the building. And questioning the building made any questioner irresponsible by definition. He studied people the way a gambler studies tells. Not to punish them, not even to hate them. To place them. The chair of the board was a retired judge: allergic to disorder, intoxicated by continuity.

The director was charismatic: busy, adored, always in a meeting somewhere else. The donors wanted good news.

The staff wanted stability.

The clients wanted miracles on deadlines.

Armand looked at all of them and saw a single weakness: **they needed the story to stay coherent.** He offered coherence like a service. He translated trouble into manageable language, and the building rewarded him for it. This is how his mind worked: **other people were not enemies; they were variables.** He didn't think, *How do I defeat them?* He thought, *How do I route them?* That difference matters. A villain imagines opposition. A bureaucratic predator imagines workflow.

His strategy wasn't offense or defense. It was **pre-emption**: making scrutiny arrive too late to feel reasonable. He did this with three quiet purchases named as a triad - **Money, Intimacy, Procedure**. Money buys access and immunity; intimacy buys silence and loyalty; procedure buys delay and distance.

Armand's money purchase was literal. He created a "special disbursement lane" for emergency case funding. A good cause is the best hiding place because it recruits moral impatience: *If you slow this down, someone suffers.* He didn't falsify everything; he only blurred the edge cases. A taxi receipt here, an "interim consultant" there, a reimbursement coded as client support. He was careful: he didn't drain the account, he skimmed from the noise. His intimate purchase was emotional. He became the person who "handled" crises. He stayed late. He remembered birthdays. He said the right sentence at the right exhaustion point: *You're doing impossible work. Let me take this off your plate.* Intimacy hides behind care. And care, when it becomes a lever, doesn't look like a lever. It looks like relief.

Then came the procedure purchase-the most powerful one, because procedure can wear innocence. He built a calendar around himself. If you wanted to understand the accounts, you had to ask him. If you wanted to barrel funds, you had to use his lane. He wrote policies that sounded like fairness but functioned like fog. "Policy" became a substitute for reasons-the institutional anesthesia your manuscript calls out directly.

Armand's internal narrative stayed clean because he didn't tell himself, *I am taking.* He told himself:

I am smoothing volatility.

I am protecting the mission from bureaucrats.

I am compensating for a system that underfunds mercy.

Notice the elegance: he located the original sin outside himself. He was merely... adaptive. And because the charity genuinely was under pressure, his story wasn't pure fiction. It was selective truth-truth used as camouflage.

How did he think about others?

He thought most people were children around money. Not morally childish-practically. He believed they wanted comfort more than accuracy. He believed they preferred a working lie to a destabilizing fact. And he was right often enough to become dangerous.

He also believed something colder: that accountability is a luxury people invoke only when they feel safe. His job, as he saw it, was to keep them safe. In exchange, he could take what he needed. No one negotiated that exchange. That is why it is corruption.

The first warning signs were banal: a missing attachment, a delayed bank reconciliation, a line item that "didn't map." Nothing cinematic. Damp in a wall. And because it was damp, not fire, people treated it as maintenance. Armand's genius-if we're willing to use that word for predation-was that he did not primarily steal money. He stole **the right to be un-questioned**. Money was just the measurable byproduct.

If you want to understand this personality type, don't ask whether they are cruel. Ask whether they are **certain**. Some brains confuse control with probity. Armand's certainty was soothing. That is why it spread.

And then a minor event cracked the surface: a donor asked to see anonymized case-impact numbers aligned to spending. Armand produced a beautiful report-too beautiful. It read like a brochure, not a ledger. The director praised him. The board exhaled. The report did what reports often do: it created relief without creating truth.

Relief is not the same thing as resolution. It is simply the moment the mind stops asking. Armand relied on that moment.

THE WISTLEBLOWER

What truth does to a body when the institution won't file it.

Nina Koenig did not set out to be brave. She set out to be correct.

She was the internal auditor-mid-level, politely ignored, the role an organisation claims to value while quietly preventing it from interfering with the story. Nina had a partner, a seven-year-old who still believed adults mean what they say, and a habit of triple-checking figures because she was trained-like many less powerful professionals-to doubt herself first.

In the beginning, she tried the normal route: clarification emails, gentle questions, requests for missing attachments. She wrote in the language that keeps you employed: neutral tone, benefit of the doubt, "just checking." She told herself the discrepancies were a system issue, not a person.

Then she noticed the repeating shape.

The same lane. The same urgency phrasing. The same exemption logic. The same subtle resentment when she asked for backup. And she felt something hard to document: that the accounts were not simply messy. They were being **managed**.

This is where whistleblowing starts-not with a moral declaration, but with an internal sensory shift: *the room isn't behaving the way it claims to behave.*

Nina began archiving everything. Not dramatically. Quietly. Screenshots. Version histories. Calendars. Because when you sense the institution might refuse to recognize your reality, you build a second reality it can't easily dismiss. Your book describes this inner life exactly: the corridors feel like evaluation, sleep thins, reality feels negotiable when status is involved. So you become a clerk of your own pain.

Her professional consequences arrived before any official finding-because institutions punish dissent early, while it's still deniable.

She was excluded from "strategy meetings." Her requests were answered late or not at all. She was told she was "creating friction."

The board praised her diligence in public and treated her as inconvenient in private. Social cost enforces silence more efficiently than overt threats.

At home, the consequences were not abstract.

Nina stopped being present. Nina was physically in the kitchen, but her mind was elsewhere. She reran conversations, drafted future explanations, and rehearsed defenses against accusations that hadn't been made yet. She became irritably meticulous: the dishwasher loaded perfectly, the child's bag packed twice. When control leaks in one domain, the body tries to reclaim it in another.

Her partner asked, "Why don't you just let it go?" and Nina heard: *Why don't you just become complicit so we can have peace?* That wasn't what he meant. But the nervous system doesn't care about the speaker's intention. It cares what it must survive.

She developed small symptoms first: jaw tension, waking at 3 a.m., the metallic taste of adrenaline when her phone buzzed. Then bigger ones: migraines, stomach pain, a sense of being watched even in ordinary spaces. Evaluation culture does that-it makes the air feel scored.

Nina's coping mechanisms were practical rather than heroic:

Compartmentalization: she spoke about her work in sterile phrases at home to protect her family from her fear.

Documentation: she relied on records because records are the only language the institution pretends to hear.

Micro-allies: she tested trust in tiny increments-one careful sentence to one colleague, then watching their face for weather.

But the most corrosive part wasn't the stress. It was the loneliness produced by a system that treats moral insistence as a disruption to efficiency. When you cannot trust the organisation, you wonder whether you can trust your own perception. That is the institution's quiet victory: it makes the whistleblower carry not only evidence, but epistemology.

What is true if the record won't recognize it?

Did she have an arc of her own? She had to.

Because if the whistleblower's sole purpose is to expose the antagonist, the reader learns only that villains exist. The deeper lesson is what truth demands of the person who carries it.

Nina's arc was not from fear to fearlessness. It was from **compliance to authorship**.

At first, she tried to be an exemplary employee: a careful tone, procedural steps, patient waiting. She believed the institution's self-description. Then she encountered the translation machine your manuscript names: the system translating lived moral alarm into safer categories, routing it into committee time, substituting process for morality. She watched her concern get turned into a "workplace conflict" and felt something in her clarity: *this is not a misunderstanding. This is a method.*

So she changed her posture. She stopped begging the system to care and started forcing it to **own**.

Her decisive move was small but structural: she sent a memo to the board chair-not accusing, not emotional, just plain language:

Here is what is missing.

Here is what the numbers imply.

Here is the foreseeable harm if we are wrong.

Here is the irreversible step we are approaching: public reporting and donor renewals. She didn't yet use the term PRGR. She used its spine.

Because PRGR, in one sentence, is this:

foreseeable harm must have a named author, a written forecast, and a pre-committed repair trigger.

Nina wasn't asking the institution to be kind. She was asking it to become auditable.

At home, this shift changed her too. She told her partner the truth without sterilizing it:

"I'm scared, and I'm doing it anyway." The relationship didn't become easy. But it became real again. Her child saw a mother who was tired and still intact.

Is it the whistleblower to change the structure? No. And yes.

No, because asking one person to correct a system is another way of making the vulnerable do the labour of the powerful.

Yes, because if nobody insists on a structural requirement, the system continues to treat harm as weather-something that "happened," not something someone did. The whistle-blower doesn't have to be a savior. But the whistleblower often becomes the first person to demand that **the author has to exist.**

That demand is the arc.

THE INSTITUTE

A board conversation (without PRGR).

They met in a conference room with glass walls that made privacy feel performative. On the table: bottled water, printed agendas, the soothing props of governance.

There were five of them: the chair, the director, legal counsel, a donor representative, and the head of operations. They spoke in the language institutions use when they want to sound moral without risking disruption.

The first signals

Chair: "We're hearing... concerns. Nothing formal."

Director: "Armand is stressed. We've had extraordinary caseloads."

Ops: "Invoices are missing attachments. Nina flagged it."

Donor Rep: "We can't afford a scandal. Renewal season is in March."

Legal Counsel: "Let's be careful. Allegations can become liabilities."

You can hear the first translation happening: concern becomes "nothing formal," missing money becomes "missing attachments," moral alarm becomes "liability."

Chair: "Is this a competence issue?"

Director: "Possibly. Or workload. Or... Nina being meticulous."

Meticulousness framed as personality. A classic minimization: turn an inconvenient fact into a trait.

The investigation

They agreed to commission an external review, but with constraints.

Legal Counsel: "We need a narrow scope. Otherwise, it becomes fishing."

Donor Rep: "Keep it quiet. Staff morale is fragile."

Chair: "We'll ask Armand for cooperation. He'll appreciate the chance to clarify."

They wanted an investigation that preserved calm.

The external reviewer requested bank statements and expense trails. Armand produced what he could. He was helpful, even charming, because charm is a kind of camouflage: it makes scrutiny feel rude.

The reviewer asked for the "special disbursement lane" policy. Armand provided it-clean, signed, rational. The reviewer asked for exceptions. Armand explained urgency. He used the mission as a shield.

The board mistook procedural activity for moral progress. Substitution: if the meeting happened, the institution can treat itself as virtuous regardless of the outcome.

The results

The report arrived in careful language: "irregularities," "insufficient documentation," "lack of segregation of duties." It condemned without naming, enabling.

Director: "So it's controls, not malice."

Ops: "Some disbursements went to entities without contracts."

Legal Counsel: "We should avoid conclusions that imply intent."

Chair: "We can ask for repayment and implement reforms."

Notice the relief: if it's "controls," nobody has to confess betrayal. If it's "process," no one has to name a person.

Nina sat outside this room with a headache and a stomach like stone, waiting to learn if the record would include reality.

Builders must construct the bastion.

Now the board did what boards often do: it designed a bastion to be built. Not a bastion against misuse-a bastion against reputational damage.

Donor Rep: "We need messaging."

Legal Counsel: "We should say we 'followed process' and 'took immediate steps.'"

Director: "We cannot let staff gossip get ahead of us."

Chair: "We'll restructure finance. Armand will step aside quietly."

Step aside quietly. Not fired. Not named. Quietly.

Ops: "And Nina?" A pause.

Director: "We should support her. But she also... escalated prematurely."

Chair: "We can't reward internal disruption."

There it is: **the final purchase.** Procedure buys distance; distance buys forgetting. The institution will reform, but in a way that preserves continuity rather than accepting full authorship.

Outside the glass room, the organisation would continue. The website would still say "integrity." The donors would still be thanked. The mission would still be invoked. And the people who had been most accurate would learn the oldest lesson of bureaucracy:

They welcome truth as "input," as long as they can route it somewhere it won't reach consequences.

Pattern recognition

Put yourself in each position.

If you were Armand, what sentence would you use to justify the first compromise?

If you were Nina, at what point would your body keep the record for you?

If you were the board, what would you protect first: truth, continuity, or calm?

This book gives the structural diagnosis: institutions translate, route, substitute. And it gives the tool that breaks the spell: a system must name an author, not a process.

So run the trilogy again under one rule:

PRGR stands for **Personal Reason-Giving Record**-whenever an institution takes (or permits) an action that can cause irreversible harm, someone must write the reasons and sign their name to the decision. The record forces plain language, a harm forecast, rejected alternatives, and a remedy trigger that activates without begging. Then ask the question this book keeps handing back to you, the reader, like a mirror:

If you had to sign your name under the outcome, would you still accept the same shortcuts?

MATRIX 1 — INTIMACY (FAITH)

What intimacy buys, how it hides, what it leaves behind, and where PRGR bites.

Intimacy lever	What it buys	How it hides	Signature + human cost / PRGR friction
Confession / disclosure ("tell me everything")	Private knowledge; leverage; pre-emptive control	"Pastoral care," "guidance," "healing," "concern"	Leaves: notes that vanish; selective quoting; memory disputes. Cost: shame, dependency. PRGR: any adverse act tied to disclosure must be signed + foreseen harm + remedy.
Access to rites / standing	Compliance; silence; loyalty	"Unity," "avoid scandal," "forgiveness," "discernment"	Leaves: soft bans; quiet exclusions; 'no longer welcome'. Cost: social death. PRGR: restriction requires signed reasons + appeal path + independent review trigger.
Spiritual authority (absolute framing)	Obedience; moral intimidation	"God's will," "obedience," "humility," "test of faith"	Leaves: self-doubt; apologising for being harmed. Cost: moral injury. PRGR: coercive demand must be authored: what is required, authority claimed, foreseeable harm.
Private space / private access	Boundary testing; plausible deniability	"Confidential," "for your protection," "special care"	Leaves: no witnesses; 'misunderstanding' narratives. Cost: fear, hypervigilance. PRGR: exceptions to 1:1 rules must be logged; complaints produce named decision-makers.
Discretion over complaints	Delay; exhaustion; containment	"We'll handle it internally," "compassion," "due process"	Leaves: disappearing complaints; stalled timelines; informal 'resolutions'. Cost: re-trauma. PRGR: no delay/closure without signature + harm forecast + remedy trigger.
Gifted attention / chosen-ness	Attachment; grooming; silence	"Mentorship," "vocation," "blessing"	Leaves: gradual normalisation; self-incrimination. Cost:

MINI MATRIX — IRREVERSIBLE HARM TEST

A quick diagnostic to run before finality hardens.

Irreversible threshold	Required authorship (PRGR)
Before the last reversible step (sentence, removal, custody transfer)	Named author signs risk + foreseen harm; sets review date; identifies remedy trigger.
Before any closure that ends scrutiny (file 'finalised', complaint dismissed)	Signature required: why closure is chosen over re-opening; harm forecast; appeal route recorded.
Before evidence becomes unreachable (time limits, disposal, sealing)	Author signs preservation duty; independent record created; audit log enabled.
Before a credibility label becomes fate ('vexatious', 'unreliable', 'non-compliant')	Author signs evidentiary basis; makes label appealable; states foreseeable reputational harm.
Before secrecy blocks challenge (privilege, redactions, non-disclosure)	Author signs reasons; independent reviewer assigned; remedy if later shown material.

Reader check: If you wouldn't sign the harm, what would you change—more time, more disclosure, more review, or refusal?

PART III

INTIMACY / ACCESS / MORAL OUTSOURCING

THE MAMASHIMI TRUST - BRISBANE AUSTRALIA

NO QUIET EDITS

I MAY EXPLAIN. I MAY NOT ERASE.

I knew the verdict was irreversible. It wasn't a career catastrophe-I had left the job almost a year earlier. But irreversibility has its own sting: once you choose stability over reality, you don't just decide. You settle.

And what's settled becomes hard to reopen, especially when a system can point to "finality" as if it were truth. That's the PRGR point here: irreversibility.

A real PRGR doesn't let you edit the past. No quiet replacement. No anonymization. No withdrawal. You can add a dated addendum, you can clarify, you can confess-but you can't swap out the record like it never existed. I've watched reputations die from paperwork no one will later admit they authored. I've watched myself "correct the record" like a stagehand changing props mid-scene, hoping the audience won't notice the story changed. That is how harm becomes permanent while responsibility stays fluid.

Irreversibility forces the opposite. If I'm willing to cause the harm, I'm willing to leave my name on the page where future people can see what I said when it mattered.

I may explain. I may not erase.

16

"THE MONSIGNOR'S HIDDEN DESIRE"

CEREMONIAL GARMENTS USED TO HIDE ORDINARY HUMAN APPETITES.

> Misuse of spiritual authority and boundary erosion (composite case), Italy 2021, PRGR

Superb wine from Tuscany softens the mind before you notice it. The first glass tastes like sunlight trapped in liquid-bright, persuasive, warming the chest. Pecorino follows, sharp and salty, flooding the tongue so thoroughly that subtlety becomes difficult. Then come the olives: bitter, medicinal, the aftertaste that arrives too late to warn you about what you've already swallowed. Blurring is pleasant when it's confined to the palate.

Blurring is dangerous when it's applied to people. That was the problem with Monsignor Vittorio Vitelli.

He moved through the marble corridors of the cathedral with the ease of a man who believed himself untouchable. His ceremonial robe brushed stone floors worn smooth by centuries of footsteps, and the jabot at his neck gleamed under chandelier light like a polished argument. To parishioners and clergy, he embodied holiness, wisdom, continuity-an official kind of goodness. They looked at him and felt the ancient relief of order: someone is in charge, someone knows the rules, someone will protect what is sacred.

But inside Vittorio, something had blurred.

Not his intelligence-he remained sharp. Not his discipline-he maintained appearances with meticulous care. What blurred was the boundary between care and appetite, between guidance and possession. He confused his role as messenger with a private entitlement to the people who came to him in trust.

It started subtly, in the places where faith encourages disclosure. Acolytes and seminarians approached him with questions-liturgical details, moral uncertainties, family pressures, the loneliness that blooms in men trying to become something "holy." Vittorio listened with warmth and patience, nodding at the right moments, offering counsel that sounded like compassion. And because he was good at listening, they gave him more. They offered their interior lives the way one offers a candle: a small flame, trembling, asking to be sheltered.

He discovered something intoxicating: the human need for approval is as powerful as doctrine. A word from him could rearrange a person's emotions. A look could settle anxiety or ignite it. The more people trusted him, the more he felt a quiet expansion inside himself-a sense that he was not simply advising them but shaping them.

A glass of wine becomes two. Two becomes a habit you defend as culture.

Vittorio began justifying minor transgressions as pastoral care. A hand on a shoulder that lingered longer than necessary. A private conversation that kept going after the official topic had ended. They offered a "special lesson" under the guise of mentorship and held it behind a closed door because "privacy protects dignity." The narration was camouflage. That was his genius and his ruin: he could wrap desire in language that sounded holy. He orchestrated encounters the way a practiced musician rehearses phrasing: creating the moment, guiding the tempo, watching for the point where hesitation turns into compliance. Some men, eager to please, yielded without naming what was happening-gratitude and confusion braided together. Others felt discomfort like a pebble in the shoe: small, persistent, difficult to explain without being accused of imagining it. Vittorio noted these differences with interest. He learned who would comply, who would resist, and whom he could make doubt themselves.

The cathedral helped him. Not because stone is wicked, but because stone is silent. The vastness of chapels and side rooms, the echoing sacristy corridors, the thick doors-spaces built to preserve reverence also preserved secrecy. Bells tolled for prayer; the sound seemed to bless every action by association. He adjusted robes, offered counsel, whispered approval, all in plain sight. The robe and jabot were not merely clothing; they were an assumption the community made on his behalf: this man is safe.

That assumption blurred the eyes of witnesses. Here is where the microscope matters.

The microscope-whether you credit van Leeuwenhoek in the Dutch Republic, or the early Italian instrument makers like the Janssen tradition debated across histories, or Galileo's refinements-was born from the refusal to accept blur. It took the unseen and made it visible. The point of a microscope is not to create truth. It is to reveal what was already there, hiding in plain sight because the human eye prefers comfort over clarity.

Vittorio lived on the comfort side of sight. He depended on it.

But comfort is unstable. Rumours surfaced, as they always do, like hairline cracks in plaster: murmurs among seminarians, uneasy glances, small warnings shared in corridors. The hierarchy dismissed them at first-misunderstandings, youthful sensitivity, "over-interpretation." Institutions love blur. Blur allows them to keep functioning without admitting the cost.

Then, someone raised the complaint that no one could soften.

Multiple testimonies, different voices describing the same pattern: mentorship that became pressure, confession that became leverage, intimacy disguised as care, backed it. When investigators began collecting accounts, they didn't find one dramatic incident so much as a repeated method. It was like looking through a microscope at a drop of water and realising the same organisms appear again and again-consistent, undeniable, alive.

Vittorio's web came into focus.

The Church's response was decisive but discreet. The Church suspended him and prevented him from ministering publicly. Counseling and supervision became mandatory. They instituted protective measures: regulated private meetings, ethical oversight, and mandatory reporting mechanisms. Policies arrived with the predictable speed of institutions trying to outrun shame.

Yet the deepest damage wasn't administrative. It was spiritual-because what Vittorio exploited was not only bodies, but the believer's capacity to trust the sacred.

Spiritual authority's cloak can double the injury when someone is abused. There is bodily harm-fear, coercion, shame. And abuse harms meaning: it makes people feel that prayer itself has been contaminated, that confession is unsafe, and that the sacred language used to comfort can also trap. Faith becomes a room where the door no longer locks. The believer wonders whether God was present or whether God was simply a costume, the abuser wore.

That is the bitter aftertaste-the olives after wine and cheese. It arrives later, and it lingers longer.

In solitude, Vittorio tried to reinterpret what had happened the way he had always done: with narrative. He told himself he had "misread closeness." He told himself he had only wanted to guide. He told himself he was being punished for warmth. But the microscope does not care for stories. It shows structure: repeated behaviour, repeated harm, repeated exploitation of imbalance.

He grasped the reality that spiritual authority does not grant immunity; it increases responsibility. The robe and jabot that once commanded obedience now looked like a cruel joke-ceremonial garments used to hide ordinary human appetites.

His fall reverberated beyond the cathedral walls. Parishioners wrestled with betrayal. Seminarians questioned vocation. Staff wondered how many signs they had blurred into harmlessness because it was easier than clarity. The community faced the uncomfortable fact that sanctity is not a property of clothing, nor of architecture, nor even of an office. If sanctity exists in human institutions, vigilance, boundaries, and the willingness to look closely must defend it.

Some churches collapse, but people quickly rebuild them-they replace the stone, restore the timber, and return the facade to its former beauty so the community can breathe again. But scaffolding cannot rebuild some losses. When trust caves in, the reconstruction is slower and less visible. It happens inside people, where no committee can supervise and no policy can guarantee safety.

And that is why blur is so dangerous when people are involved: it turns warning signs into ambiance. It makes bitterness taste like tradition. It makes exploitation look like care-until someone finally looks through the lens and sees what was always there.

The unseen made visible.

And once it becomes visible, closing your eyes will not restore its holiness.

PRGR END-CAP - AUTHORED HARM TEST

(for "THE MONSIGNOR'S HIDDEN DESIRE")

The harm in this case doesn't begin with a seduction scene. It begins with a governance move that looks like pastoral care: **the monsignor's selection of who may come close.** Desire is private; **access** is institutional. The abuse happens where those two overlap and the institution lets "spiritual guidance" become a private corridor. **PRGR would attach authorship at the first step where Monsignor Vitelli converts spiritual authority into personal access.** In this story, the hinge-steps are practical: appointments, proximity, confidentiality, and the selective granting of reputation.

The hinge-steps where PRGR would force the author to exist

The private appointment pipeline - "spiritual direction" as exclusive channel
When Vitelli begins scheduling repeated one-on-one meetings in settings designed for privacy (office after hours, sacristy, rectory rooms) and frames them as necessary for formation, PRGR triggers. He must author:

why meetings require privacy rather than transparent pastoral structures,

what boundaries apply (open-door norm, third-party availability, documented agenda),

what the person can do if discomfort arises without risking career/standing. Because in this case, the first harm is the creation of a corridor with no witnesses.

The confidentiality capture - turning confession-like intimacy into leverage

If Vitelli invites disclosures about loneliness, shame, sexuality, family conflict, "discernment"-and later uses that knowledge to deepen dependence or silence-PRGR attaches at the moment the disclosure becomes operational. He must author: what information is necessary for pastoral purpose,

what is optional,

and what safeguards prevent that information being used for coercion, retaliation, or grooming. PRGR treats intimate knowledge as a controlled substance: once held, it must be governed.

The advancement gate - access to opportunities tied to closeness

The most institutional harm in this chapter is not the desire itself, but the **career funnel** it creates: recommendations, placements, invitations, travel, committee access, "formation opportunities." PRGR triggers at any decision where Vitelli:

selects a favored person for a role, grants special access,

or blocks someone who resists him. He must author:

what objective criteria justify the selection, what alternatives were considered,

what foreseeable harm arises if closeness is the real criterion (coercion, inequality, silence culture). This is where PRGR makes grooming legible: when privilege is administered through proximity.

The tone-and-virtue reframing - discomfort rebranded as spiritual defect

If Vitelli labels boundary-setting as "pride," "immaturity," "lack of obedience," or "confusion," PRGR attaches at the first use of spiritual language to disqualify testimony. He must author:

the claim he is making (that discomfort equals spiritual failing), the evidence for it,

and what protections exist to ensure spiritual language is not used as disciplinary weapon. In this case, the abuse is carried in vocabulary.

The reassignment / exile step - removing the problem by moving the person

If complaints trigger "reassignment," "retreat," "time away," or a quiet transfer-especially of the complainant-PRGR triggers at the memo that moves them. Someone must author:

why the person is being moved,

what harm is foreseeable (reputation damage, isolation, vocational derailment),

and why moving the monsignor is not the first option. PRGR blocks the classic ecclesial containment tactic: relocating truth instead of addressing power.

What PRGR would force in this case (matched to ecclesial mechanics)

1. **No unbounded private corridor**
   PRGR requires that spiritual direction and formation meetings operate under clear boundaries:
   opt-in with informed consent,
   transparent scheduling,
   third-party availability,
   and documented purpose.
   The goal isn't to criminalize care; it is to stop care from becoming an unreviewable corridor.

2. **A controlled-intimacy rule**
   PRGR would require explicit governance of sensitive disclosures:
   what may be asked,
   what must never be requested,
   and what happens if the cleric begins to "need" the person emotionally.
   This chapter is about hidden desire; PRGR demands that desire be treated as a risk factor, not as a spiritual mystery.

3. **A retaliation tripwire**
   PRGR would establish automatic review if any of these occur after a boundary is set or concern raised:
   sudden loss of opportunities,
   character smearing framed as "spiritual concern,"
   reassignment to obscurity,
   or pressure to withdraw complaints "for the good of the Church."
   Because harm here is administered through **vocation and reputation**, not bruises.

4. **A named author for "pastoral necessity" decisions**
   When institutions say "pastoral reasons," PRGR says:
   write the reasons and sign.
   In this case, "pastoral necessity" is the phrase most likely to be used as fog.

The questions that keep this End-Cap hyper-specific to Vitelli

If you were Vitelli: which decision are you willing to sign your name under-the repeated private meetings, the selective opportunities, or the "pastoral" reframing of someone's discomfort as a spiritual flaw?

If you were the target: what is the first hinge-step where care becomes corridor-the invitation to exclusivity, the demand for intimate disclosure, or the sudden career gate-keeping?

If you were the bishop/curia: what would you author first-the boundaries on private meetings, the audit of opportunity allocation, or the rule preventing "pastoral transfers" from burying complaints?

PRGR doesn't ask whether Vitelli "felt love" or "meant well." It isolates the moment he **converted spiritual authority into personal access**-and forces a named author to exist at the administrative step where desire becomes governance.

17

"THE PASTOR'S PRIVATE CHAMBERS"

THE ILLUSION OF MORALITY, COMBINED WITH THE QUIET EXERCISE OF CONTROL.

Clergy misconduct investigations, Netherlands, 2003-2011 (composite case)

The key was heavier than it needed to be-brass, worn smooth where fingers had turned it a thousand times. Elise felt the weight the first time Pastor Willem van Dijk set it on the table between them, as if it were a harmless gift.

"Let yourself in if you ever need to talk," he said.

The sitting room at the back of the rectory didn't look threatening. Warm lamplight. Two chairs angled toward each other like a counseling diagram. Theology books aligned with ceremonial care, spines straight as a choir in silent rehearsal.

When the door shut, the sound was soft-more hush than click-yet Elise felt it in her ribs. Like stepping into a greenhouse: air thicker, private. A small climate where the normal rules of distance could be "discussed," and then-quietly-adjusted.

The people of Middelburg admired Willem's restraint. Cassock immaculate. Collar set with crisp precision, a white geometry that suggested moral alignment. Even skeptics found him hard to dislike because he rarely performed zeal. He performed calmly.

Calm, Elise would learn, can be a technique.

He began with praise, offered the way a handler offers food to win trust. Elise was twenty-three, a volunteer with the youth choir, earnest and eager, the person institutions love because she said yes before she understood what yes would cost. Willem noticed her reliability and framed it as a vocation.

"You have a gift," he told her. "Not everyone is called to serve as you do." The compliment lifted her-then made her dependent on the hand that lifted.

After the first meeting came the second, and then the third. Each time, Willem moved the boundary by a fraction. The questions drifted from faith toward need.

Do you feel seen? Do you ever feel lonely? Have you ever wished someone would take charge of things?

He phrased it as care, but the direction was unmistakable: toward confession without a screen, toward a private bond with an educated man in a collar.

Willem spoke often about "simple souls." He used the phrase kindly, almost affectionately, when discussing parish problems with staff-people who didn't understand paperwork, people who were "emotional," people who "misread kindness." It wasn't crude contempt. It was the settled superiority of someone who believed education made him the final interpreter of other people's experience.

When Elise mentioned a friend found Willem's attention "a bit intense," he smiled as if she'd reported a superstition.

"People without training confuse guidance with intrusion," he said. "That's why the Church exists-to help them name what they can't name."

It sounded like compassion. It functioned like permission.

Institutional complacency did the rest. Willem's parish ran well. Donations were steady. A man who keeps the building quiet, is treated as a gift in a system that constantly fights fires-sometimes even when his quiet comes at someone else's expense.

The first complaint arrived from a woman who cleaned the parish hall on weekends. Her letter described Willem's habit of summoning her after hours for "private prayer": how he stood too close, asked personal questions, and turned her discomfort into guilt. The diocesan office filed it under "pastoral misunderstanding." A second complaint came from a teenage volunteer's mother-short, blunt, angry. She said Willem had told her daughter that "only immature people fear closeness," and that "obedience is love." Again: not language that detonates, just coercion packaged as virtue.

A committee met. The committee took notes. The committee asked Willem for clarification. He added, almost casually, that "some families lack sophistication" and therefore misinterpret pastoral support. Several administrators nodded, because the same bias lived in them too: the educated interpret, the uneducated feel.

Elise's turning point came not from an incident but from a realization. She had edited her life to keep him pleased-canceling plans, avoiding friends, feeling anxious when he didn't respond. His approval had become a barometer. When he was warm, she felt safe. When he was distant, she felt wrong.

She tested it once. She asked to meet in the parish office instead of the sitting room. Daylight. Open door. He looked at her for a long moment, still smiling.

"Are you afraid of me?" he asked softly.

The question was a trap. If she said yes, she was accusing him. If she said no, she was surrendering the boundary again. Elise felt the air tighten, as if a hidden valve had reduced the oxygen. In that moment she understood: he wasn't offering support. He was controlling the conditions.

She began saving messages, noting times, writing down phrases he used repeatedly-trust, obedience, special responsibility-language that sounded spiritual until you heard it as a system of leverage. With a retired parish administrator, meticulous and uncharmable, she built a pattern: Willem's "private chamber" meetings clustered around volunteers, isolated parishioners, and staff with little status. The fewer credentials someone had, the easier they were to portray as unreliable.

When the dossier reached the diocese, action finally became possible-not because conscience woke up, but because the institution now had a risk profile it could recognize.

Documentation is the language bureaucracy respects. Feelings are not.

The diocese restricted Willem from closed-door counseling. They imposed supervision. The diocese framed it as "boundary training," as if the problem were clumsiness rather than intention.

He returned to the pulpit and preached about humility. He warned against gossip. Many parishioners felt relieved; they wanted the weather to clear. They wanted normal.

Elise sat in the back pew, listening, and realized she would never again confuse calm with safety.

There is a warning in the Gospels-brief, severe-about those who harm the vulnerable and then hide behind righteousness. Willem would have known it. He simply behaved as if knowledge were an exemption.

The key still existed. The door still closed. The lamplight still made the room warm. But once Elise understood the mechanism, the room never felt private again.

It felt engineered.

18

"THE LETTERS FROM THE CONFESSIONAL"

THE ROBE IS ONLY CLOTH-UNTIL THE SYSTEM MAKES IT A BLINDFOLD, AND THE WEARER LEARNS TO LOVE THE DARK.

Confessional boundary violations and emotional grooming (excerpted from the private journal of a composite character)

Dear Diary,

March 2, 2024

The church is quiet in the way a courtroom is quiet: not peace, but containment. Stone absorbs sound until you almost believe sound never existed. The candles do not flicker; they perform steadiness. Incense is a kind of curtain-sweet, ancient, and practical, as if scent can persuade God to look away.

I write with hands that would seem calm if you didn't know what they are capable of.

The robe and the jabot are not clothing. They are an argument. They tell people, This man is safe; this man has been allowed.

When I pass through the nave, faces soften as if I carry a solution. I have learned, with shame, how little is required to become a "solution" in an institution that runs on symbols.

Parishioners come to me with their lives folded into confessions: names, anxieties, secrets, the exact places where their strength fails. I hear all of it, and the hearing changes me.

That is the first thing no one tells you: knowledge of the vulnerable is an intoxicant. It is wine without a glass. It warms the chest and blurs the border between compassion and possession.

I tell myself my duty is to guide them to the light.

I also know-already-that I have used light like a lamp in an interrogation room.

At first it was small: a hand held a second too long; a gaze stayed where it shouldn't; a blessing turned into a lingering touch disguised as reassurance. The institution has a word for such things when it wants to preserve itself: misunderstanding. I can feel that word waiting in the walls, ready to protect me if I speak it in the right tone.

The frightening truth is: I am not confused. I am choosing. And yet I still tell myself I am not.

April 15, 2024

The letters arrived today: sealed envelopes, no names. The handwriting changed from one to another-some careful, some furious, some shaking on the page. They all said the same thing in different languages of fear: You made me doubt my perception.

That line sits in me like a splinter. Doubt is a clever wound. It doesn't bleed in public. It festers in private. One writer described leaving confession and feeling as if she had stepped out of a room with no windows. Another said she could no longer pray without remembering my proximity. Someone wrote: I came for absolution and left with shame that belonged to you.

The letters are evidence, but they are also mirrors. And the most unbearable part is that they do not shock me. They confirmed what I already knew.

I expected guilt to feel like collapse. Instead, it feels like a second heartbeat-present, constant, and oddly functional.

I read the letters again and felt two things at once: horror and a dark, involuntary thrill.

That is the beginning of the sickness, I think-not the act, but the way the mind lives with it.

May 3, 2024

Confession after confession, and I become fluent in weakness. I notice patterns in people the way a judge notices patterns in testimony: hesitation here, an overly precise detail there, the tremor in the voice that betrays the body's refusal to be edited.

The rituals do not protect me from temptation; they structure it.

When the choir rehearses and the nave fills with sound, the music creates a false innocence-harm can happen beneath hymns because hymns convince the eye that nothing ugly belongs in the room.

When I teach catechism, the children look at me as if I am a storybook. Their parents look at me as if I am insurance against chaos. I receive all that trust and my first impulse is not gratitude-it is use.

I hate writing that, but it is true.

The institution gives me invisible keys: access, privacy, the benefit of doubt. People want the church to be clean so badly they will polish the priest instead of asking whether the cloth hides rot.

I catch myself thinking in administrative language: Pastoral care. Boundary misinterpretation. Complex situation. No malice intended.

These are not explanations. They are disinfectant sprayed into air without cleaning the wound. And the worst part is that the disinfectant smells like holiness.

June 21, 2024

The first complaint reached the bishop.

I wore the robe, and jabot pressed to perfection, as if ironed fabric could flatten reality. The diocesan office smelled of paper and old polish-bureaucracy's incense. There were files on the table already, thick enough to feel like a verdict. Someone had arranged the documents in neat stacks. The neatness felt obscene.

I spoke the way institutions teach you to speak when you want to survive:

"I never intended harm." "My pastoral approach has been misunderstood." "Confession is sacred." "I have served faithfully for years."

The bishop listened with a face that belonged to governance, not faith. He did not rage. He did not comfort him. He performed the calm of a system protecting itself from scandal while pretending it is protecting souls.

Then he said quietly, "Intent does not erase pattern." Pattern. The word struck harder than an accusation.

A pattern is what you can't talk your way out of. A pattern is what institutions recognize only when they can no longer deny it.

I walked back through the city afterward and saw my reflection in shop windows. The robe made me look whole. Inside, I was disintegrating in slow motion.

July 10, 2024

The church has taken me off pastoral duties.

The church is still here, unchanged. The altar cloth is still white. The candles still burn. The saints in stained glass still hold their calm faces as if nothing human could touch them. The building continues to perform purity even as it has become, for some, a trigger.

I wander the nave after hours like a man haunting his own crime. The pews are empty, but I can still feel the people I hurt-like warmth left in fabric after someone stands up.

My robe hangs in the vestry now. The jabot is crisp. I look at it and feel something close to grief. Not for the garment itself, but for what it used to promise people. It promised safety. It promised refuge. It promised careful handling of vulnerabilities.

Instead, I turned vulnerability into leverage-sometimes erotic, sometimes psychological, always selfish. I keep reflecting: if someone had caught me sooner, would I have stopped?

Or would I simply have become more careful?

That question terrifies me because I do not know the answer.

August 1, 2024

Counseling has begun for the parishioners.

I am not part of those rooms, but I hear the reports filtered through institutional language: "distress," "confusion," "loss of trust." The words are small compared to the harm, like calling a fire "heat exposure." Additional measures are being installed-supervised meetings, reporting channels, ethics training. The church announces these reforms the way a courthouse announces new protocols after a scandal: We have corrected the system. But I know what reforms often are: new locks installed after the theft, while pretending the theft never happened.

Some priests avoid me with professional caution, as if misconduct is contagious through proximity. Others show me quiet sympathy, the kind that feels like complicity because it asks me to keep my shame private for the sake of the institution's smooth surface.

I understand something that makes me sick:

The church is not only a sanctuary. It is also a machine. Machines do not feel remorse. Machines protect continuity.

And continuity, when worshiped, becomes its own moral disease.

September 15, 2024

I have recognized the shape of my own contradictions.

I preached repentance and lived appetite. I offered absolution while manufacturing doubt. I spoke about sin as if it were an external enemy when, in truth, I had installed it inside the very structure people trusted to protect them.

I used to think evil arrived like a stranger-obvious, dramatic, foreign.

Now I see how it arrives: as familiarity. As permission. As a small rationalization repeated until it becomes architecture.

There is a line in me I crossed and then stopped noticing. Psychologists would call it habituation. The church would call it temptation. I call it what it is: practice. I practiced harm until it felt like ordinary life.

And still-this is the humiliating truth-I cannot heal myself.

I know the steps to repentance as well as I know the liturgy. I can recite them. I can describe them. I can even perform them.

But performance got me here.

The sickness isn't ignorance. It's appetite tied to authority, and the way authority makes appetite feel entitled. The hardest admission:

I do not fully trust my desire to be forgiven.

Because forgiveness, too, can become a tool-another way to avoid consequences while looking holy.

October 30, 2024

I am leaving the diocese.

The robe lies folded. The jabot's press completed it. The departure is tidy because institutions adore tidy exits. A clean line on a spreadsheet. A sentence in minutes. A problem converted into an administration.

They will say: We responded. They will say: Safeguards are in place. They will say: The Church is healing. But healing is not a press release.

The faithful carry what happened in their bodies. Some will never return. Some will return and feel their throats tighten at the smell of wax and incense. Some will stay because leaving feels like losing a limb-because people cling to institutions the way sailors cling to wreckage: better splinters than drowning.

I keep thinking of the old line about Peter: the rock, the foundation. People repeat it as if "rock" means unbreakable.

They forget rocks split from tension inside them. Water finds a hairline crack, freezes, expands-quiet physics, devastating result. A church can fracture the same way: not from an invading army, but from small permitted failures swelling in the dark.

I did not fall because I misunderstood.

I fell because I understood and kept going.

That is the part that does not absolve. The part that makes holy language taste like metal. The part that turns confession into theatre when it should be surgery.

The institution did not create my appetite. It did something worse: it dressed it. It gave my weakness a costume and called it calling. It gave me privacy and called it trust. It gave me deference and called it reverence. It taught everyone-me included-to mistake the garment for the man.

The robe is only cloth-until the system makes it a blindfold, and the wearer learns to love the dark.

The gatekeeper is required to permit any action that affects an individual's future, stating, "I am using access as leverage; I accept responsibility for the harm it may cause." Under this rule, "care" can't appear as camouflage, and silence can't be purchased with proximity.

What's happening in your body right now-tightness, recognition, disgust? If you were the victim, what would you need to feel safe?

If you were the bystander, what would you risk interrupting it?

Where do you tolerate "small" boundary crossings because it's easier?

19

"THE MUFTI'S TURBAN"

GUIDANCE SHOULD BE A LANTERN, NOT A BANNER WAVED BY WHOEVER PAYS FOR THE POLE.

Composite patterns of "fatwa for hire," prestige capture, and political pressure on religious opinions (fictionalized).

In the high desert spring, wind arrives like a messenger with no manners. It pushes dust into doorways and leaves the horizon trembling. By noon, heat turns streets into a mirage; by night, cold returns and reminds everyone how thin comfort is.

Mufti Yusuf Karim lived between those extremes. When he walked from his study to the lecture hall, his white turban sat perfectly, layered cloth gathered like a crown made of restraint. People greeted him with lowered eyes-the habit of reverence.

His fatwas were lanterns: guidance for lives tangled in inheritance disputes, divorce, loans, and medical ethics. Yusuf's answers were often wise, sometimes strict, always calm. Calm can soothe. Calm can also seduce a society into forgetting its questions.

The first approach came as flattery. A minister requested counsel about a "reform" and hinted the public needed reassurance. Yusuf listened, then said, "If it resembles riba, they need protection, not slogans." The minister smiled anyway, as if refusal were a negotiable starting point.

Afterward, Yusuf stood at his window watching wind lift sand in pale sheets, erasing footprints as quickly as they formed. Societies love erased footprints, he thought-outcomes without accountability.

Then the businessperson arrived.

Hassan Nouri owned warehouses, import licenses, and a smile that never looked rushed. He donated to the seminary and posed for photographs beside Yusuf at charity dinners, as if generosity were proof of purity.

Hassan requested a formal fatwa declaring a new financing product permissible. Lawyers brought diagrams and spoke of "fees," "services," "risk-sharing." Yusuf asked questions that made them sweat.

When Hassan left, a "gift" appeared: a carpet for Yusuf's study. Yusuf returned it. Days later, an "anonymous donor" funded repairs at Yusuf's sister's home in the old quarter, including a new roof and new wiring.

Influence liked indirect pathways; it kept hands clean by keeping gifts deniable.

Yusuf tried to push back. He sent money through an intermediary to reimburse the repairs. The intermediary returned it. "The donor refuses," he said, eyes carefully blank.

Pressure followed in softer forms. Newspapers hinted Yusuf was "obstructing progress." A scholar began giving lectures about "rigid elders." The minister's office floated the word retirement like a warning wrapped in courtesy.

On a night when wind rattled shutters, Yusuf met with his juristic council. Some urged firmness. Others urged nuance. Yusuf heard the deeper question beneath their arguments: was a mufti meant to protect doctrine from society, or society from doctrine?

He wrote the fatwa with careful constraints. He did not call the product pure. He called it conditionally permissible under strict requirements and warned against exploitation. He believed he had built a fence. Hassan's media printed only the first sentence.

The product spread. Families signed contracts they did not understand. Fees multiplied like weeds after rain. When complaints rose, the banks pointed to the fatwa, stamped with Yusuf's authority like a seal.

A teacher named Mariam came to Yusuf's study with a folder of cases-missed payments, penalties, quiet desperation. She spoke without drama, which made her more dangerous.

"Mufti," she said, "your words are being used as a net." "I added conditions," Yusuf replied. "They removed them," Mariam said. "As wind removes footprints."

A dust storm rolled in that afternoon, thick and brown, turning day into dusk. People shut windows and waited. After the storm passed, grit remained in every corner, proving that some of what enters is impossible to fully sweep out.

That week, regulators opened an inquiry into predatory lending and political collusion. Yusuf received a summons from regulators. They summoned him as a symbol, not a criminal. Cameras waited. Regulators asked questions about gifts, family repairs, and "relationships." The public wanted a simple villain; Yusuf was something harder: a scholar who believed he could temper power with nuance, and discovered power used his nuance as camouflage.

The banks invited Yusuf to a public forum "to explain the fatwa." The hall was full, fans pushing warm air in slow circles. Yusuf sat beneath a banner printed with his name and felt the humiliation of being turned into marketing. He spoke of restraint and warned against exploiting need.

Applause came in the wrong places-at "permissible," not at "strict." An elderly man clasped Yusuf's hand afterward and whispered, "You have made it easy for us." Yusuf did not know how to answer without sounding like a man retracting his own blessing.

A month later, the first defaults hit the neighborhood like cracks in clay. One shopkeeper lost inventory to penalties. A couple sold jewelry to keep up. Yusuf visited homes quietly, bringing food parcels and listening to shame spill out in broken sentences.

Each visit felt like trying to cup water in his hands-helpful, but leaking. When the council amended the fatwa publicly, attaching the missing conditions in bold, the banks simply changed brochures. They labeled the restrictions as "recommended guidance." He understood what the wind had been teaching all season: if authority does not bind itself to transparent process, it becomes available to whoever is strongest in the room.

After the hearing, Yusuf removed his turban and set it on his desk. The cloth looked suddenly ordinary-just fabric, just folds. The moral became clear to him with bitterness: a society hungry for reassurance can consume religious authority as a commodity. And when systems prefer rescue-investigations, statements, scapegoats-over protection, clear boundaries, disclosure, independent review; the damage spreads quietly, contract by contract, household by household.

At dawn, wind moved through the empty courtyard, lifting sand into thin veils.

Yusuf watched it and thought: guidance should be a lantern, not a banner waved by whoever pays for the pole.

20

"THE CLERK AND THE CANON"

PEOPLE WANTED TO BELIEVE THAT SANCTITY WAS VISIBLE.

Clerical sexual misconduct scandal, Australia, 2010s (composite case)

Sydney has a way of disguising danger.

On bright mornings the harbor looks harmless-blue glass, ferries cutting slow white seams, gulls circling as if the sky itself were generous. But beneath that surface, currents run in directions that don't announce themselves. A rip can pull a strong swimmer away from shore without sound, without drama, with nothing more than steady insistence.

Canon Michael O'Reilly built his authority in the same way.

At St. Mary's Parish, he was magnetic. He wore the cassock with tailored care, his stole neatly arranged, his gestures controlled enough to read as discipline. Parishioners loved his sermons because he could make hardship sound meaningful. He had the calm voice of a man who seemed to carry answers in his pockets.

Too many, he looked like safety.

Sarah arrived as a theology student on placement, twenty-two years old and hungry to do good work. She volunteered with youth outreach, helped organize events, and said yes to every request because she believed devotion meant availability. She admired Michael the way people admire a lighthouse: not for intimacy, but for certainty.

Michael noticed that admiration quickly. He also noticed the vulnerability beneath it-the eagerness for approval, the desire to be seen, the willingness to work past exhaustion if it earned praise from someone respected.

His attention began as a blessing.

He complimented her in front of others, singled her out for "maturity," asked her opinions during planning meetings as if she were already a colleague. He invited her to private "formation" sessions framed as mentorship: conversations about prayer, purpose, and spiritual discipline. In that setting, intimacy could be justified as care. The language itself was a permission slip.

Sarah felt honored. She told herself she was lucky.

Michael was patient. He did not rush. He did not leap. He shaped.

In biology, conditioning works best when rewards arrive unpredictably: not every time, but often enough to keep the nervous system waiting. Michael's praise followed that pattern. He warmed, withdrew slightly, warmed again. He offered affirmation like sunlight through clouds-intermittent, precious, addictive.

Soon Sarah measured her days by his tone. A brief smile made her buoyant. A delayed reply made her anxious. She adjusted her schedule around him, then her thoughts, then her friendships. When family and friends suggested she seemed distant, she defended him instinctively. "He's just guiding me," she said. "He's helping me grow."

The parish environment reinforced the story. People trusted the collar. People trusted the stole. People wanted to believe that sanctity was visible.

Michael's requests grew gradually. A late-night call "because he sensed she was struggling." A home visit "for spiritual support." A private walk after an event where he spoke about loyalty, about how few people truly understood vocation, about the dangers of outside influence.

He framed dependence as devotion.

In one sermon-almost casually-he spoke about hypocrisy and appearances, about the danger of being a "whitewashed tomb": polished on the outside while hollow within. The phrase landed in the congregation as moral instruction.

In Sarah, it landed as confusion she couldn't name.

Because Michael's exterior was immaculate. His behavior, however, felt like a hand closing around her choices. He never threatened openly. He never demanded bluntly. He suggested. He implied. He made approval contingent on compliance while leaving just enough ambiguity for her to blame herself.

He praised her "discernment" while quietly implying she might resist the very guidance he had given her. When she expressed discomfort, he responded with wounded disappointment-an emotion that made her rush to repair him.

The tipping point came during a weekend retreat for volunteers.

It rained hard on the second night. The gum trees outside the lodge hissed with wind. Water ran in rivulets down the windows like faint handwriting. After the evening session, Michael asked Sarah to stay behind. He spoke softly about her "gifts," about how rare it was to meet someone truly committed. Then his voice tightened into certainty.

"Not everyone can guide you," he said. "Not everyone understands what you're called to. Trust me completely." In that moment, the language of care became a lock.

Sarah felt the room shrink. She realized he presented her with a Hobson's choice: comply with his version of trust or lose the spiritual approval she'd been trained to crave.

That night she did not sleep. She listened to the rain and felt something in herself reassemble-fear becoming clarity. She understood that what had happened was not sudden. She constructed it.

She contacted the diocesan safeguarding office and, because she needed an outside anchor, a dean at her university. She did not tell a dramatic story. She gave facts: messages, meeting times, patterns, quotes she could remember. She described the emotional weight as carefully as she described the schedule.

Investigators trained in boundary violations recognized the structure immediately. The case did not require sensational details to be serious. It was serious because it was strategic: an authority figure using spiritual language and institutional trust to build emotional captivity.

The diocese responded with administrative precision. The diocese removed Michael from direct contact with interns and volunteers. He was required to undergo supervised reflection and pastoral ethics training. His public role continued, but his access narrowed. The institution protected itself while quietly acknowledging the harm. Sarah left the parish.

She held both relief and grief: relief because she had identified the situation, and grief because her freely given trust had become a bargaining chip. She learned that people can easily perform virtue, and that explaining coercion is difficult when it appears as kindness.

Michael maintained appearances. He continued preaching with composed warmth. People still admired him. Memory, like weather, moves on.

But for those who had seen the pattern up close, the stole no longer looked like a pure symbol. It looked like a mask that had worked-too well-for too long.

The scandal became a quiet warning in Sydney's ecclesiastical circles: authority does not always arrive as force. Sometimes it arrives as praise, carefully rationed, until dependence feels like faith.

THE LACE ACROSS THE DOORWAY

INTERLUDE I

Three thresholds. Three doors. Three versions of authority putting itself on.

Only now there is a fourth garment.

Not on the body-on the record.

A single page stitched into the system like lace: delicate enough to look ornamental, strong enough to snag.

And used.

They did not wake up thinking, *Today I will cross the line.*

They woke up thinking, *Today I must keep the institution stable.*

And then-before the first small decision could quietly harden into fate-someone placed a thin sheet of paper in their path.

A PRGR.

Not a policy. Not a training module. Not a committee minute.

A page that requires a human name.

The lace doesn't look like force.

It looks like paperwork-thin, decorative, easy to ignore.

But it does one thing optics cannot: it makes the choice name itself.

The doors open anyway.

The light does its flattering work.

21

"THE DEAN'S COMPROMISED AGENDA"

CEREMONY CAN BE IMPECCABLE WHILE THE STRUCTURE BENEATH CORRODES.

University corruption and Criminal/Corporate exploitation, United Kingdom, 2013 (composite case), PRGR

The gala looked like success.

Crystal glasses caught the light.

Donors laughed in clusters.

The university's banners hung like clean flags of purpose.

On stage, Dean Margaret Whitmore spoke about opportunity, innovation, and "ethical leadership" with the polished cadence of someone who knows which words reassure. Applause rose on cue-warm, practiced, generous.

Outside the ballroom, a late-season drizzle stippled the windows and slid downward in thin, obedient lines. Inside, they engineered the lighting to flatter: it was soft enough to erase fatigue and bright enough to make everything sparkle. It was optics, not truth-re-fraction, not revelation. Under chandeliers, even questionable people can look philanthropic.

Behind the ballroom walls, the university's finances were less elegant. Budgets are rarely glamorous. They are often what forces moral choices to reveal themselves.

The board hired Whitmore to deliver stability: new funding streams, stronger partnerships, and improved rankings. And she delivered-fast. That speed was her advantage and her trap.

She cultivated donors aggressively. Some were respectable. Others arrived with wealth that seemed to have no origin, like groundwater that appears clear until you test it.

Shell companies offered grants. Private foundations offered sponsorship. Intermediaries offered "consulting support" with fees that looked like normal administrative friction.

Whitmore told herself the money would serve the institution. She told herself she was protecting jobs, research, and student futures. She told herself she was doing what leadership requires: making unpleasant compromises so others don't have to.

And then, quietly, she enjoyed it.

Not simply the money-the leverage. The ability to say yes or no. The ability to steer projects toward donors' preferred narratives. The ability to move people in and out of promotions, committees, and awards. The power to make obstacles disappear for those who were useful.

It wasn't only ambition. It was the seduction of systems.

Once you learn which valves control the flow-funding, prestige, access-you treat people like variables. In any lab, you can force a result if you're allowed to adjust enough conditions: temperature, pressure, time.

Whitmore learned to adjust conditions in the same way.

A department chair who questioned a sponsor's "reputation" suddenly faced a delayed renewal. A skeptical committee member found their pet initiative quietly unfunded. The committee rewarded a compliant voice with "opportunity."

In chemistry, there is a principle that dilution can make toxins harder to detect, not less toxic. Committees, intermediaries, and documents diluted Whitmore's compromise. Every individual decision looked reasonable. Together, they formed an agenda.

Some research outputs aligned too neatly with sponsor interests. The researchers postponed certain critical findings under "additional review."

A compliance officer raised concerns and found doors closing gently. Someone told the senior professor, who was asking about transparency, not to be "negative."

In the weeks after the gala, the campus looked normal in the daylight-students hurrying between buildings, bicycles chained to railings, the library buzzing with routine.

But underneath, the institution behaved like metal under repeated stress: no single blow, just micro-fractures. Small compromises, repeated, create fatigue. Not the dramatic kind you can photograph-just the slow weakening that makes a structure fail when it finally matters.

Then, an accounting firm looking into something else discovered unusual patterns in how donations were handled: money went through several organizations, there were bills for "services" that didn't clearly match any work done, and payments to consultants seemed like a way to disguise illegal money through official-looking documents.

The university quietly hired a private investigator, Clarke Wilson, to map relationships the institution didn't want to map itself. He traced connections: sponsors linked to environmental violations, intermediaries with histories of fraud allegations, entities that existed primarily to move money without scrutiny.

The deeper he went, the more the network resembled an engineered structure-like scaffolding built behind a facade to hold something unstable upright.

When the findings reached the board, the reaction was immediate and predictable: contain the liability, protect the brand, promise reform.

The board suspended Whitmore pending review.

Public statements emphasized procedure. Internal messages emphasized calm. Committees formed. Policies went public. The university acted as though the problem were a set of technical failures rather than a human willingness to accept money without demanding truth about where it came from.

Whitmore defended herself in the language of necessity. She argued universities survive in a competitive market and that partnership is essential. She insisted that she never intended wrongdoing, that she made choices for the "greater good."

But the inquiry revealed deliberate concealment: altered documentation, suppressed concerns, strategic framing of contracts.

Not every action was criminal. Many were "defensible" in isolation. But the totality was undeniable: Whitmore had built and protected a system where external interests could buy influence under the mask of philanthropy.

Her resignation came later, after the institution had time to arrange the narrative.

In the months after, reforms were authentic enough to matter: strengthened disclosure rules, independent donor vetting, separation of fundraising from academic decision-making, mandatory transparency around consultancy contracts, and clearer whistleblower protections.

And yet, among faculty and students, the deeper lesson lingered like rust after rain: Ceremony can be impeccable while the structure beneath corrodes.

Rust is chemistry made visible-oxygen, water, time, and a slow surrender of strength. The university spoke about "values" the way it spoke about "excellence": as a brand asset.

It had assumed that because it was educated; it was immune-too sophisticated to be bought, too prestigious to be fooled.

That contempt for ordinary suspicion was part of the problem. Uncouth nuisances were how people treated those who asked basic questions.

Meanwhile, the truly dangerous people were speaking the institution's favorite language: opportunity, investment, partnership.

Whitmore's robe, her authority, her speeches-none of it had been proof of integrity. It had been proof of presentation.

The university recovered. Institutions often do.

But the people who watched the gala lights and later discovered what transactions took place under that glow did not forget so quickly.

They had seen, up close, how easily ambition can dress itself as stewardship-and how quickly ethics can become a slogan when money flows.

PRGR END-CAP - AUTHORED HARM TEST

(for "THE DEAN'S COMPROMISED AGENDA")

The harm in this case doesn't begin with a bribe in an envelope. It begins with a respectable word: **agenda**. A dean can do enormous damage without touching money directly, simply by deciding what is discussable, what is postponed, and what is framed as "not the right moment."

PRGR would attach authorship at the moment the Dean converts scheduling power into outcome control. In this story, the hinge-steps are procedural on the surface and deeply consequential underneath: committee calendars, agenda items, minutes, and the strategic use of "process" as anesthesia.

The hinge-steps where PRGR would force the author to exist

The first deferral - moving a conflict-of-interest item "to next meeting". When the Dean receives the initial signal (a complaint, an irregular procurement note, a staff warning) and defers it rather than table it with defined action, PRGR triggers.

She must author, in writing:

why deferral is justified,

what harm is foreseeable during the delay (continued exposure, retaliation, document loss),

and what interim safeguards are activated immediately. Here, delay is not neutral. Delay is the first instrument of harm.

The reframing move - converting "integrity risk" into "workplace conflict" If the Dean describes whistleblowing as "interpersonal tension," "miscommunication," or "team dynamics," PRGR attaches at the first time he uses category shift to control response. He must author:

what evidence supports the reframing, what factual allegations are being set aside, and what independent channel will examine them. PRGR blocks the classic containment technique: turning misconduct into a personality problem.

The committee composition step - who gets a seat, who gets excluded
A compromised agenda often requires compromised attendance. If the Dean selects sympathetic members, excludes difficult staff, or sets quorum rules that ensure predictable outcomes, PRGR triggers at the decision to constitute the committee.

She must author:

why these members were chosen, what conflicts exist,

and what safeguards prevent capture. This is where PRGR makes "neutral governance" legible as design.

The minutes and record step - what is written, what becomes vapor
In this chapter, the record is the battlefield. If the Dean directs secretarial staff to "keep the minutes light," omits dissent, or avoids naming the allegation in writing, PRGR triggers at the instruction about documentation.

She must author:

what is being excluded and why,

how excluded concerns will be recorded elsewhere,

and who is responsible for follow-up.
Because in this story, the harm is not only what happens-it is what cannot later be proved.

The "internal resolution" push - pressuring the reporter into silence
If the Dean urges a staff member to "handle it internally," discourages formal reporting, or suggests reputational consequences for escalating, PRGR triggers at that conversation.

She must author:

what he advised, why he advised it,

and what protections exist against retaliation. PRGR treats "quiet" as a decision with a harm forecast, not as a virtue.

The allocation harm step - budgets, roles, and career throttling

If the compromised agenda results in concrete penalties: a research budget delayed, a committee role removed, a contract not renewed-PRGR triggers at the decision that changes access.

She must author:

the objective basis,

the alternatives considered,

and the foreseeable harm to career and speech climate. Because this is how agenda control becomes discipline without saying the word discipline.

What PRGR would force in this case (matched to university governance)

1. **Deferral becomes a signed decision with a timer**
   PRGR would require that any deferral of an integrity allegation includes:
   a written reason,
   an interim safeguard list, and
   a hard review date. No "we'll revisit." No floating fog.

2. **An "agenda integrity" log**
   PRGR would create a visible record of:
   items proposed,
   items accepted/rejected,
   reasons given,
   and who made the decision.
   Because the dean's power here is not speech; it is sequencing.

3. **A conflict-of-interest firewall**
   If the Dean has any ties-funding relationships, personal loyalties, reputational stakes-PRGR requires automatic recusal from agenda decisions on that topic and appoints an independent convener. The key point: *you cannot manage your own* allegations *through the calendar.*

4. **A retaliation tripwire tied to access changes**
   PRGR would impose an automatic review if, after a report or dissent:
   someone loses committee roles,
   budgets shift,
   performance concerns suddenly appear,
   or contracts become "uncertain."
   Because this case is about silent punishment disguised as routine management.

The questions that keep this End-Cap hyper-specific to the Dean

If you were the Dean: can you write and sign the reason you moved the allegation off the agenda-knowing that the harm of delay (retaliation, evidence loss, continued exposure) is foreseeable and attributable?

If you were the reporter: what is the first hinge-step you must force into the record-the deferral, the reframing as "conflict," or the omission from minutes?

If you were the faculty board: what would you treat as the true misconduct-the original financial/ethical problem, or the governance act of making it un-discussable?

PRGR doesn't say "agendas are bad." It isolates the moment the Dean **uses scheduling to become an outcome-maker**-and forces a named author to exist at the administrative step where delay and omission become institutional policy.

"POLICY" IS NOT A REASON

THE EUPHEMISM WAS DOING MORAL LABOR.

If you're noticing that each story has the same shape-translation into safer language, routing into procedure, substitution of process for morality-you're seeing the machine. It doesn't need villains. It needs habits.

I learned its rhythm on paper. I didn't have to read the "motivation." The last lines of a verdict were enough: the cadence that turns a choice into something that sounds inevitable. I knew the closing sentences of my own matter before I opened the envelope-not the outcome, the language. The same anesthesia. The same calm.

In my case, the calm arrived with a timetable. Thirty minutes per complaint. Twenty minutes for the hearing. Ten minutes to deliberate. Preferably less. Five counsel members consolidated into one face-attentive neutrality, practiced speed. I was not a person in that room so much as a unit of work. When the verdict came, my name appeared once at the top; after that I became "he," "the defendant," an object the institution could move without having to imagine what it felt like to be moved.

And the most unsettling part is that I recognised myself in the machine-not only as its target, but as one of its trained operators. I had written the same kind of clean sentences for other people. I had used the same vocabulary that makes harm sound like administration: "for reasons of efficiency," "in the interests of consistency," "given the standard." I had called it restraint. I had called it professionalism. Only later did I notice what those sentences were doing: they were shrinking a human problem until it fit the available procedure, a policy of bureaucratic insurance. They were turning a choice into weather.

That is the PRGR point I'm pulling from these chapters and from experience: justification must be substantive, not procedural. The signatory must answer three questions in plain words-what harm will this cause, why accept it rather than prevent it, and what less harmful alternative did you reject, and why. "Policy requires" and "procedure dictates" are not reasons. They are camouflage.

I've written memos that sounded righteous while saying nothing human. I've watched others do it and call it professionalism. PRGR calls that bluff. It forces the author to exist. It forces the decision to be addressed, at least in imagination, to the person who will carry it.

So when you feel the story repeating, don't ask, "Why is this happening again?" Ask, "What sentence keeps getting used as anesthesia?" If you replace the euphemism with plain language and the moral picture sharpens, the euphemism was doing moral labor.

22

"THE DEAN WHO SOLD KNOWLEDGE AND TRUST"

SIGHT IS A KIND OF TIME TRAVEL: EVERY PERCEPTION IS ALREADY THE PAST.

Academic abuse of power and patronage systems (composite case)

The complaint letter arrived on a chilly March morning, slipped beneath the door of the university ethics office. It was brief, typed with trembling hands: "Professor Dietrich has coerced students, exploiting grades for favors. I fear others, but I am afraid to speak." For years, the name Dietrich had been synonymous with prestige. The black academic robe, the meticulously pleated jabot at ceremonial events, and his booming voice at lectures all conveyed authority, wisdom, and moral gravitas. Yet, behind that facade, human failings had quietly festered. Outside, the campus looked unchanged-bare branches scratching a pale sky, bicycles chained in neat rows, the river carrying winter's dull light downstream. Students crossed courtyards with coffee cups steaming like small chimneys. The universe continued its indifferent motion, and this indifference makes institutions dangerous because they can keep functioning while people inside them suffer harm.

The investigation began in fragments. Complaints trickled in from former students, their stories at first dismissed as misinterpretation of academic rigor. But patterns emerged:

the same courses, the same seminars, the same subtle coercions. Dietrich had mastered the art of using his robe and ceremonial presence as shields, presenting mentorship while demanding compliance. He adjusted grades, granted research privileges only to those who tolerated his inappropriate attention, and withheld recommendations from those who resisted.

The narrative of misconduct unfolded through the eyes of a single student, Lena, whose story interwove fear, ambition, and betrayal. She had admired the professor, attending late-night seminars, asking questions that revealed intelligence and promise. Dietrich had smiled, praised her work, and invited her to private consultations. Slowly, the mentorship blurred into manipulation. He hinted that academic advancement, scholarships, and opportunities for publication depended on more than study-they depended on her compliance.

Dietrich's abuse of power was insidious. Unlike overt criminal acts, this misconduct thrived on implication, on suggestion, on the careful use of ambiguity. The robe and jabot, symbols of scholarly authority, lent legitimacy to his words and gestures. Students felt trapped in a system where the same symbols that inspired learning could also intimidate, pressure, and confuse. Silence became survival; conformity, a necessity for progress.

And here is where the universe offers an uncomfortable metaphor. What we see is always unreachable. The light from a nearby building reaches our eyes a fraction of a second after it leaves its surface; the light from a star arrives years, centuries, millennia after the star has changed or died. Even the moon we admire is a version of the moon that no longer exists in the instant we are looking. Sight is a kind of time travel: every perception is already the past.

So was the university's understanding of Dietrich.

For years they had been admiring an image delayed by distance-distance not measured in space, but in deference. They saw the professor as he had been "supposed to be," not as he was. Prestige acted like cosmic dust, scattering clarity. Each ceremony, each lecture hall applause, each polished reference letter added another layer between reality and observation. The misconduct was happening in the present tense for victims, but for the institution it remained "unconfirmed," which is another way of saying not yet real to us.

The university's internal investigation, initially hesitant, grew methodical. Investigators collected, cross-referenced, and anonymized statements. Evidence included emails, research log entries, and sworn testimony. The pattern was undeniable: the professor had leveraged academic authority for personal gratification, intertwining coercion with professional opportunity.

As the case moved to disciplinary proceedings, Dietrich attempted to maintain the appearance of innocence, delivering formal lectures with ceremonial attire meticulously arranged, projecting the scholarly poise he had always cultivated. But behind closed doors, the institution documented harm: careers derailed, confidence shattered, trust in the academic system undermined. His robe and jabot, once symbols of intellect and ethical rigor, now framed a man who used his power like a lever on human futures.

The impact extended beyond individual students. Faculty colleagues, blinded by prestige, confronted systemic vulnerabilities: the absence of checks on mentorship, the lack of safe reporting structures, and the subtle ways authority can exploit. Policies now include mandatory reporting, external review boards, and clearer ethical boundaries.

Yet even reforms obey the physics of time. They are always answers to what has already happened. Institutions like to speak of "preventing tomorrow," but tomorrow is not a place you can step into and renovate. Tomorrow does not exist in our hands; it exists only as a concept. All action occurs in a vanishing present that immediately becomes the past. The most we can do is make choices now that we hope will reduce harm in the next sequence of moments-but "next" arrives without warning, and consequences are already moving toward us like light from a distant star.

For Lena and others, recovery was neither immediate nor simple. Counseling, peer support, and professional guidance helped restore confidence. Yet the experience left indelible marks. These marks remind us that power can weaponize opportunity, that learning environments can become private theatres of control, and that shame, mistrust, and self-doubt represent the invisible currency for this cost.

Dietrich faced dismissal, loss of tenure, and public censure. Critics now scrutinized previously celebrated academic publications for ethical violations. The ceremonial garments, stripped of their power, remained in university archives, silent witnesses to human failure. He understood, belatedly, that authority is not absolute; robes and jabots inspire respect but cannot compensate for moral decay.

The case became a template in ethics courses: power dynamics, consent, mentoring responsibility. And the bitter cosmology beneath it remained: institutions live in delayed light. They admire the image and miss the reality until enough evidence collapses the distance.

Ultimately, the robes and jabot had ceremonial survival, but their meaning irrevocably shifted. They no longer symbolized unassailable wisdom; they marked the fragile intersection of human desire, institutional power, and accountability. For those who suffered, the lesson was not abstract. Painfully, the unseen can remain hidden for years, but it is still real while it is hidden-and when it becomes visible, it is already too late for the past that shaped it.

23

"THE PROFESSOR WHO MISLED"

PRESTIGE AND SYMBOLISM ARE NO SUBSTITUTES FOR ETHICAL RESPONSIBILITY.

Academic misconduct and career destruction, Germany, 2011 (composite case)

Professor Helmut Krämer was a distinguished figure in Berlin's prestigious university, the man whose name seemed to arrive in a room a second before he did. In his ceremonial robe and starched jabot, he presided over lecture halls, seminars, and doctoral defenses with a practiced gravity. Students revered him, colleagues deferred, and visiting academics sought his endorsement the way sailors seek a lighthouse-less for its warmth than for its promise of direction.

Berlin, in late autumn, often wears a lid of cloud. The sky sinks low and grey, and the city's breath condenses on tram windows in pale ghosts. On those mornings, the campus courtyards felt like a laboratory dish left slightly uncovered: damp, cold, and quietly reactive. Krämer liked this season. Fog made everything look more serious. It made his silhouette-robe swinging, jabot white as a small flag-appear carved out of certainty.

Yet beneath the ceremonial dignity, Krämer's arrogance, negligence, and selective mentoring would irreparably damage the lives of those under his influence. His laboratory was a machine for reputation: grant applications, high-impact submissions, keynote invitations. He spoke about rigor the way some people speak about faith-absolutely, publicly, with an implied accusation toward anyone who questioned him.

The first warning signs were subtle. Graduate students noticed data discrepancies, suppressed results, and vague attribution of credit. A chromatogram would show a shoulder peak that shouldn't be there. The scientist would have to remove it. An NMR spectrum would look too clean for a synthesis that someone did in a rushed afternoon. Error bars would shrink across drafts, as if the students could edit out uncertainty itself. Krämer, absorbed in building his reputation and securing funding, often appropriated ideas from students and junior researchers without acknowledgment. He called it "integration" of the lab's work, as though minds belonged to him the way reagents belonged to a shelf.

His robe and jabot amplified his perceived authority, deterred complaints, and created an environment where people muted scrutiny. In meetings, he would lean back, listen to a student's concern with a slight smile, then deliver a verdict that sounded almost philosophical: "You are confusing noise with signal." It was difficult to argue with a man who made doubt feel like incompetence.

Doctoral candidate Lena Vogel was brilliant in the particular way chemists can be: precise, patient, comfortable with the slow truth of molecules. She worked on organometallic catalysts-finicky complexes whose yields changed with trace water, tiny temperature shifts, the invisible mood of the glove box. Lena kept notebooks like maps, documenting every anomaly and deviation, because she understood what Karl Popper insisted: science advances not by confirming our preferences but by risking falsification.

One winter evening, when wind scraped leafless branches against the lab windows and rain tapped the glass like impatient fingers, Lena stayed late to rerun a reaction Krämer wanted submitted as "robust." The replicate didn't replicate. The product distribution shifted, and the supposed breakthrough looked like a fragile artifact.

The next morning she entered Krämer's office, clutching printouts.

"Professor," she began, "the catalytic turnover numbers don't hold. I ran three independent repeats. The third collapses. I think the mechanism differs from we claimed."

Krämer glanced at the graphs as if they were mildly insulting. "You are overfitting your doubt," he said. "One weak replicate does not rewrite a story."

"It's not one," Lena insisted. "It changes with humidity. The oxygen sensor spiked last night. The complex may oxidize."

He cut her off gently. "Lena, you are too close to the bench. Step back. We have a narrative. We have reviewers. We have a deadline."

Narrative. The word landed wrong in a lab, like perfume in a clean room.

Lena's academic career stalled in slow, bureaucratic ways that felt like weather: her conference abstract was "reconsidered," her co-authorship moved to a middle position, her travel funding delayed until it became pointless. Krämer never threatened her directly. He didn't need to. He simply distributed opportunity the way a high-pressure system distributes clear skies-selectively, predictably, toward those who pleased him.

Another junior researcher, Jonas Weber, faced similar challenges. Jonas worked on data analysis-kinetic models, statistical fitting, computational predictions meant to align with wet-lab results. He believed, naively, that numbers were safer than personalities. He learned otherwise.

Krämer wanted a high-profile journal submission and needed "clean significance." Jonas's model showed that the claimed effect was marginal-p-values flirting with the arbitrary threshold, confidence intervals wide as Berlin avenues.

Krämer slid a marked-up draft across the table. "Tighten this," he said. "Reduce the outliers. The trend is obvious."

Jonas hesitated. "Those aren't outliers, sir. They're measurements. If we drop them, the fit improves, but it becomes... selective."

Krämer's smile was thin. "Selective is what intelligence is. You filter noise." Jonas swallowed. "But if the effect depends on which points we remove-"

Krämer's voice cooled. "Do you want to finish here? Do you want my recommendation? Then stop moralizing statistics."

In the months that followed, Jonas watched his own caution dissolve under pressure.

He felt that compliance was not a choice but a climate-an atmosphere the lab created. Like humidity, it got into everything. He learned "researcher degrees of freedom," the gentle euphemism for shaping reality until it resembled what his supervisor wanted. Later he would recognize the philosophy of it: not Popper's falsification, but the cynical inversion-protect the hypothesis and call it progress.

The broader ramifications became apparent when investigative audits arrived, triggered by a whistleblower complaint and a failed replication attempt by an external collaborator. The inquiry moved like a cold front: quiet at first, then abruptly transforming the air. The investigators requested data repositories. The team compared raw instrument files to published figures. Researchers examined lab notebooks for gaps. Email chains revealed "suggestions" about how to present inconvenient results.

The audit uncovered a pattern of misconduct that was rarely theatrical but consistently corrosive: cherry-picked runs, massaged baselines, blurred authorship, selective citation of internal validations that never actually occurred. The researcher misled multiple students and postdocs. Funding agencies expressed concern. Journals retracted publications. Collaborations froze like ponds under sudden frost.

Krämer's reputation, previously unassailable, came under intense scrutiny. In public he became philosophical, quoting Kant about duty and insisting the university had to protect scientific integrity. In private he blamed students for "carelessness" and accused critics of jealousy. He spoke as if truth were a possession, not a practice. Yet the human cost was severe. Lena Vogel lost years of careful work to contamination-both chemical and institutional.

Her confidence took on micro-fractures: she began second-guessing her instincts, her methods, her right to speak. Jonas Weber, once proud of his precision, developed a persistent insomnia, lying awake as if listening for the sound of his own conscience. Grants, employment prospects, and international collaborations suffered. The lab's atmosphere had not only altered data; it had altered people.

Colleagues reflected on the paradox: authority and symbolic attire in academia convey credibility, inspire respect, and structure mentorship, but they also create vulnerabilities when wielded without ethical vigilance. Krämer's robe and starched jabot had functioned like laboratory shielding: not protecting those beneath, but protecting him from direct impact. The deference they commanded was a reagent in its own right-catalyzing harm.

The aftermath prompted institutional reform. Berlin University implemented stricter oversight of supervisory practices, anonymous reporting mechanisms, and formal accountability structures. Authorship policies became codified. Data verification procedures became mandatory. Mentoring responsibilities became clear through a protocol, making them reproducible, auditable, and less dependent on personality.

Still, reforms arrived like rescue teams after a storm-necessary, visible, late. The tragedy was not only that a system corrected itself. It was that it had failed to prevent the damage, preferring prestige until evidence forced humility.

Professor Helmut Krämer remained a cautionary figure: ceremonial and authoritative, inwardly negligent and exploitative. In the end, the lab returned to science's oldest discipline: reality.

You can polish a narrative like glass, but nature-whether in clouds or catalysts-does not honor titles. It honors only what holds under pressure.

24

"THE PROFESSOR'S LAB EXPLOSION"

THEY WERE THE HUMAN COST OF A SYSTEM THAT HAD MISTAKEN REPUTATION FOR SAFETY.

Academic accident and institutional negligence, Germany, 2012 (composite case)

The explosion didn't end in the laboratory. It propagated outward like a verdict, turning an enclosed academic mishap into a campus-wide rupture. The blast wave punched through the corridor windows, and a second later the building itself seemed to flinch-lights flickering, ceiling tiles shuddering, sprinklers coughing into life as if the structure had suddenly remembered it could bleed. A plume of grey-white vapor-chemical fog threaded with smoke-unfurled into the hallway and then up the stairwells, an unnatural cloud that doesn't just obscure vision but rearranges instinct.

People didn't run at first. They froze, listening for what the mind refuses to accept: the groan of stressed metal, the crackle of fire finding purchase, the irregular popping of smaller reactions continuing after the initial detonation, as if the room were still arguing with itself.

Then the alarms began in earnest: harsh, relentless, impersonal. The building's siren did not care who was senior faculty and who was a first-year student. It announced only one truth-evacuate-repeating it with the cold certainty of a machine designed for disasters the institution always insisted were "unlikely."

Students poured into corridors with sleeves over their mouths, blinking through tears, some barefoot from slipping shoes on as they fled. A graduate assistant tried to shepherd them, voice breaking as he counted heads, losing track, starting again. Someone shouted that Reinhardt was still inside. Someone else shouted that the chemical storage was near the lab.

Panic took on a choreography: stumbling, grabbing, pulling one another forward. In the stairwell, the air turned hot and sour, a mix of burnt plastic and something sharp and metallic that made the throat recoil.

Outside, the courtyard filled with displaced bodies-clusters of people looking back at the windows as if the building might explain itself. Soot flecked those closest to the doors. The fire singed one student's hair into uneven curls; another held both hands over her eyes, rocking, whispering that she couldn't see. The professor's ceremonial attire-usually a symbol of calm command-was now only a rumor of fabric, torn and scorched, indistinguishable from the chaos. In that moment, the regalia of expertise meant nothing.

Authority could not calm a nervous system saturated with terror.

The first fire truck arrived with a howl that sliced through the crowd's confusion. Then another. Then the ambulances-blue lights strobing against the stone facades, sirens bouncing off the old university buildings as if the campus itself were amplifying the warning. The sound did something primal: it turned students and professors alike into bystanders of their own vulnerability.

The presence of emergency vehicles carries a specific humiliation, acknowledging that your trusted system failed and that trained professionals were called upon after failing to ensure your safety.

Firefighters surged in with practiced urgency, faces already masked, moving toward the entrance while the rest of the university moved away. Their equipment clattered like punctuation. A supervisor barked orders, and hoses unfurled in sweeping arcs, dragging across the pavement, biting into corners. Another crew established a perimeter with a bright tape that looked absurdly thin against the possibility of another blast. A medic knelt beside the student, covering her eyes, speaking in a low, steady cadence meant to anchor a panicked mind.

More students sat down wherever there was ground-steps, curbs, patches of grass-because their legs had stopped receiving instructions.

Within minutes, the university's normal rhythm collapsed. An administrative email went out, then another: immediate closure, all classes suspended, buildings evacuated, the campus shut down until further notice. The library emptied. The cafeteria doors locked mid-service. The university sealed the research lab. Security escorted international visitors off-site. The institution that had marketed itself as a fortress of reason and order suddenly operated like any other frightened organism: retract, contain, survive.

And that was the symbolic revelation the explosion made impossible to ignore. The university had always spoken the language of protection-risk assessments, compliance forms, safety committees-yet what arrived in the decisive moment was not protection but rescue. Rescue is reactive. It is dramatic, expensive, and visible.

Rescue brings sirens and stretchers and commands shouted through megaphones.

Protection is quiet and boring and rarely applauded; it requires that systems do their job before anyone is hurt, that protocols feel non-negotiable even when deadlines loom, that funding isn't allocated only when tragedy forces the hand.

In the aftermath, people kept returning to the same image: a crowd of brilliant minds standing behind a strip of tape while strangers in helmets walked into danger on their behalf. It exposed a collective dependency the system preferred to conceal. Institutions often present themselves as competent, using policies, titles, prestige, and the solemn theater of expertise. However, those garments can become a type of camouflage, hiding the places where they traded prevention for optimism.

When the investigations began, the questions weren't only about one reaction gone wrong. They were about the culture that made "minor procedural safeguards" feel optional under pressure, about the way deference to a revered professor can corrode scrutiny, about the bureaucratic habit of accepting risk until risk becomes catastrophe.

Reinhardt's injuries, and the student left blind, were not just tragic outcomes; they were the human cost of a system that had mistaken reputation for safety.

Later, long after the fire department extinguished the fire, people still remembered the sirens. Not just as noise, but as an accusation: proof that the university's promise of order had been contingent all along. The emergency vehicles had not arrived to protect the community from harm. They had arrived to collect the broken pieces after harm had already been done.

And that, more than the shattered glass or the blackened lab benches, became the enduring drama of the event-a symbol of how often humans require rescue because the systems meant to protect them choose, again and again, to wait for the alarm.

THE FIRST CONSTRAINT

INTERLUDE II

Bellini skimmed the agenda in the antiseptic language of procedure. A clerk approached-not his usual choreography, but with an added object: a PRGR already labeled with the decision that would normally pass without confession.

Decision: "Proceed with [X] while complaint remains 'insufficient information.'"

Foreseeable harm: "Silencing; deterrence; repeat access; retaliation-by-absence."

Alternatives considered: "Interim safeguards; inquiry; record-building; pause."

Remedy trigger: "Automatic review at defined doubt threshold; preservation order."

Responsible signatory: Giovanni Bellini.

The paper looked wrong against the polished timber. Too plain. Too direct. Too... human.

His hand hovered.

A moment-the smallest moment-where he could have done what he always did: keep moving.

But the system did not let him.

The decision could not pass the last reversible step until the lace existed.

He reached for the old defense-the elegant fog: *procedure, discretion, professionalism* -the language that makes choice feel like weather.

The PRGR didn't argue.

It waited.

So he wrote.

Not "the court finds," not "it is determined," not "insufficient information," not "for administrative reasons."

He wrote in the first person.

And the first person made his stomach tighten.

Reed opened the shared drive and saw the folder renamed overnight-cleaner, sponsor-safe.

A junior staff member stood beside his desk with the PRGR already open, the way a nurse holds a consent form before anesthesia.

Decision: "Rename and reframe dataset folder; alter summary language for sponsor-facing report."

Foreseeable harm: "Misleading downstream research; reputational lock; policy based on softened truth."

Alternatives considered: "Disclose uncertainty; separate raw and interpreted data; delay publication."

Remedy trigger: "Reopen if edits occur without disclosure; public correction."

Responsible signatory: Jonathan Reed.

He tried the old move-make it smaller.

"This is just standardization."

The PRGR offered no room to hide.

If it was "just standardization," he could sign it plainly, with harm written in honest language.

He read the harm line again.

He felt-briefly-how ugly it sounded when translated out of prestige.

And for the first time he understood the cost of manipulation:

Not that it deceives strangers.

That it forces the manipulator to live inside his own sentence.

Gregorios listened to numbers whispered like confession-debt, repairs, delayed salaries. Then came Petros' call: soft voice, hard confidence. A small request: reassign a priest because he was "difficult."

His instinct rose automatically: *unity, avoid scandal, protect the faithful.*

A deacon brought the PRGR sheet as if it were fragile-as if naming responsibility might tear it.

Decision: "Reassign Father Andreas after donor request."

Foreseeable harm: "Career derailment; silencing dissent; donor-hostage governance; ongoing vulnerable access."

Alternatives considered: "Refuse request; disclose conflict; independent oversight; restrict donor influence."

Remedy trigger: "Automatic review if donor-linked personnel changes repeat; external audit."

Responsible signatory: Gregorios Kalogeris.

The lace was visible now: a delicate border that made the page look almost ceremonial.

But it was used-creased, smudged, fingerprinted like a prayer book.

This wasn't an idea.

It was a practice.

And a practice leaves marks.

He stared at the word *harm* as if it were impolite.

He tried to replace it with something softer.

The form did not allow euphemism.

He could only sign what he was willing to own.

The form is filed. The pen is capped. The corridor looks unchanged.

That is always how it begins: the surface remains immaculate.

PRGR does not dirty the marble.

It only insists that if someone uses the building as leverage, the record must show a hand.

25

"THE JUDGE'S SECRET"

MISCONDUCT CAN HIDE IN NARROW SPACES–BETWEEN IMPLICATION AND DEMAND, BETWEEN REPUTATION AND REALITY.

Judicial sexual and financial misconduct, Switzerland, 2021 (composite case)

In Zürich, order isn't just policy. It's scenery. Trams slide into stops with quiet certainty, doors opening like clockwork. Sidewalks look rinsed clean. The river-cold, steady, exact-threads between stone embankments as if it, too, has agreed to behave.

And beyond the city's precise geometry, the mountains hold their patient perimeter: pale ridgelines in winter light, dark forests rising in steps, snowfields that make the sky look even sharper. On mornings when the wind comes down from the heights, the air tastes newly made-clean enough to make every sound feel distinct.

Footsteps on pavement. A bicycle bell. A distant church chime. Even in winter, the faint scrape of a chair across a courtroom floor.

Judge Matthias Keller belonged to that environment the way granite belongs to a slope.

He presided with a calm precision that felt almost scientific. His black robe was always immaculate. His white jabot sat perfectly arranged, symmetrical to the millimeter-so orderly it suggested moral alignment. He spoke in measured tones, never wasting a word, and he made the courtroom feel like a machine engineered to produce fairness: inputs of evidence and argument, outputs of reasoned judgment, all lubricated by quiet discipline.

That was the visible surface-the Zürich that visitors photograph and residents rely on. Beneath it, Keller ran a private system built on leverage.

He understood what institutions often refuse to name: authority doesn't compel only through rules. It compels through the fear of consequences. A judge doesn't have to shout. He doesn't even have to threaten. The possibility of a ruined career, a lost case, a stalled promotion-those are pressures strong enough to bend people without leaving fingerprints.

Keller exploited that pressure with methodical consistency. He cultivated the same atmosphere he projected in court: deliberate, controlled, difficult to accuse. Lawyers seeking favorable rulings, procedural leniency, or an advantage in complex matters found themselves drawn-almost gently-into private meetings. He framed them as "strategic discussions" or "administrative clarifications." Invitations arrived like honors: discreet, flattering, wrapped in the language of mentorship.

Sophie Baumann was a junior attorney when she received one.

She entered Keller's chambers expecting guidance. The room smelled faintly of old paper and polished wood, a scent that suggests tradition rather than danger. Outside the window, the river moved like dark glass. Farther off-if the day was cloudless-the mountains stood with their indifferent calm, as if the world beyond the city had no interest in human arrangements.

Keller didn't raise his voice. He didn't make vulgar demands. He suggested-carefully-that her professional trajectory could improve with the right "cooperation." He spoke of how competitive the field was, how many careers ended quietly, and how reputation depended on relationships. He mentioned names in passing, as if casually listing weather patterns. Then he allowed a pause long enough for the implication to settle.

Sophie felt the ground shift.

In physics, ice doesn't always break loudly. Sometimes tiny disruptions called micro-fractures form and spread beneath the surface, undermining the structure's integrity. Sophie felt a fracture inside herself: the moment trust in authority becomes awareness of danger. The moment a place designed for justice becomes a room in which you must calculate survival.

She tried to resist without provoking retaliation. She avoided being alone with him. She limited contact. She rehearsed polite exits and professional excuses. Yet in a system where one person's discretion could shape outcomes, avoidance itself carried risk. A judge can delay a filing, scrutinize a motion, raise an eyebrow in a hearing, and change the air in a room. He can make you feel watched without ever looking directly at you. And Keller's pressure did not stop with Sophie.

The court staff and junior magistrates subtly contributed financially to private funds, "projects," and administrative initiatives, which seemed harmless but proved beneficial, always orbiting Keller and his inner circle. Those who questioned the requests found their work suddenly under a brighter lamp. Their schedules became less forgiving. The people who questioned the requests found that their work suddenly came under more scrutiny. The unforgiving schedules highlighted their smallest mistakes as evidence of incompetence. Prospects dimmed not with a bang but with a slow, steady reduction of oxygen-like climbing without noticing the altitude.

What enabled it was not ignorance. It was a deference.

Colleagues noticed irregularities. Staff heard rumors. Oversight committees sensed discomfort the way you sense an approaching storm: pressure changes, a strange stillness, people lowering their voices. Yet the robe and jabot carried cultural weight. Keller's public demeanor made accusation feel implausible. Zürich's reputation for precision made disorder feel like a personal failure rather than a systemic risk.

Reporting channels existed, but fear made them brittle. Institutional loyalty turned them into glass: present, transparent, easily shattered. In a city that values cleanliness, people learn to hide mess. In a system that prizes decorum, people learn to keep quiet.

Keller maintained control by living just inside the line of explicit illegality. He relied on suggestion, on ambiguity, on the victim's calculation that the cost of refusing might exceed the cost of enduring. His genius-if one can use that word for such a practice-was restraint. He did not force a door open; he made people feel the door would close on them if they didn't walk through it willingly.

For victims, the toll was profound. It wasn't only professional pressure. It was the psychological weight of being forced to negotiate dignity against survival-to decide, again and again, whether a principled choice was worth the professional damage that might follow. The mind becomes its own courtroom, staging arguments for resistance, arguments for caution, arguments for silence. The verdict is never clean.

Exposure came the way it often does in disciplined systems: through documentation.

Not rage, not spectacle-paper. Emails. Calendar invitations. Financial records. Whispered accounts that, once collected, formed a pattern strong enough to hold. Investigative journalism and whistleblower reports gathered enough testimonies to break the illusion of isolation. Individual experiences, once separated by fear, assembled into a single picture. What no one dared claim alone became undeniable when set beside other stories that matched in structure, timing, and technique.

Once the story entered public view, oversight moved quickly. The court suspended Keller and removed . Investigations followed.

Reforms included stronger independent reporting mechanisms, better monitoring of discretionary decisions, and greater financial transparency within judicial administration. Committees held meetings. Statements were issued in careful, measured language-the institutional voice of a city that tries to repair damage with precision.

But reforms cannot erase what happened.

Distorted careers haunted them. Trust sustained damage. Traumas didn't vanish because an inquiry reached conclusions. People who had learned to measure every step in a courthouse did not suddenly regain the ability to walk without flinching. The psychological aftermath lingered like a cold draft in an otherwise perfect room.

Keller's case underscores a harsh paradox: ceremonial authority signals restraint, ethics, stewardship. Yet it can magnify coercion when combined with unchecked discretion. Symbols do not protect; they persuade.

In Zürich, where the air can feel so clean it hurts to breathe, misconduct can still hide in narrow spaces-between implication and demand, between reputation and reality, between what a city believes about itself and what it refuses to see.

Outside, the mountains remain. They do not speak. They do not judge. They simply hold their line against the sky, indifferent to human ceremony. Below them, the river keeps moving, cold and steady, as if discipline alone were enough to keep things pure.

The robe remained what it always was: cloth, tradition, performance.

What changed was what people learned to see beneath it-and what they decided, finally, not to ignore.

MATRIX 2 — IRREVERSIBLE HARM TEST (LAW)

When harm cannot be undone, authorship must rise with it.

Point of no return	What it buys / enables	How it hides	PRGR friction (authorship + remedy)
Charging decision / theory of case hardens	Frames reality; sets the tunnel	"Discretion," "public interest," "standard practice"	Named author signs: charge chosen + foreseeable liberty loss + disclosure duties; independent review trigger.
Disclosure failure (exculpatory withheld or delayed)	Asymmetry becomes fate	"Not material," "late discovered," "administrative error"	Authored reasons for withholding; audit log; automatic remedy path (reopen, sanction, compensation).
Plea pressure / coercive bargaining	Speed + certainty for system	"Efficiency," "risk management," "advice of counsel"	Require authored record of pressure points + risk disclosures; remedy if later contradicted by evidence.
Credibility inversion (victim/accused discredited procedurally)	Turns person into problem	"Unreliable," "non-compliant," "vexatious"	Any adverse label must be signed, evidenced, and appealable; harm forecast required.
Judicial sealing / deference / refusal to reopen	Finality over truth	"Finality," "no jurisdiction," "interests of justice"	Signature must state: finality chosen over truth + foreseeable harm; mandatory independent review for irreversible penalties.
Sentence / custody / removal (irreversible window closes)	Institution 'moves on'	"Order made," "procedure followed"	Authored harm statement + remedy trigger before the last reversible step (stay, review, preservation of evidence).

PART IV

PROCEDURE / ERASURE / CATASTROPHIC ENDPOINTS

THE MAMASHIMI TRUST - BRISBANE AUSTRALIA

BOILERPLATE IS A KIND OF LYING

THEATER IS ONE OF THE OLDEST WAYS POWER STAYS CLEAN.

By now, I can predict the institutional voice: polished, calm, faintly injured that anyone would even ask. Just like my verdict. It wasn't about the other ninety-nine percent of my work as a lawyer. It was about the one percent they disliked, isolated and enlarged until it could carry the whole story.

And I recognise the craft, because I was trained in it. The words repeat because they're meant to. Repetition is how institutions manufacture the feeling of certainty: the same phrases, the same framing, the same conclusion dressed as inevitability. Once the template is in place, judgment becomes a clerical act.

So my PRGR point here is a defense against that reflex: anti-boilerplate controls.

If copying last week's phrasing can complete this week's justification, PRGR has already failed. The system needs resistance built in-plain-language rules that forbid euphemism as a substitute for reason, mandatory alternative analysis that cannot be satisfied by "none appropriate," and repetition audits that flag identical passages the way financial systems flag identical transactions. When the same sentence appears again and again, it should trigger discomfort, not acceptance. It should force the author to re-enter the decision as a human being. I'm deliberately making these stories feel like repeats because that is how harm travels: it migrates, changes names, finds a new corridor, and wears the same sentences like gloves. Boilerplate is the glove. It lets someone handle a person without feeling skin.

If I want to know whether an institution is serious, I listen for the moment it stops speaking in templates and starts speaking in owned, specific, human claims: what I chose, what it cost you, what I rejected instead-and why.

Until then, I'm reading theatre. And theatre is one of the oldest ways power stays clean.

26

"THE ADVOCATE'S DARK DEAL"

THE COURT ITSELF WAS DEFENDING SOMETHING IT WAS NEVER MEANT TO PROTECT.

> Legal misconduct and organised crime, United Kingdom, 2010 (composite case), PRGR

London can make anything look official.

When mornings are damp, the city's edges soften, as if the weather itself is trying to be polite. The Thames turns pewter, holding the grey sky like metal in a basin. Fog presses against stone facades and slips into the seams of the old city, blurring the sharp lines of monuments into silhouettes. From a distance, everything appears calm-historic, stable, civilized. Even the noise feels muffled, like a verdict spoken through heavy cloth.

Inside court, Edward Carmichael traded in that illusion.

He was one of the city's most formidable barristers: sharp-eyed, articulate, precise. In his black gown and immaculate collar, he carried the confidence that makes juries lean forward and judges listen. He spoke with controlled elegance, as if he had weighed every word on a scale, polished it, and placed it exactly where it would do the most work. The effect was not charm so much as inevitability. When Edward rose, the room instinctively prepared to agree.

Clients wanted him because he radiated certainty: a sense that whatever had happened, however ugly, he could translate it into something survivable. At first, his work stayed within the familiar orbit of white-collar crime-fraud, theft by deception, financial misconduct. He was excellent at taking complicated schemes and turning them into doubt. He identified procedural weaknesses the way a physicist finds stress points in a bridge, tapping lightly until the structure revealed where it would fail.

But reputation attracts gravity. As his name rose, so did the quality-and danger-of his company.

Some clients arrived with money that did not smell like banks. They came through intermediaries who spoke in half-sentences. They carried names that were never spoken in full, names that felt less like identities than warnings. They expected not only defense but protection: strategy beyond the courtroom, insulation beyond the case. They were not interested in the romance of justice; they were interested in results.

Edward told himself he was doing his job. Everyone deserves representation. The law is adversarial. His duty was to test the prosecution's case, to force the state to prove what it claimed, to protect the principle that accusation is not truth.

That was the respectable story-neatly pressed, easy to recite.

The shift happened quietly, the way London's fog crosses a street with no one noticing the exact moment visibility changes. Edward's counsel stopped being reactive and became enabling. He advised on asset concealment before warrants were served. He coached clients on how to structure payments so they resembled legitimate fees, as if laundering were merely a matter of correct formatting. He suggested where a document might be "misplaced," how a timeline might be "clarified," someone who was not technically part of the legal team might approach indirectly which witness. He spoke in euphemisms the way old institutions do-softening the language until the act sounded like administration.

He learned quickly that the law could function like chemistry: add the right compound and the reaction changes. Edward became that compound-a catalyst. He did not commit the underlying crimes. He lowered the barrier that kept criminals from turning violence into paperwork, theft into invoices, and intimidation into silence. The genius of it-its seduction-was that it felt clean. No blood on the hands, only ink. The courtroom remained a room of polished wood and controlled voices. And Edward remained, outwardly, a man of procedure.

He enjoyed the elegance of it.

What protected him was not only secrecy but costume. In court, the gown and formal posture offered legitimacy like a shield. Outside court, the same reputation made institutions hesitant to suspect him. He was a man the system recognized as one of its own, fluent in its rituals, awarded its trust. In London, recognition is currency; it buys silence, delays questions, makes suspicion feel improper. A barrister of his stature could pass through rooms the way fog passes through gates-unhindered because it belongs to the atmosphere.

Naomi Blake noticed first.

She was a solicitor tasked with reviewing files and correspondence-exactly the diligent worker most people never notice until they disrupt something. Naomi didn't have Edward's aura. She had something less glamorous and more dangerous: attention. She began finding patterns that didn't match the official narrative. Evidence referenced in emails but absent from the file. Witness statements edited in ways that softened critical details.

Instructions to delay service until "after the weekend," as if justice were a scheduling preference. Small choices, which, if considered individually, could be justified. Taken together, they formed a design.

At first, she assumed an error. Then she saw repetition.

London's professional world trains people to accept polish as proof. Naomi tried to do that, too. She told herself there was a benign explanation, a bureaucratic oversight, an assistant's mistake. But the same "mistakes" kept benefiting the same kinds of clients. The omissions always landed in the same direction, like a compass that never wavered.

Naomi began copying communications, noting dates, saving drafts. She did it cautiously because Edward's stature made the risk enormous. Reporting him could end her career. Staying silent would make her part of the machinery. The fear wasn't dramatic; it was practical. London has a thousand ways to close doors without making a sound. A reputation can fall victim to whispers. A reference can vanish. Whispers can quietly fold away a future.

The breaking point came with a case involving a regional crime figure whose reach extended far beyond the courtroom. Edward's strategy seemed less like defense and more like orchestration. A key witness failed to appear after receiving "advice" from unknown contacts. Evidence custody became muddled. Timelines blurred. The case did not collapse by accident; it eroded by design, like stone worn down by persistent rain.

Naomi went outside the firm-quietly, carefully. She contacted regulators and provided documentation that linked Edward's actions to broader financial irregularities already under investigation. She didn't frame it as vengeance or outrage. She framed it as what it was: a pattern. Proof. London cannot dismiss the written thing. Once authorities looked, the protective fog lifted.

Financial regulators and law enforcement compared notes. Transactions once hidden behind vague descriptions came into focus. Professional conduct bodies reviewed communications that revealed a pattern of facilitation: not a single lapse, but a method. There were too many coincidences clustered in one place, too many decisions that benefited the same people. The story stopped being rumor and became record.

The scandal broke fast. Newspapers love a fall, especially when the fallen wears ceremonial authority. Articles appeared with the familiar tone of moral surprise-shocked, satisfied, hungry. Headlines reduced complexity into a single narrative: a trusted lawyer betrays trust. Edward's name symbolized how an entire ecosystem could be condensed into one man's corruption.

Edward faced disciplinary proceedings and removal from practice. Public language dissected the details. This language tried to sound outraged while also sounding familiar, because institutions like to pretend betrayal is rare, even when it follows a pattern as old as power itself. His gown and collar, once symbols of professional integrity, became props in a different story: the story of someone who used the appearance of justice to lubricate injustice.

In the aftermath, the legal community argued in predictable ways. Some called Naomi courageous. Others called her disloyal, as if loyalty to a firm should outrank loyalty to the law. Firms tightened compliance. Training sessions multiplied. New policies appeared, crisp as freshly printed forms. The system modernized its defenses and reinforced doors that should never have been left unlocked.

The deeper lesson was older and darker: professionals can weaponize their authority with precision. The law does not always fail through chaos. Sometimes it fails through expertise. Sometimes the people most capable of defending the system are also the people most capable of exploiting it-because they know exactly where the rules bend, where interpretation becomes opportunity, where procedure becomes camouflage.

Edward Carmichael did not wake up one morning and decide to become a villain. That is the comforting myth institutions tell themselves, because it keeps evil extraordinary. In truth, he moved step by step, each step justified, each choice softened by language, each compromise small enough to tolerate-until the sum of them created something catastrophic. And London, with its fog and ceremony, helped him. It always does. It makes the unacceptable look formal, makes complicity look like professionalism, makes wrongdoing look like a mere matter of discretion.

In Edward Carmichael's case, the boundary between representation and complicity didn't shatter in a single loud moment. The court's quiet dissolution of the boundary, akin to ink spreading through water, led it to defend something it was never meant to protect.

PRGR END-CAP - AUTHORED HARM TEST

(for "THE ADVOCATE'S DARK DEAL")

The harm in this case doesn't start when the advocate takes the deal. It starts when he **changes the boundary of loyalty**-when "client interest" becomes a mask for a private bargain, and the courtroom becomes a marketplace without price tags.

PRGR would attach authorship at the first hinge-step where the Advocate turns representation into leverage for a side arrangement.
In this story, the hinge-steps are practical: conflicts, confidentiality, strategic choices, and the quiet use of procedure to hide intent.

The hinge-steps where PRGR would force the author to exist

The first undisclosed conflict - accepting the case while already entangled

If the Advocate has any hidden tie (financial exposure, personal dependency, prior work, promises, threats), PRGR triggers at the moment he takes instructions. He must author, in writing:

what the conflict is (at least to an independent reviewer, even if not public), why he believes he can act independently,

what safeguards exist (co-counsel, supervision, recusal),

and what harm is foreseeable if independence is compromised. Because in this case, the "deal" doesn't begin with action. It begins with **concealment**.

The confidentiality capture - using client secrets as bargaining chips

The Advocate's special power is access to damaging information. If he uses any of it-directly or indirectly-to signal value to a third party (a fixer, an opponent, a criminal network, a political patron), PRGR attaches at the first "information transfer," including subtle forms:

hinting,

selective omission,

steering a narrative that protects the third party.

PRGR forces authorship of the question the profession hates to name:

Whose interests are being served by this strategy choice? What information is being withheld or redirected, and why?

The strategic sabotage step - the moment the case is quietly bent

Most dark deals are implemented through ordinary legal decisions that can be defended after the fact:

not calling a witness, delaying an application,

discouraging a client from a complaint, "forgetting" a remedy,

pushing a plea,

conceding a point that doesn't need conceding. PRGR triggers at the first *material* choice that reduces the client's position or legal options. The Advocate must author:

the reason for the choice, the alternatives rejected,

the foreseeable harm to the client,

and confirmation that no external interest influenced the decision. This is where PRGR makes "tactics" auditable.

The money movement - the payment that pretends to be something else

If the deal involves cash, invoices, "consulting," referral fees, loans, gifts, or any third-party payment connected to the case, PRGR triggers at the first transfer (or promise of transfer). The Advocate must author:

what the payment is for, who benefits,

why it is legitimate,

and why it does not create divided loyalty. PRGR is blunt here: **a hidden payment is a hidden author of the case.**

The pressure-on-client step - steering consent through fear or fatigue

Dark deals often require the client to "agree" to a weaker path. The Advocate may pressure by:

exaggerating risks, withholding information, framing resistance as irrational,

or saying "this is the best you'll get." PRGR triggers at the moment the client is pushed into an irreversible choice (settlement, plea, withdrawal, silence). He must author:

what the client was told, what options were presented,

what information was withheld (if any),

and why the recommendation serves the client rather than the Advocate's hidden arrangement.

The cover story - using procedure to erase motive

If the Advocate uses "professional judgment," "strategy," "client instructions," or "time constraints" as fog, PRGR triggers when that explanation is used to block scrutiny (by colleagues, court, regulator). He must author:

the factual basis of the explanation, why it accounts for the decision,

and what independent review is permitted. Because in this case, procedure is not a neutral container; it is the laundering mechanism.

What PRGR would force in this case (practical safeguards matched to advocacy work)

1. **A "conflict declaration" that cannot be self-certified**
   PRGR would require that any advocate with potential conflict files a sealed declaration to an independent ethics officer/board reviewer. Not public, but authored and time-stamped. The point is to prevent the classic defense: *nothing*

was written, so nothing existed.

2. **A "material decision log" for high-stakes cases**
   PRGR would require a short, contemporaneous note for the decisions that change outcomes:
   witness decisions,
   plea/settlement recommendations,
   major concessions,
   delays that forfeit rights. This is where the dark deal lives: not in drama, in choices.

3. **A third-party payment firewall**
   No money linked to a live case without:
   written justification,
   disclosure to the client (and/or independent reviewer),
   and separation from decision-making.
   If the Advocate can't explain the money, PRGR treats it as a risk trigger, not a clerical oversight.

4. **A retaliation/pressure tripwire for client complaints**
   If the client expresses discomfort and is then: dropped,
   discouraged from reporting,
   pushed into "final" decisions quickly, PRGR triggers automatic external review-because coercion in this case is often disguised as "advice."

The questions that keep this End-Cap hyper-specific to the Advocate's deal

If you were the Advocate: which exact decision did the deal require you to make-delay, omission, concession, pressure toward settlement? Can you write it down and sign it without hiding behind "strategy"?

If you were the client: what is the first hinge-step where representation stops feeling like representation-when options narrow, when information goes missing, or when money appears in the background?

If you were the Bar/institute: would you rather punish the obvious bribe, or the quieter harm-the authored legal decisions that bent a case while remaining technically defensible?

PRGR doesn't ask whether the Advocate is "bad." It isolates the moment he **converted the client's case into a bargaining chip**-and forces a named author to exist at the precise strategic step where the client's future was traded for a private arrangement.

27

"THE SIX QUIET CASE FILES"

EACH MECHANISM CAN BE JUSTIFIED WITH TRUE GOODS.

SIX CASE FILES, ONE MECHANISM

Six case files once sat here as separate chapters. You could read them one by one, nodding at each costume: cassock, collar, bench, committee. But read that way, repetition can feel like texture rather than diagnosis. This consolidation reframes repetition as pattern recognition-by design. The question is not only what happened in each scene, but what the institution did with what happened-how it translated the human into a category, routed the category into procedure, and let procedure stand in for morality. Because the mechanism is portable, this braid must represent all three arenas: law, faith, academia. The costumes differ. The purchases are consistent.

Keep one object in mind as a visible reminder: a folded white neckband, linen pressed into neatness. It sits near the instruments of power in each scene. It stays immaculate while people do not.

Read the following like a montage. Let scenes overlap. Listen for the recurring verbs: "reviewed", "noted", "handled", "no breach", "process followed". These verbs are how institutions launder moral choices into neutral grammar.

PRGR END-CAP - AUTHORED HARM TEST

Primary mechanism: PROCEDURE - the decision-maker's decisive step is where PRGR would force an author to sign the downstream harm.

Sector: CROSS-SECTOR

PRGR trigger: any decision-point likely to cause irreversible harm (to liberty, livelihood, reputation, safety)-including "temporary" steps that become permanent.

Required signatory: the person with final authority (and the office that executed the decision).

If a PRGR had been mandatory here, the signatory would have had to write-and sign-a short record stating:

- what action was taken (and why this step, now)
- the foreseeable harm to the person downstream
- the alternative considered and rejected
- the remedy trigger that halts the process if harm becomes irreversible

What the institution hides: reassignment, delay, "process," fragmented ownership, and paperwork that insists nothing is decided while outcomes harden.

Counterfactual: the decision-maker would have been forced to name the harm as his-not the system's. Pause: locate the moment you wanted to look away. That is the moment PRGR is built for.

Ask yourself:

- Which procedural move made harm irreversible: a reassignment, a denial, a timing decision, a "routine" closure?
- Who benefited from the fog-and who paid for it-the person downstream?
- Which single step would you make signable first: the delay, the denial, the

reassignment, or the closure of the file?

THE CHANTER'S BLACK CASSOCK

(FAITH)

Begin with sound. Not a scream-those are easy for institutions to treat as emergencies. Begin with a voice trained to soothe. The chanter's black cassock is a uniform of continuity: it tells the room that what happens here belongs to a sacred order, and that messy questions must not disturb the sacred order.

In this terrain, authority is atmosphere. A person in a cassock can be near bodies, near confession, near private grief, and people code this nearness as care. That is why boundary violations here are so devastating: they are not only acts, they are inversions. The offered protection becomes access.

Notice the institution's priority: not the harmed person, but the room. The congregation. The community. The institution issues a statement that sounds like virtue and functions like anesthesia: "We take this seriously." The key move is translation. The lived event turns into a manageable category: a "misunderstanding," a "pastoral complication," a "private matter." Once translated, it can be routed into familiar processes- private meetings, internal handling, confidentiality reframed as charity.

Then the moral lapse: continuity becomes the highest good. The institution does not ask, "What would repair require?" It asks, "What would keep the community intact?" The harmed person feels it immediately: the group's peace is being purchased with their silence.

Subtle coercion follows. Someone warns you about gossip. They ask you to be "forgiving." You are told not to scandalize the faithful. The role's language makes resistance feel impious. The cassock becomes a shield that turns the harmed person into the threat.

By soothing, faith language allows the institution to smile. It can sound compassionate while distributing pressure. That is how the mechanism stays invisible: it looks like care.

Cross-sector mirror: a court calls it "protecting the integrity of proceedings." A university calls it "protecting the department." A Church calls it "protecting the faithful." Each phrase means: protect the institution from accountability.

Once you see the trick, you can name it: the institution treats the public's trust as an asset to be defended, rather than a responsibility to be earned.

The Folded White Neckband lies nearby, immaculate-an emblem of office that never looks like harm.

INTERLUDE (INNER LIFE)

After the announcement, devotion becomes physical. A hymn lands like a weight. The smell of incense becomes an ambush. They chose seats near the exit. They rehearse a neutral face. They keep a phone in hand like a talisman. They doubt their own memory, not because it changed, but because the institution's calm treats their distress as exaggeration. The shame migrates from the office that abused it to the person who names it.

How do you feel when you read a "pastoral" statement that asks for prayers but never names responsibility? Have you been told that naming harm is "divisive" while the harm itself could continue?

Where have you seen tone-calmness, politeness, "maturity"-used as proof of virtue?

Parallel: In faith settings, intimacy and community provide concealment. Authority enters private life while calling itself care.

Parallel: The harmed person's distress is treated as disorder; the institution's calm is treated as morality.

Reader exercise:

Replace every institutional euphemism with plain language. "Pastoral complication" becomes "a misuse of office." "Handled internally" becomes "kept away from scrutiny." Does the moral picture sharpen? If so, the euphemism was doing moral labor.

THE JUDGE'S FATAL ERROR

(LAW)

Now move to a court file. Here the uniform is not cloth but procedure. People respect procedure because it appears fair: it is numbered, scheduled, and recorded. That cleanliness is why it can become an alibi. A fatal judicial error is rarely a single betrayal. It is a chain of small permissions: a late disclosure that becomes "not significant," a missing note that becomes "not determinative," a witness reduced to a paragraph, a risk accepted because everyone is busy and the consequences are abstract-until they are not.

Then comes the sentence that ends the human part: "the process was followed." It replaces the question of truth with the question of compliance. If they followed the process, no one must confess choice. No one confesses that convenience beat accuracy. Courts have a unique power: they can convert uncertainty into finality. A judgment crystallizes a life into a label. Once the court declares finality, the system can treat remaining suffering as noise.

Error thrives on tempo. Courts operate on calendars and queues. A harmed person operates on a nervous system. The institution's defense is to make the harmed person live at institutional speed until exhaustion looks like consent.

Cross-sector mirror: universities bury complaints in meetings; Churches bury them in "discernment"; courts bury them in adjournments and thresholds. The burial is orderly. That order is a disguise. At the end, paper becomes moral proof. The institution can point to the file and say: look, it is complete. The harmed person's ruined life allows them to point and say so. The file wins because it is official.

The Folded White Neckband lies nearby, immaculate-an emblem of office that never looks like harm.

INTERLUDE (INNER LIFE)

After the decision, they reread the ruling not for meaning but for the place where their life was reduced to a paragraph. They begin a ritual of checking-dates, calls, forms-because paper is the only language the institution seems to hear. At night: "If I had used a different word, would they have listened?" Hope arrives in the morning and drains by midday. The institution's calendar becomes their nervous system.

When you hear "they followed the process," do you feel reassured-or do you hear a refusal to own consequences?

Have people ever punished you socially for insisting on accuracy?

If you had to sign your name under the outcome, would you still accept the same shortcuts?

Parallel: Procedure buys plausible deniability. It lets the institution look clean while distributing harm. Parallel: They reclassify the harmed person as a disturbance to efficiency.

Reader exercise:

Imagine the ruling written in first person: "I chose to treat this as insufficient grounds." Does it still feel neutral? If not, the neutrality was a performance.

THE DEAN'S ACADEMIC WEB

(ACADEMIA)

The university's polished, almost tender voice speaks for the institution. The institution mentions "values." It convenes "reviews. "It forms "panels." The dean's web is made of relationships that never appear on charts.

A web does not announce itself. You discover it when you move and feel resistance: a grant stalled, a reference cooling, a rumor arriving wearing the badge of "concern." The punishment is deniable because it is distributed. Policy becomes the chosen shield. The institution says: "we found no breach." Not: "we found no harm." Policy is a minimum standard, not a moral one, but the substitution is convenient.

Prestige is the hidden currency. A university can tolerate internal damage as long as external legitimacy remains intact. So it converts the human event into an administrative shape it can manage, then calls management "ethics."

Money appears without being named. Funding lines become levers. Lab space becomes leverage. Authorship becomes ownership. Reframing a complaint as "performance" affects career survival.

Academia's foundation in evaluation means the harmed person cannot avoid measurement. Their reaction becomes evidence. Their distress becomes unprofessional. Their insistence becomes "a pattern." The institution has an endless language for making a human response look like a defect.

The Folded White Neckband lies nearby, immaculate-an emblem of office that never looks like harm.

INTERLUDE (INNER LIFE)

After the panel email, corridors feel like evaluations. They read faces for weather. They speak more softly, smile more carefully. Work tastes like metal. Sleep thins. Reality feels negotiable when status is involved.

Where do you live inside evaluation culture-and what truths does it train you to swallow? Have you seen policy used to silence a moral claim?

What happens to truth when prestige is at stake?

Parallel: "Rigor" can function as an alibi like "procedure" and "unity." Parallel: Social cost enforces silence more efficiently than overt threats.

Reader exercise:

Name a moment you stayed silent because you feared reputational cost. What story did you tell yourself to make the silence feel "responsible"?

INTERLUDE: THE TRANSLATION MACHINE

Now pause the case files and watch the machine that sits underneath all six. It works in three stages, and once you see it, you will recognize it everywhere.

Stage 1: Translation. The institution translates a messy, bodily, and morally loud lived event into a category it can handle without changing itself. In a court: "procedural issue", "credibility problem", "insufficient grounds". In a Church: "pastoral matter", "boundary confusion", "internal dispute". In a university: "policy question", "workplace conflict", "professional conduct concern". Translation is not neutral. It selects the aspects of the event that are easiest to process and discards the aspects that demand repair.

Stage 2: Routing. Once translated, the procedure routes the event. Routing is where urgency goes to die. The routed event becomes a meeting, a letter, a committee, a timeline. Notice how routing changes the emotional climate: what was once about a human now becomes about a calendar.

Stage 3: Substitution. Procedure substitutes for morality. If the meeting happened, if the institution sent the letter, if the institution cited the policy, it can treat itself as virtuous-regardless of outcome. Therefore, an institution can look clean while leaving harm intact.

If you feel angry here, ask yourself why. Is it because the technique is foreign? Or because you recognize it? Because you have seen it, and perhaps used a smaller version of it, when you wanted to avoid owning a conflict. The court explained, "We adhered to the process."

Now put yourself in the room. - You are a clerk watching a file close. You feel relief because closure means the queue moves. Do you ask what the closure does to the person outside the room? - You are a parish council member hearing a pastoral statement. You feel relief because conflict threatens unity. Do you ask what unity is being purchased with? - You are a department administrator receiving a complaint. You feel relief when it becomes a policy question because policy has checkboxes. Do you ask what the checkboxes cannot measure? Money, Intimacy, Procedure: the triad is not theory. It is a set of purchases.

Money buys continuity and leverage. Intimacy buys silence and access. Procedure buys delay and immunity. Each purchase has a hidden method. Money hides behind budgets, donations, "resource constraints." Intimacy hides behind care, counsel, and mentorship. Procedure hides behind "fairness," "due process," "policy compliance."

What makes the triad brutal is that each mechanism can be justified with true goods. We need budgets. We need care. We need procedure. So the institution does not need to lie outright. It only needs to overvalue the good that protects it and undervalue the good that would repair the harm.

Here is a self-reflection prompt you can try with no institution at all: Think of the last time you did harm unintentionally. How did you respond? Did you reach for procedure ("that's the rule"), intimacy ("I meant well"), or money ("I'll make it up")? Did any of those become a substitute for ownership?

The folded white neckband is the symbol of that substitution. It is the object that lets a person speak in a role. A role can say things a person would be ashamed to say. A role can close a file. A role can protect the community. A role can cite policy. Roles make cruelty possible without feeling cruel.

Ask yourself: what is your own "neckband"? What title, tone, or professional habit allows you to speak while avoiding the consequences of what you say? Would your emails reveal your conscience or just your compliance if they were read aloud?

So the case files are not entertainment. They are training. They rewire what you call "normal." Once you can see translation, routing, and substitution, you stop being soothed by calm language. You look for signatures. And signatures are where the institution resists hardest.

Because as soon as someone must sign, procedure can no longer pretend to be fate.

THE CANON'S HIDDEN CHAMBER

(FAITH)

A hidden chamber is not only a room. It is a permission structure: who may be alone, unobserved, unquestioned? Architecture shows you which doors are not meant for you to question.

The canon's chamber teaches that discretion is holiness. The canon's chamber frames secrecy as protection. But secrecy is also how power keeps its tools.

Compare the chamber to courthouse private spaces and university closed-door panels. "Confidential" is a door. "Internal" is a door. "Process" is a door.

Confidentiality is offered upward to power, not downward to vulnerability. The attacker violated the harmed person's privacy; the institution's privacy becomes sacred.

When the harmed person speaks, the institution applies moral pressure as concern: "be careful", "don't accuse", "think of the community."

The Folded White Neckband lies nearby, immaculate-an emblem of office that never looks like harm.

INTERLUDE (INNER LIFE):

After the closed door, they distrust rooms. Certain corridors. Certain quiet. They plan escape routes. They speak in half-sentences. They learn self-surveillance.

What rooms in your world are off-limits by culture rather than law? Who benefits when there is no record?

Would you recognize "for the good of the community" as coercion if it demanded your silence? Parallel: Architecture is a procedure.

A room can be as decisive as policy. Parallel: "Privacy" becomes a weapon when monopolized by power.

Reader exercise:

Ask: "Why must this be confidential?" Separate reasons that protect the vulnerable from reasons that protect the institution. Which dominates?

THE JUDGE'S SECRET LEDGER

(LAW)

A ledger is ordinary. That is why it is dangerous. A "secret ledger" can be a filing practice, a classification, or a decision about what counts.

When an institution hides behind records, it can claim objectivity while quietly shaping what counts. "No evidence" often means "no record we recognize."

Across sectors, the ledger changes name: docket, minutes, metrics. Columns make harm look like administration, and administration looks clean.

The hidden lapse is authorship. Someone decided what to record, omit, and label as "unfounded."

The Folded White Neckband lies nearby, immaculate-an emblem of office that never looks like harm.

INTERLUDE (INNER LIFE)

They fear not being recorded. They archive everything. They become a clerk of their own pain because the institution will not file it.

Have you ever tried to prove something true to a system that only recognizes certain kinds of evidence? If the record is wrong, what does "truth" mean inside that institution?

Who controls the official version of events in your workplace or community? Parallel: Whoever controls the record controls reality's official version.

Parallel: They treat the absence of documentation as the absence of harm.

Reader exercise:

Identify a record that shapes reality in your life. Who writes it? Who can contest it? What happens when the record outranks the lived event?

THE JUDGE OF CLEAN ILLUSION

(CROSS-SECTOR)

Clean illusion is the aesthetic of innocence: decisions made with no chooser visible. Sanctity, rigor, objectivity-three costumes for the same concealment. The institution invites you to admire the illusion: calm as virtue, order as justice, continuity as care. Because those are real goods, the invitation is persuasive.

The lapse lives in the gap between appearance and consequence. The institution looks clean; the harmed person is cast as the disturbance.

Anytime a system says "we regret any distress" without naming responsibility, it is attempting clean illusion. The Folded White Neckband lies nearby, immaculate-an emblem of office that never looks like harm.

INTERLUDE (INNER LIFE)

After the illusion is declared clean, people ask them to remain calm while they treat them like a problem. Suffering becomes a mess.When did someone ask you to be "reasonable" in the face of something unreasonable? If silence produces calm, do you sometimes mistake calm for goodness?

Would your judgment change if you had to sign your name under it? Parallel: "Clean" often means "unaccountable."

Parallel: Institutions prefer language that turns harm into weather rather than authorship.

Reader exercise:

Rewrite an institutional sentence in first person: "We found no breach" → "I chose not to treat this as harm." If it feels brutal, the original was concealment.

Step back. The six scenes are one conversion repeated: a human truth translated, routed, substituted, and silenced. If you can recognize the conversion, you can interrupt it-first in your own daily life, then in the institutions you inhabit.

QUESTIONS YOU CANNOT OUTSOURCE

How do you feel when an institution speaks in a calm voice-calm enough to make you doubt urgency? Does your body relax because calm sounds like safety, or tense because calm sounds like self-protection? How would you solve the problem if you could not add more rules? Only one lever: authorship. Who must sign? Who owns the consequences?

Is this something you recognize in daily life? Where have you seen harm turned into administration-and what did you do when you saw it? Where have you benefited from the mechanism-when silence arrived as relief? What did that relief purchase, and who paid?

Who signed the choice? Who will own the outcome?

And if it were your name required-your hand, your signature-would you still call it "process"?

28

"THE WRONGLY CONDEMNED"

SYSTEMS DON'T RUN ON REPENTANCE. THEY RUN ON RISK MANAGEMENT.

Wrongful conviction and judicial misconduct, United States, 2010 (composite case)

The first thing he noticed wasn't a smell. It was a sound.

A low electrical whine that never stopped, like a mosquito trapped behind glass, living on the nervous system. It threaded through the corridor, through the metal doors, through his teeth. By the time they brought him to his cell, the sound had already started rewriting his thoughts into shorter sentences.

The officer at intake spoke with the bored pace of someone reading ingredients on a cereal box. Rights. Rules. Timetables. The officer didn't intend for people to understand the instructions. They survived.

"Questions?"

He had a hundred. He swallowed them. In places like this, people treat questions as a kind of arrogance, and arrogance earns you friction-extra minutes standing, extra searches, extra delays that have nothing to do with safety and everything to do with reminding you who gets to set the temperature of your day.

They gave him a uniform that smelled of industrial detergent and long storage, cloth that repeated washings had thinned to the point of surrender. His street clothes disappeared into a bag with a number clipped to it. Not his name. A number. A tag you could hang on anything.

This is how a person becomes manageable: you reduce him to inventory.

At night, what returned wasn't the evidence, not the testimony, not the photographs. It was a rhythm.

The prosecutor's rhythm-how she paced each point as if she were placing stones across a river: step here, step here, step here. No urgency. No cruelty. Just the confident tempo of someone who knows the current will do the rest.

His own lawyer-public appointment, new suit on credit, eyes that kept flicking to the clock-had a different rhythm: the frantic tapping of a pen, the shuffling of papers like a deck of cards in a magician's hands. He wasn't incompetent. Exhaustion preceded his start. The state brought a full orchestra; the defense brought a cracked violin and a chair missing a leg.

In court, the accused learned something most people never learn: "truth" is not a substance. It's a performance standard.

If you hesitate, you look guilty. If you speak in loops, you look guilty. If you can't explain yourself in the polished shape the room expects, the room assumes you're hiding something.

He watched jurors lean forward when the prosecutor spoke, then lean back when he tried. Their bodies decided before their minds admitted it. He could feel their discomfort like heat on skin. He didn't have the vocabulary to name what was happening, only the instinct to recognize it: the room preferred people who sounded like the room.

His family didn't fracture all at once. It came apart the way dry bread breaks-quietly, without drama, leaving crumbs everywhere.

His mother stopped answering certain phone calls because the neighbors had asked questions with smiles that weren't smiles.

His sister came to the first hearing after sentencing with a baby on her hip and mascara that had run down one cheek. She sat there for an hour, staring at the floor, then stood up and walked out before they called his name. Later she said she felt sick. Later, she stopped coming. Shame is expensive, and it charges interest.

His partner tried harder than anyone else . She learned the rules through a laborious process, similar to how one acquires a foreign language one never desired: she memorized which forms to use, which deadlines to meet, which offices closed early, and which person behind which desk could be persuaded to stamp something today instead of next month. She learned that every attempt to help him required her to plead with strangers whose job was to remain unmoved.

Then their child began calling him "that place" instead of "dad." Not out of cruelty-out of practicality. Children choose the language that hurts less.

Condemnation expands the punishment outward. It drafts everyone who loves you into a war they never enlisted for.

Time inside does not feel like time outside. It doesn't move in days. It moves in compliance.

A door opens if you are compliant. Food arrives if you are compliant. Phone privileges exist if you are compliant. A guard says "morning" if you are compliant.

His body adapted, and that adaptation was another kind of humiliation. He stopped expecting kindness. He stopped expecting explanations. His sleep became shallow, then fragmented, then ritual-two hours here, an hour there, drifting only after the mind surrendered.

Hope didn't disappear. It became a superstition.

He learned to fear good news because good news meant someone could take it away. The fresh evidence did not come like thunder. It came like a misprint.

A small legal nonprofit sent a letter detailing a new comparison method for old traces, a database update, and a match that shouldn't have been possible when he was tried. There was another man, another pattern, another timeline.

He read it, and nothing happened at first. He stared at the paper the way you stare at a lottery ticket you're afraid to scratch.

Then his hands started shaking so hard he had to sit on them. He laughed once-an ugly sound that scared him. The laugh was not joy. It was a body relearning a chemical it had stopped producing.

He did not call his family right away. He waited until he could speak without breaking.

That's what confinement does: it teaches you not to share your heart until you've confirmed the world won't punish you for having one.

The state did not argue that he was guilty. The state argued that it was too late to ask.

The response was a wall of perfect paragraphs. Deadlines. Technicalities. Proper channels. The writing was clean enough to frame. It offered no rage, no insult, no acknowledgment of the human stakes. It treated the possibility of a wrong man facing death as a scheduling inconvenience.

The institution wasn't even pretending to hunt truth. It was guarding its paperwork like a relic.

This is the part no one wants to admit: systems rarely collapse because they love evil. They collapse because they love continuity.

Reversal is contagious. If one conviction is wrong, others might be. If one process is flawed, the public might look too closely. So the system behaves like a body protecting an infection-not by curing it, but by isolating it, sealing it, calling it "controlled."

Behind the scenes, his lawyer tried to push the new evidence forward. Motions. Hearings. Requests for resources. The same gates, the same locks, the same polite refusals. And when the lawyer made noise-too much noise-there were consequences that had nothing to do with the case and everything to do with discipline: complaints, reviews, whispers about "professionalism," as if persistence were a personality defect.

He watched the people fighting for him get punished for fighting.

It was hard not to conclude the obvious: the machine does not thank the hands that try to jam its gears.

The hearings that followed had the feeling of a ritual designed to look like fairness. A panel. A transcript. A schedule set months away. Everyone spoke in measured tones, as if the calmness of their voices could prove the health of the process.

And then-because it always comes-there was the statement.

"We take this seriously," someone said. Someone stated that lessons would be learned. "We will ensure this cannot happen again," someone said.

The sentence landed with the soft comfort of a blanket. And it was just as useful.

Because he already knew: those promises are not medicine. They are perfume. They are for the audience. They are for the institution's reflection in its own mirror.

He had seen the cycle from the inside: a tragedy, a report, a reform memo, a training seminar, a press release. Then another tragedy. Another report. Another memo.

They chose not to warn people not because of neglect-because issuing warnings costs little, while modifying the power structure requires significant expense.

Systems don't run on repentance. They run on risk management. They don't prevent harm. They contain publicity.

His mother's voice changed when he finally told her. Not joy. Not relief. A cautious, bruised quiet. "Don't get excited," she whispered, as if excitement were a sin the world could punish. "Just... don't." That was the real sentence the system had written into her: believing is dangerous.

His partner cried, then apologized for crying, as if tears were another administrative failure. Then she started listing tasks-people to call, papers to find-because action felt safer than faith.

It's a special cruelty to make an entire family afraid of hope. In the end, what he understood was simple and unbearable:

A wrongful conviction isn't a mistake that ends when someone discovers it. It's a climate that settles over everyone involved.

It changes how people speak. It changes what they dare to imagine. It teaches the innocent to behave as if they've done something shameful.

And when the institution finally admits error-if it ever does-it will not feel like triumph. It will feel like waking up after a long illness and realizing you don't remember what health felt like.

The system will write a careful statement. It will promise vigilance. It will announce additional safeguards with confident verbs.

And somewhere else, in another building, someone will turn another person into a number, and someone will again say that it will never happen again-meaning it with their mouth, not with their structure.

Because structures don't "mean." They persist.

And persistence without conscience is just a slower form of violence.

TRACEABILITY

INTERLUDE III

Lucia watched the PRGR do what procedure had never done:

It made the powerful slow down.

Not out of virtue.

Out of friction.

Emily looked at her spreadsheet and felt, for the first time, that doubt did not have to become personality. The system had built a channel where doubt could become record without becoming rebellion.

Andreas stood in a side chapel and felt obedience, holiness, and silence begin to separate cleanly.

Not because the bishop had become good.

Because avoidance had become harder than honesty.

PRGR did not make saints.

It made authors.

And authors are exposed to consequence.

In three rooms, three people asked the same question:

What am I seeing?

This time the answer could not be:

- Nothing.
- Tone.
- Misunderstanding.
- Complexity.
- Internal matter.
- Too junior.
- Pastoral.

Because each of those words is a curtain-and PRGR is designed to pull curtains down.

Bellini understood: if he chose inaction, he would have to sign the foreseeable harm of inaction.

Reed understood: if he dismissed accuracy as immaturity, he would have to sign that harm too.

Gregorios understood: if he used compassion as leverage, he would have to sign that he had made the vulnerable into hostages.

Truth was no longer offered a chair against the wall.

Truth was handed the pen.

Nothing exploded.

That part stayed the same.

Institutions still preferred process to confession. They still reached first for reputation, then delay, then reframing.

But now, each time they tried, the record contained something stubborn:

- A human name.
- A sentence in the first person.
- A harm forecast written before the harm, not after.
- A remedy trigger waiting like a fuse.

This didn't guarantee justice.

It guaranteed traceability.

And traceability is the enemy of the invisible hand.

Institutions love ideas because ideas cannot be subpoenaed.

They cannot be cross-examined. They cannot be made to sign.

PRGR is how you remind a system of its oldest inconvenience:

ideas don't answer phone

29

"THE JUDGE'S COMPLICIT COURT"

THE SICKENING EMBARRASSMENT OF RECOGNITION: WE BELIEVED BECAUSE IT WAS EASIER THAN QUESTIONING.

Judicial corruption and organised crime, United Kingdom, 2012 (composite case)

The first thing London teaches you is that courage is often a costume.

Not the cheap kind-no capes, no speeches-just a national posture, a practiced steadiness inherited like weather. The old stories are full of it: Celts holding hills as if stone were kin, Scots tightening their grip on the line and refusing to step back, that island stubbornness that becomes myth-no fear, even when fear is the sensible response. Over centuries it hardened into civic ritual: you stand, you endure, you don't flinch. The city's buildings take part. They look permanent. They look certain. They teach you, without ever saying it, that the system is stronger than the men inside it.

Judge Richard Holloway understood that lesson. He also understood its flaw.

One of London's busiest criminal courts, where time functions as both weapon and currency, fell under his presidency. On the bench he wore the black robe, the Victorian-styled wig, the crisply folded white jabot-centuries of theater made a room behave. When he entered, lawyers straightened as if pulled by strings. Clerks quieted. Defendants watched him with the old instinct people still have for symbols: this is the face of the law. Holloway cultivated that image with a artisan's care. His voice was calm. His rulings sounded methodical. His patience felt like nobility. The public saw him as the embodiment of the English bargain: we exchange the chaos of personal vengeance for the calm of procedure, and in return, we receive protection. The courtroom's rituals-robes, wig, jabot-reassured citizens that the judge is not merely a person but a function, a safeguard, an idea.

But ideas don't answer phone calls. People do.

The entanglement began with minor interventions, the kind that never make headlines because they never look like crime. Low-level intermediaries approached Holloway, seeking favorable scheduling, small procedural adjustments, and lenient pre-trial rulings. They did not arrive as gangsters; they arrived as "fixers," the sort of men London produces in every era-polished enough to enter respectable rooms, anonymous enough to disappear from memory afterward. They spoke softly, like people who understood that the true center of power prefers quiet.

At first, Holloway rationalised the favors as pragmatism. A moved hearing could ease a congested list. A delayed motion could prevent "unnecessary" disruption. A gentle bail decision could avoid "worsening" a defendant's circumstances before trial. These were the excuses that let him sleep: not greed, not corruption-efficiency. He told himself he was keeping the machine running.

And the machine rewarded him.

Not with money at first, but with something more persuasive: the sense that he could bend time itself. In a court, time is a lever. Delay can starve a case. Speed can suffocate a defense. A scheduling change can erase a witness. A procedural ruling can turn evidence into noise. With a private thrill, Holloway realized how easily decisions that looked technical on paper could shift lives. The wig and jabot didn't restrain him; they disguised him, turning preference into precedent.

Soon, intermediaries were no longer asking only for convenience. They were asking for outcomes. Holloway's office became a nerve centre of covert influence. Public proceedings remained formally correct while private notes, coded correspondence, and timed procedural decisions directed results in the background. The court's symbols-robe, wig, jabot-worked like stained glass: they coloured everything the public saw, making even questionable decisions look part of a holy architecture. When Holloway "managed" a case in favor of criminal affiliates, he experienced a satisfaction no praise could match: mastery without fingerprints.

The pattern was subtle enough that most people missed it. Certain cases involving known organised crime figures were repeatedly delayed. Occasionally, someone misdirected evidence into administrative fog. Pre-trial motions inexplicably favored defendants with connections. But the system trains people to interpret irregularity as bureaucracy rather than malice. Clerks assumed someone else had allowed it. Lawyers assumed it was a quirk of docket pressure. Journalists assumed the court had reasons too complex to explain.

And Holloway assumed he would remain unchallenged because the city needed him to be unchallenged. A judge in a wig feels like an anchor. Anchors are supposed to be heavy enough not to move.

Then a different courage entered the story-less romantic, more methodical.

Investigators within the Ministry of Justice were tracking organised crime patterns, looking not at individual scandals but at correlations-the strange way certain defendants seemed to slip through procedural seams. It was not a single complaint that raised the alarm; it was mathematics. A clustering of delays. A repetition of favorable bail conditions. A sequence of evidentiary mishaps that always seemed to fall in the same direction. The investigators followed the trail with the patience of people who understand that powerful corruption rarely announces itself; it leaves gradients, not explosions.

The Chief Justice allowed access to the files.

The investigators expected incompetence, perhaps. They found design.

There were timings that made no sense unless they were intentional. Notes that referenced communications that should not have existed. Decisions that appeared legally permissible in isolation yet, when seen as a series, formed a map-a route carved through procedure to deliver advantage to the same network again and again. The shock was not only that a judge had facilitated criminal objectives; it was that he had done it while remaining, to the public, the picture of impartial calm.

The city reacted like a body discovering an infection beneath perfect skin. At first, disbelief. Then anger. Then the sickening embarrassment of recognition: we believed because it was easier than questioning. London's trust-so dependent on the ritual of seriousness-eroded. You could feel it in the newspapers, in the mutter of barristers in corridors, in the way people looked at wigs and robes with a faint new suspicion. The symbols that had once reassured now felt like concealment.

Holloway faced suspension. Inquiry followed inquiry. The story widened. Names surfaced. The inquiries confirmed patterns. Yet the legal complexities-the careful way he had stayed within procedural ambiguity-made criminal prosecution difficult. It was the oldest trick of institutional wrongdoing: use the system's own language to make harm look like interpretation.

And then the human cost arrived in a way reforms never fully account for.

Holloway, stripped of his daily stage, faced a silence he could not manage. Men like him survive on control, and when they lose control, they are left with themselves. The public imagined a monster. But what remained was a man confronted by two unbearable facts at once: he had used the court to shelter criminals, and he had done it while preaching the dignity of law. The contradiction was not merely ethical. It was existential. He could no longer inhabit the story he had told himself-that he was the guardian, the stabiliser, the calm hand.

In the end, he ended his life.

It was not a gesture of repentance so much as a last assertion of agency: a last moment in which he decided the timing, the outcome, the closure. Even that, tragically, echoed his pattern-control as refuge, control as addiction.

Afterward, the legal community shifted into repair mode. The legal community modernized procedures. Digital systems streamlined filings. They randomized case assignments to reduce influence. The legal community fortified oversight mechanisms-on paper, impressively so. They delivered reform speeches with the same solemn cadence judges use when delivering verdicts. They praised courage, celebrated vigilance, and invoked integrity like incense.

Yet beneath the surface, a troubling truth remained: structural changes often arrive as cosmetics, not confessions. New software does not fix old deference. Randomisation does not repair a culture trained to treat symbols as proof. Oversight does not matter if the people tasked with oversight are afraid of the room they must walk into.

London likes to tell stories about fearless ancestors-Celts, Scots, the old island grit that refuses to bend. But Holloway's scandal revealed a quieter national habit: not fearlessness, but faith in ceremony. The city believed in the wig and jabot because belief is efficient. Doubt is expensive. Doubt requires you to imagine that the people who look like guardians might use the gate for their own passage.

And that is the ultimate irony: the system that enabled Holloway remained standing, almost untouched, while the man who exploited it collapsed. The robes and insignia survived as symbols, but symbols do not guarantee worthiness. They guarantee only a performance. The difference between justice and its imitation is not in the costume. It is in what the costume may hide-and how long the public calls that hiding "tradition."

30

"THE JUDGE WHO TURNED BLIND"

THE UNIVERSE DOES NOT FLINCH WHEN WE RUIN EACH OTHER.

Judicial misconduct and systemic prejudice; Tunnel vision; United Kingdom, 2010 (composite case)

Judge Alistair Hargrove was the man London likes to imagine it produces at its best: measured, lucid, unruffled. He wore the black robe and immaculate bands in the Crown Court, seeming to have already reached a conclusion. The cloth did what cloth has always done for institutions-it made a human being look like a principle. People mistook his calmness for fairness. They mistook his control for thoughtfulness. They mistook the ritual for a guarantee.

What was wrong with him was not theatrical. That was the danger.

A poor judge is easy to hate when he is loud. Hargrove was quiet. He never banged the bench. He rarely scolded. He simply narrowed the world until only his preferred version of it could fit.

Outside, London did what London does: rain lingering as a thin film on stone, buses dragging their breath through wet streets, blackbirds hopping beneath clipped hedges as if the city had harmed no one. The air smelled faintly of soot and damp wool. Inside, the court smelled of old paper, floor polish, and something else-confidence held too long in a closed room.

At first, his record looked unremarkable. Minor trials. Sentences that matched the precedent. Decisions that read like any other judge's decisions, tidy and correct on the surface. That is how this kind of pathology survives: by mimicking normal.

But patterns are not single moments. They are weather.

Over the years, certain defendants seemed to enter his courtroom already half-convicted: LGBTQ+ people, ethnic minorities, those whose presence made the state's story feel less stable. Not that Hargrove openly declared disgust. He did something more sophisticated. He made doubt feel "unnecessary." He treated alternative explanations as sentimental. He treated defense objections as clutter.

The question that hovered around him-asked quietly by the damaged, not loudly by the comfortable-was not simply, Is he biased? It was: Is this an illness or a wiring?

You could imagine a disease: a tumor pressing on empathy, a degenerative change flattening nuance, a depression calcifying into contempt. Those things happen. Brains are organs. Organs fail.

But Hargrove did not look like a man losing function. He looked like a man perfecting it.

His mind seemed built for a particular pleasure: the pleasure of certainty. Some people chase sex. Some chase money. Hargrove chased the feeling of being right-and the deeper drug of having others treat his rightness as law.

Psychologists have names for parts of this. Cognitive rigidity. Confirmation bias. Authoritarian traits. Sometimes, in darker rooms, you hear the word sociopathy thrown around like a stone. But the truth is more unsettling: you don't need a spectacular disorder to produce spectacular harm. You need a small deficit-empathy that does not fully ignite-and an environment that rewards it. You need a man whose internal alarm system does not ring when he is about to ruin someone's life, and a system that calls that silence "professionalism."

Hargrove's courtroom rewarded the absence of tremor. It rewarded decisiveness. It rewarded what looked like strength. Every time he made a harsh ruling, and the room complied, his brain received the simplest reinforcement: This works. This is who I am.

And each reinforcement tightened the wiring.

The high-profile burglary case began the way many wrongful convictions begin: with a story too convenient to question. Police arrested two men, David Morris and Stephen Patel, based on circumstantial evidence. They stitched together a police narrative that sounded complete, ignoring what was missing. A witness "thought" he saw them. A hoodie. A time window. A few vague associations. The case that should have been porous to doubt.

But in Hargrove's courtroom, doubt had to apply for a visa.

Defense counsel tried to widen the frame: alternative suspects, inconsistent timings, the fragility of memory under stress. Hargrove listened with the mild patience of a man enduring weather he believes will pass. "Counsel," he said at one point, voice level, "we are not here to speculate."

It was a neat trick-calling investigation "speculation" and treating the prosecution's assumptions as solid ground. When the defense sought to cross-examine a key witness on prior misidentifications, Hargrove curtailed it: "We will not descend into character assassination." When counsel raised the lack of forensic corroboration, Hargrove nodded once, as if acknowledging a minor aesthetic flaw, then moved on.

He did not need to shout to tilt the scales. Procedure is heavy. A small thumb is enough.

The court convicted David and Stephen. A pen stroke, so clean it barely left a mark on the paper, took years from David and Stephen. Their families learned the particular grief of bureaucratic injustice: the way you can scream into an institution and hear only the echo of your own voice.

Then there was Clara Benson.

Clara, a transgender woman, faced theft accusations-an allegation that a system recognizing vulnerability could have addressed with proportionality and care. In Hargrove's court, her identity became an invisible contaminant. He never mocked her. He did something worse: he treated her as inherently less credible.

He allowed the prosecution to linger, subtly, on insinuation-tone, appearance, "lifestyle." He framed his instructions to the jury in language that sounded neutral but shaped perception: emphasis on "public confidence," on "order," on "deterrence." His sentencing remarks were polished, even compassionate in cadence, yet the outcome landed like a stone: disproportionate, punitive, dressed as principled.

This is how prejudice often moves now-not as a slur, but as a posture.

The robe and bands made it difficult to see him as human enough to be flawed. That's the institutional magic trick. Ceremony creates a distance where accountability loses traction.

Junior lawyers noticed the pattern and swallowed it. Challenging a judge is a career risk. Clerks noticed and told themselves it wasn't their role. Colleagues noticed and retranslated discomfort into reverence: "He's old-school." "He's strict." "He runs a tight ship." The institution took his rigidity and called it stability, the way a family excuses a violent uncle by saying, That's just how he is.

Meanwhile, Hargrove's internal world narrowed further because no one forced it open.

There's a point in the psychology of wrongdoing where the person stops distinguishing between what they believe and what is real-not because they hallucinate, but because they curate reality so aggressively that it becomes indistinguishable from their preference. It's not psychosis. It's a private mythology held together by professional reinforcement.

To Hargrove, he wasn't harming anyone. He was protecting the court from chaos. He was protecting society from "narratives." He was protecting the public from weakness disguised as nuance. He had his own moral robe beneath the physical one, and he wore it more tightly.

The pattern might have continued indefinitely if not for outsiders-investigative journalists, civil rights organisations, appellate lawyers with the patience to read transcripts like weather maps. They collected what the institution refused to see: repeated curtailments of defense, repeated deference to prosecution assumptions, repeated disproportion when the defendant belonged to certain categories.

It wasn't one dramatic scandal. It was an accumulation. Like damp in a wall. Like soot in lungs.

The review's findings, when they finally arrived, used the language institutions employ to condemn without admitting enablement: "procedural irregularities," "appearance of bias," and "inadequate management of equality considerations." Suspended temporarily. Sent to training, as if the harm were a misunderstanding that a seminar could correct.

The people he had harmed did not get seminars. They got years. They got ruptured families. They got the mistrust that leaks into the rest of life: if a court can be this wrong while looking this calm, then where else is the lie hiding?

And here is the undressed conclusion your book has been walking toward, story after story, robe after robe: Institutions do not fail only when bad people arrive. They fail when good people outsource their judgment to symbols. When they choose comfort over confrontation. When they treat authority as a substitute for scrutiny. The robe and bands are not evil, but they are catalytic: they speed up whatever reaction the wearer brings into the room.

Was Hargrove ill? Possibly. Some brains are wired for low empathy and high certainty. Some personalities are built to confuse control with probity. But even if you found a name for his wiring, it would not absolve the system that let that wiring steer lives like a ship with no lighthouse.

Rain hung by the station steps when the first of the exonerations finally came. Blackbirds moved under box hedges, indifferent, as if the city did not know how many futures a judge's certainty had folded away.

And maybe that is the last cruelty: the universe does not flinch when we ruin each other. Only people do-when they still remember they are human.

Run the scenes again under one rule: harm must have an author. Money can't buy fog. Intimacy can't buy silence. Procedure can't buy clean hands. If the institution still chooses the same outcome, it must choose it openly, with a name attached-so the victim isn't the only one who carries consequences. How would you solve it-what single rule would you enforce first? What would you change tomorrow in your own workplace/community to make harm harder to "disappear"?

31

"THE WARNING LETTER OF THE QUIET ERASURE"

MY OATH HAD NOT BEEN A GATEWAY. IT HAD BEEN A HINGE.

The author's experience, Netherlands, 2004-2014 (memoir), PRGR

The day I took my oath, the sky looked scrubbed clean - a hard February blue that makes you believe, for a moment, that institutions are as honest as weather.

I wore my new fine-wool toga for the first time. The white neckpiece sat at my throat like a small flag of belonging. I walked towards the district court's signage - a modest panel of metal and paint set along the road, about a hundred metres from the main entrance. Between the sign and the building lay a pond, and in the pond a fountain hurled up a continual plume, breaking the water's surface into bright shards; like the files I would hold in my hands, intangible pieces, true and produced ones. A thin mist drifted downwind. A coot cut a black line across the ripples and vanished into the reeds along the far bank.

My employer wanted photographs for the firm's website: 'new colleague, first day, proper kit'. So I stood near the sign, trying to look like someone who had always known where to place their hands. The lens kept catching droplets. I wiped it on my sleeve and tried again. The toga was heavier than I expected - warm, dignified, faintly theatrical - and I felt that old, foolish thrill: the sense of stepping into a role that mattered.

Two days later, a letter arrived.

The sender was the staff holder. The tone was courteous, with a faint lift of humour, and yet the message landed like a slap: my toga and bef were not a carnival costume. This was an official warning. I read it twice, then a third time, as if repetition might reveal the joke I had somehow missed.

There are warnings that correct behaviour, and there are warnings that teach you your place. This was the latter. It was not about fabric. It was about ownership. The clothing did not belong to me; it belonged to the system, and the system would decide what the clothing meant.

I kept the letter. I still have it. Not because I enjoy resentment - resentment is a kind of servitude - but because it was the first plain evidence of a rule nobody states aloud: in the theatre of law, the costume is sacred, and the actor is replaceable.

I told myself it was an oddity. A bureaucratic twitch. An overzealous official searching for a minor infraction to prove their vigilance. I wanted that explanation because it preserved the story I had grown up believing: that the profession disciplines itself for the sake of justice.

I did not yet understand how they used discipline. The staff holder's term ended. A new one was 'elected', and another one - the person who would later file complaints against me.

During my early years, I joined, on invitation, a committee that had the responsibility of reviewing the local Bar's financial statements prior to their presentation to the members at the annual meeting. It was dull work. Columns, categories, footnotes. The quiet labour that, done properly, prevents scandals you never hear about.

In 2011, I chaired that committee. With the chair came a script.

Each year, they expected the chair to read a prepared text - polished smooth by repetition, emptied of risk but heavy with reassurance. The only things that changed were the numbers, the names of committee members, and the annual membership fee. The performance was part of the ritual: the words said, 'all is well', regardless of whether it was.

That year, I carried the script to the meeting and did not tell anyone what I intended to do. The room was bright with overhead light. The management table sat at the front like a raised platform. Behind it, the members of the Supervisory Board arranged themselves with the composure that reads as virginity when you are still naive.

I stood. I felt the paper in my hands. I had the option to read the familiar lines and receive applause for my compliance.

Instead, I spoke plainly.

I described what I had found. I said what the numbers supported. I asked questions that the script had avoided. I treated the ceremony as a forum rather than a performance, and that - in institutions built on appearance - is the unforgivable sin.

The reaction was almost physical. Robes stiffened. Faces flushed, not with shame, but with outrage. People who had been relaxed moments before sat upright, as if an invisible string had yanked them. The air grew thinner.

And then something remarkable happened: members called for an independent committee to explore my findings. A ripple of courage moved through the room - brief, imperfect, but real. For a few minutes, the choreography broke.

None of it appeared in the minutes.

In the official record, the meeting remained open. The forum became a performance again, and the disruption vanished like breath on a mirror.

Not long after, the staff holder came to see me. A member of the Supervisory Board accompanied him. Afraid of not having a witness or to counter any argument. Their message came wrapped in courtesy, the cadence of guidance, as if they were offering help rather than laying down a threat.

I could, the member said, become the lawyer with the most complaints on record. They had a plan.

A prediction offered as advice. A warning wrapped in civility. The sentence that allows the speaker to deny intent while ensuring the listener cannot misunderstand. They reminded me - without raising their voice - that the robe protects those who obey and bruises those who do not.

When they left, the corridor seemed suddenly longer. Outside, the winter light had slid behind the building, and the courthouse windows reflected only sky.

The cost was my position. The grinding continued.

In the 2012 National Bar Exam's Professional Conduct paper, my surname inexplicably appeared in a case file given to candidates. This was not a mistake; it was deliberate. The official explanation was "pure coincidence." Yet one member of the Exam Committee came from my local Bar, and my surname is exceptionally rare-only two lawyers share it with 3,512 people in a population of seventeen million.

What makes it even harder to dismiss is that the scenario in the question closely resembled a matter I had just dealt with, with no repercussions. It's infuriating that chance could dismiss something so improbable, given the stakes. They smiled, accentuated with a sign of loose control when my eyes met theirs.

I understood then that my oath had not been a gateway. It had been a hinge. And the gate started to close.

By October 2013, I decided to leave my profession.

Maastricht was already in its wet season-thin rain that doesn't fall so much as cling, turning the old stones darker, making every surface look newly scrubbed and newly accused. The courthouse stood as it always had in my mind: sober, contained, a place where language is supposed to behave. Yet outside, the city carried its deeper memory. Two thousand years ago the Romans had established a crossing here, a hinge point over the Maas, a place of gates and passage. Even now, walking through the streets, the logic of it remained palpable: walls, thresholds, the designation of who they permitted in and who they sent back.

My ancestors had been gatekeepers in the seventeenth-and eighteenth centuries. Shifting the appreciated, and those who formed a risk to the city. That thought came to me not as pride but as irony. Gatekeeping, I realized, is not always a job. Sometimes it is a habit of institutions-deciding who counts as legitimate, and then enforcing that legitimacy through ritual rather than reason.

In the courtyard outside the office, a ginkgo tree dropped its fan-shaped leaves onto the wet paving stones. They fell one by one-small, precise departures-and collected in bright drifts that looked almost celebratory until you stepped on them and felt the slick give beneath your shoe. I watched them and told myself I would do this clean. Change course. Inform the staff holder responsible for my file. Allow the institution to do what it claimed it did: record facts, respect decisions, move on. I still believed candour had a place inside the folds of the system.

I was mistaken.

The next complaint arrived like an administrative shrug, framed in the language institutions prefer when they intend to harm while appearing neutral: failure to comply with instructions to hand over private and office financial records.

The refusal was real. The reason was simple. It was the fourth request within twelve months.

Three inspections had already taken place. Each time, the process had been thorough enough to disrupt life and vague enough to be unlimited-questions reaching past professional boundaries, demands for records with no clear endpoint, the steady implication that innocence is something you must keep proving. Each time, the result was the same: no findings, no fault, no stain on the cloth. And yet the hands kept returning to the same pocket, as if persistence might conjure guilt where evidence could not.

Standing in Maastricht, a city built on controlled entry, I understood the pattern with sudden clarity. This was not an oversight as safeguard. This was a gate being closed-slowly, politely, with paperwork instead of iron. Procedures can sand things down. It leaves no single cut you can point to, only a gradual abrasion until you are raw enough to comply or exhausted enough to disappear.

By the fourth request, I said no.

I refused because I recognised the choreography: the warning letter, the missing minutes, the corridor "advice" that I could become the lawyer with the most complaints. An institution turned my private decision to resign into an institutional act. It gave the pursuit a respectable shape. It allowed those involved to speak of "integrity" and "standards" while they did what had been set in motion earlier: punishing someone for stepping where they weren't meant to look.

I asked the National Bar of Advocates to end my registration as a lawyer, effective 31 December 2013. I chose to walk away. And yet, external pressures also pushed me. That is the contradiction that lives in the body: you decide to leave a room, and the room decides-at the same time-to throw you out. From the outside, the result looks identical. Inside, it feels like a gate slamming behind you.

My fall from their graces was not spectacular. No scandal. No crime. No smoking gun. Just the quiet mechanics of erasure. But that erasure did something they did not expect: it freed me. It sharpened my sight-how authority hides inside ritual, how moral language launders fear, how "oversight" becomes a private weapon while remaining publicly virtuous.

This is where my professional story is often said to end. It does not.

PRGR END-CAP - AUTHORED HARM TEST

(for "THE WARNING LETTER of THE QUIET ERASURE")

This case is about the writer of this book. That matters, because it shows the mechanism from the inside: not the scandal people imagine, but the slow administrative conversion of a private decision into a public erasure.

Primary mechanism: PROCEDURE - discipline framed as "oversight" until oversight becomes a gate.

PRGR trigger: any professional-regulatory step that foreseeably causes irreversible harm (loss of livelihood, credential, reputation lock, financial collapse, long-term psychological injury)-including "routine" requests that become endless audits.

Required signatory: the smallest role with real stop-power at each irreversible fork (the staff holder/initiator of the complaint; the decision-maker who authorizes repeated inspections; the tribunal chair or panel member who imposes the final sanction).

If PRGR had been mandatory here, the institution would have had to write to the person-not to the archive-and sign the harm in plain language.

The hinge-steps where PRGR would force an author to exist

The first warning letter (symbol enforcement disguised as professionalism)

- Action: issuing a formal warning about dress/role compliance.
- PRGR would require: why a warning is necessary, what conduct is actually being regulated, and what downstream escalation path is being initiated by putting this on a file.

The missing minutes / the script (when governance becomes theatre)

- Action: omitting inconvenient concerns from the record; expecting ritual reassurance rather than factual accounting.
- PRGR would require: a signed explanation for any omission of material points

raised at an annual meeting, and an automatic disclosure obligation to members when governance questions are raised.

- Repeated financial inspections after "no findings" (oversight as harassment)
- Action: requesting the same private/professional records repeatedly without new grounds.
- PRGR would require the requestor to state: (a) the new factual basis, (b) the defined scope and endpoint, (c) why prior clean inspections are insufficient, and (d) the foreseeable harm of persistence (reputational insinuation, stress, time-cost, chilling effect on dissent).
- Remedy trigger: if an inspection yields no findings, any subsequent inspection within a defined window automatically escalates to an independent reviewer who must approve scope and necessity.

The reframing move: "non-compliance" as character (procedure laundering motive)

- Action: converting a refusal (after repeated clean audits) into an allegation of misconduct or unfitness.
- PRGR would require: the exact instruction refused, why it is lawful/necessary, what less harmful alternatives were considered (targeted request, supervised access, anonymized sampling, third-party accountant), and why those alternatives were rejected.

The final irreversible step: removal of credential / registration (the career death sentence)

- Action: ending the right to practice.
- PRGR would require a signed forecast that names the foreseeable harms explicitly (loss of livelihood, status, future employability, reputational stain, family impacts, financial instability) and states why the institution believes those harms are justified despite the risk of error.
- Required disclosure: what evidence the panel relied on; what evidence it dis-

counted; what uncertainty remains; what the affected person can do to trigger review.

- Remedy trigger: a pre-committed reopening pathway if later facts show procedural irregularity, bias, missing records, or disproportionality (automatic rehearing, record correction, reinstatement pathway, compensation/assistance where permitted).

What the institution hides (and PRGR makes visible)

- Harm dispersed into "process" so no one person owns it.
- Time used as a weapon (repeated requests, delays, fatigue).
- Reputation locks created through labels ("non-compliant," "unfit") that become destiny.
- The quiet conversion of governance disagreement into discipline.

Counterfactual (what changes if PRGR exists)

Someone would have had to sign, in plain language: "We are choosing a human cost, we believe it is justified, and we accept accountability if we are wrong." If they could not write that without hiding behind ritual and abstractions, the mechanism would be exposed as theatre rather than ethics.

Pause

Locate the moment in this chapter where you felt the shift from "oversight" to "erasure." That is the exact moment PRGR is built to catch.

32

"THE LAWYER WHO SENT THE INNOCENT TO DEATH"

THE SYSTEM PERFORMS BLAME REDISTRIBUTION AND CALLS IT INTEGRITY.

Wrongful death sentence, United States, 2009 (composite case), PRGR

The photograph lay face down on Randall Kerr's desk because he enjoyed deciding when to look. He liked control in small ways-like a chemist deciding when to add the catalyst, or a pilot deciding when to drop below cloud cover. In his office, everything suggested clean thinking: binders aligned, framed diplomas hung at exact heights, a small American flag angled as if patriotism had a preferred geometry.

Kerr was a prosecutor, which meant he was a lawyer who could speak death into a room and have the room treat it as procedure.

He turned the photo over with two fingers. A living room. A body. The scene that makes the air feel wrong even through glossy paper. The victim, a woman, had been found after midnight; the neighborhood had been loud with sirens and the buzz of porch lights switching on like startled insects.

Kerr stared at the image with practiced stillness and thought, not about grief, but about traction. A capital case was gravity. Once it started moving, everything else bent around it.

The suspect was Marcus Hill-twenty-six, warehouse worker, no prior felony record, a man whose resume carried nothing but unglamorous labor and gaps that could be called "inconsistency" by someone in a clean suit. Marcus's interview footage showed a frightened face, a voice that reached for words and found them too late.

Kerr watched it twice, listening to the pauses and the stumbles the way an angler listens for a line tightening. "He's not sophisticated," one detective said, almost kindly.

Kerr nodded as if that settled something. In his world, sophistication was credibility. Education didn't merely confer language; it conferred innocence-by-style. Marcus had neither.

That was the first advantage.

The second arrived when the lab report came in. Trace fibers. Partial prints offered interpretative possibilities. A hair sample that a state analyst called "consistent." Not definitive, but suggestive-the forensic language that functions like fog: it obscures while pretending to illuminate.

Kerr knew the difference between "consistent" and "certain." He also knew juries don't. Juries hear science and assume purity. They don't think about contamination, bias, or the way a human mind can steer a microscope.

Kerr believed the public was a child that needed firm storytelling. He called it serving justice. He also enjoyed it.

The defense attorney appointed to Marcus was Thomas Price, a man with a tired tie and a stack of files too high for one body to carry without dropping something. Price was not incompetent in the lazy sense. He felt overwhelmed by the institution, a system designed to move faster than poor defendants can keep up. At the first pretrial conference, Price asked for more time. Kerr smiled and objected with polished patience. "Your Honor," he said, "the community deserves closure."

Closure. A word that sounds humane and behaves like a weapon.

The judge, already drowning in docket pressure, agreed. The trial would proceed on schedule. That was institutional complacency in its most common form: a court mistaking speed for virtue.

Kerr built his case the way engineers build bridges: distribute the weight so no single beam looks responsible. A jailhouse informant claimed Marcus had "confessed." A neighbor recalled seeing a man "like him" near the apartment. A detective testified that Marcus "seemed deceptive" because he didn't make eye contact consistently. The forensic analyst repeated "consistent" with the seriousness of scripture.

Each piece alone was thin. Together, they created the illusion of thickness.

When Price attempted to challenge the informant, Kerr leaned into the microphone and spoke with mild disdain that the jury could feel.

"Mr. Price is trying to distract you," he said. "This isn't a college debate. This is a murder."

The line did two jobs at once: it diminished the defense, and it implied that only educated gamesmen question authority. Ordinary people, he suggested, should trust the state.

The most dangerous evidence never made it to the courtroom at all.

A supplemental report noted that investigators found another man's prints near the victim's window-partial, smudged, "inconclusive." A bloodstain examined, not belonging to the victim or the accused, never made it to the ledger.

Kerr shredded nothing. He didn't need to. He simply decided what counted.

In chemistry, you can shift a reaction's outcome by changing conditions rather than ingredients: temperature, pressure, concentration. Kerr changed conditions. He set the atmosphere so doubt felt irresponsible.

During closing arguments, a thunderstorm rolled in. Rain hammered the courthouse windows in bursts, and the jurors flinched at the sound as if the world outside were agreeing with the drama inside. Kerr used the moment instinctively.

"Some storms," he said, his voice steady, "are not accidents." They are intentional acts.

He pointed at Marcus. He spoke of "predators" and "choice" and "accountability." He did not speak of probability or uncertainty. He did not speak of reasonable doubt as a scientific standard. He spoke of evil as a simple mechanism.

Price's closing was earnest and fragmented. He tried to explain the holes, but he couldn't make the holes feel heavier than Kerr's narrative. He lacked time, resources, and-most importantly-social authority. He sounded like a man asking educated people to listen to the less educated.

The jury convicted. The penalty phase followed like an inevitable second act. Kerr argued for death with the calm certainty of someone who believed punishment purified the state. Marcus sat motionless, as if his body had turned to stone to survive what his mind couldn't. When the judge pronounced the sentence, the courtroom air felt colder, like a pressure drop before a new front moves in. Kerr closed his folder and shook hands with the victim's family. Cameras captured his solemn face. The headline the next day called him "relentless." It was intended as praise.

Years later, when doubt surfaced-DNA advances, a new witness, a confession from another man-Kerr responded with contempt.

He called innocence claims "games." He called defense lawyers "opportunists." He implied that the public was too gullible to understand how the system worked. He had built his identity on being right. And like certain brittle materials, once that identity hardened, it could not flex without cracking.

Marcus's life shrank to a cell. Kerr's life expanded-promotions, interviews, a future built on the confidence that he had served justice.

The tragedy was not that Randall Kerr was a villain in the theatrical sense. The tragedy was that he was ordinary in the institutional sense: a lawyer who learned that if you speak with enough authority, the system will treat your story as physics and everyone else's doubt as noise.

PRGR END-CAP - AUTHORED HARM TEST

(for "THE LAWYER WHO SENT THE INNOCENT TO DEATH")

The harm in this case is not a single error. It is a sequence of *ordinary defense decisions* that-under capital pressure-become irreversible. The lawyer doesn't "pull a lever" marked *execution*. He makes smaller choices that narrow the world until the state's narrative becomes the only one left standing.

PRGR would attach authorship at the first hinge-step where counsel accepts an irreversible disadvantage as "normal." In a death case, "normal" can kill.

The hinge-steps where PRGR would force the author to exist

The funding request denial - and the moment counsel continues anyway
When counsel requests funds for investigators, mitigation specialists, or independent forensic testing and is denied, the danger is not only institutional. The danger is what happens next: the case proceeds as if the denial were weather.
PRGR triggers the moment counsel chooses to go forward without escalating, documenting, or forcing the denial into a higher record.

He must author:

what resources were requested and denied,

what foreseeable harm follows (unchallenged forensic claims, missed witnesses, inadequate mitigation), what alternatives exist (continuance motion, renewed request, appellate writ, co-counsel support),

and why proceeding is still ethically defensible.

In this case, *the denial itself is authored harm by the system*, but PRGR also forces counsel to author the downstream choice: **to accept the denial as final reality**.

The missed investigation step - the witness not interviewed, the lead not chased
If counsel does not interview the state's informant, does not track down alibi leads, or does not test alternative suspects because time/resources are insufficient, PRGR triggers

at the decision to triage.

He must author:

what was not done, why it was not done,

what harm is foreseeable (unrebutted testimony, unchallenged credibility),

and what mitigation measures were attempted.
PRGR is not naive about constraints; it is strict about **naming the constraint as causal** rather than letting "strategy" become a cover.

The forensic challenge step - the moment science is treated as authority rather than claim
When counsel does not obtain independent testing, does not consult experts, or does not meaningfully cross-examine forensic testimony, PRGR triggers at the point the state's science becomes unopposed. He must author:

what specific forensic assertions will go uncontested, what the jury is likely to infer,

and what alternative actions were attempted (Daubert/Frye motions, limited-scope expert consult, pro bono expert outreach). Because this is where "I couldn't" becomes indistinguishable from "I didn't."

The late motion / procedural default step - the deadline that becomes fate
If a motion is filed late, a disclosure request is missed, or an objection is not preserved, PRGR triggers at the moment the deadline passes.

Counsel must author:

why the deadline was missed,

what harm is foreseeable (loss of suppression, inability to raise on appeal),

and what immediate corrective steps were taken (motion for leave, continuance, record preservation). In capital cases, default is not a technicality. It is a locked door.

The plea advice / mitigation decision - the moment "pragmatism" narrows life
If counsel pressures a client toward a plea or fails to develop mitigation adequately

(trauma history, mental health, family context), PRGR triggers at the moment counsel recommends an irreversible path.

He must author:

what options were presented, what risks were explained, what mitigation was pursued,

and what information the client lacked when deciding. PRGR forces the record to show whether "pragmatism" was a reason or a surrender.

The institutional scapegoat step - when the system turns structure into personal failure
After the verdict, the discipline process often performs its own translation: underfunding becomes "poor performance," systemic inequality becomes "lack of competence." PRGR triggers at the committee's decision to punish counsel without naming the structural causes.

The committee must author:

what resource constraints existed,

why those constraints are not causally decisive (if that is their claim),

and what reforms they will implement if they truly believe standards were breached. Because without authored structural responsibility, punishment becomes theater.

What PRGR would force in this case (capital-specific protections)

1. **A "death-case irreversibility log"**
   PRGR would require a contemporaneous log of decisions that cannot be repaired later:

   funding denials and escalation attempts, forensic testing decisions, key witness interviews, preservation of objections, mitigation development steps.
   This makes the case auditable *before* the body is buried.

2. **Resource-denial authorship rule**

Any time a court denies necessary defense resources, PRGR forces a signed record by the denying authority (judge/administrator):
what was denied, why, and what foreseeable harm is accepted as a consequence.
If the state insists on death, PRGR insists the state must sign the cost of under-funding.

3. **An automatic escalation trigger**
   PRGR would require an automatic mechanism:
   "If a death case proceeds without independent forensic capacity or adequate investigation funding, an external oversight review is triggered."
   No reliance on a single exhausted attorney to be a hero.

4. **A post-verdict accountability symmetry**
   If the institution disciplines defense counsel for failure, PRGR requires parallel authored review of:
   prosecution disclosures, court funding decisions, and structural constraints.
   Otherwise, the system performs blame redistribution and calls it integrity.

PUT THE BRAKE INSIDE THE PROCESS

A VETO LANE PREVENTS THE MACHINE FROM COMPLETING ITS FAVORITE SENTENCE.

One judge left before my case even started. She stepped back. We knew each other in a professional capacity. Her preference for Mars bars was something I knew. Brain fuel which she shared during the long days we spend in the court room. Another energy filled that room: mutual respect. I still don't know whether it was a conflict of interest handled properly, or a refusal she couldn't explain without naming a moral line. Or did she not want to become an author of the system? That uncertainty is its own lesson. When a decision happens offstage, the mind fills the silence with possibilities: Was the outcome already set? Was the judgment drafted before the file was even opened? I've seen it before-language prepared in advance, waiting only for names and dates to be dropped in like variables.

Somewhere in this stretch, "accountability later" becomes accountability never. Reviews arrive after exits. Reports arrive after careers end. The harmed person is trained-by delay, by polite deferral, by the endless promise of a timeline-to stop expecting rescue before the committee has even convened.

So my PRGR point here is structural. PRGR must be a system, not a document: a pipeline with gates the institution cannot pass through until it has named the harm, faced the alternatives, and attached authorship to the choice. Not after. Before. While the decision still has the power to be different.

And the key piece of that pipeline-the one I keep thinking about as I write these chapters-is the veto lane: the step where the process stops until the moral work is done on paper. The veto lane is not drama. It is friction. It is the moment the institution is denied its easiest escape: proceeding on momentum while promising reflection later.

If you're wondering why the stories sound like repeats, it's because institutions have their own routing: the meeting, the adjournment, the "we'll get back to you," the panel, the timeline. Routing is where urgency goes to die.

A veto lane prevents the machine from completing its favorite sentence: "The process was followed."

33

"THE NOTARIAL KNAVE"

STANDARD IS A DANGEROUS WORD WHEN THE PERSON SPEAKING CONTROLS THE DEFINITION.

Notary misconduct investigations, Netherlands & Belgium, 2001-2010 (composite case)

Notary Pieter Van der Meer kept the stamp in a velvet-lined drawer, cradled like a relic. Notary Pieter Van der Meer would open that drawer slowly, almost ceremonially, as if the object inside held holiness rather than authority. The stamp's handle was dark wood that use had polished. Engravers inscribed his name and office in sharp, official letters on the metal plate beneath it.

When he pressed it into ink and brought it down onto a deed, the sound was satisfying-brief, final, decisive. A tiny impact that made strangers believe they had settled their lives correctly.

Pieter liked finales. He liked people who didn't argue.

In Antwerp, his office sat above a narrow street where bicycles hissed over wet cobbles and rainwater collected in seams. Inside, the air conditioning kept the air cool and dry. Framed certificates, Latin mottos, and photographs of Pieter shaking hands with people who looked important lined the walls. In this room, clients lowered their voices automatically, as if volume itself were disrespect.

Pieter cultivated that reflex.

His arrogance was quiet but constant. He spoke to clients as if they were students who had missed the lecture. When they didn't understand terms, he didn't translate; he repeated the same sentence more slowly, adding a faint smile that made their confusion feel like failure.

"Don't worry," he would say. "It's standard."

Standard is a dangerous word when the person speaking controls the definition.

His favorite clients were the ones most vulnerable to shame: widows, immigrants, tradespeople, anyone who feared looking ignorant in front of an educated man in a suit. He understood that fear and used it like gravity, pulling them toward compliance.

Marcel Verhoeven came to Pieter after his wife died. Marcel's hands bore the small scars of mechanical work-oil and metal, years of practical labor. He brought a folder of documents and grief, both slightly disorganized.

He apologized too often, a habit of people who've learned that institutions punish inconvenience. Pieter treated him with genial condescension.

"You're doing the right thing," Pieter said, and gestured to a chair as if granting permission. "We'll make everything tidy."

He said tidy the way a surgeon says sterile-implying safety, implying professionalism, implying there's no need to ask what happens behind the curtain.

Marcel signed where Pieter showed. Initialed where Pieter pointed. His pen hesitated once, not from doubt but from the weight of not knowing what he was agreeing to. Pieter noticed and leaned in slightly.

"It's just a formality," he murmured. "If you'd like, I can explain it, but it will only confuse things." Confuse things. Meaning: you will feel small.

Marcel signed.

What Pieter inserted wasn't a dramatic theft. The clause, which was clean, technical, and apparently reasonable, created a "contingency administration fee" that future "complexities" would trigger. Complexities can delay estates. Someone can request the documents again. A missing signature can be "discovered." The system is elastic in the hands of someone who understands where to pull.

In physics, a lever doesn't need much force if the fulcrum is placed correctly. Pieter's fulcrum was language. Legal phrasing, politely delivered, made ordinary people feel that resistance was both futile and embarrassing. He expanded from wills into real estate closings, where desperation is common and time pressure does half the coercion. He routed clients toward "preferred" surveyors and accountants who returned favors invisibly. He split invoices to avoid attention. He offered "expedited processing" for a fee that was always just low enough to feel normal and just high enough to sting.

When a couple questioned a charge, Pieter smiled as if indulging children.

"You must understand," he said, "property law is not something you learn from the internet."

That sentence carried the social hierarchy in miniature: educated authority above, ordinary people below, their questions treated as insolence.

Complaints surfaced, predictably, among those least equipped to complain. A widow felt the notary had overcharged her but could not articulate how. An immigrant family who couldn't afford a lawyer to challenge a notary. A contractor who noticed odd "consulting fees" but lacked the vocabulary to make it sound serious.

The Chamber of Notaries received these complaints and responded with the complacency of a guild protecting its own reflection.

"They misunderstand the process." "They're emotional." "They don't know what they signed."

They didn't know. That was the point.

Anouk Janssens, a notary-in-training, noticed what the Chamber preferred not to. Anouk was first-generation university educated, raised by parents who cleaned offices and drove deliveries. She had grown up hearing people like Pieter speak down to her family with polite smiles. She recognized that smile immediately.

Working under Pieter, she saw repeating structures across files: identical clauses appearing where they weren't necessary, vendor names recurring like a refrain, "administrative fees" rising sharply in cases involving vulnerable clients. It wasn't sloppy. The document was deliberately patterned.

She tried raising the issue gently. Pieter reacted with amusement.

"You have a strong sense of justice," he said, as if complimenting a child's drawing. "But you'll learn that clients are... unpredictable. They imagine harm when they're anxious."

He said: "Imagine as if the harm existed only in the minds of the uneducated."

Anouk stopped seeking his approval and started documenting. She compared templates. She tracked invoice structures. She noted which clients were steered toward which vendors. Her work was boring in the way evidence often is: repetition, spreadsheet logic, quiet arithmetic that doesn't care how charming someone is. When she submitted her file to the Chamber, the response was initially dismissive. Pieter had a stature. Pieter had photos with important people. Pieter had the office that persuades committees to believe their own comfort. But Anouk's documentation forced an audit.

Pieter performed innocence beautifully. He presented immaculate binders and spoke in formal language peppered with Latin phrases-unnecessary, decorative, designed to create altitude. He treated the auditors as colleagues and the complainants as inconveniences. He framed every charge as standard practice, every clause as prudent protection.

In chemistry, some toxins are colorless. They do not announce themselves with an odor. They simply accumulate until the body reacts.

The audit identified "irregularities." The word was chosen carefully-soft enough to avoid scandal, firm enough to justify restraint. Pieter received a reprimand, mandatory ethics training, and monitoring. Mediation agreements that included confidentiality clauses allowed the offer of partial reimbursement to several clients.

The Chamber protected the profession's image by letting the worst edges of Pieter's practice be sanded down. Pieter remained in the ecosystem, now operating more cautiously. He moved into consulting and training, showing notaries the "best ways" to work, with a smile that made him seem like a protector of good behavior, but in reality, he had been punished for using people's lack of understanding to his own benefit.

Anouk advanced, slowly, labeled "difficult" in the way institutions label anyone who insists that professionalism is not proof of respectability. She learned that the cleanest harms are often the easiest to excuse, because they leave no bruises-only receipts. Outside Pieter's office, rain kept falling onto cobblestones, water finding the smallest grooves and making them deeper. Pieter's work behaved the same way.

Not a flood. A drip. And an institution that treated dripping as normal until someone finally listened to the sound.

34

"THE MISSING VENOM"

TIMING IS WHERE OUTCOMES ARE SHAPED WITHOUT ANYONE NEEDING TO FALSIFY FACTS.

> Patterns of "soft corruption" in common-law courts-favor-trading, procedural gaming, and discretionary justice that stays just inside the line.
> New Zealand, 2010s (composite case)

New Zealand has no snakes. That absence becomes a national metaphor if you let it. In summer, children push through long grass without the reflex that Australians inherit-the quick recoil from a rustle, the half-remembered warning passed down like a family prayer. In Wellington, danger rarely arrives with a hiss. It arrives as weather: wind that changes direction without asking, rain that comes horizontal, and a cold that finds the seam in your coat.

Some visitors like to turn it into theology: Australia as hell, New Zealand as heaven. But heaven is not a place without venom. It is a place that admits what can poison you and builds its defences before the bite.

On Lambton Quay the wind can pick up a paper cup and carry it like a pale ghost down the street. It can make you blink, water your eyes, and question what you saw. The city teaches a small lesson in perception: the wind can push you off course without ever touching you.

The courtroom in Wellington was a contained world designed to feel safer than the street. Polished kauri benches held the light like honey. High ceilings drew every cough upward, making it seem smaller, less human. Old leather lingered in the air with a faint sweetness, as if age itself were respectable.

People entered and unconsciously straightened, surrendering a fraction of their posture to the architecture. Magistrate Henry Kavanagh was part of that architecture. He no longer wore a wig-an emblem of modern restraint, of adapting tradition to time. His black robes fell in clean lines. The plain white shirt and band were unadorned and severe, a visual promise that nothing about him was for sale.

He had a reputation for decorum. More importantly, people knew him for his calm demeanor.

It is difficult to fear a man who never raises his voice, who never looks hurried. Calm reads as competence. Competence reads as safety. And people crave safety when they walk into a room where a stranger's sentence can change their future.

Kavanagh built his reputation on that craving.

He spoke often about the difference between law and justice, as if he were careful not to confuse them.

He used words like "balance," "proportion," "mercy"-terms that sounded pastoral in a secular room. His colleagues described him as "measured." Lawyers described him as "fair." Defendants described him, when they dared, as "hard to read."

His secret relied on that last quality.

It began with kindness that looked ordinary.

A local business owner appeared on a minor tax matter and received an adjournment that was granted with a tone of patient understanding. A man caught with drugs was guided toward rehabilitation rather than formal sentencing; Kavanagh spoke about "turning points" and "community health," and the family wept with gratitude.

Another defendant, with no one to advocate well for him, received a harsher penalty for a comparable offence-delivered with the same tone, the same calm, the same measured gaze.

These were not bribes. These were not threats. They were differences in weight applied to the scale, tiny adjustments that looked like discretion and felt like fate.

Kavanagh told himself he was doing what the law could not: adjusting for the human texture of each life. It was not corrupt; he argued inwardly, to be merciful. It was, if anything, a correction to the system's bluntness.

But mercy has a shadow. It creates gratitude. Gratitude becomes loyalty. Loyalty becomes expectation. Expectation becomes leverage.

He learned which people returned favors. Which people could make introductions? Which people, given a nudge, would donate to the charities that made him look civic-minded without asking too many questions? He learned how generosity could become a chain without ever looking like one.

And because New Zealand has no snakes, the courtroom had fewer people trained to spot a hidden bite. Kavanagh kept a ledger.

Not a crude list of payments-nothing so easy to prosecute, nothing that would make a headline in a clean moral font. His ledger contained coded, neat annotations. These annotations could have been case summaries if one lacked the specific knowledge. A star beside a name. A notation about "character."

A line that read like an administrative reminder: Follow-up-community support. A page reference that meant something only to him.

It was, in its way, a second court: private, personal, unappealable.

The ledger noted favors, similar to weather records, by tracking patterns, pressure systems, and how a case might be steered. It tracked who owed him respect and who might repay "mercy" with access. It was obsessive, careful, almost tender in its detail. A man can do terrible things with tenderness.

The authorities assigned Sophie Miller to assist him when the courts were tightening processes, modernizing filing, and digitizing what they could.

Sophie was not naive. She had watched enough procedure to understand how easily it becomes religion-how the system can worship itself. But she still believed something simple: the record matters.

She noticed small abrasions against that belief.

A case file signed out without the usual notation. A witness subpoena delayed and then "unnecessary." A prosecutor who changed tone after a private word with the magistrate-nothing overt, just a soft pivot, like a compass pulled by a hidden magnet. A defence lawyer who won too often, not through brilliance but through timing.

It was the timing that bothered her most. Timing is where discretion hides. Timing shapes outcomes with no one needing to falsify facts.

She brought up one anomaly lightly-testing the water.

Kavanagh smiled, the sort of smile that makes people apologize for questioning. "You'll find," he said, "that law is also logistics."

It sounded like mentorship. It landed like a warning.

Sophie's doubts did not arrive as a single revelation. They arrived like Wellington rain: gradually, then all at once. She kept her own notes-dates, file movements, the small irregularities that seemed to orbit the same names. She told herself she was simply being diligent, that this was what competence looked like.

But at night, walking home through wind that smelled of salt and cold iron, she felt the heavier meaning: she was documenting a pattern because her instincts were no longer willing to be soothed by calm.

The ledger revealed itself by accident, as most secrets do-through the arrogance of the person who thinks concealment is permanent.

A joiner repaired a panel in the magistrate's chambers after a minor leak. A join line sat slightly misaligned. Sophie noticed because she noticed everything. When she opened the storage space to retrieve a box of archived notes, she saw the false panel behind it-wood that looked too clean, too deliberate.

Behind it, wrapped in a plain folder with no label, was the ledger.

Its pages were dense with shorthand. It looked, at first glance, like a scholar's private work: neat, systematic, self-contained. But the pattern-names recurring, outcomes aligned, annotations matching the anomalies she'd tracked-made the air in her chest tighten.

It wasn't a diary. It was a map. And she had just found the path the magistrate used to walk around the public records.

Sophie sat still, hearing the building's quiet hum-electricity, distant footsteps, the slow breath of institutions. Then the harder thought arrived: what if she had it wrong? What if she had misread the code? What if this was simply an eccentric way of organising judicial notes?

That is how power survives: by making the observer doubt their own eyesight.

Outside, the sky over Wellington can look like a blank slate. Clouds move fast. Light changes abruptly. People describe the city as "honest" because it cannot hide its weather. But Sophie realised that a system can have honest weather and dishonest rooms.

She confided in a senior judicial ethics officer-someone older, steady, someone the institution itself treated as trustworthy. Even then, as she handed over copies and observations, a second doubt rose: could she trust this person? Or would the machine protect itself, using her evidence as a sponge and her career as a mop?

In a world that values decorum, people often view truth as a disturbance.

The investigation moved carefully, almost politely. The investigators cross-referenced each annotation with the files. The investigators measured each "coincidence" against the next. Kavanagh continued to preside, face calm, robes immaculate, the white bands as crisp as ever. He seemed like a person who had never been asked anything, which was precisely why he had not anticipated it.

When they asked him about irregularities, he answered with the same calm that had built his reputation. "You are mistaking discretion for misconduct," he said. "I am not a machine."

The line was clever. It wasn't false. That's what made it dangerous.

Discretion is necessary. Human judgment is necessary. And because they are necessary, they can be weaponized with no one wanting to believe it.

The tribunal's conclusion used careful language-the kind that allows institutions to sound decisive without sounding self-indicting. "Impermissible pattern of influence." "Failure of impartiality." "Breach of judicial ethics." No criminal charge-no one wanted to claim something poisonous had bitten the court, especially not in a country proud of having no snakes.

The authorities reprimanded Kavanagh. His discretion underwent restrictions. They imposed oversight like a fence, building it after the livestock had already wandered into the ravine.

He remained on the bench.

That was the part that split the public into three camps, as institutions always do. Some people insisted the system had worked: oversight had found the breach and corrected it. Others insisted that the system had guarded itself; a different person would have been destroyed. Many-perhaps most-simply went quiet because it is exhausting to hold both truths at once.

Sophie did not feel victory. She felt a tightening in her understanding of the world.

In her memory, the ledger wasn't just evidence. It was a mirror held up to a culture that confuses calm with goodness and tradition with virtue. She had learned that a country lacking snakes could still harbor hidden venom. Not in the grass, but in the gentle rooms where decision-makers convene.

Afterward, the courtroom looked unchanged: kauri still gleaming, leather still sweet with age, ceiling still drawing sound upward. Kavanagh still entered his robe, white bands framing his face like punctuation. But the room's meaning had shifted, as meanings do-quietly, almost invisibly.

New Zealand, Australia-heaven, hell. Sophie found she could no longer tolerate the simplicity. The difference between places is not whether danger exists. It is whether you learn to name it when it wears the uniform of safety.

And the hardest lesson of all, the one the ledger made unavoidable, was this:

A system can be proud of what it keeps out of the country-snakes, weapons, disease-while failing to notice the infection it grows inside its own walls.

Because not every poison arrives with fangs. Some arrive with decorum.

35

"THE QADI'S SIGNET"

WHEN A SEAL BECOMES MERCHANDISE, TRUTH BECOMES A RUMOR.

Composite patterns of court corruption and "paper legality" used to launder wrongdoing (fictionalized).

The river ran low that year, stones exposed like knuckles. Hot wind carried the smell of dry reeds into town, a reminder that nature keeps its own ledgers.

Qadi Salim Najjar kept ledgers too-bound in leather and stamped with authority. His power lived in a small object: a silver signet ring engraved with a geometric seal. When he pressed it into ink, paper became law.

The case that changed him began as a property dispute. A widow named Huda claimed her late husband's orchard, which his brothers had seized. The brothers arrived with crisp documents and confident witnesses. Huda arrived with her son and a folder of handwritten receipts, her scarf pinned tight as if to hold herself together.

Salim listened, asked questions, then postponed. Postponement is a quiet form of power: it drains the weak and strengthens the patient. Outside, the orchard ripened. Huda returned, each visit thinner with expense.

Meanwhile, the brothers' lawyer became a frequent presence in the court's corridors. The first "gift" came as civic generosity: a donation to the court's library. The second came as a convenience: a promise of a municipal job for Salim's nephew. No one addressed any of it to Salim directly. That was how corruption kept itself polite. Salim told himself he could accept "support" without selling judgment. He told himself he merited respect because of his burden. Most dangerously, he told himself his intentions were pure, and therefore his actions could not be impure.

A junior scribe named Rafiq noticed the drift. He watched certain filings receive immediate stamps while others stalled in trays that always seemed to sink. When he asked the senior clerk why, the clerk shrugged. "Some people know how the world works."

Rafiq answered, "Isn't this why we have a court? So the world works differently here?" The clerk smiled only.

On the day Salim was to issue his verdict, he sat alone with Huda's file open. The receipts were messy, but the story was consistent. He knew she was right. He also knew that ruling for her would make enemies with deeper pockets than her truth.

He reached for the signet ring. The metal was cool, reassuring: a tool that could end uncertainty. He stamped the verdict against Huda.

The language was careful: "insufficient documentation," "customary settlement," "debts outstanding." It sounded neutral. Neutrality is how injustice dresses itself when it wants to sleep. Huda did not cry. She simply looked at the paper as if it had become a weapon.

Weeks later, the orchard was sold. Men who did not know the trees' history harvested the pomegranates. Huda moved into her sister's cramped apartment. Her son left school to work in the market. The court record showed an orderly resolution. Reality showed erosion.

On Eid morning, the town dressed itself in brightness. Children ran with sweet bread in hand. Salim stood in the front row at the prayer ground, and men greeted him with respect as if respect were proof. Huda stood at the edge with other women, face lowered. Her son avoided the qadi's eyes. Salim felt a flicker of discomfort and drowned it in ceremony. A flock of birds wheeled overhead, shifting direction as one body, as if the sky itself obeyed a silent command.

Rafiq could not let it settle. He began copying case numbers, dates, and patterns. He noted which attorneys appeared repeatedly and which verdicts carried Salim's seal after short hearings. It wasn't one bribe; it was a weather system.

Rafiq, meanwhile, felt watched. A stranger lingered by his door. His father warned him to "leave it." Friends advised patience. Rafiq kept writing anyway because he understood that silence is also a verdict. In the evenings he walked to the riverbank where water slid around exposed stones, never stopping, never apologizing. He took it as instruction: truth does not need to shout; it needs to persist.

When auditors from the capital announced surprise reviews of local courts, it felt, to the town, like thunder from a clear sky. Officers requested disclosures and traced "donations" linked to families who kept winning disputes. They asked about the nephew's job. They asked why so many cases ended with the same firm's "settlements."

Salim insisted he was innocent. He spoke of tradition, community support, and misunderstandings. He spoke about procedure-every step recorded, every stamp allowed. He did not understand that the procedure was now the blade, because it had been used to cut away a widow's rights while smiling.

Rafiq submitted his notes anonymously. He expected relief. What he felt instead was grief: for Huda, for the orchard, because the seal meant fairness.

The inquiry did not end the court. The inquiry quietly removed Salim, using official language about "administrative review."

The town split: some said politics scarified the qadi; others said everyone had known and simply preferred the peace of denial.

The market kept selling fish.

The river kept running low.

At home, Salim slipped the signet ring off and placed it in a drawer. Without it, his hand looked smaller. Outside, wind moved through reeds, making them bow and rise in waves. Without bribery, nature bends tall things and exposes hidden things.

The moral settled slowly, like silt after a flood: when a seal becomes merchandise, truth becomes a rumor.

And when a system prefers rescue over audits, removals over protection, independent oversight, transparent gift rules, real access for the weak, the river keeps running low, and the stones keep showing through.

36

"THE MAGISTRATE'S SECRET"

BOREDOM IS HARDER TO EXPLOIT THAN INTIMACY.

Judicial sexual and financial misconduct, Italy, 2021 (composite case)

Magistrate Lorenzo Bianchi of Naples presided over his courtroom with a presence that demanded space. His black robe and precisely arranged bavaglino carried the weight of inherited ritual-centuries of law translated into cloth and posture. Attorneys adjusted their tone when they addressed him. Defendants watched his hands as if hands could reveal fate. Court staff moved with extra care, not because he shouted, but because he rarely had to.

Naples itself seemed built for double truths. The city's light can dazzle even when the streets feel bruised. Vesuvius sits beyond the bay, serene and unsentimental: a reminder that calmness isn't innocence, only dormancy. On humid days the air smells faintly of salt and exhaust, and the sea breeze brings relief that never quite cleans.

People here know that beauty and danger can share the same skyline.

Bianchi's misconduct was deliberate and methodical. Those seeking favorable rulings or procedural leniency, Bianchi pressed into compliance and financial "contributions," though the coercion almost never wore a blunt face. He preferred the softer instruments: implication, timing, private access.

He designed a world where refusal did not result in an obvious strike but led to a thousand small frictions, such as postponements, missing signatures, sudden strictness, and an inexplicable chill that spread quietly through administrative channels.

He told himself stories to keep the mirror usable. He wasn't taking; he believed-he was "managing." He wasn't coercing, he insisted inwardly-he was "testing loyalty." He didn't think of himself as a predator; he thought of himself as a realist in a city where everyone, he assumed, wanted something. This was his first human weakness: the need to believe his own appetite was wisdom.

His second weakness was vanity, more fragile than it looked. The robe and bavaglino weren't merely uniform; they were a daily confirmation that he mattered. In chambers, he enjoyed the micro-movements of deference-the pause before someone contradicted him, the quick nod when he spoke, the way juniors laughed a little too hard at his mild jokes.

He could not tolerate feeling ordinary. He kept himself above the crowd partly because he feared how replaceable he was within it.

Giulia Romano, a newly appointed junior judge, received an invitation to his private chambers under the guise of discussing case strategy. The invitation was framed as an opportunity: "I want to help you learn how to navigate." That phrasing-help, learn, navigate-activated another weakness: ambition mixed with gratitude. She arrived with a file and a careful, professional smile.

The room itself felt like a lesson in boundaries. The windows remained shut. The air carried the faint scent of cologne and old paper. Bianchi spoke at first about procedural options, then drifted toward her future as if he were already writing it. Compliments arrived in the language of authority-measured, flattering, plausible. "You have instincts," he said. "Don't waste them."

"I'm focused on the client," Giulia replied.

Bianchi's gaze held too long. Clients come and go. Bianchi built careers.

Giulia understood the subtext without being given a line to quote. It was not a proposition made in crude words; it was an atmosphere built to corner her. Her clients' outcomes, her reputation, her trajectory-those were the levers he had. The cruel part was how easily the system made that leverage feel natural. A single person controlled too many doors, and the institution had taught everyone to accept it.

Here, doubt entered her life as something almost companionable-an inner figure she privately called L'Ombra, the shadow, because it followed her everywhere and lengthened at night. Doubt did not deny what she felt; it complicated it. It offered counterarguments like a defense counsel for fear: Maybe you misread. Maybe you're overreacting. Maybe this is just the way powerful men speak. Maybe someone will brand you difficult. Maybe the court will close ranks. Doubt was not stupidity; it was a survival instinct trained by hierarchy.

Meanwhile, the financial extortion ran like an underground stream. The magistrate encouraged clerks to "support the magistrate's initiatives." Attorneys were quietly advised that "contributions" smoothed processes. Even peers felt pressure to take part in dinners, associations, committees that seemed civic on the surface but functioned like tribute.

No one payment looked dramatic; that was the design. It relied on another human weakness: the temptation to tell yourself it's only this once, because "only once" is how habits are born.

People build systems, and people comprise existence, enabling him. Some staff stayed silent because they wanted promotions and feared being sidelined. Some stayed silent because they didn't want to be the first to speak and become a target. Some stayed silent because acknowledging the truth would force them to admit they had benefited from it-small favors, accelerated paperwork, a relative's internship quietly approved.

Even the decent ones were vulnerable to the oldest weakness of all: the desire to keep life uncomplicated. Reporting channels existed, but they were thin reeds against a powerful tide. Complaints required names, signatures, and risks. Anonymous whispers were like smoke: irritating, easy for people to wave away. Bianchi understood this. He kept records-notes, messages, dates-less as evidence for court and more as insurance for himself.

People who comply under pressure often leave a trace of that compliance, and he collected traces the way a fisher collects nets.

Giulia fought in the only way that didn't immediately crush her: she became meticulous. She saved emails. She wrote times and contexts. She asked for meetings in the presence of others. She moved conversations into spaces with witnesses. She made her practice boring on purpose-because boredom is harder to exploit than intimacy.

A clerk named Paolo-quiet, conscientious-noticed her caution. One evening, as rain rattled the courthouse windows and the corridors emptied, he paused beside her desk.

"You're being careful," he said, barely audible. Giulia looked up. "I have to be."

Paolo hesitated, the hesitation of a man fighting his own fear. Then: "You're not alone."

That sentence did more than comfort her. It gave her doubt a counterweight: if others saw it too; it wasn't imagination. Paolo's weakness had been fear; his strength arrived late, but it arrived.

Eventually, investigative journalism and whistleblower reports forced the story into the daylight. Once it became public, the pattern sharpened. What had seemed like isolated discomforts revealed a consistent mechanism: private access used as pressure, procedure used as threat, ritual used as camouflage. Official inquiries corroborated multiple accounts.

This time, denial had less room to breathe.

Bianchi's suspension and prosecution followed. The government announced reforms: oversight, transparent reporting, and monitoring. The court spoke the language of repair. Yet the contradiction remained plain. The institution could move quickly once exposed, but it had moved slowly when people first hinted at harm.

Rescue was dramatic; prevention would have been quiet and inconvenient-limiting private meetings, rotating power, protecting complainants before the headlines arrived.

Giulia's career continued, but not unchanged. She gained credibility and lost innocence. Paolo kept his job, but his hands shook less when he walked past Bianchi's former door. The courthouse returned to routine-the great anesthetic of bureaucracy-yet certain staff now insisted on written instructions, open doors, and documented decisions. It was a modest shift, but meaningful: a refusal to let symbolism substitute for safety.

Outside, Naples kept doing what it always does-sea wind, street noise, volcanic calm. Vesuvius remained on the horizon, indifferent. The city offered its oldest lesson: what looks stable may only be sleeping. Silence does not keep something quiet forever-it simply waits for when enough human weakness, stacked together, can no longer hold the weight.

DON'T SCAPEGOAT THE POWERLESS

WHO HAD THE ACTUAL ABILITY TO STOP THIS—AND DIDN’T?

Was I powerless? I don’t think so. The institution didn’t treat me like a weak person. It treated me like a risk-because I challenged them with proof. The imbalance wasn’t in intelligence or status. It was in stop-power. I could show. They could decide. I noted; they watched; they concluded I was a threat.

These chapters carry a particular cruelty because the pattern is so familiar: systems protect themselves by offering up the smallest person who can plausibly be blamed. The institution stays spotless by sacrificing someone who never had the power to prevent the harm in the first place.

So here is my PRGR point: **authorship without scapegoating.** The responsible signatory must be the smallest role with real stop-power-the person who can halt, modify, delay, or force higher review. Not the clerk who typed the letter. Not the junior who followed an instruction. Not the staff member positioned as a convenient container for institutional discomfort.

If I force a powerless person to sign, PRGR dies. I’ve seen "accountability" used as a disciplinary weapon aimed downward because it’s safer than aiming at the people who actually steer. A signature becomes a trap. "You signed it" becomes the excuse that protects the architects.

PRGR is meant to do the opposite. It is a mirror held up to power, not a punishment for staff trying to survive. The repetition across chapters isn't accidental. It's the exportable architecture of blame: keep authority diffuse, keep consequences concentrated. If I catch myself searching for the villain in each story, I pause. The more reliable question is simpler and colder:

Who had the actual ability to stop this-and didn't? That is where authorship belongs.

37

"THE MAGISTRATE'S WHISPER"

POWER DOES NOT NEED TO SHOUT TO DOMINATE.

Judicial misconduct investigations, Netherlands, 2004-2012 (composite case), PRGR

Builders constructed the courthouse to dampen sound.

Thick stone walls absorbed footsteps, varnished floors swallowed echoes, and the high ceiling scattered voices until they arrived softened, almost courteous. On humid days, when the air pressed inward and refused to circulate, even raised voices lost their edge. It was a building designed for gravity, not noise. In certain corners the air smelled faintly of limestone and old paper, as if the place were a cave that had learned bureaucracy-layers accumulating, moisture held in, light rationed. Even the fluorescent fixtures seemed to hum at a low frequency, the kind you feel more than hear, like an institutional heartbeat insisting on calm.

Magistrate Pieter de Vries understood this architecture the way some people understand music. He did not merely work inside the building. He tuned himself to it.

He rarely raised his voice. He didn't need to. His power worked better at low volume. His father-an earnest man who believed in rules the way believers believe in prayer-used to say that shouting was what people did when they had already lost control. Pieter carried that sentence like a small, polished stone in his pocket. When he was young, he had watched louder men lose arguments to quiet ones. He had decided early what kind of man he would become.

From the bench, he appeared meticulous-black robe uncreased, white bef centered with geometric precision. The visual language was exact: symmetry, restraint, education. To outsiders, he looked like justice made legible. To the staff, he looked like someone whose approval mattered more than written policy.

The arrogance was not loud. The arrogance was curated.

De Vries believed in hierarchy not as ideology but as **hygiene**. Without it, he thought, everything decayed: courtrooms into chaos, language into noise, people into impulse. He feared disorder the way some people fear illness. It wasn't that he hated others; he distrusted what he called *untrained minds*. He did not use that phrase in public. He preferred gentler words: *professionalism*, *standards*, *rigor*.

In private, he was less gentle.

He had a habit, when a person hesitated, of adjusting his cuff as if aligning himself with procedure. The gesture was small, almost elegant. It signaled impatience without ever becoming anger. It let him perform superiority while remaining polite.

His interactions followed a pattern that few noticed until they were inside it.

An intern would be invited into chambers "to talk about career development." The door would close-not dramatically, just firmly enough to signal privacy. De Vries would sit with his hands folded as if he had all the time in the world, and he would lower his voice as if he were doing the intern a favor by confiding something true.

"You have potential," he would begin. Praise came first. Then calibration.

"You're very capable, but you doubt yourself." "You need to learn how this place really works." "Not everyone is suited for responsibility."

He spoke as though uncertainty were a character flaw rather than the nervous system's accurate response to power. The intern would leave feeling seen and unsettled, unable to name what had happened. That was part of the technique: if you cannot name the harm, you cannot report it without sounding unstable.

Sometimes afterward, the intern would find a small "opportunity" waiting-access to a hearing list, an introduction to a judge, a compliment repeated in public. Like a variable reward in conditioning experiments, it made the mind search for the rule that would keep the reward coming.

De Vries enjoyed that search.

He liked watching a young person attempt to become legible to him, the way defendants attempt to become credible to the court. He did not think of it as cruelty. He thought of it as instruction. The intern's discomfort was proof-proof that the lesson was taking.

In psychology, this is a known effect: cognitive dissonance amplified by authority. The mind tries to reconcile approval with unease and often resolves the conflict by blaming itself.

De Vries relied on that resolution. He cultivated it. He made self-blame feel like maturity.

With defendants, his approach was different but equally precise. He addressed them slowly, carefully, as if translating complex ideas for a child. His questions were shaped to make ignorance visible.

"You understood the terms, didn't you?" "You read the document before signing?" "You know what consequences mean?"

The courtroom heard neutral questions. Defendants heard accusation. When they hesitated, he would sigh softly-not with anger, but with disappointment. The sigh conveyed a message: you are not equipped for this world. He never mocked them outright. He used something colder: the suggestion that their confusion was proof of their inferiority.

His favorite phrase-always delivered gently, like advice-was: "We must be serious."

He said it to defendants. He said it to interns. He said it to clerks who questioned him. It made seriousness sound like a moral category that only he could grant.

Colleagues noticed his manner and dismissed it as rigor.

"That's just his style," one senior clerk said. "He expects professionalism." "Some people need to be guided firmly."

This was institutional complacency at work-not denial, but rationalization. The system preferred to believe that authority, properly dressed and properly credentialed, could not be misusing itself. After all, de Vries possessed a formal education. Measured. Civil.

And civility is often mistaken for ethics.

The first formal complaint came from Marieke van Damme, a court clerk with twenty years of service and no taste for drama. She didn't accuse de Vries of anything sensational. She described patterns.

Staff leaving chambers shaken without being able to say why. Interns becoming unusually dependent on his approval. Defendants describing hearings that felt less like procedure and more like interrogation.

Marieke's report was factual, restrained, and deeply inconvenient. She wrote it the way a biologist records symptoms in a population: not one animal, not one incident-an observable drift in behavior that suggests something in the environment is wrong.

Oversight responded cautiously. Investigators reviewed schedules, emails, and case flows. Nothing illegal appeared. Nothing explosive. De Vries's communications were immaculate-professionally phrased, legally defensible, emotionally invasive only in tone.

But tone is not nothing.

In physics, pressure doesn't need impact to cause damage. Sustained force, applied slowly, reshapes structures just as effectively. De Vries applied pressure in precisely this way-through implication, through silence, through the strategic withholding of reassurance. Like humidity working into wood, it did not crack the surface at once; it warped it.

When questioned, he defended himself with polished superiority.

"These are misunderstandings," he said calmly, adjusting his cuff. "Younger staff today lack resilience." "People misinterpret mentorship."

He spoke as if discomfort were evidence of immaturity rather than misuse of authority. He framed criticism as ignorance. He implied that those lacking legal training shouldn't be trusted to interpret their own experiences. He smiled once, briefly, as if he were indulging them. "We cannot run a courthouse on feelings."

That sentence-spoken quietly-shifted the inquiry.

Because it revealed the premise beneath his conduct: education as entitlement, and emotional reality as irrelevant data.

The investigation expanded. Investigators interviewed former interns away from the courthouse, where the walls no longer pressed inward. Patterns aligned. Language repeated. Emotional responses matched with uncanny consistency.

No one described shouting. No one described threats. Everyone described the same internal collapse.

PRGR END-CAP - AUTHORED HARM TEST

(for "THE MAGISTRATE'S WHISPER")

The harm in this case doesn't begin with a shout or a slur. It begins with a subtler instrument: **tone used as governance.** De Vries doesn't need to break rules loudly; he makes people *blame themselves* for feeling the rule being bent.

PRGR would attach authorship at the first hinge-step where the magistrate converts institutional tools-private chambers, questioning style, access decisions-into pressure that changes outcomes. In this story, the harm is administered through **humidity**, not impact: sustained force that warps people until they stop trusting their own perception.

The hinge-steps where PRGR would force the author to exist

The private-chambers "career development" invitation

When De Vries begins inviting interns into chambers for private "development" conversations, PRGR triggers at the decision to create a closed-door corridor.

He must author:

why the meeting requires privacy, what legitimate work purpose it serves,

what safeguards exist (open-door default, third party available, documented agenda),

and what the intern can do if uncomfortable without career penalty.
Because in this case, the first harm is unreviewable access.

The variable-reward access step - granting opportunities after compliance

De Vries's leverage is not overt threat; it is **selective oxygen**: access to lists, introductions, compliments repeated in public after a private meeting.
PRGR triggers at the moment he grants a career-affecting "opportunity" tied to personal proximity rather than objective criteria.

He must author:

why this intern receives access, what criteria were used,

what alternatives exist (rotation, transparent selection),

and what foreseeable harms follow (dependency, coercion, chilling effect on dissent). PRGR forces him to name whether access is reward-or merit.

The questioning-as-humiliation step - extracting ignorance as evidence
With defendants, De Vries's questions are formally neutral but structurally loaded: they force the defendant to display lack of education and then treat that display as credibility failure.
PRGR triggers at the moment he adopts a questioning style that predictably produces self-incrimination or shame through misunderstanding.

He must author:

why this line of questioning is necessary,

what safeguards ensure comprehension (plain-language explanations, interpreter support, confirming understanding),

what foreseeable harms exist (false admissions, coerced agreement, procedural surrender).
This turns "neutral questions" into **audited pressure**.

The sigh / disappointment tactic - tone used to steer outcomes
In this chapter, the sigh is not decoration; it is the method. It signals incompetence without stating it, pushing defendants and interns to scramble for approval. PRGR triggers when tone becomes a repeatable steering tool-when the magistrate's disappointment reliably produces compliance. He must author:

what objective basis exists for the implied judgment,

and why the same message could not be delivered through clear procedural explanation instead of insinuation.
PRGR forces the institution to treat tone as action when tone functions like action.

The retaliation-by-access step - who is excluded after discomfort or complaint
When staff begin leaving chambers shaken, and then-quietly-some interns stop being offered opportunities, PRGR triggers at the access decision. Someone must author:

why the intern's exposure changed (assignments, lists, introductions), what evidence justifies it,

and what harm is foreseeable (career derailment, silence culture).
Because in this case, punishment arrives as absence, and absence is easy to deny unless decisions are forced into record.

The institutional containment step - "style" used as an exemption
When colleagues dismiss patterns as "just his style" and oversight responds with careful procedural language, PRGR triggers at the decision to treat patterned harm as personality.

The institution must author:

what patterns were identified,

why they do not constitute misuse of authority (if that's the claim),

and what safeguards will prevent recurrence if they do constitute misuse. PRGR prevents the classic wash: civility mistaken for ethics.

What PRGR would force *in this case* (matched to courtroom power)

1. **No unreviewable private corridor with interns**
   PRGR would require default transparency: scheduled meetings, agenda-noted purposes, optional third party, open-door norm unless justified in writing.

2. **A "career oxygen" log**
   Because the harm channel is access, PRGR would require documentation of: internship opportunities,
   shadowing assignments, introductions, speaking roles, with objective criteria and rotation rules. This makes selective reward auditable.

3. **A comprehension safeguard for defendants**
   PRGR would require a plain-language confirmation step for high-stakes questions:
   "Explain in your own words what you understand," interpreter checks, recorded explanations.
   The point is to prevent ignorance from becoming an involuntary confession.

4. **A retaliation tripwire tied to access shifts**
   If any intern or staff member reports discomfort and then experiences access loss, PRGR triggers automatic review-because retaliation here is administered through "normal" discretionary decisions.

The questions that keep this End-Cap case-specific to De Vries

If you were De Vries: can you write, and sign, why an intern was granted or denied meaningful access-without relying on "fit," "tone," or "seriousness"?

If you were an intern or clerk: what is the first hinge-step you would force into authored form-the private meeting, the selective opportunity, or the subtle exclusion afterward?

If you were oversight: are you willing to author that "style" is harmless-knowing the foreseeable harm is a courthouse culture where people learn resistance is unreasonable?

PRGR doesn't accuse De Vries of shouting. It isolates the moment he **turned low-volume authority into sustained pressure**-and forces a named author to exist at the exact step where access and tone became instruments that reshaped careers and outcomes.

38

"THE CHANCELLOR'S DECEPTION"

AN ECOSYSTEM WHERE FEAR REPLACED HONEST CHALLENGE, WHERE DEFERENCE REPLACED VERIFICATION.

Academic corruption and misconduct, People's Republic of China, 2020 (composite case)

Beijing winters have a particular way of making certainty feel official. The air turns brittle. The trees hold their branches like spare scaffolding. On the campus of Beijing University, the old stone buildings and new glass towers sit side by side as if time itself has agreed to cooperate. In that cold, discipline looks like virtue, and hierarchy looks like order.

Chancellor Li Wei moved through it all in a robe and ceremonial jabot that seemed to translate prestige into gravity. When he entered a hall, people adjusted their posture without thinking. Students lowered their voices. Junior faculty smiled carefully. Visiting scholars spoke of his "vision" with the same tone they used for the university's history-as if both were forces you did not question.

To the public, Li Wei's attire symbolised mentorship, fairness, and the ethical stewardship of knowledge. Inside the institution, it functioned like a seal. It marked him as untouchable. And because it looked like legitimacy, it encouraged others to outsource their moral judgment to the costume.

He kept a ledger.

Not an accounting ledger alone-though it held numbers-but a private register of compliance: who owed him, who had yielded, who had been "supported" and at what cost. In the language of power, it was a map of leverage. In the university's language, it was invisible.

Li Wei's misconduct was deliberate and sustained. The professor pressured graduate students into sexual compliance under the guise of mentorship, affecting their pursuit of scholarships, lab placements, conference travel, or career advancement. Junior faculty seeking promotions and funding contributed to personal initiatives and took part in projects that merged Li Wei's network, which were framed as "donations." Refusal didn't trigger dramatic punishment. It triggered a colder kind: stalled approvals, missing signatures, postponed meetings that never returned. In a bureaucracy, delay is a blade that leaves no blood.

Ying Zhao, a doctoral candidate in biomedical sciences, first recognized the coercive nature of his "guidance" during a routine supervisory meeting. His office smelled faintly of polished wood and expensive tea. On the wall behind him hung framed photos-handshakes, awards, international panels-proof that the world already believed in him.

He didn't ask plainly. He didn't need to.

When he spoke about her future, it sounded like a gift he could either unwrap or keep sealed. He mentioned her grant renewal. He mentioned lab access to a new sequencing platform. He mentioned an overseas placement at a partner institute. Each promise landed with the same quiet implication: I can make you real-or I can erase you. Ying felt the room psychologically shift, similar to how a floor seems to move when you realize a door has locked.

The next weeks taught her how power spreads through an institution like cold through concrete. People around her became careful. A friend stopped replying to messages. A lab manager suggested she should be "flexible." A senior postdoc-eyes tired, voice low-said only, "Don't fight him. The building always wins." It wasn't advice as much as surrender, passed hand to hand like contraband.

The university maintained formal reporting channels, of course. Posters about ethics. Emails about transparency. Training modules with cheerful icons. But those tools were not built for extraordinary problems, and Li Wei presented an extraordinary problem. He was part of the university's self-image. Removing him would feel, to administrators, like tearing down a gatehouse because one gatekeeper abused the key.

So the system protected the symbol.

And then science went wrong-not philosophically, but in the most concrete way possible: data that should have saved lives instead endangered them, because of a single person's choice.

It began with a breakthrough project, the kind universities love because it converts prestige into funding. A team under Li Wei's patronage was developing an experimental viral-vector therapy-promising results in animal models, glowing presentations, careful language about "translation" to human trials. The project attracted a major grant. The cameras visited the lab. Students took selfies near the new equipment. The university's communications office prepared phrases like "global leadership" and "historic milestone."

Behind the glass of those narratives, the work was fragile. Biomedical science is not a cathedral; it's a scaffold. Every step depends on the last. One small deviation can propagate into catastrophe.

A quality-control assay-routine but essential-flagged an anomaly in an early production batch. Nothing cinematic: several ranges, a curve that looked wrong, a warning light in the world of statistics. The lab's biosafety officer recommended quarantining the batch, repeating purification, and delaying shipment to the collaborating clinic.

Delay meant that reporters would postpone the headlines. Delay meant the grant timeline might slip. Delay meant Li Wei's planned announcement-complete with visiting dignitaries-would become awkward.

And Li Wei decided.

He insisted the anomaly was "noise." He leaned on the team lead with the authority of someone whose signature controls careers. He reminded them of the stakes. He spoke about confidence, momentum, and the danger of "overcautious thinking." Then he did what powerful people often do when reality threatens them: he reframed caution as incompetence.

The batch was cleared.

This is where the metaphor becomes science, not poetry. In chaos theory, there is an image people repeat because it's easy to remember: the butterfly's wings that help shape a hurricane. The point isn't that butterflies cause storms; it's that in complex systems, tiny perturbations can grow. A single choice-small in the moment-can alter trajectories downstream in ways no one can fully predict.

Li Wei's choice was perturbation.

The trial began with restrained optimism. Participants signed consent forms. The first participant received the therapy. For a brief window, everything looked normal. Then the adverse event arrived-unexpected inflammation, a severe immune response, the clinical turn that makes doctors' voices tighten. Although the participant survived, the harm proved significant. This resulted in prolonged hospitalization, lasting complications, and a life that the participant was forced to reorganize around a side effect the medical team should have prevented.

Regulators paused the trial. Regulators demanded answers. Independent labs conducted the tests. Independent labs retested the archived batch. The anomaly was no longer a whisper; it was a warning siren. Contamination. Incomplete purification. A quality-control step that should have been non-negotiable, they treated as an inconvenience.

A single decision had become a cascade.

The consequences spread outward with a logic that felt, to those inside it, like an avalanche. Funding agencies froze accounts. Partner institutions cut ties. Journals that had accepted early papers demanded raw data. An acclaimed preprint was quietly withdrawn, then publicly retracted. Students who had built their futures on the project watched their work become radioactive. Careers bent, then broke.

Ying Zhao watched all of it with the particular nausea of someone who understands how harm travels through hierarchies. The patient who suffered would never know the university's internal politics, never see Li Wei's ledger, never hear the conversations in corridors where people decided not to push too hard. They would only carry the bodily cost of a decision made far above them, by a man whose robe and jabot signalled trust.

And then, as often happens, the institution searched for a sacrifice that wasn't the center.

The committee blamed the postdoc for "procedural oversight." Li Wei continued to appear in public for a time, face composed, voice steady, speaking about "rigorous review" as if he had not been the one who turned caution into a liability.

But patterns do not stay buried forever. They surface the way ice cracks when spring insists.

Whistleblowers emerged. Journalists followed the money and the timeline. Internal audits connected the ethical misconduct-the coercion, the financial steering, the ledger of compliance-to the scientific failure. Not because one directly caused the other in a simple chain, but because both were symptoms of the same structure: an ecosystem where fear replaced honest challenge, where deference replaced verification.

In such a place, imperfect science doesn't require stupidity. It requires silence.

The authorities suspended Li Wei, removed him from office, and subjected him to a criminal investigation. The university announced reforms with predictable speed: independent oversight, mandatory reporting, transparent monitoring of research funds, clearer boundaries between administrators and labs. Posters appeared again.

Training modules multiplied. The institution spoke of renewal.

But for those harmed, the damage was not abstract. Ying's colleagues had left. Some of her peers disappeared into other countries, other careers, carrying the quiet shame of having been part of something poisoned. And one patient-one human body-had paid for the moment a powerful man chose narrative over reality.

That is what it looks like when science goes completely wrong because of a single person's choice: not a mad experiment, not a cartoon villain, but an ordinary administrative decision-ship the batch, keep the schedule, protect the image-made inside a hierarchy that trained everyone else to treat the decision as inevitable.

Outside, the campus remained beautiful in winter. The trees still held their branches.

Snow still softened the edges of buildings. From far away, it all still looked solid.

But solidity is not the same as safety. Even mountains avalanche when pressure accumulates in hidden layers. Even the most prestigious institutions fracture when one person treats ethics as optional, and everyone else, through fear or ambition, trains themselves to call that optionality "leadership."

39

"THE BISHOP AND THE CARTEL"

EROSION TAKES TIME, SOMETIMES ETERNITY.

Church corruption and criminal networks, Mexico, 2011 (composite case)

In the northern reaches of Mexico, where the desert presses up against the towns like an old truth no one can fully escape, Bishop Ricardo Alvarado presided over his diocese with an air of solemn dignity. He moved through the cathedral in a ceremonial cassock heavy with symbolism, the regalia that makes people lower their voices without realizing they've done it. Parishioners kissed his ring. Visiting clergy treated him like a fixed point. In public, he looked like a man appointed to stand between ordinary life and chaos-an emblem of order, morality, and protection.

But beyond the sanctuary doors, where incense could not reach and light fell differently, Alvarado had entered an alliance that belonged to shadow. The cartel that controlled the region did not arrive with guns and demands; it arrived with an offer.

The church needed renovation-cracked plaster, a roof that leaked in the brief rains, electrical wiring that sparked behind the walls. The diocese had submitted requests for funds for years and received delays, partial approvals, polite refusals. Then, through intermediaries, the cartel offered financial support. Quietly. Efficiently. No forms. No waiting. Just money, presented with a smile that suggested generosity while implying ownership. Alvarado told himself he would take what the state and the Church bureaucracy would not provide and turn it toward holy ends. He imagined himself redirecting a storm, channeling dangerous force into something useful. The desert wind, when it blows, can fill your mouth with dust, but it can also cool the heat. He persuaded himself that the same principle applied to men.

At first, the arrangement seemed contained: a donation for construction, a contractor "recommended" by the donors, a few grateful words spoken from the pulpit in vague terms-benefactors, supporters, community friends. But the relationship grew, as such things do, by incremental steps that never feel like leaps. The cartel leaders began requesting concessions in the same tone they used for gifts: softly, courteously, as if they were asking for a favor rather than collecting a debt.

Property transactions came first. Parishes leased or transferred their buildings, which featured thick walls and pleasant locations, using the language of "community support" and "restoration." Certain suppliers always won bids. Quiet, compliant, pliable priests found themselves promoted, while others who asked too many questions faced reassignment "for pastoral reasons."

Alvarado facilitated it all with practiced calm. He believed, or claimed to believe, that his dealings mitigated violence. If he cooperated, the community would be safer. If he resisted, the cartel would turn its teeth on the parishioners. In his own mind, he was not corrupt; he was pragmatic. He was governing. He was protecting. Yet there was another truth he didn't name aloud: he liked it.

Not the crude pleasure of cash, but the private thrill of being consulted by powerful men who bowed their heads-briefly, strategically-in his presence. He enjoyed the sensation of moving pieces on a board no one else could see. The cassock and regalia became more than symbols; they became instruments. A request from him could sound like a blessing while functioning as a command. Every clandestine meeting reinforced the dual life he had built-a spiritual leader by day, a covert broker by night-until he no longer felt he was crossing lines. He felt he had simply learned how the world really worked.

Along the desert edge of his diocese, the land itself seemed to preach without words.

Wind moved over mesquite and scrub like a slow, dry liturgy. Dust drifted across the roads in pale veils, as if the earth were forever trying to cover what men insisted on exposing. At dusk the mountains held the last light like embers, and the sky bled from brass to violet-beautiful, indifferent, eternal. Alvarado often stood at the rectory window and watched that horizon, telling himself the cartel was like weather: something you could not stop, only negotiate with. But storms do not bargain. They arrive, and change overtakes what they touch.

The first real disturbance came from someone the bishop had learned to overlook: Sister Helena Augustus, a nun tasked with parish administration. Her work was quiet, detailed, unglamorous-exactly the labor institutions rely on and rarely honor. She began noticing discrepancies. Donations earmarked for community projects appeared to detour toward "consultants" and "vendors" with familiar connections. Accounts balanced too neatly. Receipts repeated. Projects that should have been simple always required extra fees, extra signatures, extra intermediaries.

More troubling were the meetings. Men arrived at odd hours, names absent from official schedules, ushered through side doors into the bishop's office. Alvarado called them "local leaders." Helena saw the way the priests avoided the corridor afterward, eyes down, shoulders tightened.

She began documenting everything: dates, amounts, participants, outcomes. Her notes weren't dramatic. They were worse-precise. She understood what many people refuse to admit until it is too late: ceremonial authority can be a facade, and a facade is easiest to maintain when everyone agrees not to look too closely.

Anonymous tips eventually reached the Corps of Gendarmerie of Vatican City. The Corps of Gendarmerie of Vatican City eventually drew in Interpol. The Mexican Policía Federal followed the money and the property lines like trackers reading prints in dry ground. When investigators turned their attention to Bishop Alvarado, his first instinct was not confession but preservation. He pointed to Helena.

The accusation landed like a stone thrown into a still pool. For a moment, the institution seemed tempted to accept the simplest narrative: the faithful bishop, the rogue administrator. But Helena had her records. She presented them with a steadiness that made the room feel colder. Dates aligned. Names matched. Transfers connected. The pattern appeared, undeniable: Bishop Alvarado had not merely accepted cartel funds; he had facilitated their operations, laundering money through sacred channels and lending legitimacy to what should have been plainly condemned.

When the scandal broke publicly, it did not feel like a courtroom drama so much as a sudden clearing of the air after months of oppressive heat. People whispered names in hallways, and these then became statements in reports. Accountants stripped accounts padded with holy language-"restoration," "community support," "charity"-down to their bare transactions. It was as if the diocese had built itself on sand, and now the first hard rain had come. A house built upon the sand, the Gospel warns, falls when the floods rise-not because the builders were unaware, but because they preferred appearance to foundation.

Parishioners felt Alvarado and others betrayed them easily by using sanctity as cover. Clergy argued late into the night about complicity and survival, about the line between prudence and surrender. Ecclesiastical authorities formally investigated and removed Alvarado from administrative duties. The Vatican's protective walls shielded them as they revoked his titles decisively yet distantly, leaving an ambiguous residue like dust settling after the wind stops.

Sister Helena, walking the courtyard after long interviews, heard doves flutter from the eaves and thought of another biblical image: wolves among sheep. The cartel had not burst through the church doors with weapons raised; it had entered with envelopes, smiles, and the promise of protection. That was the cruel irony-Alvarado had offered his people the illusion of safety by inviting the very hunger that feeds on fear. Whitewashed tombs, Christ said of those who looked righteous but concealed rot within; and in Helena's mind the phrase became not insult but diagnosis. The cassock and regalia had functioned like plaster-smooth, respectable, concealing cracks until the wall could no longer hold.

The diocese responded the way institutions often do when forced into daylight: with reforms. Oversight protocols tightened. Financial transparency increased. The diocese formalized reporting requirements. Anonymous channels' creation ensured that fear would not silence truth. The Church reaffirmed that ceremonial authority does not equate to moral integrity, and that courage sometimes looks like division-the metaphorical sword of Matthew 10:34-because confronting power can fracture families, parishes, and hierarchies before it heals them.

In the weeks that followed, the diocese tried to return to normal, but nature refused to cooperate with forgetfulness. A brief rain-rare, sudden-turned dust to mud and carved thin channels through the streets like ink lines on a page. It felt like a parable of erosion: not one catastrophic collapse, but the steady insistence of consequences. Erosion takes time, sometimes eternity.

Like heat trapped in stone, the deeper question lingered: why must we rescue communities after damage instead of protecting them before it? The answer was uncomfortable and therefore instructive. Systems often prefer ceremony to prevention, reputation to truth, and quiet compromise to difficult obedience. In the end, Bishop Alvarado remained a complex figure-outwardly dignified, inwardly compromised-a reminder that authority without accountability becomes a conduit for moral and criminal compromise. His story did not end only in revoked titles and revised protocols. Documents told a story that served as a warning-and so did the wind, water, and relentless desert light. Together, they testified that time eventually reveals what is hidden.

40

"THE JUDGE'S HIDDEN LEDGER"

UNABLE TO BREATHE INSIDE THE SAME STRUCTURES THAT HAD HARMED THEM.

Judicial sexual and financial misconduct, United States, 2016 (composite case)

Judge Raymond Whitaker presided over his courtroom with an air of authority steeped in the weight of judicial history. Clad in a black robe, he embodied impartiality and the solemnity of the law. Attorneys, defendants, and clerks approached him with a mix of respect and trepidation, fully aware of the ceremonial power his position conferred. Yet beneath this facade of dignity lay a darker reality-a ledger, both literal and metaphorical, that chronicled favors, compliance, and extortion in a tally that would devastate lives and careers.

The courthouse sat in a city that liked to imagine itself orderly: neat grids of streets, trimmed hedges, a river whose surface looked calm from a distance. But order can be a surface phenomenon, like a planet seen from far away-smooth, pale, convincing-until you fly closer and discover craters and fractures. Whitaker's courtroom was the same. At the bench he looked like a fixed star-constant, reliable, a reference point by which everyone oriented themselves. And that was the danger: people navigate by what they believe cannot move.

There are phenomena in astronomy that teach the same lesson-gravitational lensing, for example. When a massive object sits between an observer and a distant source of light, the object bends the light's path. The star behind it appears displaced, stretched, doubled, even brightened into a ring. Nothing about the source has changed; the path has. The observer receives a distorted image and, unless they understand the invisible mass at work, they mistake distortion for truth.

Whitaker functioned like that invisible mass.

He applied methods that were both calculated and insidious. Those seeking leniency, advancement, or procedural advantages found themselves subtly coerced into financial "contributions" or sexual compliance, always cloaked in the language of cooperation. He rarely used explicit threats. He preferred implication-the kind that allows him to claim innocence while victims carry the full weight of understanding.

A public defender named Tessa Lane learned this early. She had come to the courthouse with idealism tempered by fatigue, the kind that makes you practical without making you cynical. Her first cases in Whitaker's court proceeded unusually: sharp skepticism met motions that should have been routine; timelines stretched for no apparent reason; clients received outcomes that felt punitive beyond the facts. Then a senior attorney took her aside near the elevators, muttering as if the building itself listened.

"He likes... respect," the attorney said. "I respect the court," Tessa replied.

The attorney's eyes flicked away. "Not that. He likes cooperation."

Tessa didn't understand until she did, and understanding arrived with a sick, bodily clarity.

Whitaker's robe and jabot, symbols designed to represent fairness, amplified his coercive influence. The clothing acted like an aura of legitimacy around his requests. When a man who looks like justice asks for "cooperation," resistance feels like rebellion against the system itself. Victims often couldn't even name the coercion out loud, because naming it required admitting the unthinkable: that the symbol of protection had become the mechanism of harm.

The systemic nature of Whitaker's misconduct made it durable. Junior clerks and interns noticed irregularities but stayed silent, deferring to his authority and fearing retaliation. The courthouse ran on small dependencies: recommendations, informal mentorship, reputational whispers. Whitaker controlled enough levers to make those dependencies feel like chains. People who refused him did not always suffer dramatic punishment. Instead, they experienced slow strangulation-stalled promotions, hostile scheduling, professional coldness that made them doubt their own competence.

That slow harm resembled another astronomical phenomenon: orbital decay. A satellite doesn't fall from the sky in one spectacular plunge. It loses altitude in tiny increments, dragged by thin atmospheric resistance, until one day it burns up. Whitaker's targets didn't always implode publicly; they drifted downward in private-confidence thinning, opportunities fading, their careers losing height until recovery became nearly impossible.

Financial extortion permeated the system with alarming ease. Whitaker and a small circle of loyalists benefited when court personnel and attorneys were pressured to contribute private funds. A clerk would be asked to "support a judicial education program." A struggling attorney would be invited to a "fundraiser" where attendance was remembered and absence noted. The language remained respectable; the consequences were not. Resistance meant unfavorable rulings, delayed promotions, or quiet ostracism.

This was where Whitaker's ledger mattered. It wasn't only a record of money or sex-it was a record of leverage. Like a navigator's chart, it showed where he could steer people. Names, dates, amounts, favors owed. The ledger transformed human weakness into a usable resource. Everyone has something: ambition, fear, debt, a secret, a vulnerable family member, a desire to belong. Whitaker didn't invent these weaknesses. He simply harvested them.

In astrophysics, there is a concept called the event horizon-the boundary around a black hole beyond which information cannot escape. It's not a physical wall, but once you cross it, your ability to signal outward collapses. Whitaker's courthouse had its own event horizon: the moment a victim complied once. After that, they often felt they couldn't speak without condemning themselves. Compliance became gravity. Silence became orbit.

Yet even systems built on fear have instabilities.

The turning point began, as it often does, not with a victim but with an outsider-an investigative journalist who didn't need Whitaker's favor and therefore didn't fear losing it. The journalist received a tip, then another, then a bundle of materials that made the pattern hard to deny. The ledger-credible evidence that Whitaker's demands were not "misunderstandings," not "rumors," but a structured practice.

The story broke publicly. The courthouse atmosphere changed overnight, like the sky before a solar eclipse. An eclipse does not destroy the sun; it simply reveals what normally can't be seen because the light is too overpowering. When the moon slides across, the glare drops, and suddenly the corona-those delicate, hidden structures-becomes visible. Whitaker's power had been glare. It kept people from looking too closely. When the glare dimmed, the hidden filaments of his network appeared: patterns in case outcomes, sudden promotions of compliant staff, repeated favors to certain attorneys, and the consistent punishment of those who wouldn't "cooperate."

Federal investigations ignited. Witnesses, once isolated, discovered they were not alone. And that changed the physics of fear. Fear thrives in solitude. When people realize others share their experiences, fear loses mass.

The institution suspended Whitaker. Criminal charges followed. Disbarment arrived not as a moral judgment but as an administrative conclusion: the institution could no longer carry him without collapsing its own legitimacy. The robe and jabot-once weapons of intimidation-became evidence in the public imagination, symbols of how authority can camouflage predation.

But the fallout for victims remained profound. Victims' careers were rerouted. Reputations damaged. Some had left the legal profession entirely, unable to breathe inside the same structures that had harmed them.

Psychological scars persisted in the body: flinches at authority, distrust of closed doors, the sense that every compliment could be a hook.

And here was the paradox that refused to go away: the system that promised protection often staged rescue only after catastrophe. Oversight committees, reforms, new reporting channels-these appeared in the aftermath, when damage was already done. Prevention is quiet, unglamorous work. Rescue is visible and therefore politically useful.

Whitaker's story became a kind of cosmology lesson for the legal community. Not because courts are galaxies, but because power behaves like mass: it bends trajectories. It distorts what people perceive as "normal." It can trap voices beyond an event horizon of shame. It can create false images-like gravitational lensing-where the public sees a bright, stable star and mistakes brightness for potency.

The ultimate cruelty was that Whitaker's crimes did not require him to break the law loudly. They required him to inhabit the spaces where law becomes discretionary, where procedure becomes a blade held with a smile. He turned symbolism into camouflage and turned trust into leverage. And the most sobering truth left behind was simple: a robe and jabot can represent justice, but a costume can also wear them.

The difference is not the fabric.

The difference is the presence-or absence-of accountability strong enough to prevent the bending of lives before it becomes visible in the wreckage.

41

"THE MAGISTRATE'S PRIVATE FANTASY"

WHEN A THREAD IS ALL THAT SEPARATES REALITY FROM THE STORY WE TELL OURSELVES, THE SMALLEST TUG IS ENOUGH TO TEAR IT.

Judicial corruption and extortion, South-Africa, 2019 (composite case)

Magistrate Thabo Mbeki presided over his courtroom in Johannesburg with a presence that demanded respect. His flowing black robe and crisply tied jabot symbolised centuries of judicial authority and moral rectitude, reinforcing the perception of impartiality and integrity. Lawyers, defendants, and court staff approached him with deference, assuming his office represented fairness and justice. Yet beneath the ceremonial dignity lay a ledger of coercion, carefully maintained to track compliance, favors, and payments.

Johannesburg light can be deceptively clean in winter-blue sky, sharp shadows, air dry enough to make everything look crisp. From the outside, Mbeki's courtroom matched that clarity: wood polished, microphones aligned, files stacked with geometric precision. He spoke in sentences that sounded balanced even when they were cutting. His robe seemed to seal the room like a boundary line: inside, order; outside, chaos.

What made him dangerous was not that he looked monstrous. He looked reasonable. And the psychology of wrongdoing often begins there: not with obvious evil, but with tiny "reasonable" exceptions-small bends in a principle that feel justified in the moment. The thin line between right and wrong is rarely a cliff; it is a shoreline that erodes a few grains at a time. You don't notice the land disappearing until the house is suddenly too close to the water.

Mbeki's misconduct was systematic, deliberate, and multilayered. Lawyers seeking high-profile cases or promotion felt subtle pressure to provide financial "donations" to his personal projects, which were always framed as administrative necessity or community benefit. Graduate clerks and attorneys coerced him into sexual compliance, packaging it as mentoring, guidance, or "opportunity."

The black robe and jabot amplified his authority, turning symbolic power into leverage few dared resist. His genius lay in making coercion feel like the cost of entry-an ugly toll road everyone pretended not to see.

He also had another skill: he could rewrite the emotional meaning of his actions in real time. In psychology, people don't simply commit wrong acts and then accept they are wrong; they often protect their self-image by changing the story. This is not psychosis. It's far more common and more subtle: moral disengagement, rationalisation, compartmentalisation. When a person repeats a rationalisation long enough, it stops sounding like an excuse and starts sounding like truth.

That is where the line gets thin: not between right and wrong as abstract ideas, but between reality and the narrative we build to tolerate ourselves.

Naledi Khumalo, a promising advocate, first realised the full extent of Mbeki's influence during her second year at the bar. Invited to his chambers ostensibly to discuss a case, she quickly recognised the implicit demand: continued career advancement, access to high-profile clients, and favorable scheduling could be granted or withheld like oxygen. Refusal would not lead to dramatic violence. Refusal would cause professional invisibility. The worst threat in a hierarchy is not always a slap; it is being quietly erased.

Naledi left that meeting with a strange sensation: her mind split in two. One part of her insisted, This is wrong. Another part replied, This is how it works. The second voice is the one institutions cultivate without admitting it. It's the voice that makes people adapt. It's also the voice that, over time, can make the intolerable feel ordinary.

Mbeki understood this split. He relied on it. He didn't need victims to believe he was good; he needed them to believe resistance was futile. He would speak of mentorship while arranging dependence, praise while planting insecurity. He made compliance feel like gratitude. And once someone complied once-once they crossed the line-the psychological terrain changed. Shame and fear operated like guard dogs. The victim's world became smaller.

Financial coercion accompanied the sexual exploitation. He redirected discretionary court funds, fines, and administrative allocations to his personal ventures or distributed them to associates in his network. Any resistance resulted in stalled promotions, adverse rulings, and professional ostracism.

The robe and jabot, outward symbols of judicial integrity, lent an air of legitimacy to abuse while silencing dissent. People saw his attire and assumed the system had already vetted him. That assumption is another form of blurred perception: the brain uses symbols as shortcuts. It's efficient. It's also how predators hide in plain sight.

Systemic enabling magnified the harm. Clerks, colleagues, and administrative staff observed irregularities but deferred to Mbeki's authority, fearing reprisal or institutional censure. Reporting mechanisms existed on paper, yet failed in practice-because paper systems collapse when human incentives oppose them. Everyone had something to lose. Everyone had a mortgage, a reputation, a future application, a professional ally. Corruption thrives not only on wickedness but on ordinary self-preservation.

This is where the question of reality versus fantasy becomes more than a metaphor.

When does someone cease to differentiate between what is real and what is imagined?

In clinical psychology, true loss of reality-testing-psychosis-means hallucinations, delusions, and fixed beliefs that persist despite evidence. That was not what happened to Mbeki. His was a more common and more chilling phenomenon: he maintained contact with reality while surrendering contact with moral reality. He didn't fail to understand facts. He failed to experience them as constraints.

He began treating other people's pain as something abstract-an administrative side effect. He told himself that those who complied "wanted it," or that they were "ambitious," or that the system required "loyalty." Over time, these justifications can form a kind of private fantasy that runs parallel to the real world, like a second courtroom only he can see-one where he is not coercive but necessary; not predatory but pragmatic; not corrupt but corrective.

That is the thin line: the moment a person's internal narrative becomes so protected that it no longer absorbs moral information. They still perceive reality-deadlines, money, reputations-but they no longer perceive the humanity of others as real in the same way. Other people become instruments, not persons. In that mental framework, wrongdoing doesn't feel like wrongdoing. It feels like management.

Mbeki's ledger-kept hidden-was not only a record of payments and compliance. It was evidence of a mind that had made exploitation routine. A ledger is a tool for accounting, for bringing balance. His ledger did the opposite: it made imbalance systematic. It converted fear into a schedule.

Victims suffered profound personal and professional consequences. Naledi endured psychological stress, reputational risk, and the moral conflict of compliance. Her career choices narrowed under a constant, draining calculation: If I refuse, what happens to my clients? To my future? To my name? Several attorneys with a stronger tolerance for loss left the profession altogether, unwilling to participate in a system that punished integrity and rewarded complicity. Their departure was another quiet violence. It removed good people and left the ecosystem more hospitable to predators.

Eventually, investigative journalists and anonymous whistleblowers brought Mbeki's misconduct to light. Reports corroborated accounts of sexual coercion and financial extortion. The Judicial Service Commission intervened, suspended him, and started proceedings. Reforms followed: oversight committees, reporting channels, audits.

The system finally behaved as a system should-after the damage had already ruined careers, frayed nerves, and poisoned trust.

And that is the ultimate contradiction: institutions often prefer rescue to prevention because rescue is visible. Prevention is invisible work-boring, procedural, unglamorous. Yet the victims did not need to be rescued in the aftermath. They needed protection before they crossed the first line.

Mbeki's story sits precisely on the psychological threshold you asked about. He did not lose the ability to distinguish facts. He lost the ability to feel the moral weight of facts. His fantasy was not that the ledger didn't exist-it was that the ledger proved competence, not cruelty. Once that inversion takes hold, a person can live inside contradiction without discomfort. They can speak of justice while practicing domination. They can wear the robe and jabot and believe, sincerely enough to be convincing, that they are still the guardians of order.

To everyone else, the line between right and wrong looks obvious from a distance.

Up close-inside a hierarchy, inside fear, inside ambition-it can thin to a thread. And when a thread is all that separates reality from the story we tell ourselves, the smallest tug is enough to tear it.

42

"THE JUDGE'S NETWORK"

ACCOUNTABILITY THREATENS THE COMFORTING BELIEF THAT INTEGRITY IS AUTOMATIC.

Judicial corruption, Brazil, 2011 (composite case)

Judge Carlos Mendes was a fixture of the São Paulo courtroom. His black toga and neatly dressed white shirt with tie made him instantly recognisable, a symbol of law and authority. Visitors, lawyers, and litigants treated him with practiced deference; his measured voice and calm gestures reinforced the perception of impartiality. To the public, Mendes embodied the integrity of Brazil's judicial system-the man journalists quoted when they needed reassurance that institutions still held. Yet beneath the ceremonial exterior lay a network of subtle influence and concealed compromise that worked best when it looked like nothing at all.

São Paulo is a city of competing tempos. At street level, horns and motorcycles, and vendors create a constant pulse. Above, corporate towers gleam like promises. In the rainy season the air becomes heavy and electric; clouds build in slow layers and then collapse in sudden sheets, washing gutters and carrying oil-slick rainwater into storm drains that groan under the weight. It's a city that teaches you an uncomfortable truth early: what is visible is rarely the whole mechanism.

Mendes was a master of procedural nuance. He orchestrated hearings to privilege those with connections, scheduled testimony strategically, and guided attorneys with faintly suggestive words. The power he wielded was almost invisible to casual observers, but palpable to those who knew where to look. He strategically scheduled a case for a time when a key witness was travelling. An objection would be "noted" and then quietly drowned under procedural timing. They treated a filing as late in one matter and as "substantially compliant" in another.

Wealthy defendants and political figures benefitted as if the law had a softer grip on them, while ordinary citizens met the full, uncompromising weight of the system. The toga helped; it turned his choices into tradition. Mendes explained it to himself with the language of balance. He believed the legal system had many inefficiencies and injustices, and subtle intervention was his method for guaranteeing "proper outcomes." But beneath the civic story lived something simpler and more human: the satisfaction of exercising unchecked power, the pleasure of moving pieces without being seen moving them.

Each case he shaped without exposure reinforced his sense of mastery, and mastery can be addictive precisely because it feels like competence.

The first person to truly notice was Clara Ribeiro, a senior court clerk who had outlasted three reforms, two chief judges, and a parade of lawyers who treated documents as mere props. Clara trusted paper more than personalities. At least one could check the paper. She documented patterns-not because she wanted a scandal, but because her instincts told her the court's rhythm had become... curated.

She saw the same names appearing in Mendes's docket with odd regularity. She saw filings inexplicably "misplaced" for certain cases and miraculously recovered when the right attorney called. She saw delays that always seemed to relieve pressure for particular defendants. Over months, she traced the orchestration to Mendes's private communications and calendar. It was not a single smoking gun; it was a constellation of small lights that, once connected, formed an unmistakable shape.

Clara made a mistake at first: she assumed that if she had enough evidence, the system itself would want to know. That was her first encounter with contradiction. Institutions praise integrity in theory, yet in practice they often prefer calm. Calm is easier to administer than truth.

So she sought a person of trust. His name was Dr. Paulo Siqueira, an old friend from university days who now worked in compliance for a public anti-corruption initiative, adjacent enough to the judiciary to understand its culture, distant enough not to be bound by its everyday loyalties. Paulo was careful by temperament, the man who listened longer than he spoke.Clara trusted him because he had once helped her through a family crisis without asking for anything in return. He had a reputation for being the rare professional who didn't collect favors like trophies.

They met after hours in a small cafe where the air smelled of burnt sugar and strong coffee. Rain hammered the awning outside, turning traffic into a blur of headlights and water spray. Clara slid a folder across the table and watched Paulo's face as he read.

At first, he said nothing. Then, softly: "This is serious." "I know," Clara replied. "That's why I'm here." Paulo tapped one page with his fingertip. "This could ruin you." Clara held his gaze. "Or it could ruin the people who keep losing because they're not connected."

Paulo exhaled slowly, and Clara saw something she hadn't expected: hesitation. Not disbelief-hesitation. It was the hesitation that comes from understanding, in your bones, how many systems are held together by mutual silence.

"Clara," he said, "I believe you. But you have to understand what happens when you move against a judge with allies."

"Allies," she repeated. "Or accomplices."

Paulo didn't answer immediately. That silence carried its own warning.

For the first time, Clara felt her trust wobble-not because Paulo seemed dishonest, but because the world around them had trained her to question every motive. Who benefits from what? Who stays clean by staying quiet? In a city where personal gains intertwine with professional networks, people never offer pure trust. Trust is always tested.

Clara asked him directly. "Are you afraid for me-or for yourself?"

Paulo's eyes flicked down to the folder, then back up. "Both," he admitted. "And that's the point. We all have something to lose, which is why men like Mendes win for so long."

His admission didn't comfort her, but it clarified something essential: trust isn't a guarantee. It's a choice you make with incomplete information, hoping the other person is choosing decency under pressure.

Mendes, meanwhile, maintained impeccable private records in a logbook-neat, obsessive, almost beautiful in its order. Each entry was a triumph of discretion: dates of hearings, outcomes predicted, procedural "adjustments" recorded in coded shorthand. The ledger functioned as both tool and trophy, cataloging invisible manipulation.

In his mind, the public saw justice; he saw engineering. The toga didn't merely clothe him-it permitted him. It made his control look like a duty.

The tipping point arrived when a politically sensitive corporate fraud case reached his courtroom. The defendants had connections; the public had anger. Mendes manipulated schedules so key witnesses could not testify, dismissing procedural objections as "speculative" and "disruptive." The verdict, though technically legal, leaned so heavily toward the defendants that even veteran attorneys murmured in the hallways. The murmur was not outrage; it was worse-recognition.

Clara, now armed with meticulous evidence and corroborating documents, submitted a confidential report to the federal judicial oversight commission. Paulo helped her structure it, stripping it of emotional language and anchoring it in timelines, discrepancies, and cross-references. He insisted on precision because precision survives retaliation better than indignation. Still, Clara could sense his caution shaping every step. Sometimes he would delay a message. Sometimes he would suggest "one more piece" before proceeding. His carefulness was rational-and it also fed her doubt. Was he protecting her, or buying time for himself to assess the risk?

The investigation was painstaking. Mendes's reputation, intellect, and educated public image slowed momentum. His colleagues respected him, and his subordinates feared him. The judiciary's instinct to protect its own surfaced in polite forms: requests for more documentation, concerns about confidentiality, warnings against "misinterpretation." Yet the file was too consistent to dismiss. Patterns emerged that defied explanation as administrative accidents.

While authorities did not pursue criminal charges because the manipulations were too subtle to make up obvious prosecutable offenses, Mendes faced formal disciplinary action, including restrictions on independent decision-making, removal from certain sensitive cases, and enhanced oversight. The result was neither total collapse nor total exoneration. It was the institution's compromise with itself: acknowledge enough to restore legitimacy, preserve enough to avoid looking fragile.

Public perception shifted slowly, like weather changing over a city. Mendes continued to appear in court, toga spotless, posture serene. But those who knew watched him differently. His authority still filled the room, yet it now carried a faint static-a sense that he might be engineering the calm.

Clara's actions earned recognition in careful tones. Some praised her courage. Others treated her like a disruption. She discovered a final contradiction: people claim to want accountability, but they often resent the person who brings it. Accountability threatens the comforting belief that integrity is automatic.

Paulo remained in her corner, but not without complications. He had done the right thing-yet Clara never fully stopped measuring his silences, his cautious pauses, the moments when he seemed to calculate. That suspicion didn't mean he was untrustworthy; it meant the world had trained her not to romanticize anyone's motives. Even allies, she learned, carry their own private negotiations.

And that became the real question the case left behind in São Paulo's legal circles: in a world where contradictions multiply-public virtue, private gain; formal rules, informal networks-who can be trusted? The unsettling answer was not a single name. It made up a discipline: people must pair trust with verification, loyalty with documentation, and admiration with scrutiny.

Symbols-the toga, the calm voice, the measured gesture-can inspire respect, but respect is not the same as safety. Safety is built slowly, by systems that don't require whistleblowers to be brave.

PRGR MUST STRENGTHEN DUE PROCESS, NOT REPLACE IT

"AND HERE IS WHY I BELIEVE THE HARM WAS JUSTIFIED."

Would the outcome of my case have been different? I can't know. Without PRGR it's all counterfactual-another kind of court language, another way to keep the past sealed. But I can say what would have changed even if the result didn't: the institution would have had to own its choice in a form that couldn't hide behind calm and inaccessible files.

In these chapters, the institution often defends itself with one holy phrase: **due process**. Sometimes that phrase is proper. Sometimes it's a curtain. Either way, people get hurt while the system congratulates itself for being "careful."

The PRGR point here is protective: PRGR must not replace due process. It must expose the human choice inside it.

If hearings are available, the PRGR is issued **after** the person has responded-except for interim emergency measures. Those measures require an interim PRGR now and a final PRGR later, once the response has been heard. The record must show not only what was done, but what was done *before the person could speak*, and why that risk was accepted.

PRGR also requires workforce protections: indemnifying good-faith signatories, protecting refusal-to-sign when honest justification is impossible, and resourcing the work so it isn't used as punishment. Otherwise authorship becomes a trap, and the system will aim it downward at the safest targets.

I'm emphasizing this because institutions love false choices: either we're fair, or we're accountable. Either we protect staff, or we tell the truth. That's a lie. PRGR makes fairness sharper by making authorship unavoidable. And if these stories feel repetitive, it's because the same defense keeps appearing in different uniforms: "We followed process." PRGR forces the next sentence-the one the institution avoids because it sounds human: "And here is why I believe the harm was justified."

43

THE RECEIVER'S INVOICE AND THE COURT'S SILENCE

THE ROBE AND THE LEDGER - TWO STORIES, ONE MECHANISM

Two stories, same court, different lawyers, Netherlands, 2008-2013

The first thing people misunderstand about a receiver is the arithmetic.

From the outside, it looks like authority: a court appointment, a list of clients, an office, a title that sounds like power.

From the inside, it is fifty euros per client per month to hold someone else's life together.

Fifty euros to pay staff, rent, tax, insurance, software, travel, postage, banking, reporting, printing, phone calls that turn into counseling because nobody else is answering, and the quiet hours that disappear when a client's electricity is cut and you are the only person who can stabilize the situation before it becomes a crisis.

Fifty euros to be blamed later for any crisis you could not buy your way out of.

That is where this story begins: not in a courtroom, but in the gap between what the system demands and what it funds.

1) The email

The email came from Roger's assistant.

Not long. Not polished. The message written by someone who has stopped hoping that courtesy will help. Roger needed a lawyer for the appeal.

I learned quickly that I wasn't the first door.

Lawyer number one had said no. Then another. Then another. Some of them were afraid of the publicity-too much negative weather in the newspapers, too much certainty in the way strangers say "misuse" when what they mean is "I read a headline." Some had conflicts: they had taken over some of his clients, or wanted them. Interests would bounce. Others simply didn't want to stand beside a man the system was already preparing to display.

There was also the simplest reason: Roger didn't have the money to pay a lawyer. Defending himself would have been possible, but a bad idea. A lawyer representing himself becomes both witness and weapon. The court hears your legal argument and judges your character in the same breath.

Roger Liefhoudt was a receiver and a lawyer for over thirty years. I didn't know Roger then. No history, no loyalty, no friendship. Just a lawyer from the same jurisdiction, a file and a human being behind it.

I wrote back: "Come along, and we'll see."

He arrived the next day.

He didn't carry himself like a man who expected justice. He carried himself like someone to whom the role of the example had already been assigned. His heart did not cooperate. Hospital visits had already begun. And behind the case was a divorce-his private life collapsing as his professional life was being stripped down to accusations and sums.

You can survive a storm if you still have shelter.

Roger didn't.

PRGR highlight - *Trigger: First irreversible trajectory*

When a person's livelihood is on a line that can't be un-drawn-removal, repayment orders, reputational labeling-PRGR requires one thing before the machinery accelerates: a named author writing clear reasons in real time, not after the damage is done.

2) The ten-euro fee (and what it actually bought)

Roger had around one hundred and fifty clients with serious debts. A proper office. A real caseload. A constant stream of human emergencies.

He had invested his own money in automation. Not because it was fashionable, but because without it the role couldn't be done at scale. In those days, "automation" wasn't a shiny subscription with a marketing video. It was something you built, patched, tested, and defended-often with no applause and plenty of suspicion from anyone who equated "proper" with paper.

The law said that a receiver may charge costs to a client that are necessary. Roger charged ten euros per client for the automated administration. Clients could opt in or not. There was a choice.

And that ten euros didn't buy comfort. It bought visibility.

The system allowed clients to follow their files day by day. Not every detail-life is never that neat-but enough to stop the most corrosive part of debt administration: the guessing. They could see what had come in, what had been paid, what was still pending. They could upload invoices and documents instead of sending them into the void and waiting. They could lodge questions in writing, attached to the thing that worried them, instead of sitting on hold for an hour-listening to music that makes you feel smaller-only to reach someone who can't answer without the file.

And they didn't have to wait three months for a report that arrived like a weather summary after the storm had already hit.

In theory, a receiver manages money.

A receiver manages uncertainty-and uncertainty eats people alive when they are already in debt.

Roger understood that. He wasn't building a gadget. He was building a way for frightened people to stop living in the dark. Practical experience turned into a workable, manageable system-something that could be tracked, explained, audited; something that replaced silence with something steadier.

And then the court ruled: not necessary. Pay it back.

That sentence sounds clean from the bench. "Not necessary." Two words, one line, no mess.

But in practice it meant: return to the old world-quarterly reports, hours on hold, clients who have no clue what is happening inside the machine that decides whether the electricity stays on. It meant demanding modern administration while forbidding the tools that made it possible.

***PRGR highlight** - Trigger: Feasibility ruling disguised as "interpretation"*
When a court labels a cost "not necessary," it isn't merely classifying a line item. It is issuing an operational command. PRGR forces the author to write: what the court believes is realistically possible without that tool, and what harms are foreseeable if it is forbidden.

3) The earning model nobody names

By the time a file reaches a receiver, the debt is rarely just a debt.

It has already been turned into an earning model.

Collection fees are added on top of the original amount. Interest is added on top of that. Then come the bailiff's charges, the service costs, the "handling" costs-layer after layer until the debt becomes a machine that eats the cheese from the bread. What began as a missed bill becomes a structure that grows by feeding on the person who can least afford to feed it.

And the justice system is not outside that structure. It is one of the gears.

Orders, writs, enforcement steps-each of them "lawful," each of them "procedural," and each of them carrying cost. A legal pathway with toll gates at every turn.

This is the obscenity at the centre: almost everyone in the chain is allowed to earn from the debt. Collectors, bailiffs, sometimes lawyers, sometimes the state itself through fees and formalities. The judges, who count on their salary every month. The only two parties who are supposed not to eat from it are the client and the receiver. The client is meant to survive it. The receiver is meant to administer it. Both are expected to do that inside a system that rewards everyone else for the debt's continued existence.

Debt should never be an earning model.

When debt becomes a business, it hollows livelihoods. It kills families by inches. It separates people who were already stretched. It pushes children into poverty as if poverty were hereditary. It overloads the health system-because stress is not a metaphor; it is physiology. And it increases suicides because despair is a financial product once the system has priced it into "fees."

I watched that model in Roger's files. And I watched what happened when Roger tried, in small practical ways, to reduce its harm-by bringing clarity, speed, and human judgment into places the system prefers to keep foggy.

PRGR highlight - *Trigger: Profit incentives masked as "procedure"*
When a system's procedures predictably generate profit for third parties and predictable harm for the person in debt, PRGR demands that the author of each step write-not abstractly, but concretely-what harm is foreseeable, who benefits financially, and why the step remains justified despite that incentive structure.

4) The fifty-thousand figure (and the mirror the statute refused to name)

The headline number-around fifty thousand euros-was something else entirely.

Many of Roger's clients were engaged in legal proceedings. Governmental contributions financed some of the legal procedures, but these contributions did not cover all costs. Creditors don't pause because a subsidy has limits. Roger, also a lawyer, took on cases and charged clients for the costs that weren't covered.

The law said: if a receiver starts a legal procedure, the magistrate must give permission.

Here was the bottleneck: receivers do not start most proceedings. Creditors start them. Enforcement starts them. The world starts them, and the receiver inherits them.

The statute said nothing about that mirror situation.

So the court made the mirror itself.

It treated creditor-initiated proceedings as if the receiver had started them. Therefore: no permission. Therefore: improper. Therefore: repay.

This is how a silence in the law becomes a weapon in the hand of a court: not by admitting it is creating policy, but by calling analogy "obvious" and punishing anyone who didn't anticipate the "obvious."

PRGR highlight - *Trigger: Analogy that creates liability*
When the law is silent and the court "fills the gap," PRGR requires the author to write, plainly: this is analogy; here is why it is justified; here is the notice given; here is the safe-harbour for actions taken under a reasonable reading; here is the remedy if the analogy proves wrong.

5) The groceries (and the disgrace nobody likes to quantify)

Somewhere along the line, the story grew another layer: that the court had had serious doubts for nearly two years because debts for a "relatively large number" of clients had increased.

I have seen the papers. There was no signal. Not a single sentence that performed what oversight is supposed to perform: a contemporaneous warning, a documented concern, a line drawn early enough that correction is possible.

If a court truly doubts someone for two years and says nothing, then the court is not supervising; it is waiting.

Waiting is not neutral. Waiting is a choice to preserve a future ambush.

And the "increasing debts" claim-this is where people who have never sat with debtors reveal themselves.

There is no statutory minimum amount that must be left to a client per week. Judges mostly decide. In those days they allowed amounts that could be brutally low. Food and personal expenses were treated like a rounding error. The ledger stayed tidy while the fridge emptied.

Judges do not pay less for groceries because a blue-covered book says so.

Clients do.

I know first-hand that Roger bought groceries for some of his clients with his own money. Not as performance. As triage. Because when you leave a household too little to eat, you are not managing finances. You are managing a slow emergency.

Roger did not always follow the system.

He followed the interests of the client.

And the system does not forgive that when it wants an example.

PRGR highlight - *Trigger: "We had doubts" without dated notice*
A later claim of long-standing doubt is meaningless unless it is anchored to dated communication. PRGR requires the author to write: when the doubt began, what was communicated then, what remedy was offered then, and why silence was chosen if silence was chosen.

6) The appeal becomes industrial

I read the initial judgment. I read the law. I studied jurisprudence and history-the roots that courts often forget they are standing on. I told Roger: "Let's do it."

I wrote the appeal the way I write when the room is already hostile: structure first, emotion last. The economics of the role. The legal basis for necessary costs. The mirror problem in creditor-started procedures. The difference between funding and expectation. The way compliance has been confused with welfare.

But the system had already chosen what Roger was going to be.

Not someone corrected.

Someone displayed.

The appeal wasn't one case. It was a procession.

About one hundred and thirty cases.

Three judges. One clerk. Me with a trolley of files and, only sparingly, a lawyer for the clients. In the beginning, the talks were longer. Later, less than five minutes per case.

Facts. Calculation of the sum. The court did what courts do when they have chosen their destination: it reduced everything to arithmetic.

Roger's heart didn't cooperate. He ended up in hospital several times. I went with him to court once, and then I asked the court to allow him to be absent for the rest of the time. Watching your own life being reduced to line items is not required by law, but it is a kind of punishment.

Less than five minutes per case.

I caught myself thinking about the one thing Roger had tried to give people-simple, day-by-day visibility-because here everything moved in reverse: away from knowing, back into the old fog where outcomes arrive first and explanations limp after them.

We had about seven days to clear them.

Seven days to manufacture finality.

PRGR highlight - *Trigger: Mass processing*
When adjudication becomes industrial, PRGR forces the author to write: what safeguards preserve individual review, what errors are foreseeable under time compression, and what repair trigger exists when the foreseeable error happens.

7) The lunch break file

One day I didn't have a file with me.

It happens. You're carrying a small library, and sometimes a book is missing.

The chair suggested we take a lunch break and offered me the court's copy so I could study it.

It sounded reasonable. It sounded trust. It sounded even courteous.

I opened the file.

And there it was: the raw model of the verdict. Only a few spaces left open-those for the data we were "discussing." Names, dates, numbers. Like a mail merge.

The verdict was ready before the case was brought before the court. The case was closed. The hearing a circus act and I was the clown.

I said nothing.

I couldn't concentrate. I listened and answered. I performed my role.

The question that followed me all day was brutal: Do I tell Roger?

I decided: not yet. The verdict was there; we had to finish the week; maybe we could appeal again. Reduce harm before you add truth that cannot help him in that moment.

When the box with the verdicts arrived, I didn't make coffee.

I showed Roger the copy I had made instead.

It was one of my last cases. Meanwhile, it was October 2013. Time to go.

Not only did his business go bankrupt. He was also ordered to pay personally all the money owed. The judgment followed him into private life. He filed for bankruptcy.

He kept fighting, literally for his life and for justice.

He lost both.

I learned he died a few years later. He left a beautiful daughter and son as his heritage. His DNA untouched. His character lives on.

PRGR highlight *- Trigger: Pre-formed outcome*
PRGR doesn't accuse; it demands authorship. If a decision template exists before the hearing, PRGR forces the author to write: what is genuinely open to argument, what safeguard ensures the hearing can change the outcome, and what remedy exists if it cannot.

8) The earlier collision: when it happened to me first

Roger was not alone.

Before Roger, I had already met that same institutional reflex.

I was available as a curator - a liquidator - at the same court. In the beginning, everything was fine. I received enough cases to justify investing in hardware, software, and self-developed applications. Everything we did was electronic-unusual around 2008–2009.

Every three months I had to lodge a report to the court's clerk office. My secretary emailed them. No one complained.

Then, after about six months, a clerk emailed on behalf of a supervising judge: it wasn't allowed to send reports by email.

Fine, I thought. We'll switch to paper.

We did. And I explained our progressive approach.

Then the assignments dropped dramatically.

Then to none.

I'm a person of numbers. I don't handle patterns by pretending they aren't patterns. I looked into distribution. Heavy cases were being appointed to big firms. Smaller offices got scraps. And in insolvency, scraps can mean no payment at all. We got nothing.

I wrote to the President of the District Court. I asked to discuss my findings.

He agreed to a meeting.

What he did not say was that on arrival the room would contain four or five judges and the head of the bureau.

I asked why I hadn't been informed. At least I could have brought a colleague, three ears instead of two. They said each judge had a function in the insolvency section. Perhaps. But the function of that room was not discussion. It was pressure.

Instead of engaging with the distribution, I was personally attacked. I was told another judge-absent-had stripped me from the pool because I wasn't following rules, and another judge, other location, disliked me for being too human. "Disobedient. Emotional." That word "disobedient" again, like a stamp that makes everything else easy.

I thanked them for their time and left. Five minutes. A chapter closed.

But one paragraph followed: the absent judge ruled against my clients in all subsequent cases. Every time I appealed, an overturn occurred. Again and again.

Eventually, in one obvious case, I wrote that I was in serious doubt of his independence.

He replied I was an unsatisfied and unprofessional "client of the court" who could not accept a loss.

Then he withdrew from that matter, another judge assigned, and I won.

And I never had him as judge again.

I survived.

Roger did not.

But the mechanism was the same: the institution kept its hands clean by using ordinary tools-allocation, labels, silence-until the outcome looked inevitable and the person looked like the cause.

PRGR highlight - *Trigger: Retaliation by invisibility*
Case allocation, access to work, reputational labels-these can punish without a trace. PRGR forces the author to write: what objective criteria were used, what deviations occurred, and what review exists when "ordinary management" becomes invisible discipline.

PRGR END-CAP - AUTHORED HARM TEST

PRGR isn't interested in theatre. It's interested in the hinge-where a system converts discretion into destiny while keeping the file surface clean.

In this chapter, the harm isn't only the repayment numbers or the removal. The harm is the pattern that makes those outcomes feel "inevitable" after the fact:

- silence where warnings should be,
- analogy where law is silent,
- labels where reasons should be,
- templates where hearings should be,
- industrial pace where individuality should be,
- profit incentives disguised as "procedure."

PRGR trigger questions that would have changed this chapter while it was still changeable:

1) If the court "had doubts," where is the dated notice?

Name the date. Name the author. Name what was demanded. Name the deadline for remedy.
If the answer is silence, then silence must be authored and justified.

2) If the automation fee was "not necessary," what reality model supports that?

Write down the court's operational assumptions: what a receiver can deliver on the fixed fee without tools.
Write down foreseeable harms if tools are forbidden. If the foreseeable harms are accepted, the author signs acceptance.

3) If creditor-started proceedings are treated as receiver-started, admit the analogy.

State plainly: this is a gap-fill. State why it is justified and what notice was given.

State what safe-harbour exists for reasonable prior conduct.

4) If debt collection is generating profit at each procedural step, name it.

Who earns at each stage? What fees are being added? What interest accrues? What harm is foreseeable, and what incentive exists to prolong the debt?
PRGR forces the author to justify continuing a pathway that predictably grows the debt.

5) If 150 cases are processed at speed, where are the safeguards?

Name the mechanism that prevents errors. Name the trigger that reopens a case when the error occurs.
If there is no trigger, the author signs the risk.

6) If a verdict exists in template form, what can the hearing change?

List what is open and what is not. If nothing is open, then the hearing's purpose must be written in honest words.

7) If a label is applied ("non-compliant," "unprofessional"), how is it removed?

Labels that can't be appealed are punishments pretending to be descriptions.
PRGR demands the unlocking mechanism.

PRGR doesn't stop courts from deciding. It stops them from deciding in fog.

Because the most dangerous sentence in this chapter is not "pay it back."

It is: "We had doubts for two years," written only after the harm is irreversible.

44

"THE PROSECUTOR'S GAME"

IN A WORLD BUILT ON PROCESSING, THE WORST HARM OFTEN ARRIVES WITH PERFECT PUNCTUATION.

> Prosecutorial misconduct investigations, Germany, 2007–2015 (composite case), PRGR

A street fighter and a prosecutor both know the same first lesson: if you control the space, you control the outcome.

The street fighter learns it with knuckles and pavement. The prosecutor learns it with calendars, charging decisions, disclosure timing, and a sentence that begins, The State submits... One fights in alleys, one fights in corridors lined with framed oaths. One wears bruises; the other wears a robe. But strip the costumes away and the mechanics rhyme: pressure, leverage, dominance, reputation.

The difference isn't "good versus bad." It's which violence society permits-and how cleanly it can be denied. Where the divergence starts: heritage and hunger.

A street fighter usually forges his morality close to the ground. Heredity and environment forge it: a neighborhood where respect is currency, where fear acts as a kind of insurance, where the future is not promised, thus the present becomes the only law. Their code-if they have one-is tactile: you don't snitch, you don't touch kids; you pay your debts; you answer disrespect. It's brutal, but it's legible.

Abstraction often shapes a prosecutor's morality. They inherit institutions: universities, chambers, professional language that turns people into "subjects," "offenders," "risk profiles." Hunger looks different there. It's less about survival and more about status: conviction rates, public trust, career trajectory, press coverage, "impact." The code is dressed as principle, but it can become just as primitive: win, don't embarrass the office, protect the narrative, protect the machine.

The street fighter may be born into a fight. The prosecutor chooses a role that contains the fight.

That's why prosecutors like Johannes Krüger can feel righteous while drifting into cruelty. Not because they are monsters, but because the environment rewards a particular coldness and calls it "professionalism."

Where they meet: the shared machinery of coercion

Krüger's gift-his pathology, if you want the darker word-was spatial control without visible fingerprints. He didn't need to threaten. He built atmospheres.

A street fighter squares his shoulders, holds his gaze a half-second too long, and lets the other person imagine the pain he will inflict before throwing a punch. Krüger did it with a raised eyebrow, with disappointment that sounded parental, with "mentorship" that cut confidence into manageable pieces. In both arenas, the victim supplies half the harm by anticipating it.

That's a moral convergence point: both understand that fear is cheaper than force.

And both exploit the fact that human beings are social animals. We will endure absurdities to avoid being excluded from the pack.

Is the moral difference an illusion? Sometimes it is.

Because the prosecutor has a unique advantage, the street fighter rarely gets: legitimacy. The prosecutor can harm you while looking like order. The prosecutor can make your despair appear procedural.

A street fighter can beat you. A prosecutor can ruin you and have the room nod along.

That's why institutions are so dangerous when they rot: they launder harm through ritual. The robe becomes a detergent. The white tie becomes a disinfectant. And the public, desperate to believe, inhales the clean smell and calls it justice.

Criminal organisations vs. governments: the same cold arithmetic, different branding.

Criminal organisations treat people as numbers openly. They keep ledgers. They assign value to a life with a price tag and a deadline.

Governments pretend they don't-then do it anyway, with different stationery.

They call it "resource allocation." "Operational priorities." "Collateral impact." "Acceptable risk." When a government shuffles people under snow-buries them in files, delays, appeals, policy thresholds-it can do what a cartel does with bullets, just slower, quieter, and with better lighting.

The difference is not that one is moral and the other immoral. The difference is accountability and visibility. Cartels fear rivals. Governments fear headlines.

But when both stop fearing anything, they resemble each other: a system of extraction, dressed in either terror or bureaucracy.

The snow metaphor: what disappears doesn't stop existing.

Snow is a kind of mercy that lies. It makes a city look pure. It smooths the jagged edges of harm. Under snow, everything continues: rot, footprints, blood, discarded evidence, lost names. This is how institutional harm appears when it operates "properly." People are not executed; they are archived.

Administrative winter shuffles them.

Krüger's office was that kind of climate. He didn't break bodies. He chilled them. He made staff second-guess their own memories. Ten ears heard different things, and the committee cooked one meal: a verdict. Two eyes read it. One brain interprets it. DA career becomes a paragraph. People left behind chapters.

And because it's tidy, it's easy to swallow.

If a street fighter and a prosecutor can share methods-pressure, spectacle, intimidation-then the actual dividing line isn't the job title. It's whether the person can still feel the human cost as real.

The moment someone treats suffering as a unit-one file, one statistic, one acceptable sacrifice-the orchestra loses the tone. The notes remain correct. The performance becomes monstrous.

Krüger likely knew what he was doing. The more frightening possibility is that he also believed he was "maintaining standards." That is the most common self-portrait of institutional predators: not villains, but custodians.

So where do they differ?

A street fighter usually knows he is fighting.

A prosecutor can convince himself he is merely processing.

And in a world built on processing, the worst harm often arrives with perfect punctuation.

PRGR END-CAP - AUTHORED HARM TEST

(for "THE PROSECUTOR'S GAME")

The harm in this case isn't a single unethical act. It's a **sequence of tactical choices** that remain individually defensible while collectively rigging the field. "Game" is the right word because the prosecutor treats procedure like a board: not as a constraint, but as a set of moves designed to corner the defense until "truth" becomes whatever survives.

PRGR would attach authorship at the first hinge-step where the prosecutor converts discretionary power into engineered disadvantage. In this story, the hinge-steps are not dramatic-they are the everyday mechanics of prosecution: charging, disclosure, plea pressure, witness handling, and timing.

The hinge-steps where PRGR would force the author to exist

The charging escalation - selecting the maximum threat to control behavior When the prosecutor chooses an over-inclusive charge set or stacks enhancements primarily to increase leverage, PRGR triggers at the charging memo. He must author:

why each charge is necessary and proportionate, what evidence supports it,

what foreseeable harms follow (coerced pleas, trial penalty, inflated sentencing risk),

and what alternative charging options were rejected and why. PRGR forces the prosecutor to sign what is usually left implicit: *I am using threat as a tool.*

The disclosure timing step - "compliance" used to create surprise
If the prosecutor discloses exculpatory or impeachment material late (or in a way that is technically compliant but practically unusable), PRGR triggers at the disclosure decision.

He must author:

what was disclosed,

when and why timing occurred,

what the defense can realistically do with it,

and what harm is foreseeable (inadequate investigation, ineffective cross, lost motions).

PRGR doesn't accept "we turned it over" as an ethical endpoint when timing makes it functionally inert.

The witness control step - incentives, shaping, and selective memory
When witnesses are handled through informal incentives (charging discretion, immigration help, benefits, "we'll talk to the judge"), PRGR triggers at the benefit authorization.

He must author:

what was offered, why it was necessary,

what safeguards ensure accuracy (full recording, disclosure to defense, corroboration requirements),

and what foreseeable harm follows if incentives distort testimony. This is where the "game" produces story-like evidence.

The plea leverage step - making trial too expensive to choose
If the prosecutor offers a plea that is nominally "fair" but paired with a trial penalty that makes refusal irrational, PRGR triggers at the plea offer record.

He must author:

what sentencing delta is being imposed for going to trial, why that delta is justified,

what harm is foreseeable (innocent pleas, coercion, unequal justice by risk tolerance),

and why alternative resolutions were rejected.

PRGR forces the prosecutor to name coercion if coercion is the functional mechanism.

The motion warfare step - using volume and timing to exhaust
If the prosecutor uses repeated filings, late responses, or procedural fights not to clarify law but to drain defense capacity, PRGR triggers at the pattern threshold: once the tactic is recognizably exhaustion-driven.

He must author:

why the motion posture is necessary, what issues it truly turns on,

and what safeguards prevent "resource advantage" from becoming the deciding factor. PRGR makes "gamesmanship" traceable instead of deniable.

The narrative lock-in step - public messaging that contaminates neutrality
If the prosecutor briefs the press or uses public statements to frame the defendant as guilty before trial, PRGR triggers at the communications decision.

He must author:

why public comment is necessary,

what safeguards prevent prejudicing jurors or decision-makers,

what harm is foreseeable (tainted pool, pressure on witnesses, institutional bias). Because in this story, the "game" extends beyond the courtroom.

What PRGR would force in this case (matched to prosecutorial power)

1. **A "leverage disclosure" requirement**
   PRGR would require prosecutors to record explicitly when a decision is being used primarily for leverage (charging, plea deltas, enhancements). Not to ban it automatically, but to make it **owned** and reviewable.

2. **A "usable disclosure" standard**
   Disclosure is not merely timely by rule; it must be timely enough to be *actionable*. PRGR would require the prosecutor to certify usability (or explain why usability is not possible).

3. **A witness-incentive ledger**
   Every material benefit to a witness requires a signed record with rationale, disclosure obligations, and corroboration notes. No informal "understandings" that later become deniable.

4. **An exhaustion tripwire**
   If defense resources are visibly outmatched and the prosecution increases procedural volume, PRGR triggers automatic oversight review-not to protect the defense from losing, but to protect the process from becoming a contest of stamina rather than evidence.

The questions that keep this End-Cap hyper-specific to "the game"

If you were the prosecutor: which move was the game's hinge-charge stacking, late disclosure, witness incentives, plea delta, or motion warfare? Can you write the reason in plain language and sign it?

If you were the defense: which single prosecutorial move, if forced into the authored record, would have changed your ability to respond-usable discovery timing, benefit disclosures, or charging proportionality?

If you were the supervising office: are you willing to author that "winning" justifies tactics that predictably coerce pleas or distort testimony?

PRGR doesn't moralize about ambition. It isolates the moment the prosecutor **turned discretionary power into engineered inevitability**-and forces a named author to exist at the exact step where procedure stopped being law and became a game board.

45

"THE LAWYER WHO DANCED WITH THE CARTEL"

IF YOU LEND YOUR ROBE AND JABOT TO DARKNESS OFTEN ENOUGH, THE CLOTH STARTS TO REMEMBER THE SHAPE OF IT.

> Mexico has a long history of narco-influence, "narco-lawyers," and using institutions as costumes.

Mexico City has two kinds of music.

There is the bright kind-the mariachi that flares in plazas and restaurants, trumpets cutting through the air like sunlight.

There is the Jarabe Tapatío, the dance that turns courtship into choreography: step, retreat, turn, approach again. It looks playful, almost innocent, yet it demands precision.

Miss a beat and the entire performance collapses into embarrassment.

And then there is the other music-quieter, older, a pulse you feel beneath concrete. It rises when a funeral procession passes, when candles are lit on Día de los Muertos, when the living speak to photographs as if the dead are only in the next room.

In Mexico, the line between here and there has always been thin, a veil you can lift with memory and sugar and marigolds.

Diego Márquez believed he could live on that line.

He walked into his firm each morning with the assurance of a man who thought elegance could arrange the world.

The black robe for court hung like a second skin; the jabot sat at his throat as if it were an emblem of discipline rather than decoration. He looked like law made human-meticulous, articulate, unhurried.

Judges greeted him with the warm professionalism reserved for someone who "understands the system." er lawyers watched him the way musicians watch a conductor: waiting for the cue, learning the tempo.

But Diego's genuine talent was not law. It was rhythm.

He knew when to lean into a conversation, when to pause, when to let silence do the threatening so he didn't have to. He understood procedures aren't just rules; they are steps. If you learn the dance, you can lead.

The first invitation came like a casual melody.

A call from Ernesto, an old acquaintance-mid-level, the man who never said the cartel's name aloud, as if naming it might summon it. Ernesto asked for "advice." Nothing dramatic. A bail issue. A procedural question. A prosecutor who needed to be "reminded" that discretion exists.

Diego said yes because saying yes felt like competence.

He told himself what professionals always tell themselves when they slide: I'm not doing anything illegal. I'm merely explaining the law.

That is how the Jarabe begins: one small step that doesn't look like commitment. Soon the meetings were no longer in his office.

They took place in restaurants where the servers moved like ghosts, and the private rooms had no windows. They took place in suburban houses with ornamental fountains and men who didn't smile. They took place on ranches where the air smelled of dust and gun oil, and where the "security" was a row of rifles leaning against a wall like upright saints.

Each time Diego arrived, he felt two sensations at once-fear and the thrill of being wanted. Not wanted like affection. Wanted like utility. Wanted like leverage.

Ernesto began bringing others. Men with clean shirts and soft hands who spoke politely and carried violence inside their courtesy, as if it were a second language.

They asked for things that weren't framed as demands: a motion filed at the right time, a witness credibility "reframed," a plea bargain negotiated not with law but with suggestion.

Diego complied. There is always a reason. He always had a story he could tell himself.

I am preventing chaos. I am keeping things contained. I am making the best of a system already infected. And like any infection, it spread more easily because the body tried to ignore it.

He received cartel money in his accounts under names that sounded harmless: consultancy fees, research stipends, donations to "community projects." A lawyer should be paid, he told himself. A man cannot live on principle alone.

But the payments weren't just compensation. They were a leash made of silk.

The more he accepted, the more the cartel treated him as theirs-not by ownership declared, but by expectations implied.

He learned the special terror of that kind of bond: no one needs to say you belong to us when every previous yes has already said it for you.

His robe and jabot became part of the cartel's strategy.

Not because they admired the law, but because they understood the costume. In Mexico, uniforms and regalia have always been powerful.

A badge stops cars. A cassock opens doors. A robe makes a lie sound like procedure. Diego was a walking stamp of legitimacy.

He could escort dirty money into clean corridors. He could turn brutality into paperwork. He could make predators look like clients.

And the victims-those are never in the dance's foreground.

A shop owner who wouldn't sell was suddenly "under investigation." A witness who wouldn't cooperate found his testimony questioned, then his courage dismantled, then his name circulating in the wrong circles.

A family with land received documents they didn't understand until the bulldozers arrived.

Diego heard about these things the way a city hears about distant sirens-vaguely, and with the practiced excuse of helplessness. He told himself he wasn't responsible for what others did with the space he created. He told himself his job ended at the border of the courtroom.

But in truth, his job had become the border.

He had turned into the thin veil-like Día de los Muertos itself-where two worlds meet. The living and the dead. The legal and the criminal. The public and the hidden.

What he hadn't understood was that in this tradition, the dead don't just visit. They linger.

The first crack appeared in someone who still believed in daylight.

Sofía, his junior associate, had admired him. She liked the way he spoke, the way he could dismantle an argument without raising his voice.

But admiration has a lifespan when it shares a room with inconsistency.

She noticed files that returned to the office with unfamiliar staple marks. She noticed that Diego's "late meetings" were followed by sudden strategic pivots, and these choices seemed less like advocacy and more like obedience.

Then she saw him do something small and unforgivable: he coached a witness not to lie, exactly-but to forget in a useful direction.

That was the moment Sofía understood what Diego had become. Not a lawyer at the edge of compromise.

A musician playing the wrong score.

She began documenting quietly: names, dates, transfers, emails with carefully vague language. She didn't act like a hero; she acted like someone who knows that heroism gets people killed. She copied the ledger-like patterns in Diego's behaviour because she understood a simple principle: institutions don't respond to feelings. They respond to proof.

Journalists were sniffing around cartel influence in professional circles-accountants, notaries, lawyers. Federal authorities were following money flows, mapping networks the way meteorologists track storms: pressure systems, convergence points, hidden currents.

Diego didn't notice at first because he lived inside an illusion of control. He thought his intelligence was armor. Then his phone began behaving strangely. Calls dropped. Voices echoed. Cars appeared in his rearview mirror too often. He felt watched in the way prey feels watched-instinctive, humiliating, undeniable.

He tried to correct his steps, to dance backwards out of the trap.

But the Jarabe doesn't work that way. Once you've taken the lead, someone else learns your rhythm. When they arrested him, it wasn't cinematic.

It was procedural. Clean. Men with warrants, not rifles. Doors opened by keys, not kicks. The state, for once, performed its own kind of choreography-slow, deliberate, unstoppable.

The public story broke like fireworks: Prominent Lawyer Tied to Cartel Network. Commentators spoke as if they'd always suspected it.

Colleagues expressed shock with the tidy relief of those glad it wasn't them. Diego's face appeared on screens, his name turning from prestige to spectacle in a single news cycle.

At trial, prosecutors did not need melodrama. They had patterns.

They showed transfers. Timelines. Messages that danced around meaning without ever saying it. They showed how his "advice" created space for intimidation and disappearance. They showed how legitimacy, once rented to criminals, becomes a weapon sharper than any knife: it turns the victim's plea into a file number and the predator's appetite into a procedural delay.

Witnesses testified behind protective screens. Sofía testified with a voice that did not try to sound brave. It sounded careful-which is often the truer form of courage.

The conviction came like a verdict always does: a few words that pretended to contain the weight of ruined lives.

Diego's licence was taken away. Sentenced. Sealed into a cell where no robe could confer authority. The cartel adjusted, because cartels are evolutionary; they don't mourn; they replace.

And this is where Día de los Muertos returns-not as decoration, but as judgement.

In Mexico, you learn that the dead are never purely gone, and the living are never purely safe. You set out offerings because you know absence can still have hunger.

Diego had fed that hunger with legal language and ceremonial cloth, and he had told himself it was only business.

Now he sat alone, and the sounds that came to him in memory were confused: trumpets in a plaza, laughter over waffles of another country, the quiet click of a judge's pen, the soft shuffle of paper. Two worlds overlapping. Two rhythms, no longer separable.

He had wanted to be the man who could dance between opposites. But the opposite tradition in Mexico is not a joke.

It's a warning: if you invite the dead into your house often enough, eventually they don't wait for an invitation. And if you lend your robe and jabot to darkness often enough, the cloth remembers the shape of it.

46

"THE JUDGE AND THE CARTEL"

REFORMS ARRIVED, AS THEY ALWAYS DO, AFTER HARM HAS ALREADY TAKEN ROOT.

Judicial corruption and organised crime, Mexico, 2012 (composite case)

In Mexico City, afternoons can turn the street into a shimmering plane where distance looks like water. The air wavers above concrete. Edges blur. A figure seems closer than it is. A promise seems real until you reach for it. Heat makes mirages honest, especially since it doesn't invent illusions; instead, it shows how easily the eye can be convinced. It teaches, brutally, that perception is not protection.

Judge Alejandro Torres built his career with that kind of optical deception.

In court he wore the toga judicial over a white shirt and tie, the cloth falling in disciplined lines that suggested seriousness, restraint, impartiality. He had presided over high-profile criminal cases for nearly two decades. Lawyers respected him. Defendants feared him. The public recognized his name and believed the costume meant something. Torres cultivated that belief carefully, the way some men cultivate gardens: daily, patiently, with attention to small appearances that others overlook.

He spoke of order, of stability, of the judiciary as the last barrier between citizens and chaos. He ran his courtroom with meticulous control. Procedures adhered. Deadlines enforced. He corrected sloppy language. He demanded proper citations. That visible discipline became a shield for what happened off the record. People mistook severity for purity; they assumed a man who tightened screws in public would not loosen bolts in private.

Torres first felt the cartel's interest when a major trafficking case landed in his courtroom. The defendant arrived with counsel that seemed unusually confident-too calm in a room designed to intimidate. There were no flamboyant threats, no obvious bribes. Instead, intermediaries appeared the way humidity appears before rain: gradually, almost politely, as if they had always been part of the atmosphere.

They were ordinary men with ordinary faces who understood how to speak to a system that wanted to be left alone. They offered hints first: a number to call if his son ever had "trouble on the road," a friend who could "help" with a property dispute, a doctor who could "make appointments easier." They framed themselves as inevitable. This is how things work. The sentence never needed to be spoken aloud; it hung in pauses, in smiles that lasted a half-second too long.

Torres told himself he could manage it. He knew he could take what was offered and keep it contained. That he could maintain order by controlling the terms of engagement. In that self-story, he wasn't surrendering; he was negotiating with gravity.

But the deeper seduction was not money. It was power.

A ruling delayed here. A piece of evidence "reviewed" there. A witness's schedule adjusted so a key appearance became "impractical." Torres learned how small technical decisions could redirect a case's gravity. He could shift outcomes without leaving obvious traces. The toga judicial made those shifts look like judgment rather than intervention. And each time he did it without consequence, he felt an intoxicating confirmation: the system was clay in his hands.

Soon his office became a quiet hub of secrecy. Confidential files moved in and out under strange circumstances. Requests for access came from people who had no formal reason to ask. A document would appear with a different staple pattern, as if it had been briefly reborn elsewhere. Some folders returned smelling faintly of cigarette smoke, though no one in his chambers smoked. The smallest details carried their own language: misaligned signatures, overwritten dates, a memo reprinted on slightly different paper stock.

Like an invasive species finding a new ecosystem, the cartel did not need to destroy the court. It only needed to live inside it-feeding off routine, hiding in paperwork, blending into the daily hum until no one remembered the difference between normal and compromised. That is how cartels use systems: not by replacing them, but by inhabiting them. They don't always aim to overthrow the state; they aim to rent it. They learn which clerk controls the schedule, which administrator holds the keys, and which judge believes he is untouchable. They exploit the human weakness that keeps institutions running: the desire to avoid conflict, the habit of looking away, the belief that survival requires cooperation.

And they enforce their rules with a purity the law rarely achieves.

No mercy for those breaking the rules: not the cartel's rules, not the rules of silence, not the unwritten rule that says we don't speak about what we all know.

Clara Medina noticed.

She was a seasoned court administrator with a memory for details most people consider trivial: timestamps, sign-out logs, the way a clerk's handwriting changes when they are nervous. Clara had worked long enough to understand that corruption rarely announces itself. People first feel it as friction-small disruptions in patterns that used to make sense. She noticed scheduling anomalies that always benefited the same side; case files moved without proper notation; witness subpoenas were delayed. The chain-of-custody records for evidence began developing gaps like missing teeth.

At first she tried to explain it as incompetence. Everyone does. In institutions, incompetence is comforting because it's impersonal; it doesn't imply danger. But the gaps kept forming in the same direction. That directional consistency made her skin prickle.

Clara began documenting everything-quietly, methodically. She kept copies of the logs. She noted names. She saved emails. She made parallel lists: what the docket said should exist versus what she could physically find. The work felt like collecting grains of sand, but she understood grains become dunes, and dunes can bury a lie until it becomes landscape.

Then intimidation arrived-not dramatic, not explicit. A car lingering too long outside her apartment. An unfamiliar caller who hung up after she answered. A comment at work about her children's school, delivered as if it were casual conversation: "My cousin's son goes there. Nice place." The man who said it smiled politely, and the politeness was the threat. It told her: We see your life outside the courthouse.

The next day, a stray dog appeared near the entrance of her building, limping. It wasn't her dog. It stared at her with a calmness that felt accusatory, then vanished down the street. Clara later told herself the dog meant nothing. But that's how fear works: it attaches meaning to whatever it can reach, because meaning is preparation.

Clara did not need a direct threat to understand the message. She needed someone she could trust.

She chose Inspector Rafael Ibarra, a contact from years earlier when the court implemented a digital filing transition and the federal police had consulted on document security. Rafael was not a friend in the warm sense; he was a professional acquaintance with a reputation for discretion and a habit of speaking plainly. Clara called him from a payphone near a busy market, the place where voices dissolve into crowd noise. She didn't use names at first.

"I have a pattern," she said. "Not a rumor. A pattern."

Rafael's pause was momentary. "If you're calling me, it's serious." "It's dangerous," Clara corrected.

"What do you need?"

"I need to know if you can keep me alive," she said, surprised by her own bluntness.

The line went quiet except for distant traffic. Then Rafael said, carefully, "I can try. But you need to understand something: in this city, people sell truth the way they sell fruit-by the kilogram. You can't assume anyone is clean just because they wear a badge."

There it was-the doubt that arrived not as imagination, but as reality. In a world of contradictions and personal gains, who can someone trust? Clara felt her throat tighten. She had hoped for certainty. Instead, she received honesty, which is rarer and colder.

Rafael asked for evidence, not a story. Clara arranged a meeting in daylight, in a public park where families walked and vendors sold ice cream, because cartel violence thrives in private spaces where witnesses disappear. She handed him copies-logs, emails, docket inconsistencies, chain-of-custody gaps. She did not give him the originals. That was her own adaptation to the cartel's world: never hand over your entire life in one envelope. Rafael looked through the documents and said, "This isn't random."

"No," Clara replied. "It's curated." "And the judge?"

Clara swallowed. "I think he's the hinge."

"Think," Rafael repeated softly. Not skepticism-warning. "If you're wrong, they will ruin you. If you're right, they might kill you."

That was the life-threatening geometry of it: the risk existed on both sides of the truth.

After the meeting, Clara noticed two men by a food cart who seemed to watch her too long. Their attire resembled that of office workers, featuring button-down shirts and cheap watches, yet it lacked any dramatic flair. When she turned, one of them smiled as if she were a neighbor. The friendliness made her blood run cold. She walked home through streets shimmering with heat, and the mirage-like air made every distance feel unreliable. Safety looked close until she tried to measure it.

The turning point came when an anti-corruption task force probing cartel operations received anonymous tips about judicial involvement. Clara, already holding a private archive of anomalies, acted. She provided her records-dates, patterns, missing-file sequences, communications that pointed toward an internal hand guiding outcomes. Rafael delivered them through channels designed to withstand interference: encrypted transfers, redundant copies, and compartmentalized teams so no single leak could erase the whole.

Investigators followed the trail through digital forensics, witness interviews, and procedural analysis. They did not need a single confession. Confessions are fragile; they can be recanted, intimidated out of existence. They needed the shape of the pattern-and Clara had given them that.

The scope was worse than many suspected. Torres had not orchestrated violence directly, but his decisions had protected violence indirectly. By bending procedure, he had given criminal power room to breathe. Witnesses who might have testified were delayed until they disappeared. Evidence that might have convicted was "misfiled" until deadlines expired. The court did not pull the trigger; it cleared the path. The toga judicial became camouflage, and camouflage is dangerous because it makes predators look like furniture.

Then the cartel's own rulebook asserted itself.

Someone found a clerk beaten behind a warehouse one morning. He had spoken too freely in a bar and was alive but broken. The message traveled faster than any official memo. No one needed to say the cartel's name; it was present in the silence that followed. The building became more careful. People stopped using personal phones. Doors closed more gently. Even laughter in the break room sounded forced, like a performance staged for invisible listeners.

Clara pulled her children out of school for a week. She told the principal it was illness. She watched the street from behind the curtains. In the late afternoon, when the heat made the asphalt shimmer, she saw the same car pass twice, slowly. On the third pass, it didn't slow down. That was almost worse-a sign that the watchers wanted her to know they could be casual.

Rafael arranged protective measures-nothing cinematic, nothing that guaranteed safety. A change in routine. A secure location for key documents. Instructions on what to do if someone approached her with "friendliness." Yet even Rafael's help came with doubt. Clara understood that trust in this environment is never total. Trust is a series of calculated risks-choosing the least dangerous betrayal.

The consequences eventually landed. The authorities suspended Torres and prosecuted him. His career ended not with a single dramatic revelation, but with accumulated evidence that made denial impossible. The court's leadership announced reforms: strengthened oversight, improved digital tracking, randomized case assignments, and reinforced reporting mechanisms. Reforms arrived, as they always do, after harm has already taken root.

Public trust cracked. People argued in cafes and on radio programs about whether justice had ever been real or only staged. The city's heat continued to shimmer, reminding everyone that appearances can be convincing and still be false.

Torres's story remains a stark warning: ceremonial symbols can project integrity, but they cannot manufacture it. In a city where mirages are common, the toga judicial is not proof of virtue. It is only cloth-made dangerous or honorable by the choices beneath it. And when cartels learn to use systems, they buy not only outcomes; they buy silence. They turn rules into weapons, and they punish those who break them with a certainty the state often cannot match. In that contradiction, the heat does not lie. It simply shows how easily we mistake shimmer for water-until we realize thirst has been guiding our eyes all along.

47

"THE COURT THAT SOLD CHILDHOOD"

PROCEDURE IS A BLADE WHEN IT'S HELD WITH A SMILE.

"Kids for Cash" judicial-corruption scandal in Pennsylvania, USA.

Snow fell the morning the first boy received his sentence. Not the cinematic kind-no floating poetry-just a thin, mean sleet that made the courthouse steps shine like bone. Parents wiped their shoes on the mat and believed the building was built for fairness because belief is efficient. The flag outside moved stiffly in the cold, and the seal over the door looked solemn enough to promise protection.

Judge Harlan wore the black robe as if it were a natural skin. The white neckband-his small flag of office-sat at his throat with the calm geometry of legitimacy. He rarely raised his voice. He did not need to. His power was not volume; it was routine. He had the smooth cadence of a man who could turn judgment into paperwork, and paperwork into inevitability.

The hearings moved fast. Too fast.

Children stood in front of him with hands shaking in their pockets, hearing words they did not understand: "adjudication," "disposition," "placement." Harlan spoke those terms the way a butcher speaks of cuts of meat-professionally, without emotion, as if the body in front of him were already reduced to category.

Sometimes he smiled, a small, practiced curve that suggested patience, and the room relaxed because humans confuse friendliness with justice. A boy would glance at his mother, as if to ask whether smiling meant safe. A mother would nod because she wanted to believe it.

The public defender assigned that morning was late. Traffic, he said. Someone murmured that he was not assigned at all. The word "waived" slid past like a bead of water on glass. The boy did not understand the waiver. He did not understand that America's promises-due process, counsel, fair hearing-were not magic spells. They were rights that required enforcement, like locks that only work if someone checks the door.

Outside, the wind pushed icy grit along the streets like a broom trying to erase footprints. No ambulances were required. The floor remained free of spilled blood. That was the trick. The harm looked clean. The building smelled of disinfectant and old paper. The bailiff's shoes squeaked on the polished tile. Everything about the environment said order.

The sentence landed lightly, as if it were a correction rather than a removal. Placement. The word sounded like an administrative favor, not a cage. The boy was led away, and the next file came up. Harlan's pen moved. The docket advanced. The machine was efficient. Efficiency in a courtroom can be another kind of violence.

The parents who complained were told they were "emotional." The lawyers who asked for time were denied it. Continuances were treated like indulgences. The judge's patience became part of the performance-he would tilt his head, as if hearing a child's excuse, and then he would cut it off with a sentence that sounded parental: You need structure. The local paper praised him as "tough on youth crime," as if toughness were a merit in itself, as if children were simply small adults who deserved the same cold consequences.

Meanwhile, the private detention center outside town filled. Beds that had been empty became occupied. Vans arrived in the early mornings and late afternoons like deliveries. The facility sent glossy pamphlets to local agencies, promising "rehabilitation," "character building," "accountability." Its language was clean enough to pass as care. On paper, it sounded like help. It sounded like doors locking.

The pattern emerged in the way mold emerges: not as one dramatic bloom, but as an odor you can't explain until you stop pretending it isn't there. Parents began comparing notes. A boy sent away for fighting. A girl sent away for a prank. Another for truancy. Another for minor theft. No one case looked like a crisis. Together they formed a shape.

And then money entered, quietly-through intermediaries, through "fees," through friendships dressed as professionalism. The robe made the exchange feel impossible. Who imagines corruption under that kind of cloth? The community didn't want to imagine it. Imagination is expensive; denial is cheap. People preferred the comforting story: Harlan is strict because he cares.

In America, the Constitution is supposed to be the floor beneath your feet-cold maybe, but solid. It promises that the government cannot take your liberty without due process of law. It promises you have the right to counsel when the state is trying to deprive you of freedom. It promises, at least in principle, that punishment is not supposed to be purchased. But those promises are only words unless someone in the room insists they matter. Here, the court treated the words like decor by framing, citing, and ignoring them.

A court clerk-middle-aged, careful, loyal to routine-noticed that certain referrals always landed in the same place. Certain cases always ended with the same outcome. The detention center's invoices were consistent. The county's "placements" rose like a steady graph. She noticed that the judge's calendar included lunches and "community partnerships" with men who owned the very beds the children were filling. It was not proof. It was a smell. And smell, when it grows strong enough, becomes evidence.

A mother finally demanded a transcript. Another filed a complaint with the state. A journalist from outside the county asked for numbers. Once the questions moved beyond the town's polite perimeter, the air changed. The same courthouse that had felt immovable felt like a stage set: convincing from the front row, fragile when you tug at the seams.

When it broke-indictments, reversals, national disgust-people spoke as if the scandal had arrived suddenly. But it had been growing for years in plain sight, watered by deference. The shock wasn't only that money had passed hands; it was that the money had purchased something the Constitution treats as sacred: liberty.

Childhood. Time that is unrecoverable.

Families learned what "due process" means when you don't get it. They learned what it means to sign a "waiver" you don't understand. They learned what it means to stand in a courtroom without a lawyer while a judge smiles and calls it fairness. Rights that exist only on paper are like umbrellas left at home in a blizzard-comforting in theory, useless in the storm.

In the aftermath, committees assembled with grave faces. Officials spoke about reforms. There were promises of better oversight, better training, better safeguards for juveniles: ensuring counsel is present, ensuring waivers are knowing and voluntary, ensuring transparency in placements. The system performed repentance the way it performed justice-ceremonially, efficiently, with press releases.

But no press release can restore a lost year. No committee can erase the moment authorities take a child from a parent and transport them to a place that profits from the child's absence. The damage isn't only legal; it is psychic. It teaches people that authority is not protection. It teaches parents that institutions can speak the language of rights while practicing the economics of exploitation.

The snow melted. The courthouse stayed standing. Spring arrived, and the streets dried. The flag still hung outside. The seal still gleamed over the door. Tourists still walked past, assuming solidity meant integrity.

The families carried the thaw in their bodies for much longer-proof that authority can injure without striking, and that ceremony can make cruelty look like policy. The children had not needed rescue; they had needed protection. They needed a system that prevented the fall, not a committee that mourned afterward. And that is the deepest American irony of it: a nation built on constitutional guarantees still required, after the fact, apologies and reversals-dramatic forms of rescue-because the quiet duty of enforcement had failed where it mattered most.

MATRIX 3 — PROCEDURE (LAW)

What procedure buys, how it hides, what it leaves behind, and where PRGR bites.

Procedural move	What it buys	How it hides	Signature + human cost / PRGR friction
Delay / adjourn / defer	Time as punishment; exhaustion; fading witnesses	"Backlog," "complexity," "awaiting instructions"	Leaves: drifting deadlines, worn-out challengers. Cost: life on hold. PRGR: delay must be signed + foreseeable harm + review date.
Non-disclosure / partial disclosure	Asymmetric knowledge; controlled narrative	"Privilege," "sensitive material," "not relevant"	Leaves: gaps, redactions, 'missing' exhibits. Cost: defence blindfolded. PRGR: withholding requires authored reasons + independent audit trigger.
Administrative closure / file 'resolved'	Ends scrutiny; protects reputations	"Insufficient grounds," "no action," "finalised"	Leaves: no author, no remedy, only a closed file. Cost: harm becomes permanent. PRGR: no closure without signature + remedy pathway.
Delegation / diffusion (committees, handoffs)	No owner; plausible deniability	"Referred," "escalated," "outside scope"	Leaves: endless referrals, no accountable chooser. Cost: claimant disappears. PRGR: every handoff names the deciding actor + duty to act.
Procedural compliance theatre	Legitimacy without truth	"We followed process," "policy complied with"	Leaves: perfect paperwork, wrong outcome. Cost: reality loses to form. PRGR: process is invalid if harm is unowned or unremedied.
Retaliatory process (burden-shifting, credibility erosion)	Silence through risk; deterrence	"Vexatious," "uncooperative," "tone"	Leaves: character on trial, not facts. Cost: shame + withdrawal. PRGR: any adverse label must be authored and appealable with evidence.

THE TRIGGER IS OBJECTIVE, NOT THE MOOD

PRGR FORCES THE CLOCK TO START EARLIER. BEFORE THE FALL, NOT AFTER THE FUNERAL.

By now, you've seen how institutions talk themselves out of urgency. They turn injury into "complexity," then wait for fatigue to do the rest. The story repeats because the incentive repeats: delay is a weapon that looks neutral.

And I should say this plainly, because it changes how you read everything that follows: *I am not writing for revenge*. I'm not trying to humiliate the people who sat behind the bench or the committees who signed the paper. I don't need them to suffer to make my point. What I want is smaller and harder: a system that will not do to the next person what it did so efficiently to me. I want the young lawyer, the intern, the clerk, the defendant, the priest who raises a concern, the academic who refuses to flatter a superior-whoever ends up in that chair-protected by structure rather than luck. I want the outcome, whatever it is, to be owned.

So the PRGR point I want to anchor here is structural: the trigger is objective. If harm is foreseeable-liberty, livelihood, legal standing, professional exclusion, long-term reputational harm, safety-the record is required. No exemptions for urgency, hierarchy, or tradition.

This matters because discretion is where favoritism hides. If the institution gets to decide when accountability "applies," it will apply it to the weak and waive it for the useful. I've been in rooms where people argued about thresholds as if thresholds were ethics. They're not. They're strategy.

An objective trigger is how I stop ethics from becoming a popularity contest. If these chapters feel repetitive, it's because the institution keeps using the same move: treating foreseeable harm as if it were unforeseeable until after it lands.

PRGR forces the clock to start earlier. Before the fall, not after the funeral.

48

"THE BARRISTER'S GLIDE"

IT REARRANGED BLAME UNTIL IT LOOKED LIKE ACCOUNTABILITY.

Suspension of high-profile lawyer, Netherlands, 2013 (composite case), PRGR

CHAIR: Please state your name for the record.

RESPONDENT: Thomas Prins.

Thomas Prins sat in a room that smelled of copier toner and stale coffee, wearing the only suit he owned that still looked like it belonged in a courtroom.

The chair's microphone was too close; it made every breath sound like an admission. Across from him, five panel members sat in a line-five faces arranged into practiced neutrality, like masks that had learned to smile without warmth. Behind them, a portrait of the Queen stared outward like an eye that never blinked.

Prins had once been proud of what portraits like that implied: stability, restraint, fairness administered by procedure.

He had defended Marcus Hill in a capital trial in the city-appointed, under-funded, outgunned. He had made mistakes, yes, but mistakes on a battlefield designed to exhaust the defender until exhaustion became evidence of moral failure.

COUNSEL FOR THE BAR: Mr. Prins, did you request independent forensic testing?

PRINS: I requested funds. The motion was denied.

His voice came out flat, not from arrogance but from depletion. Years of speaking into rooms that treated structural failure as personal weakness had sanded down his tone.

COUNSEL: Did you interview the state's informant prior to trial?

PRINS: I attempted to. Access proved limited. Time was a constraint for me.

Time-the invisible predator in every under-funded defense case. It doesn't roar. It just shortens distances until choices become losses.

Outside, a storm was building. Prins could feel it the way bodies sometimes feel weather: pressure dropping, humidity thickening, a subtle agitation in the muscles. He had seen this pattern in court too-the storm that arrives not as lightning but as accumulation: one hostile question, then another, then another, until the air becomes unbreathable.

The committee spoke.

Not one at a time, exactly. They took turns, but the effect was collective. Five against one. Ten ears leaned forward in concert-ten ears that, Prins realised, would hear nineteen different things. Each panel member caught a different emphasis, a different stumble, a different tone. Yet when they combined their perceptions, their collective brain brewed a single drink: a verdict.

PANEL MEMBER 1: You filed the motion late. Why?

PRINS: I received the lab report late.

PANEL MEMBER 2: But you could have expected the need.

PRINS: I anticipated it. I asked for funding earlier.

PANEL MEMBER 3: Your notes suggest you "considered" calling the witness but chose not to.

PRINS: I had to triage. I had limited investigative time.

PANEL MEMBER 4: That sounds like an excuse.

PRINS: It's an explanation.

They weren't shouting. That was the cruelty of it. Verbal abuse does not require volume. It can be done with immaculate grammar, with calm voices, with questions shaped like accusations. Their technique was institutional: reduce complexity to checklists, then punish the person who couldn't satisfy a checklist built for a world where resources are equal.

The bar counsel leaned in and said the quiet part out loud.

COUNSEL: Many attorneys manage capital cases effectively within the same constraints. Why didn't you?

It was superiority disguised as inquiry-the assumption that the system's constraints were manageable if you were simply more competent. It translated the state's advantage into Prins's deficiency. It made inequality sound like a character flaw.

Prins felt anger rise like heat in a sealed flask.

"Because the constraints weren't equal," he said, and his voice finally carried something sharp. "Because the state had three investigators and a lab and unlimited motions practice. Because I had one paralegal shared with four other attorneys and a calendar designed to break me."

The chair tapped a pen gently-the small ritual of authority, calming a room without acknowledging truth.

CHAIR: Mr. Prins, please answer the question asked.

That sentence was its own kind of discipline: Stay inside our frame. The frame was the committee's power. If Prins spoke about structure, they called it evasion. If he spoke about his choices, they called it a confession.

PRINS: I did what I could within the resources provided. I decided under constraints that were not of my choosing.

PANEL MEMBER 5: Yet a man's life was at stake.

PRINS: Yes. That's why I asked for resources. The panel repeated his words back to him, distorted.

PANEL MEMBER 2: So you're saying it's not your responsibility.

PRINS: I'm saying it's shared responsibility.

PANEL MEMBER 3: Shared responsibility is another way of avoiding accountability.

Ten ears, nineteen interpretations. Their collective brain poured the same drink, anyway.

Prins explained late nights, denied funding, suppressed evidence he didn't know existed, and forensic testimony he lacked resources to challenge. He admitted what he could not defend: an interview missed, a point not pressed hard enough, a fatigue he had mistaken for endurance. Each admission landed like blood in water-immediately noticeable, immediately used.

When the hearing ended, he stepped outside into wind so sudden it felt like the world changing lanes. Rain began in sharp drops, then became a sheet. It soaked his suit and made the pavement shine like oil. People hurried past with umbrellas, protected by thin fabric the way institutions protect themselves: enough to stay dry, not enough to stop the storm.

Weeks later, the decision arrived: suspension, public reprimand, an official warning. Two eyes would read it. One brain would interpret it. And the interpretation would be simple, because simplicity is what verdicts deliver: He failed.

What the verdict did not say-what it could not say without accusing the system-was that the committee had performed its own kind of theater. It had taken the messy truth of an under-funded defense and distilled it into a digestible narrative. A scapegoat is a story you can file.

Kerr-the prosecutor who built the case-remained celebrated in many circles. Judges spoke of him with respect. The institution protected its highest-status actors and disciplined the one easiest to portray as incompetent.

Prins's fall did not free Marcus Hill. It did something else: it rearranged blame until it looked like accountability.

And that was the lesson Prins carried out into the cleared air after the storm: when an institution fails, it prefers a human container for its failure-someone with fewer allies, fewer credentials, less prestige. Then it calls the selection "standards," "integrity," "professional conduct," as if words themselves could launder discomfort into ethics.

Ten ears. Nineteen meanings. One drink poured.

The Board didn't say: "He is dishonest." It said: "He is a risk." PRGR teaches that "risk" is how institutions talk when they want certainty but cannot prove character."

And in the end, the verdict tasted exactly the way it tasted: bitter, official, and impossible to appeal to anyone who wasn't in the room.

PRGR END-CAP - AUTHORED HARM TEST

(for "THE BARRISTER'S GLIDE")

The harm in this case is not that Prins made no mistakes. The harm is **what the institution did with the mistakes once it had them**-how it translated resource scarcity into personal deficiency, and then called that translation "standards."

PRGR would attach authorship at the exact step where the committee converts structural constraint into moral verdict. In this story, the hinge-steps are not hidden. They are spoken aloud, calmly, as if calm itself makes them true.

The hinge-steps where PRGR would force the author to exist

The funding denial that becomes invisible Prins says it plainly: he requested funds for independent testing; the motion was denied. The first authored-harm step is not the denial alone-it is the system treating that denial as background weather. PRGR would trigger at the denial and require the denying authority to author:

what resources were denied, why,

what foreseeable harm the denial creates (unchallenged forensics, missed leads, reduced cross-examination capacity),

and why proceeding remains ethically acceptable. If the state insists on life-and-death outcomes, PRGR insists the state signs the cost of underfunding.

The triage moment - when "I had to" is treated as confession
Prins admits he "considered" calling a witness but chose not to; he "attempted" to interview the informant but access was limited; he filed late because the lab report arrived late. PRGR triggers at every decision that is *forced* by scarcity but later judged as choice. It requires authorship of constraint:

what the constraint was (time, denial of funds, limited access), what options were realistically available,

what harm is foreseeable from each option,

and why the selected path was the least harmful.

PRGR prevents the committee's favorite laundering move: turning "no resources" into "no responsibility."

The checklist trap - the moment complexity is reduced to a failure narrative
The committee's method is institutional: reduce the messy truth of an under-funded defense into a checklist, then punish the person who can't satisfy a checklist designed for equal-resourced worlds.

PRGR triggers when the committee adopts that frame.

It requires the committee to author:

why the checklist standard is appropriate under known resource disparity, what structural conditions would have to exist for the standard to be fair,

and what reforms they will implement if they truly believe the standard is non-negotiable. If they will not fund fairness, PRGR forces them to admit they are enforcing appearance, not justice.

The "answer the question asked" move - procedural discipline used to suppress structural truth
When Prins speaks about inequality, the Chair narrows him back into "our frame." That sentence is not neutral. It's the point where the institution refuses structural evidence and calls the refusal order. PRGR would trigger at any instruction that constrains testimony in a way that predictably excludes causal context. It requires authorship of what is being excluded and why:

what categories of explanation are disallowed,

what harm is foreseeable from excluding them (mis-attributed blame, repeated system failure), and

what alternative forum exists for structural review.

The scapegoat selection - punishment that preserves the institution

The verdict that arrives later is simple: "He failed." Not written is the institution's own role in shaping the conditions of failure.

PRGR triggers at the sanction decision.

The committee must author:

whether systemic resource constraints contributed, why they are or aren't decisive,

what parallel accountability exists for funders/administrators,

and what repair will prevent recurrence.

PRGR forces symmetry: if one actor is disciplined, the system must also name its own causal role-or admit it is reallocating blame for institutional comfort.

What PRGR would force in this case (practical safeguards matched to the glide)

1. **A "resource denial → harm forecast" record**
   Every denial of defense resources in high-stakes cases triggers a signed harm forecast by the denying authority and a mandatory escalation pathway. No denial without ownership.

2. **A "constraint-aware standard" requirement**
   Disciplinary review must explicitly state what resources were available, what were denied, and how standards are calibrated to reality. If the committee insists standards are fixed, it must author the funding and access conditions required to meet them.

3. **A structural review lane separate from personal discipline**
   PRGR would require a second track: when a case shows patterns of constraint-driven failure, the institution must initiate an institutional audit (funding, scheduling, investigative access). Otherwise discipline becomes theater.

4. **An irreversible-harm trigger**
   If a case involves "life-or-death" stakes, PRGR requires heightened thresholds:

no proceeding without minimum investigation capacity, minimum expert access, and a documented record of what is missing and who chose to proceed anyway.

The questions that keep this End-Cap specific to Prins (not generic)

If you were Prins: which decision would you force into authored form first-the funding denial, the late lab report timing, the un-interviewed informant, or the witness you triaged away?

If you were the committee: are you willing to sign a statement that your standards remain fair under the resource inequality Prins describes-and if so, what funding reforms will you author to make that statement true?

If you were the institution's funders: would you sign your name under the foreseeable harms of denying resources in a capital case, knowing that later blame will be assigned to the cheapest person to punish?

PRGR doesn't pretend humans can be perfect under constraint. It isolates the moment the institution **turns constraint into character**-and forces a named author to exist at the precise step where the system chooses a human container for its own failure.

49

"THE FILE THAT WANTED THE PERSON"

HE LOST BECAUSE INSTITUTIONS PREFER OUTCOMES THEY CAN DEFEND.

Request for rehabilitation of a lawyer, Netherlands, 2020, PRGR

Five years is a unit of time that pretends to be neutral. It looks tidy on paper. It sounds like a sentence that has ended. It fits the mouth of a committee chair. It slides cleanly into a paragraph of reasons.

Five years is an ecosystem: a slow collapse of certainty, a long improvisation of rent and reputation, and the ordinary humiliations of being uninvited to your former life. It is the time it takes for friends to become acquaintances, for savings to become stories, for the word *former* to attach itself to your name like a persistent odor.

When people say "after five years," what they often mean is: *the institution is prepared to consider you again*-not because you are healed, not because you are safe, but because the calendar has done its ceremonial work.

The Applicant

A lawyer named Bastian C. resided in a provincial city that promoted itself as orderly. His charisma, which clients felt was like oxygen, gave them the sense that someone had finally appeared who could represent them without fear, just like his father did. Bastian's voice filled rooms, sharp, exact, to the point. His suits were a kind of argument. He moved with the ease of a man who believes the law is a stage that rewards those who understand the lighting.

Then they took him away.

The story of the removal did not matter here, because it was the story that arrived prepackaged: a cluster of breaches translated into a single moral. Whether you think the decision was inevitable or vindictive depends on which side of the profession you were standing on. People always have theories about the fall of a prominent lawyer. Theories are a way of keeping the profession clean: if we can explain his collapse as a personal defect, we don't have to look too closely at the architecture that produced him.

Five years later, Bastian applied to return.

In public, this is called clemency. In private, it is called *reinstatement*. The difference between the two words is the difference between a human and a file. Clemency implies a heart. Reinstatement implies a registry.

He asked to be allowed to wear the robe again-to be licensed again to touch other people's emergencies. He did not ask the institution to admit it had been wrong. He asked it to admit he might now be fit.

This is an offer the institution rarely likes, because it contains an unspoken insult: *You decided once. I am asking you to decide again.*

The Board

The hearing took place before a body that called itself the **Supervisory Council of Appeal**-a name made of nouns stacked like boxes. The room was bright and unromantic. The elevated long table, positioned to look down, signified dominance over those below.

Water glasses aligned at attention. A wall clock that did not care about shame.

The Council did not need to shout to command a room. It only needed a procedure.

There is a ritual to professional discipline: the applicant speaks, but not too freely; the Council listens, but not too warmly. The Council speaks in questions that are shaped like conclusions. They test each answer for tone: if it is too emotional, they deem you unstable; if it is too calm, they consider you unrepentant. The Council is always calm; calm is the privilege of authority.

Cameras rolled the day of the final verdict. Newspapers later printed the reasons for refusal, and the profession's cafes retold them. The public loves the morality play of a fallen lawyer because it reassures them that the system has antibodies. The profession loves it too, for the same reason.

Among the reasons was this: **after being disbarred, Bastian filed for bankruptcy**. And in the five years that followed, **he did not pay off all debts**.

It is easy to see why this appealed to the Council.

Misconduct often complicates matters. It requires context. It requires the Council to admit it is evaluating behavior inside a profession that generates privileges, incentives, shortcuts, and temptations. Financial residue, by contrast, is clean. It is arithmetic. It is the thing you can circle in red.

A debt is a number with moral potential.

The PRGR Lens

In The *Robe and The Ledger - Robes, Jabots and Human Failure*, PRGR is not a statute. It is a pattern.

It is the engine behind many dignified decisions: **the way institutions translate messy lives into manageable risk**; the way procedure becomes a moral instrument; the way a person's history is, converts it into a forecast.
PRGR does not ask: *Who are you now?* It asks: *What can we safely predict you will do?*

And if prediction fails, PRGR supplies an escape hatch: *We acted prudently given the information.*

Therefore, disciplinary bodies prefer clean variables. They prefer evidence that is fileable. They prefer narratives they can repeat without blushing. A person is unpredictable. We can make a file look inevitable. So when the Council looked at Bastian's bankruptcy, it saw not only financial hardship. It saw:

possible dependence on others, possible pressure,

possible vulnerability to inducement, possible resentment,

possible instability.

"Financial integrity" is rarely about morality in the confessional sense. It is about independence. A lawyer who owes is a lawyer who can be pulled. The profession knows this because it has seen it, and because it fears it, and because it is easier to ban the vulnerable than to admit the profession produces vulnerability as a byproduct.

But PRGR adds something sharper: institutions are tempted to treat **the consequences of punishment as proof the punishment was justified**.

Disbar someone, and you remove their income and their identity in one motion. Many will then collapse financially. When they do, the institution can point to the collapse and say: *See? Unfit.*

This is a self-sealing loop masquerading as prudence.

What Could Have Changed the Decision?

The question is not whether Bastian should have been reinstated. The question is: **could the Council's reliance on the unpaid debts have been disrupted?**

Under PRGR, disruption rarely comes from emotion. It comes from boredom. Institutions do not relax because you suffer. They relax because the risk becomes dull.

If Bastian had wanted to reduce the weight of the debt argument-if he wanted to puncture the Council's clean narrative-he would have needed to replace ambiguity with documentation so thorough it became tiresome.

Not "I am trying." Not "I have learned." Not "I had no chance."

Instead:

A creditor schedule listing every debt, its origin, and its present status. Proof of payments over time-consistent, dated, traceable.

Settlement agreements where settlements exist, and written refusals where they do not. A formal repayment plan approved by an independent administrator.

A simple explanation of any third-party assistance: who paid, why, under what conditions, with what separation from any future practice.

A declaration of ongoing obligations that might revive (contingent claims), accompanied by evidence of how exposure is contained.

Then-crucially-a firewall.

Re-entry into the profession is not merely about morality. It is about the environment. If the Council's fear is that financial instability could compromise independence, the applicant must show not only personal intent but *structural safeguards*.

PRGR predicts a Council is more willing to accept a person back if it can tell itself: *we are not trusting character alone; we are trusting a system.*

That could mean a supervised practice arrangement that is genuinely bounded: not a symbolic "mentor," but rules that prevent an easy relapse into old habits-financial oversight, client money restrictions, periodic reporting, limitations on the kinds of matters handled, a staged return rather than a full restoration.

This is not mercy. It is engineering.

And it is often the only mercy institutions can tolerate.

Because an institution does not want to forgive; it wants to reduce the chance it will have to apologize later.

Why It Might Have Changed Nothing

But PRGR also teaches a darker lesson: sometimes the outcome is not about solvable risk. Sometimes it is about symbolic discipline.

There are cases where the Council needs the refusal to stand-not because the applicant is uniquely dangerous, but because the Council's authority depends on permanence. A famous fall must remain a warning sign. If it becomes reversible, then disbarment becomes less like a cliff and more like a penalty box. The profession cannot bear that, because it depends on the threat of exile to keep its members aligned.

In such cases, a debt becomes useful not because it is decisive, but because it is available.

The Council can say: *"We are not punishing him twice; we are protecting the public."* The language is always protection. Protection is the profession's most socially acceptable instinct.

And because debts can almost always be described as unresolved in some form-especially after bankruptcy-there is always a way to keep the refusal looking rational.

Here PRGR shows the trap:

If you collapse after sanction, the collapse becomes proof you were unstable.

If you rebuild too quickly, the rebuilding becomes suspicious: *Who is funding you? What strings exist?*

If you repay slowly, the slowness becomes proof you are not restored.

If you repay with help, the help becomes proof you are dependent.

The applicant is asked to demonstrate independence in a situation designed to produce dependence.

The Council's Favorite word

The Council's decision, when it came, used a word that institutions love because it hides judgment inside a neutral-sounding shell.

RISK

Risk is what an institution says when it wants to be firm without sounding cruel. Risk is how it avoids describing a person as beyond redemption while still keeping them outside the gate. Risk is the polite face of permanent exclusion.

PRGR insists we look at what "risk" does here. It turns a moral question-*has this person changed?*-into an administrative one-*can we defend our decision if something goes wrong?*

The Council is not only protecting clients. It is protecting itself from future embarrassment. This is not cynicism; it is organizational survival. The Council is a body of humans, and humans respond to incentives. A reinstatement that later fails is a scandal. A refusal that later seems harsh is rarely punished.

PRGR would predict the Council's caution even if Bastian had become a saint.

The Conclusion That Remains

So the analysis holds two conclusions at once-conclusions that can coexist without canceling each other.

First conclusion: The debt reason was structurally convenient. It allowed the Council to convert a messy "restoration" question into a clean "independence" question. It allowed a moral narrative to be written in numbers.

Second conclusion: A PRGR-informed strategy could have helped, but only if it replaced moral pleading with documentary dullness and real safeguards. Even then, success would not be guaranteed because the case may have served symbolic purposes beyond its stated reasons.

This is the precise cruelty of professional discipline: it pretends to be individualized while often operating as theater for the group.

The proceeding treats the applicant as a person, so it feels fair. The decision serves as a signal, making the institution feel safe.

In the end, Bastian did not lose only because he owed money. He lost because institutions prefer outcomes they can defend.

And the easiest outcome to defend is always the one that keeps the curtains closed.

PART V

CLOSE

THE MAMASHIMI TRUST - BRISBANE AUSTRALIA

THE REFUSAL ITSELF IS THE FINDING

WATCHING A SYSTEM REPEAT ITSELF ACROSS DIFFERENT INSTITUTIONS.

By the time I reach chapter 50, I've seen enough repetition to stop treating it as coincidence. My story isn't "bad people sometimes exist." My story is "institutions have learned to make harm unowned."

So the last PRGR point I want to leave you with-before the case files someone told me to ignore-comes from the red line itself: from here on, silence is no longer neutrality; it is choice, and choice has a name.

My moral test becomes brutally simple: no inquiry into intent, no romance about complexity. If an institution refuses the PRGR, the refusal itself is the finding. I'm not pretending PRGR will make the world gentle. It won't. But it draws a boundary: no more harmless harm-harm that everyone admits happened, and no one admits they caused.

And now the personal part, the part I keep trying to edit out because it makes me feel exposed: I am writing this as someone who once believed the paperwork was the work. I believed in procedure the way people believe in architecture-because it stands, because it looks stable, because it seems designed to hold weight. I learned, the hard way, that a building can be perfectly built and still be used to trap people inside it.

I don't want revenge. I don't even want apologies from strangers in robes. I want the next person who walks into the room I walked into to meet something sturdier than tone and tradition. I want the clerk who knows something is wrong to have a lever they can pull without being destroyed for pulling it. I want the decent professional-who would never call themselves a villain-to be forced, gently but firmly, to write the sentence they usually avoid: ***I chose this. I knew it would hurt you. I did it anyway. Here is why.***

That is my résumé after these chapters: not bitterness, but a demand for authorship. If, after forty-nine chapters, the scenes feel like echoes, it's because I've been watching a system repeat itself across different institutions-procedure, money, intimacy-changing costumes, keeping the same engine. The only way to interrupt an engine is to name the person with a hand on the controls.

50

"THE VERDICT THAT OUTLIVED THE TRUTH"

THE PRECISE STEP WHERE CORRECTION WAS POSSIBLE AND STILL REFUSED.

Wrongful execution and systemic misconduct, United States, 2008 (composite case), PRGR

This time, the car would not bring him back to the confines of death row. This time, the doors remained unlocked and unsecured. The car would only deliver a locked and sealed casket containing a lifeless body, a vessel from which the spirit had been cruelly extracted. The heartbeat had ceased after the poison replaced the blood, leaving behind a haunting silence. His parents received the casket containing a lifeless body like an online-ordered carton of groceries. Swift, one signature needed. Payment fulfilled.

Those who orchestrated this grim event sought solace in glasses of spirits, attempting to wash away the haunting memory of witnessing a life extinguished. They tried to erase the last flicker of life in his eyes-one moment vibrant, the next, void of existence. The system accepted the mistake as collateral damage.

Judge Thomas Whitfield's gavel struck with a sound that seemed older than the room itself-oak on oak, certainty on uncertainty. The black robe, the courtroom, the practiced cadence: all of it performed the same function as stained glass in a cathedral or a Nobel medal pinned to a lapel. It didn't prove virtue. It suggested it. It asked the public to stop thinking and start believing.

And people did.

Outside, Alabama heat held the town in a slow fist. Thunder sat on the horizon like an unanswered question. The courthouse air-conditioning hummed, trying to imitate calm. Inside, the subject sat behind the defense table with his hands folded, as if neatness might make him legible to strangers.

He was thirty-one. Black. Poor. Unfamous. The person a system can lose without losing face.

The prosecution did not need to be brilliant. It needed to be coherent. A story that the prosecution could tell in a straight line to a room of citizens, whom they had summoned away from their real lives and told that common sense would substitute for expertise.

In the jury box sat a retiree whose hands remembered yarn more than cross-examination. A landscaper who spent his days making edges look clean. A bridge engineer who understood load, strain, failure-but not the psychology of a coerced witness. Their lives had weight and dignity. None of that made them trained in the mathematics of evidence.

A Michelin-star chef does not invite a random table of diners to decide whether vibes cooked an egg. Yet the legal system does exactly that and calls it democracy.

Joshua's trial began the way so many of these begin: with a pretense of balance. Two sides. Equal time. Equal chance. But equality of arms is a phrase that collapses under inspection, like cheap scaffolding.

The state arrived with resources-police, labs, paid experts, investigators, a machinery designed to produce a single outcome and call it public safety. The defense arrived with an inexperienced public defender, Rebecca Lane, a stack of files, and a calendar that punished her for wanting to be thorough. She did the only thing she could do: she fought with facts and watched facts bleed out through procedural cuts.

She pointed out the contradictions: a timeline that didn't hold, witness descriptions that shifted, forensic language that sounded confident while actually meaning "maybe." She asked for disclosure. She asked for more testing. She asked the court to slow down long enough to be correct.

The prosecution answered with urgency, the oldest perfume of power: we must act now.

And Judge Whitfield-who believed himself impartial the way a priest believes a cassock sanctifies him-ruled again and again in the state's favor, not because he hated Joshua, but because he trusted the institution's posture more than he trusted the possibility of its rot.

The jury watched the judge. They watched how he nodded. What he interrupted. What he allowed to linger. No one tells jurors this explicitly, but the room trains them: the robe is the compass. Follow it.

The jurors did what untrained people do when facing complexity: they reached for emotion and narrative, because emotion is easier than doubt.

Doubt is working. Doubt is a muscle. Doubt requires education, time, and humility. Institutions pretend they want doubt. They want closure.

Joshua received a conviction. The word came down like a stamp-efficient, final, impersonal. The judge pronounced the sentence with ceremonial gravity, like someone reciting an ancient spell because it had always been recited.

Outside the courthouse, someone sold peanuts. Someone laughed. A mother wiped a child's face. The world kept behaving as if the system had done what it claimed to do.

But the system does not seek truth.

It seeks procedural truth-the truth that survives paperwork.

PRGR END-CAP - AUTHORED HARM TEST

(for "THE VERDICT THAT OUTLIVED THE TRUTH")

The harm in this case isn't only that the system got it wrong. It's that, once the wrongness surfaced, the system **chose stability over correction**. A verdict can outlive the truth only when multiple actors keep making the same kind of decision: *leave it as it is; the cost of change is higher than the cost of injustice.*

PRGR would attach authorship at the exact hinge-step where an institution decides to preserve a verdict it no longer fully believes. In this story, the engine is not malice; it is institutional self-protection dressed as finality.

The hinge-steps where PRGR would force the author to exist

The first suppression of doubt - the moment "new information" is treated as nuisance When a credible contradiction appears (a recantation, new forensic findings, an alternative suspect, an undisclosed benefit, a document that changes meaning), PRGR triggers at the first internal decision to classify it as "non-material," "not reliable," or "insufficient."

The prosecutor / agency must author:

what the new information is, why it is being discounted,

what foreseeable harm follows from discounting it (continued incarceration, execution risk, reputational harm, loss of evidence over time),

and what independent review channel will test the discounting. PRGR prevents "we considered it" from becoming the last line before forgetting.

The procedural barricade - using standards of review as a moral shield
This case hinges on the system's favorite move: converting truth into *timing*. "Too late." "Procedurally barred." "Final."
PRGR triggers at the decision to invoke procedural barriers to avoid factual reconsideration.

The author must write:

what procedural doctrine is being used,

why it justifies refusing a truth-focused hearing,

and what harm is foreseeable from preferring finality to accuracy.
If the institution chooses finality, PRGR forces it to admit it chose finality.

The evidence custody decision - the moment the truth becomes unrecoverable
Verdicts outlive truth when evidence decays or disappears: lost files, destroyed samples, untestable exhibits, missing notes.
PRGR triggers at any decision to:

destroy evidence, deny retesting,

block access to exhibits,

or "close" records in ways that prevent independent verification.

The author must write:

what will be lost,

why loss is acceptable,

and what harm is foreseeable (permanent inability to correct error).
Because in this case, destruction is not maintenance; it is outcome protection.

The reputational calculus - the moment the office protects itself by keeping the verdict
If officials privately concede uncertainty but publicly defend certainty, PRGR triggers at the communications decision: press statements, court filings that overstate confidence, internal memos instructing staff to "hold the line." They must author:

what they know,

what they are claiming, why the gap exists,

and who benefits from the gap.
PRGR makes the office sign the lie as an act, not as atmosphere.

The re-victimization move - discrediting the truth-bearers

When witnesses recant, or new experts contradict old testimony, institutions often respond by attacking credibility: "unstable," "seeking attention," "unqualified," "confused."
PRGR triggers at the first decision to treat the truth-bearer as the problem rather than the evidence. The author must write:

what specific credibility defects exist, why they outweigh the substance,

and what independent testing will occur rather than mere dismissal. This blocks the classic move: replacing inquiry with character assassination.

The final refusal - denying relief despite acknowledged uncertainty

The critical hinge-step is the decision that closes the door even after doubt is real: denying a new trial, denying clemency, denying a commission to review, denying exoneration because "the standard isn't met."
PRGR triggers at that refusal.

The deciding body must author:

what level of doubt exists,

why the threshold is still not met,

what harm is foreseeable from denial (continued punishment of the wrong person),

and what remedy remains available (if any) in reality, not in theory.

PRGR forces the institution to sign the sentence: *we will keep the wrongness because correction costs us.*

What PRGR would force in this case (matched to wrongful finality)

1. **A "truth persistence" obligation**
   PRGR would require that once credible doubt appears, the institution must initiate a truth-focused review track that is separate from adversarial defense of the verdict. No office should both defend the conviction and decide whether to reopen it without authored justification.

2. **A preservation-and-access rule**
   No evidence destruction, no retesting denial, no access blocking without a signed harm forecast that acknowledges: *we are choosing irreversible loss.*

3. **A "finality justification" record**
   If a court or board relies on procedural bars, PRGR requires it to write plainly: why finality is being prioritized over accuracy, and what safeguards exist to prevent wrongful permanence. Finality becomes a signed moral choice, not an invisible default.

4. **A reversal trigger tied to specific indicators**
   PRGR would define automatic triggers for independent review when any of these occur:
   credible recantation with corroboration, new forensic methods undermining prior testimony, disclosure violations, new suspect evidence, or evidence-handling anomalies.

The goal is to prevent truth from being treated as optional.

The questions that keep this End-Cap specific to "a verdict that outlived the truth"

If you were the prosecutor/office: at what hinge-step did you choose stability over correction-when you discounted new evidence, when you invoked procedural bars, or when you publicly defended certainty you no longer privately held? Can you sign that choice in plain language?

If you were the judge/review board: what does "finality" mean in human terms here-years lost, life lost, family destroyed? Would you still write "procedurally barred" if you had to write that human cost beside it?

If you were the reader: which sentence would you use to justify keeping a wrong verdict-"the standard isn't met," "we can't reopen every case," or "we must preserve confidence"? And would PRGR accept that sentence without an authored harm forecast?

PRGR doesn't ask whether the system values truth in theory. It isolates the moment it **chose a verdict over reality**-and forces a named author to exist at the precise step where correction was possible and still refused.

51

"ROBES, JABOTS AND HUMAN FAILURE AT THE HOUSE ON THE HILL" THE FINAL CHAPTER

LONG-TERM SYSTEMIC FAILURE

Long-term systemic failure in settings where the outside world is systematically excluded, France, mid '80s-2024 (composite)

The bell cut the dark like a blade you could hear.

It rang before morning had existed. It rang while the air was still a cold animal in the corridors. It rang until the novice's eyes opened in panic, because panic was the quickest way to make a body obey.

She lay for a second with her heart running ahead of her, then sat up too fast and felt the room tilt. Stone held the night's chill like a secret. The window was a paler rectangle in the wall. The bed smelled faintly of detergent and old wool, as if someone had washed the world clean of comfort.

On the chair beside her lay the robe: folded, heavy, dark as a closed door. And on top of it, impossibly bright, a small white strip of cloth meant to sit at the throat-the jabot, bib, sign. It was clean enough to make her feel dirty for looking at it. It looked like innocence made into fabric.

She touched it. It felt like nothing.

The bell rang again. It did not ask. It did not persuade. It announced that whatever she had been before this moment was irrelevant.

In the corridor, other women moved in silence. Not the relaxed silence of peace, but a silence that had undergone training until it could stand upright on its own. Faces were calm, the way masks are calm. Footsteps were small. In this place, even noise had to be obedient.

She followed them, learning their pace immediately, because learning was safer than not learning.

At the chapel, the candles shivered; their flames small and anxious. The novice knelt and tried to pray, but her mind made lists that had nothing to do with God: *Don't cough. Don't scratch. Don't look around. Don't be a body.* The robe pressed around her like a weight. The white cloth at her throat turned her pulse into something she could feel, trapped under fabric.

Someone sang. The voices rose together, smooth and disciplined, and the novice felt the relief of disappearing into a sound that belonged to everyone.

She also felt, faintly, the horror of how quickly she liked that relief.

After prayer came work. After work came prayer. After prayer came work again. The hours did not pass so much as clamp shut, one after the next, like steel teeth. The bell ruled everything; the bell was the house's heartbeat; the bell was the house's law.

By the third bell, she had flinched before it rang.

That was the first week: not a week of revelations, but a week of conditioning. A week in which the house quietly taught her that her reflexes were wrong and its reflexes were right.

Sisters corrected her for walking too quickly on the second day. On the third, for walking too slowly. On the fourth, for looking tired. On the fifth, for not looking tired enough. By the sixth, she understood that correctness was not a destination-it was a moving target designed to keep her mind bent forward, always reaching, always apologizing.

She went as if entering weather when the Mother summoned her.

The Mother sat behind a desk that held a ledger. Thick, dark, authoritative. The book lay open like scripture. A pen rested beside it, angled precisely, as if even ink must submit.

The Mother's voice was gentle in the way cold water can be gentle: it does not shout, it simply takes your breath.

She asked the novice about her family. The novice spoke, grateful for the attention. The Mother asked about attachments. The novice felt the word slide into her like a small hook. She spoke again, careful now. The Mother listened with little facial movement, and the novice understood she would never receive warmth for free. Warmth would be something you earned and could lose.

"Here," the Mother said, "we learn to die to ourselves."

The novice nodded, because nodding was what you did when someone explained the rules of gravity.

In the room's corner, two women sat still-part of the Mother's inner court. They did not speak. They watched with eyes that looked kind until the novice tried to meet them directly. Then the kindness vanished. They were not there to comfort her. They were there to remember her.

The Mother closed the ledger with a sound that felt final, and the novice's stomach tightened as if the closing of a book could close something inside her.

Outside, the bell rang again, and she realized with a flash of dread that she was already learning to measure her life in other people's sounds.

The Table (Week One)

The bell for meals did not sound like an invitation. It sounded like an inspection.

They filed in and sat as if assigned by gravity. Plates were already set. The room smelled of boiled things and restraint. A reader's voice began at once-saints, suffering, virtue-words laid over chewing like a cloth meant to hide the mouth.

The novice's spoon clinked once against the bowl. The sound was small, accidental. Still, she felt it land in the room like a dropped coin.

A woman from the inner court lifted her eyes. Not sharply. Not obviously. Just enough to let the novice know she had been recorded.

The novice ate more carefully.

Across the table, an older sister paused with food in her mouth, as if her throat had closed around it. She swallowed too slowly. The reader's voice did not stop. The room did not react. Only the Mother's gaze slid toward her with the languid attention of something deciding whether to bite.

"Finish," someone murmured-soft, almost tender.

The older sister's face tightened. She kept eating. Her eyes shone with the bright refusal of tears.

Later, in the corridor outside the lavatory, the novice heard retching behind a door. She stood still, hand on the wall, the white cloth at her throat suddenly feeling less like purity and more like a leash.

No one spoke about it at prayers.

Silence has many uses. One of them is erasure.

The Bell

The bell did not merely order the day. It ordered the soul.

It told you when to be grateful. It told you when to be silent. It told you when to kneel. It told you when to eat. It told you when your body could exist.

The bell never rang for doubt. Doubt was something you carried alone, like contraband.

In the first week, the novice learned an unknown fear: not fear of punishment, exactly, but fear of being *seen wrong*. Fear of being the person who made the wrong sound, the wrong movement, the wrong request. Fear of becoming a problem in a house that cured problems by correction.

It is difficult to describe how a place like this breaks you without breaking your bones. It does it by teaching you that your own inner alarms are unreliable. It replaces the body's wisdom with the institution's rhythm. It makes you distrust your hunger, your fatigue, your pain, because these are "attachments," and attachments are the enemy.

By the end of the week she woke seconds before the bell, as if her nervous system had worshipped it. She told herself this was progress.

The Table

Sisters arranged the table to resemble a tribunal.

Meals were silent except for the reading: stories of saints, moral tales, tidy examples of endurance and purity. Words flowed down the room while bowls passed hand to hand.

The novice had imagined simple eating, grateful eating, communal eating. She found monitored eating instead. Measured eating. Eating that carried meaning like a stone.

A correct posture. A correct pace. A correct quantity. A correct face.

No one spoke the rules aloud because people can question spoken rules. Instead, the rules became ingrained in practice. You learned them by being corrected. You learned them by watching someone else's correction. You learned them by feeling shame rise in your throat before anyone even spoke.

Sometimes the Mother watched. Sometimes the inner court watched for her.

Food became a language of power. Not dramatic power-no shouting, no slammed fists. Something worse: power administered as normality.

At the table, the body was reminded again and again: **even your stomach does not belong to you.**

And the terrible brilliance of it was this: coercion delivered with cutlery looks domestic. Humiliation delivered as "discipline" looks like virtue. A house can do unspeakable things and still feel, to outsiders, like a place of calm.

The White Cloth at the Throat

The jabot sat where voices begin.

It was supposed to signify purity. It also functioned as a quiet threat: your words must be clean, or you are unclean. Your complaints must be spiritual, not practical. Your suffering must be offered up, not spoken plainly. The novice learned the house's grammar quickly:

If the Mother corrected you, it was love. If you hurt, it was purification. If you resisted, it was pride. If you cried, it was weakness. If you asked for relief, it was attachment. If you thought of leaving, it was temptation. The white cloth made the logic feel inevitable. It made obedience look beautiful. It made the women look credible, which would matter later, when credibility became a battlefield.

At night the novice unpinned the jabot and set it on the chair. In the dark it glowed faintly, a small ghost of innocence. She began to dream of it-white cloth tightening, tightening-until she woke with her mouth dry, unable to remember what she had been trying to say.

The Ledger

The ledger was always there, somewhere. On the desk, in the office, in the Mother's hands, in the air.

The novice had surrendered worldly things at the beginning, as one does in stories: a phone, a small stash of cash, letters, objects that anchored her to the outside. She had told herself this was freedom.

Then the paperwork appeared.

It arrived wrapped in tenderness. The language was devotional: simplicity, trust, detachment, offering. The novice signed where she was told to sign. She felt virtuous for not asking too many questions. She felt relieved to be guided. She did not yet understand that guidance can be a kind of capture.

No one said, *this makes you dependent.*

But dependence grew anyway, quietly, like mold in stone.

A place that holds your money holds your future. It holds your ability to leave, to rent a room, to seek counsel, to buy time. In a closed house, the vow of poverty can become a vow of powerlessness-powerlessness administered by the ones who keep the books.

And alongside personal binding came the other ledger-story whispered in later years: decisions about property, purchases and sales that seemed to drain communal resources while privileging a small leadership circle. Not the theatrical theft of movies, but something colder: sanctioned misdirection, paperwork that turned the many into fuel for the few.

In the House on the Hill, the most important transfers were not always of money. They were of options.

The Ledger (Years Later)

The room is the same, but the novice is no longer a novice.

Her hands are older. The skin at her knuckles is dry from work and cold water. The robe fits her like a second wall. The white cloth at her throat is as familiar now as her own pulse, which she has learned to ignore.

The Mother is older too, but age has not softened her. It has clarified her. The ledger lies open again, its columns neat, its ink calm, its numbers indifferent. Clipping still keeps the garden outside the window obedient.

The Mother does not look up when she speaks.

"There is a matter of your family," she says, as if family were a minor ailment. "A matter of what the house has coming to it."

The sister across the desk-once the novice-feels her stomach drop with the old, trained reflex: guilt before understanding. She is suddenly aware of how little she knows about her own finances, how long it has been since she has seen her name in any context that did not include obedience.

She remembers signing papers when she was young. She remembers the warmth that accompanied the pen. She remembers being praised for trust.

Now the Mother's finger moves down the page like a judge's gavel, stopping on a line that contains the sister's life reduced to a number. The finger taps once softly.

"This," the Mother says. "I must arrange this."

The sister tries to ask a question. Her throat tightens against the white cloth. The words stumble out, small and apologetic.

The Mother's eyes lift at last, and the air in the room changes. The inner court-still present, always present-turns its attention toward the sister like a coordinated organism.

"What is there to ask?" the Mother says gently. "You have given everything. That is your joy." The sister hears herself agree.

Agreement is not always consent. Sometimes it is survival wearing a polite face.

When she leaves the room, the bell rings, calling her to prayer, and she feels the familiar split in her: the part that kneels, and the part that has quietly learned not to exist.

The Mother's Weather

The novice learned that the Mother's mood was the house's atmosphere.

The air warmed when the Mother was pleased. When the Mother felt displeased, the corridors tightened. A glance could act like a verdict. A pause in her voice could feel like doom.

Uncertainty became the governing principle. The novice anticipated correction and edited herself before someone else could edit her. She learned to perform gratitude. She learned to fear the soft words more than hard ones, because soft words could be used to cut without leaving marks.

The inner court carried the Mother's will through the house the way priests carry incense: gently, invisibly, everywhere.

They asked questions with concern that felt like a net. They offered "help" that felt like surveillance. They kept notes-literal or otherwise-about who struggled and who complied. They taught the younger women that safety was not a right but a reward.

And the novice discovered something bleak: pain can become a currency if belonging is rationed. A kind word after humiliation can feel like mercy. Mercy can become addictive.

This is how systems outlive outrage: they convert harm into devotion.

Widening the Lens

A first week becomes a first year. A first year becomes a lifetime. And then-quietly-becomes an inheritance. The novice grew older in the robe. She learned the house's customs the way one learns a language: not by studying, but by surviving. New novices arrived and looked at her with the same frightened hope she once carried, and she taught them how not to attract attention, how to swallow questions, how to interpret their own bodies as suspect.

This is the most frightening thing about such houses: they do not require constant aggression. They require repetition.

Over decades, testimonies would describe patterns that belonged not to one bad day but to a culture:

Physical mistreatment dressed as discipline, particularly around food and bodily control, where humiliation could be administered as "formation."

Neglect or coercion around health and medical care, where pain could be spiritualized and autonomy thinned into obedience.

Psychological and spiritual coercion, where doubts became symptoms, protest became sin, and confession became a tool for governance.

Financial dispossession and mismanagement, where vows and institutional structures blurred consent, deepened dependence, and made leaving materially terrifying-alongside decisions that appeared to advantage a small leadership circle while impoverishing the broader community.

Any one story can be doubted. A pattern is harder to dismiss. A pattern repeated over forty years is a system. And duration is its own accusation. Forty years means the harm was not a misunderstanding. It was an operating procedure.

Oversight as Politeness

A house like this does not survive only because of what happens inside. It survives because of what happens outside.

Visitors came and saw clean cloths at throats, orderly rooms, calm faces, the bell's tidy authority. Families sensed something off, but reverence soothed them. External authorities visited, listened, received assurances, and left.

Oversight often becomes a ceremony: a performance of concern that produces no consequences. Institutions prefer quiet over truth because truth is expensive. Quiet keeps reputations intact. Quiet prevents harm from becoming scandal, and scandal makes harm visible.

So the bell kept ringing.

The table stayed set.

The ledger remained closed to those who needed it most. The white cloth stayed white.

The Mirror, Late

Eventually, the congregation brought in a mirror-a formal inquiry, independent enough to gather stories side by side, to hold testimony against documents, to make the pattern undeniable.

For those harmed, the report did not invent their reality. It returned it.

That return is not small. In coercive systems, one of the earliest thefts is the theft of certainty. External recognition feels like being handed back your own eyes when you have been trained to doubt your own senses. But recognition is not repair. Recognition is paper.

Paper does not restore the years. Paper does not rebuild a body that learned to apologize for pain. Paper does not return money that became institutional property by spiritual persuasion. Paper does not heal the part of a conscience that was made to call harm "love."

And then there is the calendar-the grim institutional ally. Much is too old for court. Although the law prevents prosecution of old cases, it does not prevent repair, yet legality frequently serves as a moral shield. Time limits become the final locked door.

The past remains unlocked only for the ones who never had to live in it.

Robes, Jabots, and Human Failure

The robe, the jabot, the bell, the table, the ledger-these are not decorative details. They are mechanisms. They show how control is administered while sanctity is performed. They show how aesthetics can anesthetize judgment. They show how a community can look holy from the road while quietly teaching women to disappear.

Therefore, the story belongs in Part V.

Because it is not merely about a leader. It is about a system that made failure durable. Forty years is not an accident.

It is a design that worked.

Until it was named.

PRGR END-CAP - Authored Harm Test

Primary mechanism: PROCEDURE - the file moves while responsibility evaporates.

Sector: CROSS-SECTOR PRGR trigger: any procedural step likely to cause irreversible harm (to liberty, livelihood, reputation, safety).

Required signatory: the person with final authority *(and the office that executed the decision).*

If a PRGR had been mandatory here, the signatory would have had to write-and sign-a short record stating:

what action was taken *(and why this step, now)*

the foreseeable harm to the person downstream

the alternative considered and rejected

The remedy trigger that halt the process if harm becomes irreversible

What the institution hides

Technicalities. Delay. Fragmentation. "Nothing decided yet" paperwork. A chain of small steps, each defended as minor, until the minor steps become a life.

In the House on the Hill, the file moved in many disguises:

a "correction" recorded as formation, a health decision treated as obedience, a meal turned into discipline,

an asset transfer framed as devotion,

an exit made impossible by practical depletion, oversight visits reduced to minutes and pleasantries.

Each step could be described as administrative. Each step could be claimed as necessary. Each step could be passed along to the next desk, the next office, the next season.

And when someone asked *who did this?* The institution could answer with clean hands:

No one. The process did.

That is the genius of procedural harm: it is cruelty diffused into compliance.

Counterfactual

The word "**system**" would have been forced to name an author.

A PRGR forces the last person in the chain to stop hiding behind the chain. It drags the soft violence of process into a single human sentence: *I did this. I chose it. I anticipated the harm. I accept the remedy trigger.*

If the House on the Hill had required a PRGR at each irreversible step, harm would have had to become legible as harm-before it became history.

Pause

What are you feeling-**anger, fatigue, recognition, relief?**

Don't outrun it. The body registers what institutions try to launder. Ask yourself:

Who moved the file-and who carried the sentence?

Where in your daily life do decisions become "system decisions" so no one owns them?

If you were inside this institution, what single structural requirement would you add first?

Because this is the final diagnostic of authored harm:

When harm lasts long enough to feel like weather, it is no longer an accident. It is a procedure. And every procedure has a pen at the end of it.

PRGRR Section (Public Relations, Governance, Repair and Reform)

P - Public Relations: The Perfume of Damage Control

When a sealed house is forced open by an independent report, institutions often release familiar scents:

"We are shocked."

"We did not know."

"It was complex."

"It reflects another era."

"Some experienced difficulties."

These phrases are soft for the speaker. They are acid for the harmed.

Credible public response requires:

plain language (coercion, mistreatment, neglect, misuse), full publication of findings with privacy protections, explicit acknowledgment of oversight failures without dilution, independent survivor contact points (not internal gatekeepers), dated, measurable commitments with third-party verification.

G - Governance: How Closed Houses Become Self-Sealing

Governance fails when it becomes ornamental: leaders remain too long and shape reality; complaints are routed into the same hierarchy accused of harm; spiritual guidance becomes surveillance and information capture; finances avoid independent audit under the shelter of vows; external oversight defers to autonomy or fears scandal.

Governance that changes incentives:

term limits and leadership rotation, independent safeguarding authority with investigative power, external financial audits with published summaries, protected reporting channels that bypass internal hierarchy, medical autonomy and consent policies with independent clinicians.

R - Repair: Restitution Beyond the Calendar

Time-bars restrict courts, not responsibility.

Minimum credible repair includes: restitution funding (therapy, housing transitions, legal and career support), independent reconstruction of asset transfers and property decisions, survivor access to personal files and documentation, structured exit support for those leaving, memorialization so legal limitation does not become historical erasure.

R - Reform: Preventing Reassembly

Reform fails when it removes faces but keeps the machine.

Anti-reassembly safeguards: annual external safeguarding reviews, periodic welfare checks by qualified professionals, separation of spiritual direction from disciplinary power, a written charter of member rights (health care, finances, family contact, freedom to leave), compulsory training on coercive control and spiritual abuse for leaders and overseers.

Coda: After the Mirror

The report arrives, and for a moment the house feels lighter, as if paper can change the density of air.

Copies pass through hands that have learned to touch carefully. Someone turns pages as if turning might bruise something. Words sit on the surface of ink with the calm authority of print-words that the women once swallowed whole, words that once could not be spoken without punishment. The house, confronted with language, pretends to recognize itself.

Outside, there are statements. Regret shaped into sentences. Promises that sound clean. The familiar incense of institutional sorrow rises: *we did not know; we are shocked; we will learn; we will do better.* Some will believe these phrases because belief is easier than imagining what forty years requires.

Inside, the bell still rings.

Not because the bell is cruel. Because the bell is the point. It continues the day the way a heart continues after grief. The sound is the same, bright and metallic, slicing the morning into obedience. It calls the women to prayer, and prayer is both refuge and trap: refuge because it is the only place their minds have been allowed to rest; trap because it is where the story can be rewritten without changing the structure.

They go to the chapel. They kneel. They sing. Their voices braid together, smooth as ever, as if harmony could prove innocence. The white cloth at the throat is still white. It still looks like purity to anyone who wants purity to be visible.

At the table, bowls still travel down the line. Reading still fills the room. Silence still does its work. Some eyes are older now, sharpened by the knowledge that what was named can still continue if it is merely renamed. A spoon clinks-one small, accidental sound-and heads lift with the old reflex before anyone remembers they are allowed to be human.

Somewhere, behind a door, the ledger waits.

It is not dramatic. It does not burn. It does not confess. It sits where it always sat, thick and dark, pages lined like cells. The names inside it are not names of people, not really. They are entries. They are numbers. They are a way of making a life legible to authority and illegible to itself. The ink does not look guilty. Ink never does.

A sister walks past the office and feels the familiar tightening in her stomach, the bodily memory of permission. She tells herself she is free to knock now, free to ask for her own file, her own record, her own past. She tells herself this, and still her hand does not lift. The habit of fear is faithful. It survives long after the object of fear has shifted shape.

This is the final cruelty of long failure: it teaches the victim to carry the institution inside the ribs. Forty years cannot be undone by the revelation of forty years. Paper can expose. It cannot extract.

The question, after the mirror, is always the same: does the house change-or does it simply learn new words? The bell rings again. The women rise. The robes move like a single dark tide. The jabots flash briefly at their throats, small flags of a purity the world prefers to believe in.

And somewhere, in the quiet after the sound, the system listens to itself and decides whether it has been truly interrupted-or merely observed.

52

"WHEN TECHNICAL TRUTH GETS A CHAIR AT THE TABLE"

AND WHEN TRUTH SAYS SOMETHING ELSE, THE CHAIR BECOMES UNCOMFORTABLE.

NASA after the 2003 Space Shuttle Columbia disaster. USA, 2003

There is a moment-rare, almost always late-when an institution invites technical truth into the room. Not morality. Not conscience. Not courage.

Technical truth: the version that arrives with spreadsheets, instrument logs, timestamps, version histories, chain-of-custody forms, and the dull, unromantic insistence that we must reconcile reality with what we have said about it.

It is invited in politely. It is offered a chair.

And the institution congratulates itself for being "transparent."

The Chair Is Not Power

A chair at the table is not the same as a voice in the decision.

Institutions love chairs. Chairs are symbolic. Chairs are furniture-as-morality. A chair suggests inclusion, fairness, consultation, and modern governance. One can photograph a chair. Institutions can name a chair-Chief Data Officer, Independent Advisor, External Reviewer, Compliance Lead-and this naming feels like action.

But titles do not tame technical truth. Rules about when it may speak, how long, and what counts as "relevant" tame it.

In the courthouse, truth is procedural: admissible, timely, properly filed. A fact that arrives five minutes late in court can be treated as if it never existed. In the university, truth is publishable: polished, fundable, aligned with narrative. In the Church, truth is pastoral: softened, so it does not disturb faith or donations. In the corporation, truth is strategic: filtered through legal and reputational risk. The robe changes shape, but the habit remains.

So the chair appears, and technical truth takes a seat, and everyone smiles as if the matter is settled. Then the agenda begins.

The Room Where "Input" Becomes Truth

Institutions rarely permit truth to serve as a verdict. More often, institutions frame it as input.

"Thank you for your findings." "That's helpful context." "We'll take that under advisement." "We'll circle back."

This language is not neutral. It is a method. It keeps the institution's authority intact while letting truth appear inside the room like a guest who must not mistake hospitality for belonging.

Technical truth, in its raw form, is intolerant of euphemisms. It is unimpressed by seniority. It does not bow to robes. It does not care if someone loves the speaker, fears the speaker, or has endowed the speaker. It cares whether the numbers reconcile.

That is exactly why someone needs to manage it. And management begins with translation.

The technician arrives saying: "These graphs don't match the raw runs."

The committee minutes record: "Presentation discrepancies discussed."

The auditor says: "Layered entities handled the routing of funds."

The public statement says: "Legacy financial complexity identified."

The clerk says: "This exhibit exists in discovery but not in the trial binder."

The supervisor says: "Administrative oversight."

Truth is not denied. It is domesticated.

And domestication is the institution's most refined skill.

How Institutions Punish Accuracy

When technical truth first speaks plainly, people often perceive it as impoliteness. Institutions punish impoliteness faster than they punish wrongdoing.

A person who exposes a discrepancy is described as difficult, anxious, obsessive, uncollaborative, lacking "strategic perspective." This is the institutional reflex: to treat accuracy as a personality problem. Stubborn numbers that leave trails prevent the institution from attacking them directly. Instead, they frame the person as the disturbance. The leak, not the mold.

It is an old tactic in a modern suit:

If you cannot dispute the evidence, dispute the temperament. If you cannot refute the data, refute the data-bearer.

If you cannot erase the trail, accuse the witness of being "unhelpful."

This is how institutions preserve hierarchy while appearing rational. It keeps the focus on behavior rather than substance. It makes the whistleblower into the story, so the institution can remain the stage. Technical truth is allowed to sit-but only if it behaves like a guest. And guests do not rearrange the furniture.

The Illusion of "We Have Experts"

Institutions love experts the way they love robes: as a visual signal that legitimacy is present.

A scientist on a committee is like a jabot at the throat-white cloth suggesting cleanliness. An auditor is like a gown-black fabric suggesting gravity. A statistician resembles a seal on a document, implying the numbers gained approval.

But expert presence is not expert power.

Many institutions recruit experts for reassurance, not correction. They want a person who can speak "technical" in public and "loyal" in private. They want competence without disruption. They want the comforting performance of rigor, not the inconvenience of it.

So, we offer the chair under these conditions:

Your findings must fit within the existing narrative.

Your language must be "balanced" (which often means diluted). Your risk assessments must not alarm donors, voters, or trustees. Frame your conclusions as "recommendations," not as imperatives.

You must describe your conflict with leadership as "differences of view."

And if the expert resists these conditions-if they insist that reality is not a matter of viewpoint-then the institution talks about "tone."

Tone is the velvet glove. It is how authority protects itself without appearing authoritarian.

The Two Ways Truth Gets a Chair

Technical truth gets a chair in one of two circumstances.

First: after the embarrassment.

A scandal, a leak, a lawsuit, a headline. Suddenly the institution discovers the advantage of oversight. Suddenly it appoints an integrity panel, a review committee, an external auditor. It erects the chair like a memorial to what it should have done earlier.

This is the reactive chair: placed in the room as part of rescue after harm.

Second: before the risk becomes visible.

Sometimes an institution invites technical truth early because it senses instability-financial strain, regulatory pressure, internal dissent, an upcoming public listing. The chair is a preventive charm: "See? We have governance. We have controls. We have experts."

This is the protective chair: placed in the room to reassure observers, not to empower reality. In both cases, the chair is less about truth than about appearance.

And appearance is what institutions trade in.

The Moment That Changes the Room

Still, there are moments when the chair becomes something else. Rarely. But enough to matter.

It happens when technical truth refuses to become mere input. When it insists on being the floor, not the decoration.

A simple example: the persons with the data go beyond simply "presenting findings." They insist the decision cannot proceed until the discrepancy is resolved. They insist approvals require reconciliation. They insist that documentation is not optional and timelines are not suggestions.

This is when the room changes.

At first, leadership experiences it as insubordination. The institution's nervous system interprets constraint as threat. The reflex is to reassert authority: to remind the technician who holds the chairmanship, who sets the agenda, who signs the minutes.

But technical truth is a strange resistance because it does not argue ideology. It argues gravity. It does not claim moral superiority. It claims arithmetic.

And arithmetic is difficult to shame.

When technical truth may function-not as advice but as a threshold-something profound happens: the institution becomes accountable to reality rather than merely to itself.

This is the real meaning of "truth at the table." Not a chair. A veto.

Why Truth Needs a Veto

Institutions are designed to continue. That is their strength and their danger.

Continuity rewards those who smooth, deflect, and preserve. It punishes those who interrupt the flow. Therefore, access alone is insufficient for technical truth, which interrupts flow by identifying mismatches. It requires consequence.

A veto is not dramatic. It is procedural. It is the institutional language of power used against institutional drift. It says:

No release until replication.

No settlement until disclosure.

No procurement without tender integrity.

No trial without full discovery.

No promotion without conflict review.

No sermon about charity while the accounts remain private.

The veto is the point where truth stops being a guest and becomes a rule. And rules-unlike moral appeals-are things institutions understand.

The tragic irony is that institutions often only build vetoes after harm. They install them the way people install smoke alarms after a fire: as a way to feel safe, not as proof they were wise.

But safety and wisdom are different forces.

When Truth Is Invited Too Late

There is another pattern that repeats across robes, jabots, mantles, collars: technical truth arrives late because early truth would have required early refusal.

Refusal is the institution's rarest act.

It is easier to accept questionable money, and promise safeguards than to reject it and live with scarcity. It is easier to approve a project and manage optics than to stop it and admit uncertainty. It is easier to protect a celebrated figure than to confront them and risk losing prestige. It is easier to rescue after harm than to prevent it by being suspicious at the beginning.

Institutions frequently only seek technical truth when they have already made public, financial, or reputational commitments. By then, reality is an inconvenience, not a guide. Truth becomes a problem to solve, not a compass to follow.

Therefore, so many "independent reviews" feel like theatre. Not because the experts are insincere, but because the institution has already decided what it needs the truth to say.

And when truth says something else, the chair becomes uncomfortable.

The Chair as a Trap

A chair can also be a trap.

When a technical person enters an institution's leadership space, proximity often seduces them to power. The invitation feels like recognition. At last, they are listening. At last, the numbers matter.

But proximity has a cost. The institution asks for translation, then for softening, then for strategic framing. The expert bridges reality and narrative, and people walk on bridges.

If the expert adapts, they become the institution's proof of integrity. If they resist, they become proof of its "dysfunction." Either way, the institution tries to absorb them.

This is how technical truth sometimes becomes complicit without intending to: by accepting the chair and mistaking it for authority.

The chair feels like a promotion. It can also be containment.

The Only Reliable Test

So how do you know when technical truth truly has a seat-rather than a photo opportunity? There is one reliable test:

Can it stop the process?

Can the auditor halt the payment? Can the statistician delay the release?

Can the compliance officer block the contract? Can the clerk force disclosure?

Can the lab's integrity lead prevent publication until the methods are clean?

Can the oversight body remove a celebrated figure without requiring a scandal first?

If the answer is no, then the chair is a decoration.

If the answer is yes, then technical truth is not merely present. It is governing.

And this is the moment institutions fear-because it redistributes power from role to reality.

Why This Matters Beyond Technique

Some readers will want to believe that technical truth is a narrow thing-numbers, methods, procedures, documents. But within institutions, technical truth is never merely technical. It is ethical.

A missing exhibit is not a clerical matter when someone's freedom is at stake. A massaged graph is not a stylistic choice when patients and investors are being persuaded. A buried conflict of interest is not administrative when it shapes justice. A delayed distribution is not "timing" when people go cold and hungry in the meantime. Technique is where harm becomes legal.

That is the book's recurrent warning: institutions are most dangerous not when they break rules, but when they follow them in ways that conceal moral absence. Technical truth, when allowed to function properly, exposes concealment-not by preaching, but by making the hidden visible. And visibility is the enemy of comfortable power.

Conclusion: The Chair and the Cloth

Robes and jabots exist to turn people into roles. They compress the messy variability of human judgment into the stable silhouette of authority. In that silhouette, the institution appears clean-even when it is not.

Technical truth does something humiliating to robes: it treats them as irrelevant. It does not care how polished the cloth is. It cares about what happened.

That is why the chair matters. Because if technical truth can truly sit at the table-with veto, with consequence-then the institution becomes less theatrical and more accountable. It becomes less dependent on the sacred aura of roles and more dependent on the stubborn discipline of reconciliation.

But if the chair is merely symbolic, then the institution has not modernized. It has only accessorized. One can starch a jabot. A committee can convene. A committee can offer a chair. And still the same old machinery can run: authority protected, harm managed, truth invited only when it is already too late to prevent what it can now only document.

So we are not asking whether technical truth has been invited. The question is whether regulators permitted it to govern.

Because when technical truth truly gets a chair at the table, the institution loses its favorite privilege: the privilege of pretending.

EPILOGUE

After the Robes Are Removed

If the prologue began with a loss, the epilogue ends with the residue of that loss: a different way of knowing. I cannot return to the earlier comfort of assuming that legitimacy implies care, or that professionalism implies conscience. What changed was not my capacity to admire institutions when they function well; it was my refusal to treat their language as neutral.

My epistemic stance became procedural realism: I trust what can be owned. I trust what can be signed. I trust what survives contact with an independent record. Everything else-assurance, dignity, ceremony-may be sincere, but sincerity is not accountability. If this book does anything, let it be this: it teaches you to feel the difference, in your body, when a system is describing reality and when it is managing you.

And if you recognise that sensation in your own daily life-at work, in families, in offices, in committees-then you already know why authorship matters. The smallest act of resistance is often not heroism. It is naming the mechanism and refusing to disappear into it. When institutions fail, they rarely collapse. They continue-procedurally intact, linguistically confident, formally correct. What disappears is not order, but meaning.

This book has traced a pattern in which injustice does not erupt but accumulates, not through defiance of rules but through their faithful execution. The cases reveal how harm arises without cruelty, continues without malice, and justifies itself without dishonesty.

They reveal a world in which no one appears fully responsible-and yet nothing happens without human hands.

At the center of this pattern is a quiet transformation: individuals cease to experience themselves as moral agents and experience themselves as functions. The robe and the jabot do not corrupt; they relieve. They promise safety from doubt, shelter from blame, and distance from consequences. Over time, this relief becomes dependence.

The loss concerns answerability, not professionalism.

Institutions often insist that responsibility belongs to the system, not the person. Yet systems do not think, hesitate, or feel the weight of consequence. Only people do. When responsibility is moved entirely to structures, justice becomes something that happens-or fails to happen-with no one ever having chosen it.

The deepest failure documented in this book is therefore not legal or procedural. It is existential. It is failing to remain human in spaces that reward abstraction, compliance, and silence.

This failure is not inevitable. People cultivate this failure.

Institutions train individuals to narrow their vision, to fear deviation, to trust procedure over judgment. They reward those who do not see too much and marginalize those who do. Over time, this produces a culture in which people experience moral presence as unprofessional and ethical unease as a personal flaw.

Yet every case in this book also implies a counterfactual: moments when something else could have happened. A question might have been raised. A concern could have received serious consideration. Acknowledging a human consequence rather than processing it away was an alternative.

These moments matter because they expose a truth institutions often deny: justice does not emerge automatically from structure; it depends on human choice.

The purpose of this book has not been to demand heroism. Heroism is rare, unsustainable, and easily dismissed. The demand here is quieter and more difficult: the refusal to disappear into one's role. The insistence on remaining morally present, even when the institution does not ask for it-and especially when it subtly discourages it.

Institutions often ask, "What would happen if everyone acted on their conscience?" The more troubling question is: What happens when no one does?

The answer is not chaos. The answer is what you have read. I did not ask for a return. Consider this unique file. A lawyer is struck off. Five years pass. He applies to return. The board refuses, and one reason-quietly devastating-is financial: after disbarment he went bankrupt; he has not repaid all debts. Therefore, he is still unfit.

This is exactly the reasoning PRGR forces into daylight, because it can become a closed loop: the sanction collapses earning capacity; the collapse delays repayment; the delayed repayment is then used to justify continued exclusion. The system manufactures the condition it cites.

A proper PRGR for a refusal like this would not moralise about insolvency. It would require a signatory to write, plainly to the applicant:

"We are refusing reinstatement. The foreseeable harms are continued professional exclusion, continued reputational damage, reduced earning capacity, and-importantly-reduced ability to repay debts. We accept that our decision may prolong the financial condition we cite.

We rely on bankruptcy and incomplete repayment as evidence of risk. The specific risk we claim is not "poverty," but [state the risk model in human terms]: vulnerability to undue influence, impaired judgment under pressure, unreliability in handling client funds, or repeated disregard for obligations. We also acknowledge alternative explanations: income collapse following disbarment; unavoidable obligations; the basic arithmetic of debt repayment under restricted work. We reject these as sufficient mitigation because [specific reasons tied to evidence, not tone].

We considered a less harmful alternative: conditional re-entry designed to control the identified risk rather than permanently exclude the person. Options include: probationary licence; restricted practice areas; prohibition or tight controls around client money; supervised practice; mandatory financial reporting to an independent officer; a verified repayment plan; staged return with review points and automatic triggers for suspension if benchmarks fail. We rejected these because [specific reasons], and we state here what measurable criteria would allow return in the future."

That is what a PRGR would force: a refusal that cannot hide behind "integrity" as a mood.

It must become a disclosed calculation-risk, safeguards, thresholds, and an honest account of the harm the refusal causes.

And it would also force the board to answer the question that decides whether it is acting as a protector or as a gatekeeper of purity:

Are we managing a concrete, articulable risk-or are we using a financial aftermath, produced in part by our own sanctions, as a permanent moral verdict?

If justice is to mean more than procedure, if authority is to deserve trust, then responsibility must return-not as blame, but as ownership. Not as punishment, but as acknowledgment. Not as spectacle, but as practice.

One can wear robes. One can fulfill roles. One can follow rules. But none of these absolve the person who acts. When the robes are removed, when the files are closed, when the institution moves on, what remains is a single question-one no system can answer on our behalf:

Did we choose to remain human? This book ends there, for now.

APPENDIX A

FULL CASE FILES

CASE FILES
PART I

SETUP, FIRST SHOCKS, LENS

The Mamashimi Trust - Brisbane Australia

53

"THE MAGISTRATE'S SHADOW"

SURVIVAL SOMETIMES DEMANDS CHOICES THAT DO NOT FEEL SURVIVABLE AT ALL.

Judicial misconduct and criminal influence, Austria, 2011 (composite case), PRGR

Organised crime is not an exotic anomaly that lives only in dark alleys and foreign headlines. In one form or another, organised crime exists around every corner, as humanity anchors it. Where there is scarcity, someone will sell relief. Where there is abundance, someone will sell access.

For most, greed serves as the engine, fueling their appetite for more, despite having long reached a point of sufficiency. For some, it is a need: the pressure of survival, debt, addiction, fear, family obligation, the quiet panic of a life that has narrowed to a single desperate corridor. Most participants carry no regret; they narrate their choices as business, loyalty, or inevitability. Others are punished mentally every day-not by courts, but by conscience-living inside a sentence that never ends, forced to keep choosing the lesser evil to survive a world that keeps offering only evils.

It was in that world-ordinary, proximate, human-that Magistrate Stefan Gruber became useful.

Gruber was a figure of unwavering authority within the hallowed halls of the Austrian judiciary, renowned for his fastidious courtroom demeanour and an intellectual rigor that defined his legal philosophy. Clad in a flowing black robe with purple trim and a ceremonial tie, he embodied centuries of legal tradition; the courtroom seemed to tighten into solemnity when he entered.

Lawyers adjusted their posture. Clerks quickened their pace. Defendants fell silent, a silence born from the belief that the man behind the bench, not just the written rules, embodied the law.

His presence created trust the way architecture does-without argument. It looked stable; therefore, it felt true. And that is precisely why organised crime noticed him. Criminal networks rarely want to destroy systems outright; they prefer to live inside them. They did not need Gruber to become a gangster. They needed him to remain a magistrate-publicly rigorous, ceremonially convincing-while becoming privately permeable.

The first approaches were subtle. Low-level intermediaries came as if they were dust on a sleeve: easy to brush off, easy to dismiss. They sought minor favors on behalf of associates caught in minor trouble-an adjournment here, a scheduling preference there, the quiet softening of language in a ruling so that a procedural door remained ajar.

Gruber, ever the pragmatist, told himself these were harmless adjustments, the normal lubrication of an overburdened machine. The courts were drowning in files; small "efficiencies" felt like mercy. A late witness. A misplaced form. A sick defendant. The excuses were always plausible because real life is always plausible.

Yet the logic of compromise is geometric: one small angle changes the whole trajectory.

These favors did not remain minor. They multiplied, not by force but by familiarity. Soon the requests carried more weight: postpone this hearing until the witness relocates. Phrase that orders so the police must restart the clock. Grant bail if the statute allowed it, but where prudence would have resisted. None of it needed to look like corruption. It only needed to look like discretion.

Organised crime thrives in that grey zone-the space between what is legal and what is right. Greed loves the grey zone because it can pretend to be cleverness. Need loves it because it can pretend to be the only option. Within the confines of Gruber's office-lined with law books, certificates, ceremonial objects-the true nature of his operations took shape. Publicly, the proceedings maintained an immaculate surface. Privately, a labyrinth formed: coded messages, strategic calendar shifts, and conversations that men who treat favors as currency remembered, though they never wrote them down.

The robe and tie, symbols of judicial integrity, became camouflage. They did not merely conceal. They legitimised. The same gesture that could calm a courtroom could also intimidate a clerk into silence. Formal politeness, which signals professionalism, could also warn: you will not be believed against me.

Gruber was not naive. He knew he was stepping across lines. But the seduction was not only money. It was control-the sensation of touching outcomes with invisible fingers.

When he delayed a case and watched the machinery obey him, he felt a private thrill that was almost aesthetic, like solving a puzzle no one else knew existed. Each successful manipulation made the next easier, because success rewrites morality. A man believes that what works must be justified, because the alternative is to admit he is merely weak.

And then the other part arrived: fear.

There is a moment in many corruption stories when the relationship flips. In the beginning, the official thinks he is "managing" criminal influence. Later he realises the influence is managing him. Organised crime does not offer favors as gifts; it offers them as chains. Kindness is the hook. The hook is the leverage.

Some of Gruber's intermediaries had no remorse at all. They treated the court like any other institution to be exploited-like a loading dock or a tax office. But one of them, a courier named Tobias, carried a different punishment. He was not a mastermind; he was a man with a sick father and a debt that never shrank.

Each time he delivered a message, each time he heard the polite words that meant to do this or else, he felt his stomach tighten. His sentence was psychological: wake up, choose, carry the choice, repeat. The system of crime gives some people profit and gives others a daily corrosion of self.

Gruber liked to imagine he was in the first group-profiting. He did not want to see that he had become a node in a network that had its own rules and no mercy for those who broke them.

The pivotal moment arrived when Austria's Federal Criminal Police, already deep in organised crime investigations, detected troubling links between judicial outcomes and external influence. Patterns surfaced: cases delayed in oddly consistent ways, procedural anomalies clustering around certain names, certain lawyers succeeding in Gruber's court with improbable regularity.

Lena, a court staff member with the patience of an archivist, had kept records. She had noticed that "coincidence" in bureaucracies has a smell. The missing timestamp. The altered staple marks. The file that Lena signed out without signing back in. She documented what others ignored because ignoring was easier than confronting a powerful magistrate.

When she stepped forward, investigators could finally connect the visible dots to the invisible hand. Digital traces, witness interviews, and procedural analysis confirmed what the judiciary least wanted to admit: Gruber's manipulations-stalling prosecutions, diverting investigative efforts, widening loopholes-had materially benefited criminal enterprises.

The revelation shook Vienna's judicial community. The court suspended Gruber. The subtlety that had protected Gruber for years complicated the pursuit of direct criminal charges. But the tribunal found him guilty of ethical breaches that were unmistakable, and he served two years in prison.

Titles that had once seemed permanent were no longer his.

That stripping is always symbolic, but symbols matter. The robe and tie, which once represented integrity, now warn that one can easily wear authority like a mask.

Reforms followed: enhanced oversight, digital case management, and transparency protocols designed to reduce the opportunities for quiet manipulation. Yet reforms are always late. They are architecture built after the fire. The deeper truth remained: organised crime did not begin with Gruber, and it did not end with him. It exists because humans create it-through greed, through need, through the recurring temptation to turn power into a private instrument.

And in the wake of his fall, two kinds of people remained. Those who felt nothing-because they had sold their conscience long ago.

And those who lived with a daily punishment inside their own minds, forced to remember that survival sometimes demands choices that do not feel survivable at all.

54

"THE ARCHBISHOP'S SECRET LEDGER"

NUMBERS, LIKE SOULS, ARE SOMETIMES MESSY.

Catholic Church financial scandals, (Italy & Vatican banking systems), 1980s-2010s (composite case)

The Milan Cathedral projected an authority that required no explanation. Light fell through stained glass in orderly colors. Incense rose and dispersed as if it had received training. When Archbishop Giordano Marchetti stepped from the sacristy, the congregation read the message the vestments sent: continuity, discipline, sanctity. He understood the power of that impression. He also understood the ease with which he could spend it.

Marchetti's public work centered on humility. His sermons stressed restraint, stewardship, and the moral peril of wealth. He spoke of charity as an obligation rather than an attribute, and he delivered those lines with enough calm conviction to make them sound less like instruction than truth.

Behind the archdiocesan doors, his understanding of stewardship took a different shape.

Donations arrived through foundations with names that suggested transparency-Fondazione Santa Misericordia and similar entities that sounded as if they could only exist for good. The paperwork was immaculate. Receipts were issued. Reports were filed. Budgets were presented with careful language: education, hospitals, outreach, renovation.

But the accounting did not end where it appeared to end.

A portion of the money traveled outward in a way that never looked like theft on a single page. Consulting fees, administrative costs, and "special project" disbursements allowed them to divide funds across small transfers. They reappeared in jurisdictions that specialized in discretion-Switzerland, Luxembourg, and island accounts that existed primarily to be difficult to examine. These fake companies were like fancy glass containers: they used religious-sounding words, had convincing mission statements, and their legal structure hid what they were really doing.

Marchetti called it prudence when he explained it to himself. The Church, he believed, had to survive the world as it was, not as it wished it to be. If influence required financial leverage, then financial leverage became a form of pastoral strategy. He did not feel like a criminal. He felt like a realist operating inside an institution that rewarded realism when it remained quiet.

Only a few people had access to enough detail to notice the pattern. Fewer still had the nerve to name it. Carla Benedetti was his private secretary-efficient, methodical, the person who kept the archbishop's life smooth enough that no one thought about the effort required. Her work included preparing quarterly financial summaries that were meant, in theory, to show good governance. She had handled numbers long enough to recognize the difference between complexity and disguise.

Late one evening, while assembling a report, she saw discrepancies that resisted ordinary explanations. Renovation funds went through an allocation and then a "reclassification." Interest payments did not align with the balances they were supposed to reflect. None of it was blatantly absurd. That was what made it credible-and what made it dangerous.

She reviewed the entries again, then again, searching for the reassuring error that would let her close the file and go home.

She didn't find it.

When she finally spoke to Marchetti, she chose her words carefully.

"Your Excellency," she said, "some of these figures don't reconcile. I'm not sure how to present them."

He looked at her as though he were weighing her-not only her competence but her temperament. Then his expression softened into something paternal, gentle enough to be disarming.

"Carla," he said, "numbers, like souls, are sometimes messy. Be patient. The truth of things comes in time." He briefly put his hand over hers, an action that might be seen as kindness or control. It achieved its goal: it redirected the emotional burden back onto her. If she pressed further, she would be the impatient one, the anxious one, the person who did not understand the world as deeply as he did.

She left the office unsettled, and then-almost involuntarily-ashamed of being unsettled. That was one of Marchetti's gifts. He could make doubt feel like a personal failing rather than an institutional warning.

Outwardly, nothing changed. Marchetti attended events, hosted donors, and delivered speeches on poverty and compassion. He greeted dignitaries with practiced warmth. He wore the robe as if it were proof.

Privately, the ledger continued.

A discreet call to a banker. An instruction passed through an intermediary. Someone placed a signature where no one would ever read it aloud. The pleasure, for him, was not only the money. It was the sense of operating above ordinary scrutiny-of holding an institution's moral language in one hand and its hidden transactions in the other.

The first public disturbance came the way such disturbances often do: not through internal oversight, but through an external reader who didn't share the institution's incentives.

A journalist named Lorenzo Ricci received an anonymous tip. Ricci had covered corruption long enough to recognize a familiar structure: foundations, layered transfers, and the slow migration of money into places where accountability became a technical problem rather than a moral one. He spent months following the routes, checking registries, and tracing corporate ownership. He waited for the opportune moment to publish the story without it being dismissed as rumor.

When it broke, the headlines were blunt and humiliating. Some framed it as betrayal. Others framed it as hypocrisy. The public reaction came in predictable waves: outrage, disbelief, rationalization, and then a quieter, more corrosive cynicism.

Marchetti responded with the discipline of someone who had rehearsed crisis without expecting to need it.

He called a press conference inside the cathedral. He arrived in full ceremonial presentation, allowing the setting to suggest innocence before he said a word. He spoke in the language institutions prefer when the facts are inconvenient: complexity, misunderstandings, administrative errors, modern financial systems. He admitted "mistakes" without admitting intent. He promised an audit without conceding why an audit was necessary. He gave the crowd repentance without confession.

It was not a legal defense. It was a narrative defense.

An internal Vatican review followed. Transactions were examined. Accounts were compared. Documents were requested in the way documents are requested when an institution needs to show concern while maintaining control. The financial architecture, designed to be technically lawful, worked as intended. Prosecutors could not cleanly prosecute much of what Marchetti had done. The financial architecture had been built to live in the gap between wrongdoing and proof.

The review produced consequences, but not the kind the public imagines when it imagines accountability. Marchetti was reassigned to a smaller diocese in central Italy. The description of the move was administrative-an "opportunity for renewed focus," a "reorientation of pastoral leadership." Within the Church's internal logic, reassignment was both punishment and containment. It removed him from the direct center of the scandal while preserving the dignity of the office. It prevented a trial of the institution by allowing the individual to carry the burden quietly elsewhere.

The system remained intact.

Carla Benedetti resigned. Not in protest, not with a statement, but with the slow exhaustion of someone who realized that clarity was unwelcome. She did not become a whistleblower. She did not become a heroine. She simply stepped away, carrying with her the knowledge that an institution can absorb almost anything as long as it controls the surrounding language.

Marchetti continued to preach. In photographs, his vestments remained crisp. In public, his voice remained steady. Institutions outlast beliefs, which is why his authority continued even though people did not believe everything he said. They rely on structure, ceremony, and the careful management of consequences.

The ledger did not need to be destroyed. It only needed to be made harder to see. And so it was.

His stole stayed perfectly arranged. The stain was elsewhere.

CASE FILES PART II

MONEY, LEDGERS, DONORS, "STEWARDSHIP," AND PURCHASED

THE MAMASHIMI TRUST - BRISBANE AUSTRALIA

55

"THE BISHOP'S COMPLICITY"

UNEDUCATED PEOPLE MISUNDERSTAND PASTORAL CLOSENESS.

Church misconduct, Ireland, 2002 (composite case), PRGR

Dublin rain doesn't fall like weather. It falls like persistence.

It slicks the cathedral steps. It darkens the stone. It turns streetlights into smears. It makes the city look older than it is, and it makes secrets feel as if they belong to the architecture.

Water finds every seam. It beads, seeps, and returns, testing the same weak points until the surface yields. In that way, it is honest. It never pretends the cracks aren't there.

Bishop Patrick O'Donnell understood architecture-especially the institutional kind.

In public he was solemn and composed, cassock immaculate, stole gleaming with the careful symbolism of authority. He spoke about morality with a voice trained to sound gentle even when it was firm. Parishioners trusted him because he looked like certainty. He could stand at a pulpit and make doubt feel like a personal failure in the listener rather than a reasonable response to power.

Inside the diocese, he ran certainty like a machine.

Complaints arrived-some whispered, some written, some carried in shaking hands. Allegations against priests were recorded, filed, "handled." That word-handled-became a sanctuary for everything the Church did not want to say aloud. It was a word that sounded responsible while doing the work of silence.

When a priest drew complaints, O'Donnell did not call the police. He did not invite sunlight. He reassigned. He moved. He sealed.

He framed it as mercy.

"Authority must balance compassion with discretion," he would say, and because he said it in the bishop's tone, people mistook the sentence for wisdom rather than strategy.

He spoke as if scandal were the actual harm and exposure the real cruelty. In his logic, the institution was a living body that must not be shocked. Better to cauterize quietly than risk bleeding in public.

His private arrogance appeared in smaller ways-how he spoke about complainants.

"Uneducated people misunderstand pastoral closeness." "Some parishioners are suggestible." "Rumors spread among those who don't understand the Church."

He didn't say victims were lying. He said something worse: that their perceptions were unreliable because they lacked sophistication. It was institutional superiority dressed in clerical language-contempt delivered as pastoral concern.

And that contempt shaped procedure. Files written in careful euphemisms: "boundary concerns," "misinterpreted interaction," "unwise familiarity." Names shifted into initials. Locations were generalized. It was semantic chemistry: change the label, reduce the sting. The facts didn't disappear, but they lost reactivity-less likely to ignite action, more likely to settle into archival dust.

Father Brendan Mahon, newly assigned to the cathedral, saw the pattern because he still believed the institution meant what it preached.

He expected complaints would trigger protection. Instead, he watched them trigger containment. He watched families turn into administrative problems. He watched victims absorbed into the process and then quietly forgotten, as if paper could swallow pain.

He also watched how O'Donnell's circle behaved: the smooth coordination, the brief meetings, the polished language. There was a kind of pride in it-an assumption that governance was a higher calling than truth. They spoke about "protecting the faithful," but what they meant, increasingly, was protecting the faithful image of the Church.

Brendan began collecting what the system preferred to keep fragmented: letters, internal memos, reassignment notes, meeting summaries where the same phrases appeared like a chorus-pastoral prudence, avoid scandal, protect the faithful-as though protecting the faithful meant protecting the institution's public face.

The moral sickness wasn't loud. It was bureaucratic.

Like an infection left untreated, it spread quietly through routine. In biology, infections don't always announce themselves with fever; sometimes they settle into tissue and become chronic-pain normalized, damage ongoing, the body learning to live around decay. That is what "handled" became: chronic institutional harm disguised as management.

When Brendan raised concerns, O'Donnell's response was calm and scalding.

"You are ," the bishop said. "Your zeal is admirable. But you don't understand governance." Governance. Not justice. Not protection. Governance.

Brendan realized that procedure had become a substitute for conscience.

Completing a form made the institution feel clean. The institution felt merciful when a priest moved. If the scandal stayed quiet, the institution felt safe. It was a closed system, like a room with no ventilation: air recycled until people forgot what fresh air felt like.

The truth broke free through journalism-what institutions often call "attack" when they mean "exposure." A reporter received tips from multiple parishes and began connecting the same priestly names appearing in different towns, like migrating storms that keep forming the same shape. The reporter didn't need to invent drama; the pattern was dramatic on its own.

Moving a problem is not solving it. It is distributing it.

Brendan-terrified, methodical-provided documentation that made denial impossible. He did it the way a scientist would: not with moral speeches, but with replication.

Here is the complaint. Here is the memo. Here is the reassignment. Here is the same pattern again. Once, coincidence. Twice, concern. Three times, method.

The public reaction was grief hardened into anger. Parishioners who had deferred for years began asking questions in plain language: Why were warnings ignored? Why were priests moved? Why were families treated as inconvenient? Why did "mercy" always seem to flow upward and never outward?

O'Donnell stepped aside from administrative duties, his title intact, his authority bruised. The diocese announced reforms. Review boards. Reporting protocols. Safeguarding frameworks.

The institution did what institutions do when the tide turns: it built a barrier and called it repentance. But barriers aren't the same as repair. A watchman who sees danger and refuses to sound the alarm is not innocent simply because he stayed quiet. Silence didn't erase responsibility. O'Donnell had watched. He had seen. And again and again, he chose discretion over warning. His sin wasn't rage. It was managerial calm-the decision to treat harm as something to be contained rather than stopped.

Father Mahon paid a price for speaking. Institutions rarely reward disruption in real time. Institutions labeled him "difficult" and moved him away from central files "for his own good."

The same machinery that had moved priests to avoid scandal now tried to move him to avoid accountability. Yet his evidence forced new oversight-real scrutiny, not ceremonial reassurance.

In the cathedral, the rain continued. Dublin kept moving. The bells still rang. But the sound changed for those who learned what mercy's language had done. It carried an extra note-thin, metallic, unmistakable:

The careless handling of the note of trust prevents it from ever regaining its original shape.

PRGR END-CAP - AUTHORED HARM TEST

(for "THE BISHOP'S COMPLICITY" - case-specific, non-boilerplate)

This case isn't about a bishop "not knowing." It's about a bishop **knowing enough to act** and choosing not to-then using the institution's language to make inaction sound like prudence: discernment, patience, unity, due process, avoiding scandal.

Complicity is not a mood. It is a sequence of decisions.
PRGR bites where the bishop turns that sequence into something no one can later pin to a name.

PRGR would attach authorship at the first hinge-step where the bishop chooses **containment over intervention**.

The hinge-steps where PRGR would force the author to exist

The first credible signal - and the choice to keep it "pastoral"
When the bishop receives an initial report (a priest's warning, a staff note, a victim's account, a donor's concern) and chooses to treat it as an internal pastoral matter rather than a safeguarding / legal matter, PRGR triggers. He must author:

what he was told (category + seriousness), why he chose the pastoral channel,

what harms are foreseeable from internal handling (continued access, intimidation, evidence loss), and what immediate safeguards are implemented *that day*.

This case's danger is the gap between "I heard" and "I acted."

The "private meeting" decision - confronting power without witnesses
If the bishop meets the accused privately, accepts reassurances, and then treats the reassurance as resolution, PRGR triggers at that meeting decision.

He must author:

why the meeting was private,

what questions were asked,

what evidence was demanded,

and what was done if answers were incomplete.

Because private reassurance is the institution's easiest narcotic: it produces relief without proof.

The access-preservation step - leaving the accused in role
The most concrete harm hinge is leaving the person in a position where they can continue doing harm: ministry, school contact, finances, youth programs, counseling, access to vulnerable congregants. PRGR triggers at any decision **not** to suspend or restrict access after credible signal.

The bishop must author:

what risk model he is using ("low risk," "uncertain," "unproven"), what safeguards compensate for continued access,

what harm is foreseeable if he is wrong, and why precaution was rejected.

PRGR turns "we couldn't be sure" into a signed acceptance of risk.

The silencing move - discouraging reporting "for the good of the Church"
If the bishop or his office urges complainants or staff to avoid police, avoid formal complaint, avoid "making it public," PRGR triggers at that conversation. He must author:

what he advised, why he advised it,

what protections exist against retaliation,

and what independent pathway remains open.

Because in this story, complicity often arrives as counsel.

The transfer decision - moving the problem instead of addressing it
If the bishop reassigns the accused, relocates a witness, or shuffles roles "to reduce tension," PRGR triggers at the transfer memo.

He must author:

who is being moved and why,

why moving power is not the remedy,

what harms are foreseeable (repeat harm in new place; reputational ruin for whistleblower; loss of evidence), and what disclosure accompanies the transfer.

PRGR blocks the oldest ecclesial containment reflex: geography as absolution.

The record-thinning step - keeping notes "light"
Complicity thrives in weak records. If the diocese keeps files vague ("concerns raised," "pastoral conversation had") PRGR triggers at any decision to avoid detail. The bishop must author:

what is being omitted, why,

and what independent archive preserves substance. A thin record is not administrative style; it is future immunity.

The final posture - "we followed process" without naming the harmed
If the bishop's public statement emphasizes procedure, unity, or "we take matters seriously" while avoiding the concrete harms and safeguards, PRGR triggers at the communications sign-off.

He must author:

what was done and what was not done,

what risks remain,

and what remedy path exists for affected people.

What PRGR would force in this case (matched to complicity mechanics)

1. **A "credible signal → immediate safeguards" rule**
   PRGR requires that the first credible signal triggers non-negotiable actions

within 24 hours: access restrictions, independent intake, and preservation of evidence. No, "we'll see."

2. **A "pastoral handling" justification record**
   If the bishop insists on internal handling, PRGR forces him to sign the harm forecast of that choice and specify why external reporting is not required (and who reviewed that determination).

3. **A transfer disclosure requirement**
   No reassignment of an accused person without documented disclosure to the receiving institution and oversight review. Moving without disclosure becomes authored harm.

4. **A retaliation tripwire**
   If the reporter loses standing, roles, invitations, or employment-PRGR triggers automatic review. Because complicity is often maintained by disciplining the person who won't be quiet.

Questions that belong to this chapter (and keep PRGR from sounding generic)

If you were the bishop: which decision will you sign in plain language-the choice to keep it "pastoral," the choice not to restrict access, or the choice to discourage formal reporting?

If you were a staff member/victim: what is the first hinge-step you need forced into record-the initial signal receipt, the access restriction decision, or the transfer memo?

If you were diocesan oversight: are you willing to author that "uncertainty" justifies continued access to vulnerable people-and to sign the foreseeable harm if you are wrong?

PRGR fits "THE BISHOP'S COMPLICITY" because it treats complicity as what it is here: **a chain of inactions that function as decisions.** It forces a named author to exist at the precise step where the bishop chooses containment and then makes him sign the harm he is otherwise asking others to absorb in silence.

56

"THE DAYAN'S TALLIT"

JUSTICE IS NOT A MOOD, AND PEACE IS NOT AN EXCUSE.

Documented patterns of bribery, coercion, and procedural abuse in arbitration/religious courts and community dispute systems (composite).

The rain that morning did not fall; it insisted. It pressed against the windows of the Beit din like a steady finger, tapping out a question no one wanted to answer. Outside, puddles in the alley trembled with each drop, as if the earth itself were flinching.

Inside, everything was dry and orderly. The corridor smelled of old books and black tea. A framed verse hung near the waiting bench-letters neat as stitched thread-promising truth, promising justice, promising a world that made sense if you obeyed it.

Dayan Mordechai Feld wore his tallit when he sat in session, the folds resting around his shoulders like a banner of gravity. The fringes-tzitzit on the tallit gadol-brushed his sleeves when he moved his hands, soft reminders that law was supposed to be tethered to God. People watched the cloth and relaxed, as if textiles could guarantee integrity.

A man named Shimon Kessler waited in the corridor with his hat in his lap. His knuckles were raw from worry. Across from him sat Leah Kessler, his sister-in-law, eyes fixed on the floor. Between them, a dispute over inheritance had curdled into something ugly: accusations of withheld assets, of forged signatures, of quiet theft. When the clerk called them in, the room felt smaller than it should have. The three dayanim sat behind a long table. Feld in the center, his tallit immaculate, his expression calm. On either side, two older men listened more than they spoke, their faces like stone that had learned patience.

Feld nodded to Shimon. "You may begin."

Shimon cleared his throat. "My brother is dead," he said, voice cracking. "And I'm being told I should give up the share he promised me. But I have the papers. I have-"

Leah interrupted, sharp. "You have papers you made."

Feld raised one hand, a gentle stop. "We are not here for shouting. We are here for din, for judgment." He pronounced the word as if it were clean.

The hearing moved quickly. Feld asked questions with the precision of a man who enjoyed control. He requested documents, glanced at them, and set them aside. He spoke of community harmony, of avoiding public courts, of settling "within the house." The other dayanim nodded as if the cadence itself were proof.

During a break, Feld stepped into the small side room where tea was set out. Rain streaked the frosted glass. The door clicked shut behind him with the soft finality of secrecy.

A man in a tailored coat followed-Uri Stern, a "community mediator," though everyone knew he did more than mediate. He moved like someone who had learned to make deals in quiet places.

Uri poured tea without asking. "Hard case," he murmured. Feld did not look at him. "They're emotional."

Uri smiled. "Emotional people do desperate things. Desperate people can be... unpredictable." Feld's jaw tightened. "What do you want?"

Uri leaned closer, voice low. "I want the Beit din to stay respected. You want the Beit din to stay respected. Leah's family is generous. They fund half the scholarships. They keep the roof from leaking."

The tea's surface, rippling as though disturbed by the cup, caught Feld's stare.

Uri continued, "If this goes against Leah, you'll have drama. Headlines. Civil court. Police sniffing. You know how it goes. But if you guide it toward a 'compromise'-a settlement-everyone calms down. And," he added softly, "the roof gets fixed."

Feld's tallit did not restrain him. It decided to feel heavier-and therefore, in his mind, more justified. He told himself he was protecting the institution. He told himself he was preventing scandal. He told himself that peace was worth bending the line.

When the hearing resumed, Feld's tone had changed slightly. Still gentle, but firmer-like a hand guiding someone toward a door they didn't want to open.

"Shimon," Feld said, "I must speak plainly. Your claim is... uncertain. Your evidence is not as strong as you think."

Shimon blinked. "But you just said the signature looked-" "I said it looked similar," Feld corrected smoothly. "Not conclusive. The Beit Din cannot build on sand." Shimon's face flushed. "So what now? I lose everything?"

Feld lifted his palm again. "No. We will propose a compromise. Leah will give you a smaller amount. You will both sign. You will both move on. This is wise. The Torah's ways are ways of peace."

Leah's lips twitched with relief. Shimon stared as if the air had turned to smoke. Outside, the rain intensified, hammering the roof like a verdict.

Afterward, Shimon cornered Feld in the hallway. The clerk pretended not to see. "Dayan," Shimon said, voice shaking, "with respect-this isn't justice."

Feld's eyes stayed calm. "Justice is not always what you want. Sometimes justice prevents worse harm." "What harm?" Shimon whispered. "To whom?"

Feld's voice lowered. "To the community."

Shimon stepped back as if struck. He saw it then: his rights were being weighed against the institution's comfort, and the institution had heavier stones on its side of the scale.

A week later, Shimon met Rivka Halpern, a attorney who advised families pro bono. They sat in a cafe where steam fogged the windows and rainwater ran in brown rivers along the curb. "She says I should sign," Shimon told her. "They all say I should sign.

If I don't, they'll call me a troublemaker." Rivka's eyes were sharp. "Do you have copies of everything?" Shimon slid a folder across the table. "I kept them. I didn't know why. Just-instinct." Rivka read, then looked up. "This isn't a compromise. It's pressure." "But it's the Beit din," Shimon said helplessly. "He wore the tallit. He quoted peace." Rivka tapped the folder. "Cloth is not proof."

She asked questions the community had avoided: about donations, about intermediaries, about "fundraising dinners" Feld attended at Leah's cousin's house. She filed a complaint through an oversight channel nobody liked to mention. She contacted another Dayan in a neighboring city. She quietly collected testimonies from others who had felt guided toward outcomes that always seemed to favor the same families.

The investigation did not arrive like thunder. It arrived like damp spreading across a ceiling: slowly, then suddenly undeniable. Bank statements. Emails. Patterns of "gifts" routed through Uri Stern. A scholarship fund paid directly for Feld's son's tuition-"anonymous donor," the paperwork said, as if anonymity were innocence. The community reacted with grief and anger, not neatly separated, when they asked Feld to step aside pending review. Some said, "He did so much good." Others said, "How could he?" Most said nothing at all, because silence is the easiest garment to wear.

On a Friday evening soon after, the rain finally stopped. The street glittered under the streetlights. Water dripped from tree branches in slow, patient drops, like a metronome. Shimon walked past the Beit din and felt the strange quiet of an answered storm.

Inside, Feld's chair sat empty.

The moral didn't feel like triumph. It felt like a warning: justice is not a mood, and peace is not an excuse. If the tallit becomes a curtain, the scales will tip with no one noticing-until the weight of consequence forces them back.

57

"THE IMAM'S BISHT"

THE CLOTH THAT WARMS A LEADER CAN ALSO WARM A LIE.

Composite patterns of patronage and charitable-fund capture within religious institutions (fictionalized).

Before the first call to prayer, the town still belonged to the night. Palms hissed in the cool air, and a thin mist lay in the wadi like breath. By noon, heat would flatten the streets into a shimmer. At dawn, everything looked honest.

Imam Hamid al-Rashid liked the dawn. It made him feel clean.

On Fridays he wore a dark bisht trimmed with gold over his thawb. The moment he stepped outside, shopkeepers straightened and voices dropped. The bisht did not make him righteous, but it made righteousness look like him, and that subtle confusion was part of his authority.

New taps, leveled tiles, and bright paint marked the mosque's recent renovation. The town praised Hamid's "leadership" and did not ask how quickly the funds had appeared.

Khalil Barzan, the local construction magnate, pledged a large "gift for the House of God," through whom they appeared. They announced the pledge after Jumu'ah, and the congregation murmured approval, just as people murmur when they feel protected. Hamid thanked Khalil and prayed for him. He meant it. He also noticed how gratitude can harden into obligation.

Khalil's men began to "help." They suggested vendors, offered discounts, and arrived with solutions before problems were fully named. Each suggestion sounded harmless. Each carried a hook. Hamid told himself he could manage it-hikmah, wisdom-steering the wealthy toward good. Quietly, he enjoyed being needed by both the pious and the powerful.

Then the requests shifted.

A teacher in the neighborhood had spoken publicly about municipal corruption. Khalil did not like it. "It stirs fitnah," Khalil said in Hamid's office, voice soft as if discussing charity. "People get excited. They forget adab." "We counsel with gentleness," Hamid replied. "We do not silence."

Khalil smiled. "No one said silence. Only guidance."

When Khalil left, a sealed envelope remained on the desk-cash and a note: For the scholarship fund. Hamid deposited it under a new line item, "Youth initiatives." He did not tell the committee a request had been attached because he did not want to make it real.

But it became real on the minbar.

The following Friday, wearing the bisht, Hamid delivered a khutbah on unity and guarding tongues. He did not name the teacher. He didn't need to. People felt the direction of the wind. After the prayer, older men praised him for "calming the youth." Their faces looked away.

Two weeks later, the teacher stopped his lectures. He said he was "taking a break." In the market, people pretended it was his choice. Hamid told himself he had prevented division. In the quiet after Isha, shame pricked like grit in the eye.

Once Khalil learned the imam would lean, Khalil leaned harder. A cousin needed a marriage officiated quickly despite the paperwork. A nephew wanted the mosque hall for a "private event." A contractor wanted Hamid's public endorsement. Hamid said yes more often than not because yes is easier, and because he told himself the good funded by

Khalil's money outweighed the compromises.

Summer storms finally arrived. Rain slammed the town, turning dust to mud and carving channels through the streets. It felt like a parable: water finds the paths already cut. So does influence. So does consequence.

That week, an anonymous packet reached the regional council: receipts, procurement patterns, messages from Khalil's assistant to mosque staff. The packet did not accuse Hamid of stealing; it accused him of lending sanctity to a patronage network. The evidence was ordinary-paper, dates, stamps-which made it impossible to dismiss as rumor.

An inspector arrived, polite and relentless. He asked why the same vendors won repeatedly, why "donations" appeared right before decisions, why committee minutes lacked disclosure. Hamid answered with calm phrases about efficiency and community trust. The inspector listened like weather: patient, inevitable.

When the council suspended Hamid pending review, the town cracked. Some defended him:"He rebuilt the mosque!" Others muttered everyone had known, in their bones, that Khalil's gifts were not pure. The youth whispered that the imam had become a gatekeeper for the rich.

Hamid spent the first week of suspension walking at dawn. Mist rose and dissolved. He thought of how society is like soil: firm until a storm exposes the channels beneath. The mosque had needed protection-transparent rules, shared oversight-long before it needed rescue by inspectors and statements.

On the day he cleared his office, Hamid folded the bisht carefully. The gold trim caught the light for an instant, bright as a warning. Outside, wind lifted fresh-dried dust and carried it away, indifferent.

At the first community meeting, the convener spoke of "reassurance." Someone suggested a statement praising Hamid's years of service. An elder warned, "Do not embarrass the mosque." An older man answered, almost whispering, "Do not embarrass the poor." The room went still. Outside, rainwater dripped from the eaves in slow, counted drops.

Hamid was invited to write a letter of repentance "for the sake of unity." He drafted three versions. In each, the words tried to land on safety: I was protecting the community; I was avoiding conflict; I was preventing fitnah. None of the drafts named the simpler truth: he had allowed a donor to rent his moral authority.

In his last dawn walk before the hearing, he watched ants carry crumbs across wet sand, each one following a path laid down by others. He understood then that institutions often worship outcomes and neglect pathways. The community celebrated renovation, not governance; applause, not safeguards. And when the paths led into harm, they called the resulting intervention "mercy," forgetting that true mercy requires quiet construction before the fall.

The mosque remained. The prayers continued. However, the town understood something it should have been spared: informal purchases of authority occur, and protection before harm is not the same as rescue after it. The cloth that warms a leader can also warm a lie.

58

"THE ROSH YESHIVA'S WHITE ROBE"

PURITY DOESN'T LAST WHERE TRAFFIC IS HEAVY.

Documented patterns of academic/clerical institutions suppressing misconduct, misdirecting funds, and prioritizing reputation over protection (composite).

The first snow of the season came late, thin flakes drifting over the yeshiva courtyard like ash that wanted to be beautiful. The stone benches gathered white along their edges. A bare tree stood in the center, its branches scratching the sky as if the sky owed it answers.

Rosh Yeshiva Eliezer Weiss liked the snow because it made everything look newly forgiven.

On ceremonial days he wore a kittel-his white robe-beneath a dark coat, letting the whiteness show at the collar and cuffs. Students spoke of him with reverence. He had the kind of authority that made men sit straighter and older men speak softer.

He preached discipline as devotion. "Torah requires backbone," he told the Beit Midrash, pacing between rows of desks. "A weak spine bends toward weakness."

The yeshiva's finances, however, were bending.

A major donor had died. Tuition arrears grew. The heating bills rose. The building's old radiators clanged like complaints. The board urged Weiss to "stabilize."

A fundraiser named Mendel Raskin offered a solution: a new "learning initiative" with corporate sponsorship, plus generous private gifts routed through a foundation.

"It's clean," Mendel promised in Weiss's office, brushing snow from his shoulders. "It's respectable. And it keeps the yeshiva safe."

Weiss folded his hands. "Safe from what?"

"From scrambling," Mendel said. "From layoffs. From scandal." The word scandal hung in the air like frigid breath.

Weiss agreed. He told himself he was protecting students. He told himself that the yeshiva was a ship, and a ship needs a captain willing to make hard decisions when the sea turns rough.

The "learning initiative" arrived with banners and photo ops. A visiting benefactor posed beside students. Speakers delivered speeches about "the future." The Beit midrash was repainted, and the fresh paint smell felt like hope.

But the foundation money came with strings that were never written. Mendel suggested hires. "This teacher is excellent," he'd say. "This administrator will help modernize." Weiss, already tired, allowed it. He told himself competence was the goal.

Then certain students disappeared from the dorms-not expelled, not officially. Quietly "encouraged to transfer." The reasons were never transparent. "Not a good fit," Weiss would say, refusing detail. In the dining hall, whispers grew like mold.

A student named Yosef-bright, anxious, loyal-approached Weiss after morning seder. Snowmelt dripped from the eaves outside, forming slow drops that sounded like counting.

"Rebbe," Yosef began, "they moved my roommate out. He said someone told him... told him he asked too many questions."

Weiss looked at him, expression calm. "Questions are good. Disruption is not."

"But-" Yosef swallowed. "He was asking about the scholarship list. Why some boys lost their aid." Weiss's eyes tightened. "Yosef, you are here to learn Torah. Not to audit."

Yosef's cheeks flushed. "But isn't it written-" Weiss cut him off gently. "Do not confuse piety with suspicion." The phrase sounded holy. It was also an order.

Yosef went back to his desk and tried to learn. The letters blurred. He thought of the white snow in the courtyard and how quickly it turned grey near the street where cars splashed slush. Purity, he realized, doesn't last where traffic is heavy.

Weeks later, Yosef found a spreadsheet left open on an office computer-tuition accounts, donor allocations, "special exceptions."

He didn't intend to snoop. He intended to drop off a form. But the numbers stared at him like eyes. Sizeable sums labeled "student welfare" routed into "consulting fees." A line item for "initiative promotion" paying for Mendel's travel. A note: quiet transfers.

He felt sick. Not because money was messy-money is always messy-but because the mess was being hidden under the language of holiness.

The yeshiva told parents it was stable. It told students it was righteous. It told donors it was transparent. Yosef showed the screenshot to his friend Chaim in the dorm hallway.

Chaim stared. "Don't," he whispered. "You'll ruin everything."

"Everything's already ruined," Yosef said, voice shaking. "We just haven't admitted it." Chaim's eyes flicked toward the stairwell. "They'll say you're causing profanation of the Name." Yosef replied, "What's the profanation of the Name -truth, or theft?"

The confrontation arrived on a Sunday afternoon when the snow had melted into brown rivers along the curb. The board met in the library. Weiss sat at the head, his kittel visible at the collar like a quiet claim to purity. Mendel sat beside him, smiling as if this were a strategy session.

A board member cleared his throat. "We received... a complaint." Weiss's voice stayed calm. "From whom?"

The member glanced at Yosef, seated at the end like an intruder. "From a student."

Weiss looked at Yosef as if seeing him for the first time. "You came to the board instead of your Rebbe?" Yosef's hands shook, but he forced his voice steady. "I came because I was told not to ask."

Mendel laughed softly. "Students misunderstand budgets." Yosef slid printed pages onto the table. "Then explain these."

Silence fell. The papers sat like evidence that refused to be blessed away.

Weiss's face hardened slowly. "You don't understand," he said. "Do you want the yeshiva to close? Do you want boys on the street?"

"Do you want boys to be lied to?" Yosef shot back.

Weiss stared, breathing through his nose, then said quietly, "You have turned learning into accusation." Yosef answered, "You turned holiness into camouflage."

Afterward, the board started an audit. The yeshiva issued a statement about "reviewing governance." Mendel disappeared for a while. Weiss continued teaching, but his authority thinned. The Beit midrash remained filled with boys bent over books, yet the room's air had changed: less trust, more vigilance.

In the courtyard, the tree stood bare against a clear sky. Wind moved through its branches like a dry prayer. Yosef watched it and thought: systems prefer rescue-public statements, audits, new policies-because rescue looks like virtue.

Prevention would have required listening when the first questions were asked.

Weiss's kittel stayed white. The institution, for the first time, admitted it could still be dirty.

59

"THE ABBÉ WHO COUNTED COINS"

THE LIE ISN'T ONLY IN TAKING; IT'S IN TREATING SACRED TRUST AS A PRIVATE OPPORTUNITY.

Clergy financial misconduct, Belgium, 2002-2011 (composite case), PRGR

On winter evenings in Liège, the river looks like dull metal-pewter water sliding past stone embankments, carrying the city's cold without complaint. In the parish counting room behind St. Bartholomew's, coins made their own weather. They clinked in shallow cascades, a bright, nervous sound like hail on glass.

Abbé Lucien Moreau loved that sound.

He never said so, of course. Publicly he spoke of generosity and sacrifice with the soft certainty of a man who had never lacked either. He wore his cassock neatly, his collar crisp, his gestures economical. Parishioners admired his composure. Donors admired his discretion. Even skeptics admitted he looked "proper," as if moral integrity were a property of clean fabric.

But at night, when volunteers stacked coins into neat towers and paper bills into precise rectangles, Lucien would stand in the doorway and watch with a hunger he disguised as gratitude.

"Bless you," he would say, smiling. "Every coin counts." He meant it literally.

The parish counted in a cramped room that always smelled faintly of dust and lemon disinfectant. A portable heater clicked on and off, dry heat against damp walls. The air was thick with old paper and human breath. When you spend enough time around cash, you notice its chemistry: the coppery tang on your fingertips, the faint sourness of sweaty banknotes, and how coins tarnish where you've handled them too often. Even money corrodes.

Lucien preached about corrosion in other forms-modern cynicism, weakened faith, moral decay. He spoke about humility as if it were a practice he performed daily. People liked him for that. They needed him to be that. In a world that feels increasingly ungovernable, parishioners love a man who seems orderly.

He understood that need and used it.

His system began with small "adjustments," the kind a congregation tolerates because it doesn't want to examine its own trust. The congregation rerouted a donation earmarked for youth outreach to "building maintenance."

Lucien's genius was not theft; it was labeling.

He learned how to make money move by changing the names of containers. Like chemistry, where a harmless-looking vial can contain something volatile, the danger wasn't always in the amount-it was in the disguise. He would split invoices into smaller chunks so they slid under oversight thresholds. He would pay friendly vendors who returned "discounts" later than consulting fees. He would buy items for the rectory and record them as parish assets: a new chair, then a better chair, then a desk "for community meetings" that happened mostly with Lucien alone.

No single transaction screamed. Together, the pattern hummed.

When questions arose, Lucien used a tone perfected by institutions everywhere: indulgent superiority.

"My dear," he once told a volunteer who asked about a discrepancy, "parish finances are more complex than they look. Leave the structure to those trained for it."

The volunteer-an older woman who cleaned offices in town-blushed and apologized. She had asked a sensible question and felt crude for asking it. Lucien didn't raise his voice. He didn't need to. He used education as an altitude: from up there, everyone below looks smaller.

Institutional complacency supported him. The diocese was busy, understaffed, allergic to scandal. As long as the parish's outward metrics looked healthy-attendance stable, repairs completed, no newspaper headlines-administrators preferred not to open drawers.

The first person who refused to be soothed was Clara Van Acker, an accountant who volunteered her expertise out of stubborn faith. Clara didn't come to the counting room for warmth. She came for accuracy. She had spent years reconciling ledgers for small businesses where a missing fifty euros was a crisis, not a rounding error.

Clara noticed the pattern in the way a trained ear notices an instrument slightly out of tune. Deposits didn't align with bank confirmations. Vendor invoices repeated the same phrasing-different names, same template. "Emergency repairs" appeared again and again, always just below the amount that required a second signature. A charity allocation had been "temporarily held" for two years.

She asked Lucien politely for supporting documents.

He smiled, the patient smile of a man addressing someone he considered useful but slow. "Clara," he said, "you mustn't let numbers steal your peace."

Peace, in his mouth, meant silence.

Clara persisted, anyway. First, she wanted to see bank statements. Then, she asked for agreements with vendors. Finally, she required proof of work completed for the consulting fees. She built her own ledger alongside his, the way a meteorologist builds a forecast from pressure readings: one anomaly is noise; repeated anomalies are a front moving in.

Lucien adapted. He became warmer in public, more generous with compliments. He thanked Clara from the pulpit for her "diligence," turning her scrutiny into a badge he could wear. He invited her onto a "renewal committee," a move designed to make her complicit.

She declined.

One night, after a parish meeting, Clara lingered in the office to file documents and found a folder tucked behind a drawer insert, not hidden expertly-hidden casually, as if casualness itself were protection. Inside were letters with a foundation whose address matched a mailbox service, and a sequence of transfers that routed parish money out and back in under different labels. It wasn't only skimming. It was laundering legitimacy through paperwork.

Clara felt a tightness in her chest the way people do before a storm: pressure shifting, breath shortening, the body warning the mind.

She photocopied everything.

The diocese did not respond with righteousness. It responded with triage. A discreet inquiry. A quiet request for records. A visit framed as "routine."

Lucien met the investigators in a room filled with saints' portraits and polished wood. He wore composure like armor. He spoke about stewardship, administrative strain, and modern compliance burdens. He offered binders of paperwork-so much paper it threatened to suffocate the question.

When pressed, he admitted to "minor administrative errors." He promised reforms. He suggested that critics "misunderstood the realities of parish management." He implied, gently, that those critics-often less educated parishioners-were prone to suspicion and exaggeration.

That implication worked on some investigators because bias is not rare in institutions; it's simply unexamined. But Clara's documents were stubborn. They showed intent. They showed repetition. They showed money moving in loops designed to blur ownership and responsibility.

The outcome was quiet but real. Lucien lost financial control of the parish. Oversight came into effect. An agreement that avoided criminal proceedings allowed them to repay a portion of misdirected funds. The diocese framed the matter as "irregularities corrected," a phrase that made wrongdoing sound like a clerical typo.

Lucien remained a priest for a time, reassigned to duties that limited his access to accounts.

He preached humility in a different parish with the same calm voice. Many parishioners forgave him because admitting you were used is harder than forgiving.

Clara kept volunteering, though she no longer believed the institution's promises of transparency. Morality, she learned, is performable as beautifully as music, and coins keep time as steadily as prayer.

There is an old biblical account of a servant who ran after silver in secret and returned wearing innocence. The story's force is not thunderous. It is diagnostic: the lie isn't only in taking; it's in treating a sacred trust as a private opportunity.

Lucien had counted coins as if counting were devotion. But money, like metal, remembers.

It tarnishes in spots where the same hands have handled it too often.

PRGR END-CAP - AUTHORED HARM TEST

(for "THE ABBÉ WHO COUNTED COINS" - non-repetitive, case-specific)

In this case, the danger is not "money in a church." It is **money becoming a confessional without absolution**-the abbé learning who needs what, who fears shame, who will accept a private arrangement rather than public scrutiny, and then using that knowledge to make the parish run *through him*.

PRGR would bite at the exact moment Abbé Moreau (or his delegate) turns the coin-counting into **a private corridor of discretion**.

The hinge-steps where PRGR would force authorship (specific to the abbé's method)

The cash-handling exception that becomes habit
The first breach is usually framed as pastoral practicality: "We can't burden volunteers," "The poor give cash," "We'll reconcile later." PRGR triggers when the abbé authorizes *any* recurring practice where cash is handled without dual control (two-person count, sealed deposit bags, same-day deposit log). He must author:

why the exception is necessary,

what minimum safeguards still apply,

and what loss threshold will trigger automatic external review. In this story, "exception" is the seed of a shadow system.

The locked drawer / private envelope step
If the chapter contains the telltale detail-coins counted after hours, envelopes set aside "for emergencies," donations "temporarily" stored in a private drawer-PRGR triggers at the first time funds are removed from the ordinary chain of custody. The abbé must author:
whose hands touched the money,

where it was stored, who can verify it,

and why parish oversight is being bypassed. This is the moment where trust stops being spiritual and becomes operational.

The "directed generosity" step - deciding who receives help without trace
If the abbé dispenses aid personally (cash to a family, "quiet support" to a parishioner) and the help is real, the risk is not charity-it's **unreviewable selection**.

PRGR triggers when distribution is done without a coded ledger or independent verification.

He must author:

what criteria govern help,

what prevents favoritism or dependency,

and what privacy-preserving record exists (coded entries, two-person approval).
Otherwise relief becomes a lever: people learn that dignity depends on the abbé's mood.

The donor-intent bend - "We'll use it where it's most needed"
In coin-counting cases, the most common misuse is not theft but **repurposing**: restricted gifts quietly funding unrelated needs or smoothing budgets.

PRGR triggers at the first decision to redirect a gift away from its stated purpose (repairs, youth program, named fund).

The abbé must author:

what was promised,

why it's being redirected,

what alternative funding was rejected,

and how donors will be informed.

PRGR makes "pastoral necessity" a signed claim, not a blanket.

The silence purchase - using spiritual authority to stop questions
If a treasurer or volunteer asks for reconciliation and receives a rebuke framed as faith ("Do

you distrust your priest?"), PRGR triggers at that response.

The abbé must author:

why the question is illegitimate (if it truly is),

what transparency channel exists that doesn't shame the questioner,

and what protections prevent social retaliation. In this case, the abuse is not only in accounts; it's in the way scrutiny is made to feel sinful.

What PRGR would force in this case (tailored safeguards)

1. **Chain-of-custody rules that treat cash like evidence**
   PRGR would require: two-person counts, sealed bags, same-day deposits, independent reconciliation-because coins are not just money here, they're the medium of plausible deniability.

2. **A privacy-safe aid ledger**
   Help can be discreet without being untraceable. PRGR requires coded entries and dual approval so charity doesn't become personal dependency.

3. **A donor-intent lock with a documented override**
   If funds must be redirected, PRGR forces a written override that can be reviewed later. Not because the parish is a corporation, but because moral authority should not double as spending authority without restraint.

4. **A retaliation tripwire for questioners**
   If the volunteer who asked about the count is suddenly excluded, criticized, or removed, PRGR triggers automatic review-because this case's enforcement mechanism is social, not violent.

Questions that keep this End-Cap fresh and case-bound

If you were the abbé: which specific step are you willing to sign your name under-the after-hours cash handling, the private envelope "for emergencies," or the redirected gift justified as "need"?

If you were the volunteer counter: what is your first non-negotiable safeguard-two-person count, sealed deposits, or independent reconciliation-and what will you do when faith is used to make you feel ashamed for asking?

If you were the parish council: do you want holiness to mean "don't ask," or do you want holiness to mean "nothing here requires secrecy to survive"?

PRGR fits this case because it doesn't moralize about coins. It pins down the exact moment the abbé **turns counting into control**-and demands a named, signed reason at the step where "trust" quietly becomes an unaudited system.

60

"THE LAWYER'S HIDDEN LEDGER"

A TAILORED GARMENT DOES NOT PREVENT WRONGDOING; IT CAN MAKE WRONGDOING LOOK OFFICIAL.

Legal misconduct and organised crime, Switzerland, 2013 (composite case)

Zürich wears restraint the way the Alps wear snow: as a proof first of seriousness, as a promise of permanence. From the city, on clear days, the mountains Pilatus, Rigi and Titlis look immovable-white ridgelines cut clean against the sky, rock and ice stacked like certainty. People forget that permanence is only what survives for now. The Alps are not invulnerable. They avalanche. They shed stone. They erode grain by grain under forces too patient to notice.

That was the mood around lawyer André Keller.

Keller was a respected figure in Zürich's legal circles, the sort of man whose tailored robe seemed to tighten the surrounding air. When in courtrooms, boardrooms, or discreet restaurant rooms where deals are spoken softly, he conveyed authority, professionalism, and moral rectitude. His handwriting was neat, his arguments clean, his tone measured to suggest he had nothing to hide. People trusted him partly because trust is a social convenience. It saves time. It spares discomfort. It lets a system move.

But Keller's legitimacy was, over time, carved from within.

One could describe the arrangement's start as innocuous. Certain clients required "subtle" guidance: strategic filings, small scheduling adjustments, quiet negotiation with opposing counsel to prevent complications. Keller told himself it was competent practice, not compromise. A good lawyer expects friction and smooths it. That is what he told himself while he pushed tiny stones down a slope.

In the Alps, you can do that. You can flick a rock with your boot and watch it tumble, harmless, satisfying, no consequence. Until you understand slopes, remember. Until you understand that a slight disturbance can be the first whisper of a larger collapse.

Over months, those minor favors strengthened into systematic facilitation of criminal operations: laundering money through legal structures, advising on loopholes with a technician's calm, coordinating with intermediaries whose faces were forgettable by design. It was not dramatic. It was administrative. Illicit wealth moved through the channels of respectability like meltwater disappearing into limestone-quiet, persistent, creating hollows underneath a surface that still looked solid.

Keller's office became a hub of dual authority. Publicly, he maintained rigorous legal decorum, representing clients with diligence and skill. Privately, he kept a ledger-part diary, part instrument-that tracked intricate arrangements: favors owed, payments made, deadlines, the exact timing of procedural interventions that could tilt an outcome without leaving obvious fingerprints. He didn't call it corruption. He called it management.

And he enjoyed it.

Not in the crude way people imagine, with stacks of cash or vulgar triumph. He enjoyed the precision of it-the sense that he could control a legal climate the way a skilled mountaineer reads weather. He enjoyed the private thrill of influence, the knowledge that outward appearances remained untarnished. His robe functioned as camouflage: not hiding him from sight, but hiding his intent behind an assumed integrity.

Nadine Vogel, a junior associate, was the first to feel the ground shift.

She was new enough to take rules seriously and smart enough to notice when rules were being treated like suggestions. In Switzerland, paperwork is a kind of religion: forms, signatures, stamps, the quiet conviction that order protects people. Nadine trusted the system the way hikers trust marked trails. If something was missing, it mattered.

She began seeing discrepancies. Files moved without notation. Evidence redirected. Transactions that didn't belong in a legal file appearing in legal language-"consulting," "settlement facilitation," "retainer adjustments"-phrases clean enough to pass casual review. She noticed certain client accounts behaved strangely, as money entered, sat briefly, then flowed onward through entities that looked legitimate only because legitimate terms described them. The rhythm was too consistent to be accidental.

At first she doubted herself. That is how respectable systems defend themselves: they make the observer question their own eyesight.

She started documenting anyway. Dates. Correspondence. Access logs. Minor anomalies, collected like snowflakes. Individually beautiful, harmless. Together, capable of weight.

The Alps teach a brutal lesson about accumulation. A loud disturbance causes an avalanche; nothing more than the steady layering of snow can cause it until a weak layer-hidden underneath-can no longer hold. The surface can look calm and bright. Failure is already inherent in the structure.

Nadine found the weak layer.

She opened a drawer on instinct one evening when she was searching for a file that had been returned. Inside was Keller's ledger. Not a confession, not a melodramatic list of crimes, but a carefully constructed map: coded entries, initials, timings. It read like a professional's notebook-efficient, almost elegant. That elegance made it worse. It suggested intention sustained over years, a mind that had stopped feeling moral friction.

Nadine felt her stomach tighten. In that moment, Zürich's stability-the crisp streets, the steady trams, the clean neutrality-felt like a thin crust over a slope.

She didn't confront Keller. People who confront powerful men inside powerful systems often become the problem the system wants to eliminate. She copied what she could quietly and stored it off-site. She lived differently: changed routes home, muted phone conversations, stopped trusting casual friendliness in the office. When Keller asked her once, smiling, whether she was "settling in," she answered with polite neutrality while feeling the strange sensation of standing on unstable snow.

The turning point came from outside. Federal authorities investigating organised crime began tracing financial flows through law firms and advisory structures-following money the way glaciologists follow meltwater paths to find hidden cavities. Patterns surfaced: shell companies connected to known intermediaries, legal trusts used as temporary reservoirs, funds moved with the speed and certainty of practiced repetition.

Nadine supplied her documentation. She did not offer opinions. She offered evidence-ledger excerpts, correspondence, timestamps, the small mechanics of the system Keller had relied on to stay invisible. Investigators cross-referenced everything. The picture sharpened. Keller's office was not merely adjacent to criminality; it had become a conduit. His legal expertise had provided criminals something more valuable than advice: legitimacy.

Public exposure provoked an immediate reaction. That Swiss way-quietly, painfully, and with controlled language that could not fully conceal alarm-shook the Swiss legal community. Clients questioned trust. Colleagues looked at robes differently. Keller faced suspension, investigation, and criminal inquiry. His defenders argued technicalities, claiming that the structures were "permissible," the advice was "general," and the actions could be framed as "normal advocacy."

But the ethical breach was indisputable. The robe, meant to signify professional dignity, now read as concealment. A tailored garment does not prevent wrongdoing; it can make wrongdoing look official.

Keller himself reacted like a man watching a mountainside he thought he understood move. Not panic, at first-calculation. He tried to speak in the same measured tones, tried to treat the investigation as an inconvenience he could manage. But once authorities map a pattern, the map becomes difficult to erase. His ledger-once a private trophy of control-became the mechanism of his undoing.

Reforms followed, as they always do after people have already absorbed the damage. Law firms strengthened compliance. Bar associations implemented stricter auditing protocols. Client onboarding became more stringent. Suspicious transaction reporting expanded. The system tightened its straps like a climber checking harnesses after someone falls.

Yet the deeper lesson remained uncomfortably human: the mountains looked unmovable, but they were never invulnerable. Stability can be mistaken for safety. Respectability can be mistaken for virtue. Those who understand can exploit a legal culture built on trust; that trust is, in part, an aesthetic-something you can wear. Authority cannot substitute for ethical integrity. Robes enhance perception and credibility, but they do not prevent compromise. When oversight is lax, authority allows concealment; when ambition or gratification enters the equation, even the cleanest system can be used as a channel.

Keller's case did not destroy Zürich. The city still ran. The trams still arrived on time. The mountains still held their white lines against the sky.

But anyone who paid attention understood something had shifted: not the Alps themselves, but the belief that immovable things are immune to collapse. In the end, it wasn't a single dramatic fall that defined him. It was erosion-small choices repeated until the slope gave way. And like an avalanche, once it started moving, it carried everything with it: trust, reputation, the comforting illusion that dignity is the same as goodness.

61

"THE IMAM'S DONATION BOX"

SMALL THEFTS BECOME LARGE WHEN THE HUNGRY ARE THE ONES PAYING.

> A repeatable institutional failure mode-charitable systems with weak controls + concentrated access + social reluctance to question "the steady hand."

Before sunrise, the air outside the community center still held the night's coolness. A thin wind nudged dust and leaves along the curb in small spirals. Cars arrived quietly. People came carrying the weight of ordinary life-late shifts, sick parents, rent due-yet they entered as if crossing into shelter.

Inside, the prayer hall smelled faintly of clean carpet and sandalwood oil. Light pooled low and warm. Near the entrance stood the donation box: plain wood, a narrow slot, a modest plaque-For those in need. It looked almost shy, a quiet mouth waiting to be fed. Worshippers slipped folded notes and envelopes into it with practiced reverence, like dropping worries into a safer place.

Imam Nabil arrived a few minutes before the call. He wore a simple cream robe and a white scarf that fell neatly at his Qabba, its ends resting on his chest like a visible promise. His calm was steady, neither theatrical nor distant. He greeted people by name when he could, by face when he couldn't. In his presence, the community felt organized, contained.

Haroun Saleh, the center's director, held the keys.

He did not lead prayers. He did not preach. His authority lived in the back rooms: schedules, invoices, contractor bids, account passwords. He spoke in the language of "operations" and "compliance," words that make virtue sound like paperwork. When the heater failed or the pantry ran low, Haroun fixed it quickly, and competence is a drug. People trusted him not because they had measured him, but because they had needed him. When hardship sharpened-layoffs, medical bills, families doubling up-donations increased and requests for help multiplied. Haroun organized relief drives with brisk efficiency. He printed flyers, coordinated volunteers, and repeated the same soothing refrain at board meetings: We're managing. We're careful. We're accountable. Accountable to whom? No one asked. Hope can be a kind of exhaustion: you accept the first steady hand offered because questioning feels like another burden.

The first misdirection looked like reimbursement.

A supplier was "slow with paperwork," Haroun said. He had covered an emergency purchase with his personal card-rice, diapers, disinfectant-and needed repayment. The treasurer nodded. It was plausible. The second misdirection looked like an advance: a last-minute repair "couldn't wait for the bank transfer." The third looked like a temporary change-moving money between sub-accounts "to avoid fees." Nothing screamed theft.

Everything wore the mask of administration.

Soon the withdrawals became routine: careful amounts, always below the level that required a second signature, always close enough to a legitimate expense to resemble its cousin. Haroun told himself he would settle it later, reasoning that stress deserved compensation and that, since the center still functioned-lights on, pantry stocked, prayers held-no one was truly harmed. He used the visible good as evidence that the hidden wrong didn't matter.

But harm accumulates quietly, like carbon monoxide. You don't notice until the room feels wrong.

Layla Qasim noticed. She was a volunteer accountant, the sort who found comfort in columns that align. She didn't come looking for scandal; she came looking for order. The numbers, however, were stubborn. She saw a pattern of cash withdrawals after major donations, reimbursements without invoices, repeated wording that looked copied, not remembered. She asked for documentation. Haroun answered with warmth designed to shame her.

"Sister," he said softly, "don't let suspicion poison your heart. We're doing good work. Don't become someone who sees wrongdoing everywhere."

Suspicion, in that sentence, became sin. Layla felt heat rise in her cheeks-an old tool, shame-meant to make her retreat. For a moment, she almost did. Then she thought of the women who asked for grocery cards with eyes lowered, the father who had admitted he'd skipped meals so his kids could eat. Arithmetic, she remembered, doesn't care about charisma.

She brought her questions to the board.

The board listened the way institutions often listen when truth is inconvenient: slowly, with a concern that bends toward delay. One member said, "We should handle this quietly." Another worried about fitnah, discord, and the community's reputation. A third suggested Layla might misunderstand nonprofit accounting. They asked her to "give it time." Time-another word that smuggles permission.

Haroun sensed the pressure and adapted. He began producing paperwork that looked official: invoices with realistic formatting, receipts that arrived too neatly, vendor contacts who would sign what he asked in exchange for small favors. The fraud grew into a private bureaucracy built beside the public one.

Then a donor asked for a year-end statement.

It was an ordinary request-tax documentation-yet it became the spark in dry grass. The donor's records didn't match the center's. Haroun stalled, then produced documents that contradicted themselves. The donor pushed harder. Suddenly the board found speed it had not shown when the poor were the ones at risk. They hired an outside auditor.

The audit arrived without sirens: emails, file requests, quiet insistence. An auditor is a kind of priest of numbers-patient, procedural, unmoved by titles. Haroun tried the charm. He tried to overwhelm him. He tried to frame confusion as complexity. The auditor kept asking for originals. The gaps widened. The story, once plausible, collapsed under the weight of its own edits.

When authorities became involved, the community's reaction wasn't only anger; it was grief. People can forgive a thief more easily than they can forgive the sensation of having prayed beside one. The community shared a sharp, communal shame: the poor had suffered two thefts-one from the world and another from someone they trusted within their refuge.

Afterward, the center implemented controls that felt obvious in hindsight. Two signatures. Independent audits. Rotating access. Separation of duties. The system finally did what it should have done quietly at the start. That was the bitter lesson: the institution had been excellent at compassion, excellent at response, excellent at public unity-yet it had failed at the less glamorous work of prevention.

On the first Friday after Haroun's departure, the imam stood near the entrance, greeting congregants as usual. The donation box sat in its familiar place. People hesitated before dropping their envelopes in. Each coin sounded louder than it used to-less like charity and more like a question: Who holds the keys? Who checks the locks? Who protects us before we need rescuing?

Outside, the wind rose and dragged a ribbon of dust across the curb, erasing footprints as if the street were trying to forget. But the center could not forget. It had learned, at last, that prevention is the only mercy that doesn't arrive too late. Minor thefts become large when the hungry are the ones paying.

62

"THE BISHOP'S SILENT TRANSACTIONS"

HONEST DOUBT BECOMES THREATENING, BECAUSE IT FORCES A CHOICE.

> Church corruption and financial misconduct, France, 2012 (composite case)

Bishop Henri Marchand presided over a diocese in southern France; his ceremonial cassock and accessories projected dignity, moral authority, and centuries of ecclesiastical tradition. To parishioners and clergy, he embodied sanctity and guidance. The cathedral itself helped maintain the illusion-incense, stone, hymns, the softened light that makes every face look more patient than it is. In such places, belief is not merely an idea; it is an atmosphere.

And atmosphere is persuasive.

Marchand understood the Church is built on what people choose to believe. Not simply that God exists, but that the men at the altar are safe conduits-that the gestures mean what they say they mean, that the words correspond to the unseen. He had learned how much a cassock can accomplish before he spoke a sentence. He also quietly learned how far that same trust can stretch before it snaps.

His entanglement with criminal networks began, as it often does, under the guise of good works. Wealthy donors appeared with a kind of polished humility, offering funds for cathedral restorations, social programs, and parish support. Their money arrived as if Providence itself had wired it: timely, abundant, "anonymous" when convenient. Marchand rationalised acceptance. He told himself that the Church has always taken the world as it is and tried to redeem it. He told himself he could turn tainted wealth into clean mercy.

The first compromise is almost always metaphysical: you decide you can separate the source from the use. Gradually the transactions became more elaborate and ethically ambiguous-property transfers, investment vehicles, administrative decisions aligned with donors' personal interests. Meetings occurred in rooms that smelled of old paper and polished wood, where men used respectful language while making requests that had nothing to do with salvation. Marchand didn't accept envelopes; he accepted structures. A lease reclassified. A building sold at an "appropriate" discount. A parish hall contracted with a company "recommended" by a benefactor. All legal, all documentable, all deniable. He came to enjoy the technical elegance of it: sin disguised as administration, compromise hidden in procedure.

Here the center of the story shifts from money to belief. Not belief in God, but belief in the Church as an organism founded on something more than human appetite. Marchand's cassock became a kind of gravitational field around him. People's belief in his holiness made them less likely to imagine he could be compromised. The less they imagined, the freer he became to rearrange reality.

Sister Claire Fournier, the diocese's financial administrator, began seeing the distortions. Claire was the type who trusted ledgers because ledgers do not blush. She noticed donations appeared inconsistent with standard procedures. The financial administrator redirected funds without rational justification. Certain projects disproportionately benefited individuals with external connections that were never named plainly. The irregularities did not appear chaotic.

She documented everything: dates, amounts, approvals, strange timing. She brought it not to a journalist, not to the police, but to the Abbess of her congregation. That choice itself represented faith-faith that the Church could correct itself and that the Church would welcome truth instead of punishing it. The Abbess listened, expression still, as if prayer had trained her not to flinch. Then she transferred Claire to a project in Malawi, an act that appeared pastoral on paper but felt like burial in practice. A noble mission, yes. Also distance. Also silence.

This is the thin seam where belief becomes complicated. People often think belief is the opposite of doubt. In institutions, belief can function as a substitute for scrutiny. Doubt-honest doubt-becomes threatening because it forces a choice: either the system confronts itself, or it protects itself.

The tsunami came later, when third parties began probing clerical finances. Documentation-revealing how Marchand's authority had facilitated discreet advantages for individuals linked to criminal operations-appeared on a journalist's desk, anonymously, untraceable. The story did not arrive as a confession; it arrived as paperwork. A kind of secular gospel: in the beginning was the document.

Publications started investigations. Policing confirmed what the diocese had avoided naming: silent transactions had materially supported illicit activities while preserving the appearance of legitimate Church operations. And here the symbolism sharpened-Marchand's ceremonial attire had not merely been incidental; it had been instrumental. It gave credibility to the donors' philanthropy. It gave moral cover to the paper trail. It turned a practical arrangement into something that looked like community benevolence.

Public exposure prompted an immediate reaction. Parishioners felt betrayed. Some responded with anger; others with denial so fierce it sounded like devotion. Clergy questioned leadership in whispers that stayed carefully away from microphones. Church authorities initiated canonical and civil inquiries. The church authorities suspended Marchand from administrative duties pending review.

Then came the strangest image of all: his cassock hanging unused, collecting dust for two long years. The garment that once moved through aisles like certainty now sat inert, a costume without a role. In the Church, vestments are supposed to signify continuity-the idea that holiness is bigger than the individual wearer. But dust on a cassock means something else. It means time has stopped admiring you.

This is where your question enters: to believe or not to believe-what did Jesus mean when he established the Church "on Peter"?

Matthew's line-"You are Peter, and on this rock I will build my church"-has served for centuries as a justification for continuity, authority, and structure. Yet the same Gospel also contains a warning that cuts against complacency: Peter is not a marble statue; he is a trembling man. He boasts, he fears, he denies. The "rock" is not the fantasy of an incorruptible leader. It is something stranger: a community built on a human who is painfully fallible, and yet called to responsibility.

If the foundation were flawless performance, Peter would be the wrong choice.

So what did Jesus mean? The scandal forces a plausible reading into view: the Church is established not to guarantee its leaders will never fail, but as a structure that must constantly return to truth. Peter's strength is not that he never collapses; it's that he is confronted, corrected, and restored. The Church, if it is faithful to that origin, should not treat authority as proof of virtue. It should treat authority as a burden that requires more accountability, not less.

Marchand's case revealed the opposite impulse: the system's instinct to protect symbols rather than people. They moved Claire away after she saw anomalies. The system treated a cassock like reputation-management. Reforms arrived only after outsiders forced the truth into daylight.

The French Episcopal Conference implemented stricter oversight: audits, transparency requirements, and tighter controls. Institutional reflection followed in official language-measured, careful, almost antiseptic. No one publicly earned recognition for courage. The silence around Claire's role was itself telling: institutions often praise whistleblowers only when praise is unavoidable, and even then they prefer the whistleblower far away.

Marchand's internal world, meanwhile, became its own courtroom. In private he likely replayed his rationalisations: I helped the poor. I restored the cathedral. I kept the diocese stable. This is another contradiction at the heart of such figures: they point to visible good to excuse invisible harm. Yet the Church is not merely an NGO with incense. Its moral claim is higher. When the source of charity becomes entangled with criminal power, the charity is no longer only charity-it becomes laundering of legitimacy.

And legitimacy is more valuable than money.

In the end, the question "to believe or not to believe" did not resolve neatly for the diocese. Some parishioners left, unable to pray beneath the same vaulted ceilings without hearing the echo of deception. Others stayed, insisting faith is in God, not in men. Both responses contain truth. But neither should become an excuse. Staying must not mean forgetting. Leaving must not mean cynicism.

Marchand-now reduced from bishop to an object of investigation and rumor-embodied the unbearable tension: a man who preached moral order while engineering discreet advantage, a shepherd who made himself useful to wolves. His cassock, once a moving symbol, became a static relic, teaching a hard lesson about what Jesus may have meant with Peter: the Church is built on a rock that is human, and therefore people must build the Church with vigilance, repentance, and the courage to confront its own leaders-because belief without truth is not faith. It is fantasy dressed in vestments.

63

"THE RABBI'S WHITE SHAWL"

IF YOU DAMAGE TRUTH TO CHASE JUSTICE, YOU DO NOT STRENGTHEN THE WORLD.

U.S. prosecution of a Rabbi in a coercive "get" conspiracy.

On Yom Kippur the synagogue looked like snowfall. Men in white kittels stood shoulder to shoulder, their breath held the way people hold fragile things. A tallit rested at each neck-fringes like thin roots reaching for the floor. The lamps above cast a soft, milky light, and the hush had the density of a sealed room.

Outside, the city moved on, but inside the sanctuary time felt braided to older time, as if every whispered Vidui rose into a sky already full of confessions.

Rabbi Baruch Levin's voice moved through the room with the authority of inherited sound. He knew how to place a pause so it felt like reverence instead of rhetoric. He knew how to make a verse land without violence. People trusted him the way they trusted the Ark curtain-instinctively, without examining the stitches.

Levin believed in order. He believed in law. He also believed-quietly, dangerously-that he could force righteousness into existence the way you force a door.

He had watched too many women come to him with eyes reddened by waiting. Too many families twisted by what should have been simple. In a community that prized continuity, the get-the religious divorce-could become a choke chain when a husband refused. The cases arrived as whispers, because shame travels quickly and mercy often travels slowly. A woman chained to a marriage. A husband who enjoyed his leverage. Parents pleading for their daughter's release as if asking for the removal of a curse.

Levin listened with a face like stone warmed by compassion. He quoted the old imperative-Tzedek, Tzedek tirdof, justice, justice shall you pursue-and the words landed clean, like coins on a table. But coins can be for purchase. And anger's currency can purchase justice when it becomes a performance.

The first time Levin intervened outside the ordinary process, it felt like a correction, not a crime. He told himself he was filling a gap in the system. He told himself that delay was cruelty, and that cruelty deserved force. He said to a trusted colleague, half-joking, half-serious, "If the court cannot open the door, sometimes you need a stronger hand on the latch." The colleague laughed, because laughter is how men disguise unease.

Soon the "stronger hand" took shape as a group of enforcers-men who did not wear tallitot, who did not speak the language of study, who carried tools instead of texts. The enforcers introduced themselves as "helpers," "community protectors," "people who understand persuasion."

A warehouse became the courtroom. It was a grim parody: no Ark, no candles, no holy books-only a table and a lock on the door.

Levin did not strike anyone himself. He did not need to. The spiritual economy was enough. His presence sanctified the threat. His words gave moral permission for what followed. He told himself he was correcting cruelty with force. He told himself he was balancing the scales.

A scale, once tipped, is hard to trust.

At first, he framed it as rare. A last resort. The sort of thing done only when all else failed. But the mind adapts quickly to its own exceptions. The second case felt easier because they had already made the first one. The third felt routine. In time, Levin stopped seeing the warehouse as an emergency measure and began seeing it as a lever-a mechanism that produced results.

And results are addictive, especially to men who believe they are righteous.

A man named Avi-raised on the reverence of Torah learning, newly hired to help with community administration-noticed the drift. He was not involved in the coercion; he was involved in paperwork, where truth often betrays itself. He saw unusual payments labeled "consulting." He saw late-night calls on the rabbi's phone logs.

He heard whispers about "a team" that solved problems quickly. The older men dismissed him when he asked. "You're ," they said. "You don't understand. These women are suffering."

Avi understood suffering. That was the problem. He also understood that ends do not purify means simply because the ends feel noble. He remembered a line from the Talmud his teacher loved to repeat when students tried to justify shortcuts: "A mitzvah that comes through an aveirah is no mitzvah."

A good deed accomplished by wrongdoing is not a good deed. Levin's method might produce a get, but it also produced fear. It replaced one form of captivity with another. And fear, once invited into the community as a tool, never stays obedient.

The recordings began accidentally, the way so many exposures begin. An enforcement group member, arrested on an unrelated charge, offered cooperation as a bargaining chip. They monitored phones. They traced meetings. Levin continued believing he could manage the darkness without being changed by it, unaware that the darkness was now keeping its own records.

When the case finally surfaced in indictments and public filings, congregants reacted as if they had discovered mold inside bread. The shock was not only that coercion existed, but that it wore the language of piety. The rabbi's defenders spoke of desperate women and stubborn men, of broken systems and urgent needs. His critics spoke of violence. Both were true-and truth, in such stories, rarely comes pure.

Levin's supporters gathered outside the synagogue after a Friday-night service, faces tight with anger. "He helped people," they said. "He did what the courts wouldn't." Others stood apart, silent, their silence not approval but mourning. A woman who had once sought Levin's help stared at the synagogue doors as if they had changed shape. She sought mercy there and found a man who believed intimidation could manufacture mercy.

In the weeks that followed, the community fractured along familiar lines: those who wanted the scandal contained and those who wanted it named. Some elders argued that public exposure was itself a sin-hillul Hashem, desecration of God's name-as if truth harmed God's name more than by betrayal.

Avi recalled another stark and uncomfortably relevant Talmudic warning: "Whoever can protest and does not protest is held accountable." Silence is not neutral. It is participation.

Autumn arrived with an impatient wind. Leaves scraped along the pavement like pages torn from a book. Grey clouds moved low over the neighborhood, and rain fell in thin, cold sheets, blurring the streetlights into halos. Avi walked under that weather and felt the story's moral pressure the way you feel humidity before a storm: heavy, inescapable.

The tallit-the soft banner of devotion-remained what it had always been. But for some women, it now carried a second meaning: how easily sacred cloth can become a curtain. A tallit can symbolize covenant, but it can also function like camouflage when people treat its wearer as beyond question.

Levin's tragedy was not that he believed in justice. It was that he believed that because justice was holy, any tool used in its service would also become holy. That is not righteousness. That is self-deception dressed as devotion.

In the end, the legal process did what it always does: it reduced the story to counts, evidence, and sentencing. The community held meetings about reforms-stronger oversight, clearer boundaries, protocols for supporting women without coercion. All necessary. All late.

And beneath the procedural cleanup, a more intimate reckoning remained: the realization that someone who truly believes he is right can exploit that reverence.

Outside the synagogue, the wind kept moving, dragging wet leaves into corners. Nature continued its quiet work of erosion, wearing down sharp edges and exposing foundations.

Avi remembered a final Talmudic phrase, one that sounded less like theology and more like a civic warning: "The world stands on truth, justice, and peace." If you damage truth to chase justice, you do not strengthen the world. You weaken its pillars.

The tragedy wasn't that the community needed justice. It was that a man entrusted to pursue it chose a shortcut through darkness-and called the darkness "necessity."

64

"THE ARCHBISHOP'S SECRET BENEFACTORS"

MONEY BENDING INSTITUTIONAL DECISIONS TOWARD ITSELF, NOT THROUGH FORCE BUT THROUGH MASS.

Church financial scandal, Spain, 2013 (composite case)

Vaulted ceilings housed the gala, where candlelight lent gold a deceptive cleanliness. Incense floated in the air with perfume and expensive cologne, a mixture that felt less like worship than varnish.

Archbishop Étienne Marceau moved through the hall as if he belonged to the architecture. His robes were flawless, heavy cloth falling in dignified lines; his cross caught the light with engineered humility. He smiled gently at donors and laid his hand on shoulders with practiced warmth.

"Thank you for your generosity," he said again and again. Generosity is a word that disguises power.

Behind the cathedral offices, in a room that smelled of paper and old stone, a small ledger existed that never appeared in official audits. The ledger lacked a title. It lacked a stamp.

Marceau kept it in a drawer behind files labeled with harmless bureaucracy: "Restoration," "Outreach," "Administrative."

The ledger recorded benefactors by category, not name alone.

Reliable.

Sensitive.

Needs recognition.

Wants influence.

Must be nursed.

To Marceau, donors were not merely donors. They were instruments. Their money bought more than repairs and soup kitchens. It bought access: invitations, introductions, favorable silence. It bought the ability to shape the Church's public voice.

His arrogance showed refinement. He believed he could manage it-keep charity pure while letting influence flow underneath like a hidden current. He spoke of the faithful as "children of the Church," a phrase that sounded tender but functioned as a hierarchy. He treated skeptical journalists as "uneducated in spiritual matters." He spoke about politics with the tone of someone convinced that moral authority outranks elected authority.

And the surrounding institution-old, cautious, trained to preserve itself-preferred not to see. A cathedral needs money. Restoration is expensive. Scandal is more expensive.

So, the benefactors received a welcome.

One donor owned a construction firm repeatedly awarded church contracts at suspicious rates. Another was an industrialist under investigation for labor abuses. Another ran a private foundation that functioned mostly as a reputation wash for money of unclear origin. Their checks arrived in thick envelopes. Their names appeared on plaques. Their seats at cathedral events were "reserved."

Reserved, like a privilege, like a verdict.

A diocesan finance officer, Claire Dufour, noticed the distortion first. She was competent and careful, the person institutions rely on until that competence becomes inconvenient. She saw recurring vendor names, unusual "consulting fees," and gaps in donor disclosures. She requested clarification and received gentle deflections. "Claire," a senior administrator said, smiling, "you're very diligent. But don't confuse accounting with mission."

Mission. Like a fog machine, moral language is used to obscure mechanics.

Claire persisted. Claire questioned the exemption of certain donors from standard background checks. She asked why procurement committees did not vet "trusted partners." She asked why the archbishop's schedule included private dinners with people the Church publicly criticized.

The answer eventually became a warning.

"You must understand how the world works," she was told. "The Church cannot survive on ideals alone." That sentence carried the institutional complacency that feeds corruption: survival framed as justification. Claire began quietly building her own map: donations linked to contracts, contracts linked to intermediaries, intermediaries linked back to the same donors. The pattern resembled gravitational pull-money bending institutional decisions toward itself, not through force but through mass.

Marceau continued smiling. He preached about humility. He spoke of poverty with solemn conviction. After blessing the faithful, he met benefactors in private. Powerful people, who don't like hearing no, made requests with politeness.

A donor wanted a nephew moved into a prestigious diocesan role. A donor wanted a school contract awarded to a preferred vendor.

A donor wanted the archbishop to soften public statements about labor conditions.

Marceau made slight adjustments. He called them prudence.

Then the story leaked, not through whistleblowing alone but through competing powers. A donor, angry at being denied a particular favor, tipped a journalist. The journalist started asking questions that lacked truthful answers, unlike incense.

Claire's documentation became crucial-because institutions can dismiss accusations, but they struggle to dismiss spreadsheets.

The investigation that followed was narrow and careful. Church leadership wanted a repair without a collapse. They emphasized "review," "oversight," "financial modernization." They spoke about a few "isolated failures," as if the problem were a cracked tile rather than a foundation shift.

Marceau defended himself with a calm that sounded almost holy. He insisted he had protected the cathedral and its poor. He suggested critics were naive, that they did not understand governance. He implied gently that those outside the Church lacked the sophistication to interpret its needs. His most revealing defense was an old one: "A gift," he said, "does not buy the Church."

And yet there is a biblical warning-simple, unadorned-that gifts can blind even the clear-sighted. It isn't a sermon. It's an observation about human nature. Marceau knew the line. He behaved as if it applied to lesser men.

The outcome was institutional: Marceau had to step aside from financial authority. They reviewed some contracts. Someone quietly ended a few donor relationships. They formed a new committee. Public statements emphasized renewal while avoiding explicit naming of wrongdoing.

The cathedral remained standing. That is what institutions aim for: continuity. But among staff, something fractured permanently. They had watched moral language used as insulation. They had watched wealth treated as a choir that could sing in tune with holiness simply by being loud enough.

Afterward, when candlelight flickered under vaulted ceilings, the gold looked less clean. Not because it had changed, but because people had learned to see the residue beneath shine.

Money purchases not only stone and glass. It purchases silence. And silence, in a cathedral, carries farther than any hymn.

65

"THE BISHOP'S LEDGER"

PAPER IS THIN AGAINST A MAN SURROUNDED BY REVERENCE.

Clerical abuse and financial exploitation, Philippines, 2019 (composite case), PRGR

The air in Manila can feel like a damp cloth placed over your mouth. Heat rises from concrete. Rain arrives not as relief but as force-monsoon sheets that turn streets into rivers and make the city smell of rust, fruit peel, diesel, and incense drifting out of open church doors. In weather like that, people look for shelter. They seek a sanctuary where ritual keeps the world's chaos at bay: a nave, a choir, or a perpetually burning candle flame.

Bishop Rafael Cortez knew exactly what that shelter meant to people. He also knew how he could change its meaning.

He presided over a sprawling diocese with authority magnified by ceremonial robe and clerical jabot-a man shaped by public reverence into something larger than flesh. Parishioners spoke his name with the careful warmth reserved for saints and benefactors. Seminarians straightened when he entered a room. Priests lowered their voices as if his presence calibrated the air. The Church trained its people to see authority as safety, and Cortez wore safety like a garment.

Behind that, he kept a ledger.

Not simply numbers, but a private inventory of control: sexual compliance, financial contributions, obligations disguised as gratitude. It was the record that does not merely note events; it organises them. It turns human vulnerability into predictable outcomes.

His misconduct was systematic and sustained. Priests pressured seminarians aspiring to ordination or placement in coveted parishes into sexual acts that they framed as "obedience," "formation," and "mentorship." Donors to church projects felt pressure to contribute more. The priest redirected some of these additional funds to his personal accounts and distributed others to his loyal associates, who helped strengthen his network. He rarely used direct threats. He preferred the slow pressure that makes victims feel the decision is theirs-because the deepest coercion is the kind that can be mistaken for consent.

Ana Santos, a seminarian, first met that pressure in a private counseling session. The room was ordinary-bookshelves, a crucifix, a faint smell of polished wood-yet it felt like entering a sealed container. Cortez spoke softly about vocation, sacrifice, and humility. He asked questions that sounded like spiritual care. Then the conversation shifted, not in topic but in weight. Approval felt conditional. Her future became a door that only he could open.

He never had to say, Do this. The entire system said it for him. Hierarchy, reverence, and the fear of losing one's calling combined into a vise. Ana understood the unspoken bargain with a clarity that made her dizzy: compliance would determine her trajectory, her recommendations, her assignments, her survival within the diocesan machine. Refusal would not only harm her career; it would be framed as spiritual failure-pride, rebellion, lack of trust.

That twist is one of the darkest skills of abusive clergy: they weaponise the believer's own language against them. They don't just harm the body. They contaminate meaning.

This is where the scar goes deeper than skin.

Sexual abuse in a religious setting leaves injuries that are hard to describe to people who haven't lived them. The body remembers fear; that is trauma's most basic truth. But believers also carry a second wound: the sense that the sacred itself has become a trap for them. A confessional becomes a hunting blind. A blessing feels like a brand. The hand raised in benediction becomes a hand that took something. Even prayer can feel dangerous, because prayer requires openness-and openness resembles vulnerability.

The assault breaks not only a person's boundaries. It damages the architecture of trust by which they relate to the Divine.

Ana's confusion wasn't just emotional; it was theological. She entered the seminary thinking the Church could hold weakness without exploitation. When exploitation arrived from the very person who preached holiness, her mind tried to reconcile irreconcilable things. That reconciliation attempt is itself a kind of suffering: you revise your instincts, doubt your senses, reinterpret disgust as "temptation," reinterpret coercion as "discipline." Many victims stay silent not because they cannot speak, but because speaking would require them to dismantle the internal world that keeps them functioning.

Cortez depended on that.

Financial coercion ran alongside the sexual exploitation, reinforcing it. Funds moved through discretionary budgets and "special projects." Donations were directed toward accounts under his influence. Priests learned which building renovations received swift approval and which requests the administration delayed into oblivion. Seminarians saw which priests went to prestigious parishes and which priests the institution relegated to obscurity. The pattern taught a simple lesson: those who cooperated were "rewarded," those who resisted were "forgotten." In an institution, forgetting is a quiet form of violence.

And the jabot, crisp at his throat, made everything look official.

People around him noticed irregularities, of course. But institutions often confuse the absence of noise with the absence of harm. Administrators saw hints and looked away, telling themselves they were protecting the Church from scandal. Fellow bishops hesitated, fearing collateral damage. Oversight boards moved slowly, as if time itself were a moral defense. Reporting mechanisms existed on paper, but paper is thin against a man surrounded by reverence.

Cortez's ledger helped maintain the ecosystem. It ensured people felt individually trapped: If I speak, he will ruin me. If I resist, he will deny my ordination. If I complain, no one will believe me. That feeling of isolation is the abuser's greatest ally.

Then the story broke-not with one dramatic confession, but with accumulation. Whispers. A document. A pattern in finance. Testimonies that lined up too neatly to dismiss. Investigative journalists began asking questions that did not accept ceremonial answers. Internal audits found the seams where money had been stitched into private advantage. Whistleblowers carried fragments of truth out of closed rooms and into daylight. When investigations corroborated the accounts, the public reaction was as violent as a storm. Parishioners felt betrayed. Some refused to believe it-belief is not only faith; it is attachment. Others believed instantly because they had already sensed the rot. Priests argued over "protecting the Church" versus protecting people, as if those were competing obligations. Seminarians watched their vocation wobble on its foundations.

The Cardinal removed Cortez from office, suspended him from clerical duties, and subjected him to criminal proceedings. Reforms followed: mandatory reporting channels, independent oversight, stricter auditing, supervised meetings, explicit safeguarding protocols.

But the question you asked sits deeper than reforms: How can a messenger turn into a devil?

The blunt answer is that messengers and devils aren't different species. They're human beings with appetites. Desire itself is not evil-sexual desire is part of being human. The difference is what a person does with desire when they also possess power.

A true messenger is bound by consent, humility, and the recognition that other people are not instruments. A devil-at least in the moral sense-takes the same human appetite and fuses it with entitlement: I want, therefore I take. Power makes taking easier, and reverence makes it quieter. Over time, the abuser stops experiencing restraint as a virtue and starts experiencing it as an inconvenience. That's how the transformation happens: not by suddenly becoming monstrous, but by repeatedly choosing appetite over ethics until appetite feels like a right.

Cortez didn't fall because he "liked sex." He fell because he liked control, and he used sex as the mechanism. He turned intimacy into extraction. He turned guidance into leverage. He turned sacred language into a lock. For victims like Ana, the aftermath was not a simple return to normal. Recovery in such cases involves more than therapy and time; it involves rebuilding an inner chapel where trust can live again without fear. Some will rebuild quickly, like churches reconstructed after fire, the walls rising because the community refuses emptiness. Others will never rebuild-faith vanishes, vocation ends, prayer becomes impossible. Both outcomes are understandable. Both are forms of survival.

And that is the lasting scar on the soul of the believer: not only the memory of what happened, but the knowledge that the place designed to protect vulnerability became the place where vulnerability was exploited. When that happens, the work is not merely to punish the perpetrator. The deeper work is to restore the meaning of sanctuary-so that the next person who steps into the church to seek shelter does not find another storm waiting behind the altar.

PRGR END-CAP - AUTHORED HARM TEST

(for "THE BISHOP'S LEDGER" - case-specific, non-boilerplate)

In this case, the ledger isn't just accounting. It is **jurisdiction**. A bishop's money decisions shape who gets shelter, who gets silence, which priest is protected, which parish is starved, which complaint becomes "pastoral noise," which investigation becomes "unhelpful to unity."

So PRGR, here, must not sound like generic anti-corruption. It must target the bishop's distinctive power: **to convert spiritual governance into financial routing-and to call the routing "discernment."**

PRGR would attach authorship at the hinge-step where the bishop uses the ledger to govern people indirectly.

The hinge-steps where PRGR would force the author to exist

The "discretionary fund" decision - money without daylight
Most episcopal misuse begins with a fund that has no plain owner: "bishop's discretionary," "charitable relief," "special pastoral needs."
PRGR triggers at the creation or use of any discretionary fund beyond a minimal threshold.

The bishop must author:

what the fund is for,

who can authorize payments, what documentation is required,

and what harms are foreseeable if discretion expands (favoritism, hush payments, off-book settlements). This is the seed from which the shadow budget grows.

The first "pastoral settlement" payment - the hush hinge
If the chapter contains payments tied to complaints, scandals, or "quiet resolutions," PRGR triggers at the first settlement authorization.

The bishop must author:

what harm is being addressed,

what accountability actions accompany payment (reporting, discipline, safeguarding), why payment is necessary *and* why it isn't functioning as silence purchase,

what the recipient is permitted to say (explicitly). PRGR forces the institution to stop disguising hush as mercy.

The contractor / benefactor routing - the ledger as patronage
If funds repeatedly flow to the same contractors, donors' preferred vendors, relatives, or friendly organizations, PRGR triggers at pattern level: once the repetition becomes governance.

The bishop must author:

why these parties are repeatedly selected, what independent procurement exists, what conflicts are present,

and what harm is foreseeable (kickbacks, inflated costs, dependency relationships). Because in this case, the ledger becomes a network map.

The punishment-by-budget step - starving parishes and rewarding loyalty
The bishop's most powerful move often isn't theft; it's resource allocation as discipline:

a parish that raises concerns loses funding,

a priest who "causes trouble" is assigned to a poorer post,

a compliant region gets renovations and visibility. PRGR triggers at any material allocation difference tied to "unity," "tone," or "obedience."

He must author:

what objective criteria justify the allocation, what alternative allocations were rejected,

what harms are foreseeable (collective punishment, chilling effect on reporting, inequity disguised as management).

PRGR makes it impossible to punish dissent through the budget while pretending its neutral stewardship.

The donor-intent override - sacred money redirected by authority
If restricted gifts are repurposed ("education fund" used for legal fees, "poor relief" used for repairs, "mission fund" used for settlements), PRGR triggers at the first override. The bishop must author:

what the donor intent was, why override is necessary, why other funds were not used,

and how donors/parishes will be informed. Because in this case, secrecy is the real currency.

The record-thinning step - when the ledger is made unreadable on purpose
If entries are vague ("miscellaneous pastoral"), split across accounts, delayed, or routed through intermediaries so that no single page tells the story, PRGR triggers at the instruction or policy that permits vagueness.

The bishop must author:

why detail is being avoided,

what risks that creates,

and what independent audit will compensate for the loss of clarity.
A bishop's ledger is dangerous when it becomes a fog machine.

What PRGR would force in this case (matched to Episcopal *power)*

1. **No discretionary fund without a published rule-set**
   PRGR would require a public governance note (internally public-council/audit committee) stating limits, purposes, authorization steps, and audit cadence.

2. **A "settlement ≠ safeguarding" separation**
   Any payment linked to harm triggers two parallel records: one financial (why money), and one safeguarding (what accountability actions).
   PRGR blocks the substitution where payment becomes the only response.

3. **A budget-retaliation tripwire**
   If a parish or priest raises concerns and then experiences budget cuts, project denials, or reputational marginalization, PRGR triggers automatic review. Because Episcopal retaliation often arrives as "resource management."

4. **Donor-intent locks with override signatures**
   Overrides are allowed only if authored, time-stamped, reviewable, and communicated. No silent rerouting.

The questions that make this End-Cap belong to this bishop (not generic)

If you were the bishop: which exact ledger entry would you sign your name under in plain language-"pastoral settlement," "special needs," "miscellaneous"? What are you refusing to name, and why?

If you were the diocesan finance council: which is the real danger in your hands-missing money, or money used to buy silence and obedience? Where would you force authorship first: discretionary funds, settlements, or budget punishments?

If you were a priest or parishioner: what is the first hinge-step that tells you the ledger is being used as governance-the sudden budget shift, the repeated contractor pattern, or the quiet payment that replaces accountability?

PRGR fits this case because it doesn't merely demand "transparency." It pins down the bishop's unique mechanism: the moment he **uses the ledger to govern people indirectly**-and requires him to **author the harm at the exact allocation decision where money becomes a substitute for truth.**

CASE FILES
PART III

INTIMACY / ACCESS / MORAL OUTSOURCING

THE MAMASHIMI TRUST - BRISBANE AUSTRALIA

66

"THE PASTOR AND THE PETTY COUNCIL"

DIVISION IS THE INSTITUTION'S FAVORITE FEAR. IT MAKES MORAL COWARDICE FEEL LIKE PEACEKEEPING.

Clergy misconduct & Local government scandals, Netherlands, 2003-2010 (composite case)

The town hall chamber smelled of wet wool and cheap coffee. Coats steamed on chair backs. Outside, a low cloud ceiling pressed down on the market square as if the sky itself were leaning in to overhear.

The agenda was short-road repairs, zoning, a minor dispute over a vineyard parcel on the edge of town. The label for the last item was bland: "Community Development Proposal."

Everyone knew what it meant.

Pastor Friedrich Huber sat in the front row, hands folded, expression modest. His collar stiffened, white against the black suit, like an ethical diagram.

He did not win the election. He had no official vote. Yet half the council watched him before they spoke, the way people watch a compass before they admit they're lost.

Mayor Anneliese Kranz opened the discussion with practical language: youth facilities, community cohesion, revitalization. She spoke like a manager. Then she glanced at Huber, and the tone shifted.

"Pastor Huber," she said, "perhaps you'd like to share your perspective."

He rose slowly, as if reluctant to carry authority, which is exactly how authority likes to present itself.

He spoke about service, about the moral health of the town, about the need for spaces where people could "grow upright."

His words were gentle, but the effect was pressure. In the room's humidity, his voice seemed to travel farther, not louder-just more certain.

The proposal, formally, was simple: the council would gain a vineyard parcel-"underutilized land," the paperwork said-to expand a parish-run youth center. The parish would manage the construction. The town would provide subsidies. Everyone would benefit.

Only one person in the room looked uncomfortable: Karl Metz, the vineyard's owner, a quiet man with stained fingernails and a face weathered by sun and pruning shears. He stood when called and spoke plainly.

"My family's worked that land for three generations," he said. "It's not underutilized. It's my livelihood." Huber responded with a soft smile.

"Karl," he said, using Karl's first name as if it were kindness, "we must think of the greater good. You understand sacrifice."

Sacrifice. The word landed with a strange violence. Karl faced a request to lose property, which they presented as goodness.

This was how superiority operated in Hohenwald: the educated spoke in noble abstractions; the working man spoke in losses that sounded selfish by comparison. The council members-teachers, administrators, small business owners-shifted in their seats, suddenly eager not to appear petty.

Huber did not threaten. He did not need to. He wielded moral credibility like a currency. Those who opposed him risked being seen as ungenerous, even sinful.

In the weeks that followed, the council moved quickly. A valuation appeared that inexplicably lowballed Karl's land. The council pushed through paperwork with phrases like "community necessity." Meetings happened without Karl present. Mayor Kranz spoke of fairness while encouraging speed.

Huber visited council members privately-not with bribes, but with praise and implication.

He thanked them for leadership. He spoke about how "history remembers the brave." He suggested that resisting the project would "divide the town."

Division is the institution's favorite fear. It makes moral cowardice feel like peacekeeping.

Karl tried to complain, but the process required language he didn't speak: appeals, petitions, procedural windows. When he showed up at the municipal office, a clerk explained deadlines in a tone that made him feel stupid for not knowing them already.

"This is all public information," she said. Public, perhaps. Accessible, no.

That was the quiet cruelty: the system treated education as an entitlement, then punished those without it for failing to navigate a maze designed by educated hands.

A local journalist, Simon Meier, began digging because the numbers made little sense. Subsidies were high. Valuation was low.

Vendors bidding on construction were oddly connected-one contractor was a cousin of a parish administrator; the town had hired another repeatedly without competitive review.

Meier's articles didn't accuse. They simply compared. And comparison is dangerous to people who rely on narrative.

Huber responded from the pulpit. He preached about unity. He warned against cynicism. He spoke about "those who sow distrust," and the congregation understood the target without him naming it. The sermon was modest in volume and ruthless in implication.

Meanwhile, Karl's vineyard looked less like a property dispute and more like a case study in institutional arrogance: a town council using morality to justify political convenience, a pastor using sanctity to grease the gears, and ordinary citizens expected to accept loss as morality.

The investigation arrived not because the town discovered conscience, but because the funding trail drew outside attention. Regional auditors reviewed the subsidies. They asked why procurement procedures were bypassed. They asked why land valuation was so low. They asked why a moral project required such administrative secrecy.

Mayor Kranz performed shock. Huber performed sorrow. Both emphasized intention over outcome. "We meant well," they said, as if meaning could rebuild trust. Evidence showed nepotism, financial mismanagement, and a coordinated effort to pressure a landowner into compliance. Officials halted the project. Certain parties voided certain contracts. The committee issued a reprimand. The mayor survived politically-barely-because towns often forgive their own leaders faster than they forgive whistleblowers. The diocese reassigned Huber "for pastoral renewal." Routine is the Church's favorite disguise.

Here a biblical echo fits, quietly: the story of a vineyard taken by those with authority, justified in the language of necessity and righteousness. The lesson isn't theatrical. It's structural-power can sanctify theft if enough people prefer the comfort of believing its service.

Karl kept a portion of his land. He lost money, time, and the illusion that morality protects ordinary people from administrative machinery.

In spring, the vineyard budded again. Vines don't care who sits on a council. They respond to light, pruning, and time. But Karl knew human systems aren't as honest as plants. A vine either bears fruit or it doesn't.

A council can bear rhetoric and still be rotten.

67

"THE CURATE WHO LOVED CONFESSIONS TOO MUCH"

OVER TIME, THINGS CORRODE-NOT DRAMATICALLY, BUT INEVITABLY.

> Catholic clergy boundary violations investigations, Ireland & Canada, 1990s-2000s (composite case)

The village sat on Ireland's western edge, where weather arrived unannounced and stayed as long as it pleased. Wind off the Atlantic pushed rain sideways across the headland; gulls wheeled above the stone roofs, crying as if they were warning someone who wouldn't listen. Salt collected on windows and on the metal latch of the church door, a thin crust you could wipe away but never fully remove.

St. Malachy's was small, plain, and stubborn. The confessional booth stood to the left of the nave, a dark wooden compartment with a curtain that seemed too heavy for so modest a building. On Saturday afternoons, there was always a line. Not because the parish was unusually sinful, but because Father Brendan Callagh had built a reputation as a man who listened as if listening were a sacrament of its own.

He was warm in a way that made people feel chosen. He leaned forward. He softened his eyes. He hurried no one out of pain. Parishioners said he had the gift of "making you feel safe," and they used that phrase the way people use "healing"-as if safety were a property he carried in his vestments.

Callagh understood the confessional as a system: it concentrates vulnerability, filters it through ritual, and returns it to the penitent as relief. It's a controlled exchange-private words released into darkness, absolution offered through a screen.

For most priests, the boundary is the point. For Callagh, the boundary became the material he worked with.

The first warning came from Siobhan Keating, a thirty-nine-year-old schoolteacher with a marriage collapsing quietly in public. She confessed loneliness, resentment, the ache of a life that had narrowed without her noticing. Callagh listened with a stillness that felt almost tender. She expected a short penance, a prayer, a return to her ordinary world.

That evening she received a text message on her personal phone.

Siobhan, I hope you don't mind - but I felt you might need someone to talk to tonight. B. She stared at the screen until it felt unreal. She had not given him her number.

At first, she tried to find an innocent explanation. Priests had parish lists. Church offices kept records. Perhaps it was a clerical mistake. Perhaps it was concern. The mind looks for benign interpretations the way the body looks for warmth when the temperature drops: automatically, desperately.

But the messages continued. Late-night check-ins. Questions that sounded pastoral but landed personally: how she slept, whether she felt "seen," whether she felt "held." The tone was never obscene, never explicitly sexual. That was the trap. This space existed between care and possession, where language acts as a solvent, dissolving the boundary without showing teeth.

Siobhan's discomfort grew into dread. She felt as if the confession had not ended when she left the booth. It had simply changed form-moved out of the church and into her phone, into her evenings, into the hours when people are most persuadable.

Then she discovered she wasn't alone.

In the parish office one afternoon, she saw a notebook lying open on a desk. She wouldn't have looked, as she wasn't a snooper, but her own name, written large enough to catch the eye, compelled her to. Under it were headings in neat columns:

Triggers. Emotional pattern. Openings.

It read less like a priest's notes and more like fieldwork: a method for locating weakness, mapping it, and returning to it when needed. Like a predator that learns the timing of a flock, it wasn't about one moment. It was about repetition.

Siobhan took a photo.

The safeguarding office moved quickly but quietly. In small communities, scandal spreads like fire in gorse; the wind does most of the work.

The diocese understood that the public release of the story would spread the scandal beyond Callagh. It would turn outward, toward the institution.

They opened an inquiry without announcement. Investigators retrieved Callagh's communications. The messages, when read in bulk, were more disturbing than any single text. He tailored his language to each woman-one's loneliness, another's grief, another's shame-using the confessional's intimacy as a starting point and extending it beyond the sacrament's walls.

No explicit propositions. No crude threats. Instead: emotional proximity engineered as if it were spiritual medicine.

Biology offers a useful comparison. A parasite rarely announces itself. It survives by minimizing pain in the host while maximizing access. It persuades the body to tolerate what it should reject. Callagh's approach offered the same quiet efficiency; he gently maintained the tone while increasing dependence, allowing the relationship to slide-slowly, imperceptibly-across a line most people are trained not to see.

He told himself it was ministry. His journals, later reviewed, framed his behavior as "care" and "healing." He wrote about "souls in need of attention" the way a man might describe a project he enjoys too much. The rationalization was moral camouflage.

There is an old warning in Ezekiel about shepherds who feed themselves instead of the flock. It isn't a thunderclap. It's a diagnosis. A role meant to protect becomes a way to consume.

Callagh did not appear to believe he was a wolf. He appeared to believe he was still a shepherd-just one who had learned to take what he wanted from the act of tending.

The bishop confronted him in the rectory. Callagh denied wrongdoing. He insisted he was offering comfort. He accused the diocese of paranoia, as if the problem were oversensitivity rather than overreach. When they suspended him, he reacted with a kind of wounded innocence, asking whether compassion had become a sin.

He was told to leave the parish within forty-eight hours.

The community response split along familiar lines. Some parishioners defended him immediately, calling the women liars or attention-seekers. Others admitted-quietly-that they had always felt something overfamiliar in his manner: the lingering eye contact, the private jokes, the sense that the confessional wasn't only about sin.

Siobhan became the visible target. Hostility arrived in anonymous notes, in grocery-store silences, in colleagues who suddenly kept their distance. A few women thanked her in private, confessing they too had felt drawn too close but never dared say so. In towns like this, public truth is costly. Private truth is common.

Callagh did not return to explain himself. Under the institution's preferred language, they moved him to a retreat house on the coast for "reflection and renewal." It was containment.

Diocesan records show the institution reassigned him to administrative duties far from pastoral contact. This was an internal demotion without a public trial, a burial without ceremony.

After he left, St. Malachy's felt colder. The confessional booth sat unused more often than not. People approached it the way you approach a place where an accident occurred: cautiously, aware that the structure still stands but trusting it feels different.

Weather does what weather does. It returns. Rain keeps arriving from the Atlantic. Salt keeps settling on metal and stone. Over time, things corrode-not dramatically, but inevitably.

Trust corrodes the same way.

Callagh had taken something that no ledger could measure: the safety the people believed they were entitled to when they spoke behind the screen. He hadn't needed force. He hadn't needed explicitness.

The power imbalance itself had been enough.

68

"THE ABBOT'S SECRET ARCHIVES"

SUPERIORITY, WHEN SANCTIFIED BY RANK, IS A PARTICULARLY EFFICIENT FORM OF THEFT.

Church misconduct, Austria, 2005 (composite case)

Snow makes everything look forgiven.

At St. Michael Abbey, high in the Austrian Alps, winter arrived like a curtain drawn across the world. Pine boughs sagged under white weight. Footprints filled with powder within minutes. The mountain wind erased edges, softened stone, muffled sound-turning the abbey into a sealed organism, self-contained, warm inside, cold outside. In that altitude the sky could be painfully clear, sunlight scattering off the snowpack in sharp, glittering angles, as if purity were a physical property. But anyone who understands chemistry knows: white can be bleach, not innocence. It hides residue. It makes stains harder to see until the thaw reveals what was always there.

Abbot Josef Hartmann ruled that organism with quiet certainty.

The staff always pressed his cassock. His gestures were economical. When he walked the cloisters, he moved like a man who believed discipline was holiness. Visitors felt it immediately: the abbey's authority wasn't loud, but it was absolute. It didn't ask for agreement; it assumed it.

Hartmann loved the way people deferred.

He spoke to donors-wealthy patrons and local villagers alike-with the same gentle tone, but different meanings. With the wealthy, he was gracious. With the villagers, he was paternal. He called them "simple souls" when they weren't in the room, as if education were the same thing as moral rank.

The abbey raised money constantly: repairs, charitable outreach, scholarships, restoration. On paper, it was sacred administration. Hartmann treated the abbey's accounts like a private ecosystem-resources flowing toward what he considered "necessary," and he considered his comfort necessary.

A better chair for his office. A better car for "diocesan travel." A better wine for "hospitality." Small indulgences, made smaller by language.

The first concern surfaced in the hands of Brother Lukas Gruber, a monk assigned to the abbey's donation records. Lukas was not impressive in the way institutions reward. He didn't speak well at dinners. He didn't carry charisma. He carried patience-the kind that notices when numbers drift.

He began seeing irregularities: duplicate entries, charitable allocations that vanished and reappeared under different labels, repairs invoiced twice under different vendors. At first, Lukas assumed error. Monasteries, like forests, have deadwood-clerical mistakes, forgetful volunteers, messy archives.

But the errors had a direction. They always bent toward the abbot.

When Lukas asked for clarification, Hartmann answered with an indulgent smile. "Brother, you mustn't be anxious," he said. "Accounting is not prayer."

Monks stated it as guidance, but it came across as dismissal. Hartmann didn't need to threaten; he only needed to establish that Lukas's attention was insolence.

Still, Lukas kept looking.

One evening, instructed to retrieve binders from the library, he found a panel in the abbot's private study that didn't sit flush. He pressed it, and it shifted with a quiet click, like a tooth giving way.

Behind it was a narrow cavity-dry, cold, carefully hidden-and inside were ledgers and journals, wrapped as if they were relics.

The handwriting was Hartmann's. The entries were meticulous. Names of patrons. Notes about gifts. Amounts diverted. "Allowances" for compliant monks. A record of quiet exchanges that turned sanctity into a marketplace.

Lukas felt his throat tighten. The abbey's silence seemed louder suddenly, like a pressure change before a storm. He replaced everything exactly as he found it, hands trembling with the precision of fear.

For days he wrestled with what he'd seen. The abbey taught obedience. The world praised humility. But this wasn't humility-it was concealment. Hartmann had built a secret chamber of paper the way certain animals build burrows: not for beauty, but for survival.

Lukas thought of an old story he'd heard in Scripture study-about a man who hid forbidden spoils beneath his tent, convinced the earth would keep his secret. The story doesn't end with safety. Hidden things have a way of resurfacing, not because heaven strikes, but because lies corrode the ground that covers them. And another line returned with it, spare and cutting: what is whispered in secret will be shouted from the rooftops. Not by angels-by auditors, by files, by the ordinary physics of evidence accumulating until it has weight.

Lukas did not preach. He acted.

He copied what he could. He noted dates, amounts, and patterns. He waited for a visiting canon-an official known for strict oversight-during a regional ecclesiastical conference hosted at the abbey. While Hartmann stood before guests in ceremonial composure, Lukas passed the canon a folder in a corridor that smelled of wax and cold stone.

The investigation that followed was internal and reluctant. Institutions hate daylight. They prefer controlled lamplight, angled just so. Hartmann's defenders spoke about "complexity," "misunderstanding," "the abbey's autonomy." Some monks, fearful and dependent, insisted Lukas was misreading stewardship as theft.

It would have worked-if Hartmann had been sloppy.

He wasn't. He organized himself. And that organization became evidence.

The inquiry found enough to remove him from administrative authority. The abbey introduced stricter controls. An oversight committee installed the bishop. Some money came back. Some did not. Time, procedure, and the institution's preference for quiet resolution prevented the prosecution of certain acts.

The Church authorities reassigned Hartmann anonymously. His cassock remained anonymous. His public face remained anonymous. The mountain kept its snow anonymous.

But inside the abbey, the atmosphere changed. Monks looked at locked doors differently. They understood monks could use a ritual as camouflage, and that sanctified rank makes superiority an efficient form of theft. Lukas returned to his work with the same plain diligence as before. He gained no halo. He did not become heroic in official narratives. He simply became what every institution quietly depends on and often despises: A witness who refuses to be dazzled.

69

"THE PROFESSOR WHO CLAIMED OTHERS' GENIUS"

THE DISEASE IS NOT ONLY IN INDIVIDUALS. IT LIVES IN INCENTIVES.

Academic authorship theft and career coercion, Germany 2017 (composite case), PRGR

The presses continued their relentless operation, their vibrant covers still catching the eye. They remain oblivious to the complexities of language, equations, or statistics; their sole focus is on the tangible elements of paper and ink. Prof. Dr. Ingrid Hoffmann liked to begin every first-year lecture the same way: with a slide of a cell, magnified until the ordinary became cathedral-sized. Under the microscope, membranes looked like coastlines; mitochondria like scattered lanterns. She would pause-just long enough for the room to fall quiet-then say, almost tenderly: "Science is seeing what is there, not what you wish were there."

In ceremony, she wore the academic robe and starched jabot like a second skin. The cloth did what cloth has always done in institutions: it smoothed the edges of doubt. Students watched her cross the stage at graduation and believed they were looking at certainty. Colleagues watched her accept grants and keynote invitations and mistook momentum for merit. The robe implied a simple equation: prestige equals uprightness.

Ingrid did not correct them.

Her lab on the fourth floor had glass walls and spotless benches-an aquarium of competence. Inside, the culture controlled the way cultures always are in high-output labs: by time, by fear, by an ever-moving target called "excellence."

Experiment planned like music, each student. A musician handed a part, each result expected to land on the beat. Ingrid called it rigor. The students called it survival.

At first, the misconduct did not look like misconduct. It looked like editing.

A footnote shifted. A phrasing change "for clarity." A suggestion that a paragraph would "read more smoothly" if the introduction reframed around Ingrid's earlier paper-an innocent homage until the homage became a spine and the student's work became a ribcage hung from it. Her name appeared not as a theft, but as a slow annexation.

"Authorship is complex," she would say, smiling as if she were offering relief from confusion. "Science is a collaboration. Names are flexible."

The sentence was clever because it was half true. Collaboration is complex. Names are flexible-when power is uneven.

Lena arrived as the doctoral candidate professors like to discover: meticulous, curious, unglamorous in her ambition. She loved the unromantic parts of science-controls, replicates, the honest boredom of repeating something until it stopped being an accident. She kept lab notebooks with the devotion of an archivist. Dates, times, lot numbers, raw images. The unfiltered story.

In a sympathetic system, that kind of meticulousness becomes a foundation. In Ingrid's lab, it became a liability: too much record, too much memory, too much proof.

The first time Lena saw her data in someone else's hands, it was in a draft manuscript Ingrid had circulated to senior collaborators. Ingrid altered Lena's figure, relabeling it and making it appear as though she had created it independently. Lena recognized the blot like you recognize your own handwriting: not because it is beautiful, but because it is yours.

Her mouth went dry. She checked her own files twice, as if the theft might dissolve under scrutiny. It did not. When she brought it up, Ingrid's response was not anger. Anger would have signaled a boundary. Ingrid offered something colder: reassurance.

"My dear," she hissed, a maternal tone that made Lena feel childish for standing there. "Your contribution is valuable. But the lab's reputation must be coherent. A paper is a narrative. You don't put every instrument in the foreground. Trust me-this benefits you."

Then she leaned in, the way people do when they pretend intimacy is kindness.

"And don't be naive," she added. "If you want a career, you learn which hills are worth dying on."

That is how an institution teaches obedience: not through threats alone, but through the suggestion that dissent is suicide and compliance is maturity.

From that day, Lena noticed what she had previously filed away as "normal." Ingrid's favorite students received first authorship like blessings. The quiet ones did the work and disappeared into the acknowledgments. Access to a key reagent became conditional. The budget did not cover conference travel until loyalty was proven.

Rationing letters of recommendation, those private passports into the future, occurred like water in a drought. And there was always the grant machine.

Ingrid treated funding like oxygen. Every grant deadline was a weather system rolling in: pressure dropping, tempers rising, everyone moving faster, speaking less, sleeping in bursts. In those weeks, the lab's ethics shifted subtly, like a compass near a magnet. The lab started referring to negative results as "preliminary." Failed replicates became "technical anomalies." Data points were nudged out of plots with elegant justifications. A statistical choice here, a threshold there, until the story looked clean enough to be believed.

Science has a particular vulnerability: you can make almost anything look convincing if you control the angle of the lens and the lighting of the narrative. A microscope can reveal truth, but it can also magnify a lie into something gorgeous.

When Lena resisted-quietly, at first-Ingrid applied pressure without ever raising her voice. Lena's experiment schedule changed. Ingrid moved her bench. A reagent order "got delayed." Her manuscript draft returned with edits that rearranged credit like furniture in a locked room. Ingrid's power wasn't theatrical. It was procedural-death by a thousand administrative paper cuts.

Lena considered reporting it, then pictured the machinery that would respond.

Universities love the language of integrity. They print it on banners. They made it part of their official purpose. They host panels on "responsible conduct." But when an allegation threatens a high-output professor, the institution becomes a body protecting an organ it cannot imagine losing. Not because the organ is healthy, but because it is productive.

The first anonymous complaint landed in an administrator's inbox and was quietly "noted." The second was "reviewed." The third was "hard to substantiate." Each time, the message was the same, dressed in bureaucracy: This is complicated. Be careful. Think of the consequences.

Consequences for whom?

For a while, the system functioned exactly as systems do when they are sick: it defended the infection because the infection looked like strength. Ingrid was grants. Ingrid was prestige. Ingrid was ranking. The academic robe and jabot were not just cloth; they were camouflage made from reputation.

Lena realized that truth, in a hierarchy, is not enough. Truth must be armed.

So she began building a dossier-not dramatic, not emotional, simply factual. Original drafts with timestamps. Email threads where Ingrid "suggested" authorship changes. Lab notebook scans matched figures in published papers. A folder of raw image files compared to the "cleaned" figures sent to journals. A map of small manipulations forming a larger pattern: not a mistake, not a misunderstanding-an operating system.

An external ethics committee-brought in after a collaborator quietly raised concerns of their own-finally agreed to review the material. The meeting took place in a conference room with fluorescent lighting so flat it made everyone look guilty. Ingrid arrived in a tailored suit that mimicked the lines of her ceremonial robe: authority translated into fabric.

She smiled, even then.

When the committee displayed Lena's notebook beside the published figure, the room changed temperature. You could feel it: the moment a story stops being an argument and becomes an exhibit. Ingrid tried the usual defenses-collaboration, oversight, miscommunication-but the evidence had a cruel purity. The dates did not care about her tone. The files did not flinch. The raw data was indifferent to charisma.

For the first time, the robe couldn't do its job.

The consequences were not cinematic; institutions rarely allow cinema when they can choose paperwork. The editorial board removed Ingrid "pending review." A handful of papers went under investigation. She was required to complete ethics retraining-the modern ritual of penitence, designed to suggest repair without admitting rot.

But the shockwaves moved faster than the formal sanctions.

Students in other labs compared notes. Senior faculty spoke aloud what they had swallowed for years: that prestige can be a solvent, dissolving accountability; that metrics reward output, not honesty; that the gatekeepers of science-reviewers, journals, committees-often protect their own ecosystem before they protect truth.

Some colleagues insisted Ingrid was an outlier. Others recognized the more frightening possibility: she was not an exception. She was a symptom.

The university rolled out reforms with the speed of a building committee after a fire: new authorship policies, mandatory contribution statements, a clearer mentorship oversight structure, and independent reporting channels. It looked good on paper. It always does. The real question-Lena's question-was whether anyone would enforce it when the next celebrated name appeared on the complaint.

Because the disease is not only in individuals. It lives on incentives.

Lena finished her doctorate with a different education than the one promised on brochures. She published independently, eventually, but the more lasting change was internal: the loss of naivety, the gain of something sharper. She learned that "trust the process" is often a lullaby sung to keep the vulnerable asleep. She learned that integrity is not a trait-it's a practice, and it requires witnesses.

Ingrid still attended some ceremonies later, though less often. In photographs, she looked almost the same: composed, intelligent, dignified. The robe and jabot continued to exist, immaculate, because cloth does not blush. But for those who knew, the garments had changed meaning. They were no longer symbols of guaranteed principles. They were reminders of how easily a system can perfume itself-how quickly it can fill the air with something sweet and familiar while something brutal happens offstage.

Like strawberry candy that doesn't contain strawberries at all.

And that, perhaps, is the final cruelty of academic misconduct: it doesn't just steal credit or warp data. It warps faith. It teaches that truth is negotiable and that power is the real peer reviewer.

Science is supposed to make the unseen visible. But in the wrong hands-under the wrong robes-it can make the visible disappear.

PRGR END-CAP - AUTHORED HARM TEST

(for "THE PROFESSOR WHO CLAIMED OTHERS' GENIUS" - case-specific, non-boilerplate)

This case isn't mainly about money. It's about **authorship**-who gets named, who gets erased, and how institutions let erasure look like mentorship. The professor's theft is not taken from a safe; it's taken from a timeline: drafts, data, acknowledgments, first authorship, grant credit, the reputation that becomes future employment.

So PRGR, here, must not sound like "files moved." It must land on the chapter's distinctive hinge: **the moment the professor turns access to student work into a pipeline of uncredited extraction.**

PRGR would attach authorship at the first step where the professor converts supervision into appropriation.

The hinge-steps where PRGR would force the author to exist

The "send me your draft/data" corridor - private intake without trace
When the professor asks students to send full drafts, raw datasets, code, or lab notebooks into private channels (personal email, untracked folders, "just show me your notes"), PRGR triggers.

She must author:

what is being requested, what will be done with it,

what credit expectations apply,

and how contributions will be logged.
Because in this case, the first harm is **untraceable intake**-work entering a corridor where the professor controls the story of origin.

The "I'll rewrite it" step - editing that becomes ownership
If the professor claims that heavy editing justifies ownership ("I basically wrote it"), PRGR triggers at the first major rewrite decision.

She must author:

what contribution he is claiming,

what the student's contribution is,

what authorship criteria are being used (discipline standard),

and who is the independent arbiter if disputed.
PRGR blocks the classic theft-move: converting power to edit into power to erase.

The submission decision - choosing the author list and order
This is the irreversible hinge. The professor decides to submit, and names appear (or don't).
PRGR triggers at the moment the manuscript or grant is submitted with a given authorship order.

She must author:

why each name is included/excluded,

why the order is what it is,

what contributions map to that order,

and what the student was told and agreed to.
Because once submitted, the narrative hardens and the junior scholar becomes "difficult" if they object.

The acknowledgement substitution - "thanked" instead of credited
If the professor moves a student from author to acknowledgments ("for assistance"), PRGR triggers at that downgrade.

She must author:

why authorship was denied,

what standard justifies the downgrade,

what harm is foreseeable (career loss, grant competitiveness, future employment),

and what remedy exists (co-authorship on a parallel paper, formal contribution statement).
PRGR treats acknowledgments as a disciplinary demotion, not a courtesy.

The reference-letter gate - using future dependence to silence dispute
In these cases, coercion often arrives as a whisper: "Don't make this adversarial; I control your references."
PRGR triggers at any moment the professor links credit disputes to future opportunities.

She must author:

what was said,

what opportunities are within his discretion,

and what safeguards prevent retaliatory evaluation.
Because in academia, retaliation is usually delivered through *absence*: no letters, no introductions, no projects.

The institutional minimization - labeling it "authorship disagreement"
When the department frames the complaint as "a collaboration conflict," PRGR triggers at the categorization.

The institution must author: what power imbalance exists,

why this is not simply a peer dispute,

what independent process will determine credit,

and what protections exist for the student.

PRGR prevents the university's favorite wash: turning exploitation into "miscommunication."

What PRGR would force in this case (matched to academic extraction)

1. **Contribution logs as default, not apology**
   PRGR would require a running contribution record: dataset origin, code commits, draft versions, analysis decisions. Not bureaucracy for its own sake-an antidote to narrative theft.

2. **Authorship decisions must be signed at submission**
   No author list without a signed statement from the lead author/supervisor mapping contributions to order and confirming student review. If someone won't sign, the list isn't ready.

3. **A retaliation tripwire tied to opportunity loss**
   If a student disputes credit and then loses: lab access, project roles, conference funding, or reference support, PRGR triggers automatic external review. Because this chapter's violence is career erasure.

4. **Independent adjudication that isn't housed under the professor's network**
   PRGR requires that disputes be handled outside the department's patronage circle. Otherwise, the same hierarchy that enabled the theft decides whether theft occurred.

The questions that make this End-Cap belong to this story

If you were the professor: at the moment of submission, can you write-plainly-why the student is not first author (or not an author at all) and sign it knowing it will be reviewed against the contribution log?

If you were the student: what is your first hinge-step to document-the draft intake, the rewrite, the author list decision, or the "acknowledgment downgrade"?

If you were the institution: are you willing to author that this is "just a disagreement," knowing the foreseeable harm is a junior career erased into gratitude?

PRGR fits this case because it treats intellectual credit as what it is in academia: **the**

currency of survival. It pins down the moment the professor **converts mentorship into appropriation**-and forces a named author to exist at the precise step where someone else's genius is taken and relabeled as his own.

70

"THE PROFESSOR'S BLIND EYE"

THE BLIND SPOT-ONCE INVISIBLE-BECOMES THE VERY THING PEOPLE CANNOT STOP SEEING.

Academic misconduct, Germany, 2012 (composite case)

In Heidelberg, winter often arrived without drama-just a thin fog off the Neckar, a dampness that softened edges and made distances unreliable.

The university buildings looked as they always had: disciplined stone, clean lines, authority rendered in architecture. Inside the chemistry institute, that authority translated into a distinct atmosphere-white light, stainless steel, sealed cabinets, and the constant hum of ventilation that pulled invisible risks away from human lungs.

Professor Martin Vogel moved through that world with the composure of a man who believed he belonged to it by natural law.

He was tall, spare, and careful about presentation. At formal ceremonies his maroon academic mantle sat perfectly on his shoulders; the stole with its emblem of learning and healing lay flat at his chest like an official guarantee. He entered lecture halls the way a metronome enters a room-setting tempo, ordering attention.

Students spoke his name with a kind of reverence that was less about intimacy than distance. Colleagues deferred to him on matters large and small: reagent procurement, lab allocation, departmental politics, hiring decisions.

Pundits lauded his published work for its pioneering nature. His results, as presented, looked as clean as a well-run experiment.

That surface cleanliness mattered more than most people admitted.

Because underneath it, the system was already drifting-slowly, quietly-toward a kind of contamination that doesn't announce itself with smoke or alarms. It shows up as missing raw files, unusual edits, re-labeled samples, and explanations that are technically plausible but emotionally wrong.

Vogel's laboratory ran on junior labor: doctoral candidates, postdocs, and technicians who believed they were building careers by contributing to a larger truth. They were building Vogel's reputation.

He assigned the difficult syntheses downward and drew the narrative upward. The results that supported his hypotheses, he polished and promoted. The team treated results that didn't support his hypotheses as noise.

At first, the changes were subtle-small omissions, reclassifications, "lost" spreadsheets, a notebook page that looked freshly rewritten. An anomalous result became "operator error." A failed replication became "impure solvent." A negative finding became "inconclusive." There was always a reason, always an explanation offered with the calm certainty of authority.

In a lab, certainty is seductive. It feels like competence.

But science does not reward certainty; it rewards correction. It behaves like an immune system-flagging inconsistencies, rejecting false positives, forcing humility through repetition. Vogel had learned how to blunt that immune response. Not with open fraud, which creates heat, but with quiet edits that reduced the visibility of deviation.

He practiced a kind of institutional optics: arranging what others could see, and ensuring what mattered most remained in the blind spot.

The first person to notice wasn't a rival professor or a compliance officer. It was Lena Weber, a doctoral candidate assigned to Vogel's group-ambitious, precise, and still enough to trust that method protects truth. She began with the ordinary doubts of any researcher. A label didn't match a log. A reagent bottle was in the wrong place. A chromatogram appeared without a corresponding time-stamped run file. These were small things. Labs produce small things constantly: drips, smears, minor errors, instrument quirks. The mind tries to explain them away the way the eye fills in missing detail.

But then Lena saw a set of reported yields that did not make chemical sense.

A competitive field made the paper's acceptance for publication an enviable outcome. Vogel congratulated the group with controlled warmth.

The manuscript presented a synthesis pathway with yields that looked almost too elegant: high, consistent, and remarkably resistant to the variability that normally accompanies real bench work. Lena stared at the numbers the way you stare at a photograph that seems slightly manipulated: the lighting too even, the skin too smooth. She pulled the raw logs. Some files were missing. In other places, the timestamps did not align. In the physical notebooks, she found edits that were not in her own handwriting. A solvent listed on a key day did not match the inventory. The inconsistencies were not random but patterned.

Pattern makes doubt turn into suspicion.

She told herself she might misunderstand something. Vogel was famous. The department praised his rigor. Senior people spoke of him as if he were part of the institution's infrastructure-load-bearing. Accusing him, even privately, felt like accusing the building of being unsound.

Still, Lena followed her training and performed the test.

She repeated the synthesis. The yields collapsed. She checked the setup, recalibrated the instrument, changed glassware, replaced reagents, and repeated. The result remained stubbornly ordinary. The "flawless" yields in the accepted paper looked less like achievement and more like invention.

When she finally confronted Vogel, she chose the most conservative wording she could manage, as if speaking softly could make the subject safer.

"Professor, the synthesis for compound 47 doesn't match the raw data," she said. "There's no plausible reaction path that produces these yields."

He watched her with a stillness that felt less like listening and more like measuring. Then he gave her a faint smile-polite, controlled, and emotionally empty.

"Ah, Lena," he said, "sometimes the narrative matters more than the minutiae. Science is interpretation as much as observation. Trust the process."

It was a smooth sentence, designed to convert her concern into immaturity. It implied her excessive focus on details prevented her from understanding the whole. It also implied that his authority was the "whole."

Lena left his office with a strange physiological response: not anger at first, but a tightening in the chest, a sense of pressure without release. It reminded her of being in the lab during an unstable reaction-watching a flask that looks calm until it suddenly isn't.

She realized then that trust had become a tool.

Vogel's authority didn't need to threaten openly. It operated like gravity: constant, assumed, shaping behavior without speaking.

Students adjusted themselves around him. Colleagues avoided conflict with him. Even simple questions took on risk. His ceremonial presence-his mantle, the symbols of learning at his chest-made doubt feel inappropriate. But Lena understood something else too: once you know where the blind spot is, you can test it.

She began documenting.

Her work became meticulous, almost clinical: she made photocopies of notebook pages before Vogel could revise them; screenshots of file directories; printouts of email threads; photographs of reagent labels; dated notes of what she had observed and when.

Late nights in the lab became less about discovery and more about comparison-raw log against publication draft, data against claim, observation against narrative.

Meanwhile, Vogel remained serene.

He continued mentoring students in public. He chaired meetings with confident efficiency. In seminar rooms he spoke about ethics with the smooth authority of a man who believed ethics was a performance standard rather than a constraint. His public persona did not flinch.

The escalation came when he submitted a major grant application promising results that Lena now suspected were structurally impossible to deliver.

The proposal was ambitious-almost seductive in its certainty. The proposal seemed like a map to a future the author had already proven.

But Lena knew what the lab bench had said when it could speak honestly: uncertainty, variability, limits. The physical world had not agreed to his storyline.

She brought her documentation to the department ethics committee.

The internal response was slow, as institutional responses often are when a revered figure is involved. People offered preliminary rationalizations-Vogel was busy, Vogel was strict, Vogel had high standards, perhaps Lena was misreading. There was a reluctance to accept that misconduct could exist inside a system that so carefully advertised integrity.

Reputation exerts its own pressure, and institutions often respond to that pressure the way organisms respond to threat: by minimizing, by isolating, by trying to prevent systemic shock.

But the evidence did what evidence does when it's sufficiently specific. It accumulated.

Missing raw data. Edited notebooks. Repeated patterns of "loss" always toward cleaner results. Emails that implied a preferred outcome. A paper that the person who had actually run the experiments could not replicate. Eventually, the committee moved from discomfort to process.

An investigation became a necessity. Regulatory inspectors seized files. Students were interviewed. Data scientists analysed test results. The closer the inquiry got to the bench-level reality, the less plausible the narrative became.

Vogel's influence delayed consequences, but it did not erase them. Even in systems designed to defer to prestige, a consistent pattern functions like a leak: it widens under pressure.

The committee's conclusion was careful and institutional-serious enough to act, cautious enough to protect the department. Vogel received a formal reprimand from the board. He lost certain supervisory privileges, and they barred him from submitting further major grant applications independently. The sanctions did not read like a fall from grace; they read like containment.

Which is often how institutions prefer to correct themselves.

Lena emerged with professional respect, and with the complicated fatigue of someone who has done the right thing and paid for it in ways that don't appear on official letters. She received recognition for integrity, but she also learned what integrity costs when it threatens a hierarchy.

Vogel did not continue to teach.His lectures did no longer draw students; his name still carried weight. But the atmosphere shifted. It wasn't public outrage so much as private recalibration. People watched him differently. Conversations lowered their voices when he passed. He passed silently, defeated.

The old certainty surrounding his personality evaporated over time, replaced by a thin, persistent doubt-like a residue you can't fully clean away because it has bonded to the surface. Science depends on correction. It also depends on the courage to admit errors.

Vogel had built a career on refusing that admission, and for a time the institution had supported the refusal-because brilliance is persuasive, and because results, when polished, can look like truth.

But the physical world is patient. Chemistry does not care who wears the mantle. Data does not become cleaner because a famous hand arranges it. Eventually, reality reasserts itself, quietly, like winter fog returning to the river.

And the blind spot-once invisible-becomes the very thing people cannot stop seeing.

71

"THE PARISH PRIEST AND THE FORBIDDEN TRUST"

THE GAZE HELD JUST LONG ENOUGH TO MAKE SOMEONE FEEL CHOSEN.

Clergy safeguarding failures and private manipulation (composite case)

Father Andrés Marín used to think of himself as a careful man.

Not careful in the timid sense, but in the way a conductor is careful with tempo-how you hold a pause, how you release a phrase, how you make a room breathe at the same time.

In the sunlit nave of the cathedral, he moved with the solemnity expected of his office. Black robe. Crisp white jabot. Gestures measured, voice calibrated. Parishioners admired the cadence of his sermons and the gentleness of his counsel. When he raised his hands to bless, his certainty steadied people, as if transferring through the air. Outside, the city lived in brightness-white stone flashing in the noon sun, pigeons lifting in sudden flurries, incense drifting out of open doors and mixing with warm dust. Inside, the cathedral held a different climate: cooler, echoing, built for the human need to feel small in a way that is safe. That architecture invited confession. It made secrets feel less like shame and more like something you could finally put down.

Andrés listened.

At first, he listened in the way priests are trained to listen: as a witness, a guide, and a man who carries other people's burdens without taking them on himself. Parishioners came with the common grief of ordinary lives-infidelity, anger, despair, the slow corrosion of marriages, the silent loneliness of people who look fine in public.

Andrés offered words that sounded like healing. He spoke about mercy, about patience, about the idea that human messes do not startle God.

Then something in him shifted.

It wasn't a lightning strike of lust. It was quieter-an internal change of register. He noticed how a person's voice changed when they trusted him. How eyes softened. How hands relaxed. He noticed that a word from him could rearrange the emotional weather inside someone else's chest. And with that noticing came a feeling he had not expected to enjoy: control.

Control is an innocent word when you apply it to yourself. Discipline. Restraint. Responsibility. But control becomes another thing when it applies to other people-especially people who are kneeling, confessing, trembling. Andrés discovered that vulnerability produces a kind of power in the witness. A person tells you the truth, and suddenly you occupy a space inside them that no one else can access. You become the keeper of their private world.

He told himself it was pastoral intimacy. He told himself he was simply doing his job well.

That is how people cross the first line: they do not make a conscious declaration, but tell a story that makes crossing feel like a duty.

The next steps were small, almost invisible, like tiny adjustments in an orchestra that the audience won't notice until the sound piece sounds wrong. A lingering hand on a shoulder after absolution. A private conversation that stretched after Mass, framed as mentorship but infused with suggestion. Choir tutoring that became personal counsel. "Check-ins" that always seemed to require a closed door.

The black robe and jabot did not stop him. They helped him. They wrapped transgression in legitimacy and made parishioners doubt their own discomfort. If a priest touches you and calls it care, the believer's mind often tries to reconcile the sensation by blaming itself: I must be impure. I must be imagining it. I must be tempted.

Andrés orchestrated these encounters the way he orchestrated sermons: creating openings, guiding people into the moment he wanted, testing how far he could go forcing nothing overt. He mastered the art of "accidental" intimacy: fingers brushed as he handed back a prayer book, closeness in a corridor that he could deny as spatial necessity, and a gaze held just long enough to make someone feel chosen.

Some parishioners leaned into it, confused gratitude mixing with the old human hunger to be seen. Others pulled away, sensing the imbalance but lacking the language to name it. In a church, people train themselves to treat authority as virtue. They assume that if the man in vestments is close, it must mean God is near.

That was the seduction Andrés fell into: the ability to make his desire feel like a sacrament.

But a conductor who loses control does not simply lose the orchestra. He loses himself. The musician in him-once devoted to composition-improvises for pleasure, for relief, for ego. He reads the notes but starts missing the tone. Tempo becomes erratic. The strings hesitate. The wind comes in too sharply. The audience cannot name the flaw, but they feel it: something that should hold has slipped.

Andrés felt that slippage most clearly when he started needing the encounters, not just enjoying them.

He became restless when parishioners didn't seek him out. He scanned the congregation for faces he could draw closer-people who looked lonely, uncertain, eager for guidance. His sermons sharpened into something slightly theatrical, as if he were playing for a private audience.

He convinced himself that the affection he elicited proved his "gift." That those who resisted were simply frightened of intimacy. That his boundaries were old-fashioned obstacles to "real" pastoral care.

This is how the moral compass warps: not because right and wrong vanish, but because the self becomes the center of the map.

Whispers started as they always do-softly, indirectly. A staff member noticed who avoided being alone with him. A choir director observed the pattern of "special attention." Parents mentioned their children seemed uneasy after private guidance. A few parishioners stopped coming to confession entirely, choosing silence over exposure.

The hierarchy dismissed it at first. Institutions prefer misunderstandings to misconduct because misunderstandings do not require structural change. A cathedral can absorb gossip. It struggles to accept accountability.

The turning point came when Sofia, an acolyte, chose the hardest path: she spoke to a visiting bishop. Not in a dramatic outburst, but with the steadiness of someone who has rehearsed the words in private because saying them aloud felt like standing in front of a firing squad. She testified in detail, and her testimony was consistent. It wasn't only what had happened; it was the pattern: the grooming, the incremental pushing, the way Andrés turned spiritual care into a private corridor of dependence.

The bishop listened the way Andrés should have listened years earlier-with gravity and restraint. The diocesan office launched a formal inquiry.

Testimonies piled up. Accounts aligned with one another in the way separate instruments align when they're playing the same melody: the same cues, the same settings, the same gestures repeated across different people. When confronted, Andrés tried to do what abusers often do: he relied on the costume. He spoke of pastoral misunderstanding. He invoked the ambiguity of touch, the complexity of spiritual guidance. He tried to make the investigation feel like an attack on the ministry itself.

But the evidence had tone, not just notes. It carried the human reality of harm: shame, confusion, fractured faith. It became impossible to dismiss as "miscommunication."

As churches do silently, without tremors, they suspended him, removed him from pastoral duties, and barred him from ministry involving direct contact with parishioners.

Church' counselors offered counseling to those affected. Safeguards, including supervised meetings, clearer boundaries, oversight committees, and anonymous reporting, were installed. The cathedral-still physically luminous, still echoing with prayers-became a site of something colder: reckoning.

And here the true damage showed itself. Sexual abuse scars not only bodies. In a faith setting, it scars the soul of the believer-not in the mystical sense of "taint," but in the psychological sense of contamination. It can make prayer feel unsafe. It can turn a confession into a trap. It can make the very idea of God feel complicit because the person who claimed to represent God used that representation as leverage.

For many victims, the most painful question is not "Why did he do it?" but "Why did I believe?" Belief becomes a wound. Trust becomes something you fear.

In solitude, Andrés confronted a distinct silence. The authority that once lifted him now felt like ash in his mouth. He wandered familiar corridors and heard the echo of hymns that used to sound like affirmation, now sounding like accusation. He understood, too late, that the Church's garments are not armor. The jabot does not sanctify desire. The robe does not absolve manipulation.

He had started as a conductor who believed he could hold the composition. But once he used people's vulnerability as an instrument for his own gratification, he lost the piece entirely. The orchestra-the community-did not collapse in flames, but it learned to hear the discord. And once the orchestra hears discord, it cannot unheard it.

Some institutions rebuild trust with remarkable speed, like a church repaired after a devastating storm because the community cannot bear emptiness.

Others find that something has vanished forever-not the building, but the innocence that once lived inside it. The cathedral's walls remained. The rituals continued. But for those harmed, the sound of the music had changed. The notes were the same. The tone was not. And that is the final cruelty of a conductor losing control: it isn't only his own fall.

It is the way he teaches the musicians-believers, acolytes, parishioners-to doubt the entire composition, even when the composition itself was never the enemy.

72

"THE RECTOR'S COVERT ALLIANCE"

A BRIGHT COLOR WARNING YOU TO LOOK CLOSER, BECAUSE SOMETHING UNDERNEATH IS UNSTABLE.

Academic misconduct and Corporate/Criminal influence, Australia, 2013 (composite case)

Rector Jonathan Mercer commanded respect for one of Australia's most prestigious universities. In his vermilion ceremonial gown and precisely arranged black bonnet and hood, he exuded intellectual authority, tradition, and moral gravitas. The color alone did a kind of psychological work-vermillion like a warning flag repurposed as honor, the shade of oxidized iron and fresh blood rendered respectable by ritual. Faculty, students, and donors viewed him as a paragon of academic integrity.

Behind that ceremonial facade, Mercer cultivated discreet relationships with corporate sponsors whose operations were ethically dubious-some with indirect links to criminal activity-and he did it with the quiet confidence of a man who believed institutions forgive success.

The alliance began subtly, as it always does. Research required money. Money arrived with smiles. The university needed equipment, scholarships, visibility, "impact." Mercer welcomed private donations with pragmatic language and a cultivated shrug.

"This is the world," he would say at executive meetings, as if moral discomfort were an adolescent phase. "We can either shape industry or watch it shape us."

He repeated that line often enough that it became doctrine. People stopped hearing it as a justification and started hearing it as maturity.

At first, Mercer believed he could steer projects toward legitimate academic goals while satisfying sponsor interests. He spoke in reassuring abstractions about "mutual benefit." He talked about the university as an engine of progress. He framed the sponsors as imperfect but necessary-like fossil fuel in a transition economy: dirty, regrettable, and essential, at least for now.

Then the requests arrived.

Not crude demands. Those would have insulted the university's self-image. Instead: preferences, "strategic framing," "commercial sensitivity," "timelines aligned to market realities." A suggestion that certain findings might be "premature." A polite inquiry about whether an inconvenient dataset was "statistically robust." Mercer didn't sign a pact in any dramatic sense. He simply began allowing small distortions-then calling them leadership.

Selective interpretation here. A delayed publication there. An internal review panel stacked with the "right" voices. A grant condition quietly rewritten to channel money toward a sponsor-friendly lab. A student asked to "tighten" methods until the uncertainty narrowed into something publishable.

In science, bias rarely announces itself as bias. It enters like contamination-trace amounts at first, then accumulates until the experiment is no longer describing the world but the researcher's desire. Mercer's compromise behaved the same way. Each individual decision looked defensible. Together, they formed a system.

Mercer's office became the nerve center for that system. Sponsors held private meetings. Financial dispositions were fragmented across committees, so no single person held the entire picture. He understood institutional physiology: distribute responsibility like a diluted toxin, and no one feels accountable enough to act.

Administrators, eager to remain "team players," helped without naming what they were helping. Their ignorance was partly real, partly chosen.

They told themselves the same comforting things:

It's not our job to judge industry.

If we don't take the money, another university will. The research is still technically sound.

Nobody is forcing anyone.

That last sentence was Mercer's favorite. He used it like a disinfectant.

"Nobody's forcing you," he told a hesitant department head once, smiling as if offering freedom. "But don't confuse your personal scruples with institutional duty."

Personal scruples. As if ethics were a hobby, like hiking.

His cynicism appeared in offhand remarks-small enough to pass as humor, sharp enough to reveal contempt. "Students want purity," he said at a donor function. "Then they graduate and want salaries."

Or: "The public likes virtue. They also like results. Luckily, they can't tell the difference."

Those who laughed weren't corrupt. They were tired, ambitious, and afraid. In hierarchical institutions, laughter is often compliance in audible form.

The ceremonial regalia amplified Mercer's authority and helped deflect scrutiny. A rector in full dress looks like a person who belongs to history. People hesitate to accuse history. His gown was not merely clothing; it was a credential you could see. When he spoke about integrity, the room wanted to believe him, because believing him maintained the world as it was: stable, prestigious, reassuring.

Dr. Emily Hart, a mid-career researcher who unfortunately still cared about the difference between knowledge and marketing, revealed the irregularities. Dr. Emily Hart noticed that results inconvenient to sponsors were suppressed or endlessly "under review." She noticed students being pressured to adjust experimental designs, not to improve rigor, but to improve optics.

When Emily raised concerns internally, she met the university's quiet defenses: not denial, but dismissal. "That's above your pay grade," an administrator told her kindly.

"Be careful," a colleague warned. "They will label you difficult." Mercer himself was more elegant. He didn't threaten. He patronized.

"Emily," he said, "you're a scientist. Don't become a moralist. The university needs adults in the room." Adults. The word shamed her into silence. It implied that her insistence on integrity was childish.

Emily didn't escalate emotionally. She escalated methodically. Over months she documented dates, correspondence, funding allocations, and project outcomes.

She tracked version histories showing edits that consistently softened negative findings. She preserved sponsor emails that used polite language to exert pressure. She observed the committees that convened and those that were mysteriously bypassed by them. Her file grew into something institutions fear: a pattern.

The tipping point came when investigative journalists began probing corporate influence in Australian universities. Emily provided documentation under protective conditions. The reporting did what internal committees rarely dare: it connected the fragments. It made the network visible.

And once visible, it was impossible to keep pretending it was accidental.

The investigation revealed sponsors whose operations carried ethical rot-environmental violations, labor abuses, questionable offshore arrangements. Not every connection met criminal thresholds. But the proximity was damning, and the university's role was unmistakable: it had been laundering legitimacy.

Mercer's robe and ceremonial authority were not incidental; they were essential. They had functioned like a seal on a document-proof, for the public, that whatever was happening must be respectable.

Public reaction was swift. Faculty argued about oversight. Students expressed disillusionment in blunt language administrators couldn't reframe. Donors-some outraged, some nervous-asked whether the brand would survive. The administration intervened in the only way institutions reliably know: contain, stabilize, rebrand.

Review pending Mercer's suspension. The university announced reforms: they strengthened financial transparency, established independent auditing, improved donor vetting, separated fundraising from academic decision-making, and clarified whistleblower protections.

The announcements were bright and fast, like fresh paint over smoke damage.

But the deeper problem wasn't only Mercer. It was the institutional environment that had made him possible: ignorance cultivated as convenience, complacency rewarded as loyalty, arrogance disguised as sophistication.

People had seen enough to suspect something. They had chosen not to know because not knowing protected careers. That is how systems fail: not through a lack of intelligence, but through an excess of self-interest.

Mercer's story underscored a universal lesson: ceremonial authority cannot safeguard ethical standards. Colorful gowns amplify credibility, but they do not manufacture integrity. Authority without oversight becomes a weather pattern-pressure building, accountability evaporating, the storm delayed until it becomes expensive.

Emily's persistence mattered because she refused the institution's preferred bargain: silence for belonging. Her documentation forced scrutiny, replacing the institution's practice of treating reputation as proof.

She didn't become heroic in official narratives; institutions rarely celebrate disruption while they still need stability. But she became something more useful: a witness.

Mercer kept his title for a time in the administrative gray zone where institutions park embarrassment, but he lost credibility, influence, and moral authority.

He resigned two years later, not out of repentance, but because his presence had become a liability the university could no longer carry.

And the vermilion gown-once a symbol of prestige-took on its older, truer meaning: a bright color warning you to look closer, because something underneath is unstable.

Human desire, discretion, and complicity, combined with weak oversight, can always compromise academic, legal, and ecclesiastical authority. Institutional clothing may project respect, but it cannot conceal ethical lapses indefinitely.

Ultimately, institutions operate under the same principles as nature: concealed elements still deteriorate, ignored issues still grow, and denied facts eventually reappear, much like a tide that inevitably returns despite confident shoreline construction.

73

"THE PROFESSOR'S SILENT PACT"

A SYSTEM TRYING TO PRESERVE BLOOD PRESSURE: ISOLATE THE PROBLEM, STABILIZE THE IMAGE.

Intellectual, academic corruption and Corporate complicity, Germany, 2012 (composite case)

In Heidelberg, winter fog makes the river look like it's hiding something.

The Neckar slides under bridges in gray silence, and the old university buildings rise above it with the confidence of centuries. Prestige here is not a feeling. It's infrastructure. People's speech, their credibility, and the speed at which their doubts are dismissed are all shaped by it. Even the cobblestones seem to carry a memory of deference: footfalls slow as they approach the gates, voices unconsciously lowered near the carved stone, as if intellectual noise could disturb it. On some mornings, the fog settles so thick it beads on coat sleeves and eyelashes, turning breath into visible proof bodies exist below the level of ideas.

Professor Klaus Weber thrived in that climate.

He wore academic regalia with a polished ease, jabot neat, robe immaculate, and carried himself like a man who believed knowledge conferred innocence. In faculty meetings, he spoke about rigor and public trust. In donor dinners, he spoke about innovation and impact.

In private, he spoke about money.

It began, as these things often do, with "support." A sponsor offered funding for equipment. Another offered travel support. Another offered "partnership opportunities." Weber told the department it was a triumph-proof that their work mattered beyond the ivory tower. He framed the partnership as oxygen: without them, the lab would suffocate under budget cuts and bureaucratic inertia. And because people fear suffocation more than they fear compromise, they nodded.

Then the requests arrived.

Not explicit instructions-those would be crude. Instead: preferences. Timelines. "Strategic framing." "Commercial sensitivity." A suggestion that certain findings might be "premature" to publish. The language was always clean, like laboratory glassware rinsed so thoroughly you forget what it held yesterday. Each request came with a smile and an implied future: continued funding if the lab remained "aligned."

Weber didn't sign a pact in the dramatic sense. He simply started leaving things out.

He stopped mentioning certain sponsor communications to his team. He began nudging graduate students toward projects that aligned neatly with external interests. He delayed papers that might complicate the sponsor's narrative. He called it caution. He called it professionalism.

He didn't call it what it was: complicity.

At first, the changes were subtle enough to be mistaken for leadership style. A line removed from a draft. A limitation section shortened. A "follow-up study" promised before publishing negative results-follow-ups that were never scheduled. In biology, organisms adapt to their environments gradually: small behavioral shifts that keep them fed, sheltered, and safe. Weber adapted in the same way. He learned the ecosystem of influence and began behaving as if ethics were flexible tissue, meant to stretch rather than hold.

The university's leadership didn't want to see it. Their complacency had a financial rationale. Corporate partnerships made annual reports glow. They made the institution look modern. They made administrators feel superior to critics-especially critics without credentials.

When a journalist questioned sponsorship influence at a public panel, an administrator answered with practiced contempt:

"People who don't do research don't understand research."

The room laughed politely. Weber laughed too. The laughter had the smooth cruelty of a closed circle: a reminder that education is not only knowledge, but membership.

Lena Fischer, a researcher on one of Weber's teams, didn't laugh.

She noticed the missing raw data sets. She noticed that they indefinitely labeled negative findings "preliminary" while they rushed favorable findings to conferences. She noticed that internal discussions about methods had sounded like marketing meetings. Terms like "robustness" and "replication" now sounded like "messaging" and "positioning," as if truth were a product that needed a launch strategy.

And she noticed something else: the way Weber spoke differently to different people. With donors, he was servile. With junior researchers, he was imperial.

He treated questions from students as naivety. He treated concerns from staff as disloyalty. He called caution "cowardice," as though ethics were a weakness for the less educated-those who could not see the grand strategy. When a doctoral student raised concerns about omitting a dataset, Weber responded with a sigh that sounded like disappointment in a child.

"You'll understand when you're senior," he said. "Science is not a monastery." The line sounded worldly. It landed as permission.

Lena began compiling evidence, not out of ambition but out of necessity. In science, if you can't reproduce a claim, you don't have a claim-you have a story. She tracked version histories, funding conditions, email language that revealed external pressure, and internal decisions that showed Weber responding to that pressure with eager compliance. She documented which "premature" findings stayed buried, which "urgent" findings the researchers pushed forward, and how the timing of publications matched sponsor product cycles more than academic readiness.

She also recorded the subtler signatures: meetings that happened without minutes, "informal" donor calls that led to immediate shifts in research focus, a sudden emphasis on one dataset and sudden silence around another. The pattern was unmistakable to anyone trained to see causality rather than coincidence.

When investigative journalists began probing corporate sponsorships across German universities, Lena provided documentation under protective conditions. The reporting did what internal committees rarely dare: it made the invisible visible. It named the mechanism, not just the outcome. With dates and emails, it showed how a lab's scientific posture bent under money that arrived wearing a philanthropic mask.

The university reacted quickly, but not nobly. It moved like a system trying to preserve blood pressure: isolate the problem, stabilize the image. Pending review, the university suspended Weber. The university formed committees, as always, to polish. New transparency policies emerged, accompanied by bright words and careful timing, but without content and personal responsibility. The press release language mirrored the crispness and reassurance of Weber's jabot, implying the institution had discovered and corrected a flaw, akin to sealing a minor crack before admitting foundation stress.

Weber defended himself with the arrogance of someone accustomed to being believed. "You can't expect purity in a complex world," he said. "This is how research survives."

It was a revealing confession disguised as realism. He spoke as if compromise were maturity and principle were childishness. He implied that anyone who disagreed didn't understand how funding works-an argument that sounds sophisticated until you notice it's simply surrender dressed as expertise.

The inquiry found enough to sanction him-restrictions, oversight, loss of leadership roles. Not all actions met criminal thresholds. Much of it lived in the gray zone where institutions like to store their worst truths. Weber kept his professorship, but the cost was permanent: the trust of colleagues who could read the pattern now, the confidence of students who no longer mistook regalia for integrity, and the quiet certainty that he had traded something essential for funding that would never truly satisfy. Conferences never saw him again. His title couldn't offer protection, similar to how the university's name couldn't. The disgrace will fade eventually, long after his books are forgotten.

In chemistry, some bonds form without heat or flame. They form through proximity-molecules drifting together until attraction becomes structure. Weber's silent pact formed the same way.

No explosion. No single betrayal. Just the steady drift of ethics into fog-until the river finally reflected what had been there all along.

CASE FILES PART IV

PROCEDURE / ERASURE / CATASTROPHIC ENDPOINTS

THE MAMASHIMI TRUST - BRISBANE AUSTRALIA

74

"THE ORDINARY PROFESSIONALS"

THE JUSTICE APPARATUS IS NOT A TEMPLE. IT IS A MARKETPLACE WEARING A ROBE.

> Belgian and wider European court scandals where "respectability" becomes camouflage-and where institutional perfume covers rot rather than removing it, Belgium, 2018 (composite case), PRGR

Brussels teaches you early that symbols don't blush.

In the narrow streets near the Grand-Place, the air can turn sweet with the smell of waffles-warm butter, caramelising sugar, a vanilla note that seems innocent enough to make you forget the grit under your shoes. Tourists follow that scent like a hymn. They photograph the facades. They laugh. They buy the illusion by the square.

And then, a few blocks away, there he is: Manneken Pis.

A small boy in bronze, urinating with serene indifference into a public basin, celebrated as if shamelessness itself were a civic morality. People gather around him smiling-because the statue is "cheeky," because it is "Brussels," because it makes a joke of propriety. He is a mascot of the city's ability to mock decorum while selling it at full price.

The courthouse, not far in spirit if not in distance, operates on the opposite promise: Here, shame exists. Here, it matters. The irony is that it often functions the same way: a public symbol performing innocence while something crude continues, steady as a stream, behind the scenes.

Magistrate Philippe Leclerk understood this better than anyone.

He arrived each morning with the precision of a man who believed routine could conquer time. Black robe, folded in disciplined lines. Jabot arranged as if the throat were an altar and symmetry a form of moral proof. He spoke in a measured tone that suggested moderation, a kind of judicial temperature control. Lawyers adjusted their posture when he entered. Defendants stopped breathing properly. Clerks lowered their eyes, not out of reverence so much as training.

In a city thick with ceremony, his costume did the work before he opened his mouth.

Publicly, Philippe Leclerk was what Belgium likes to imagine itself as: orderly, principled, careful with language, allergic to excess. He had the manner of someone who could weigh competing truths and render a verdict without leaving fingerprints.

Privately, he behaved like Manneken Pis-only his stream fell upward. No laughter. Not water. Obedience.

It began, as it always begins, with "small things."

A scheduling change for a defence lawyer who "really needed it." A hint to a junior prosecutor about what the bench "preferred" to see. A defendant's bail conditions softened because the magistrate thought "rehabilitation is better than punishment."

These were not crimes. They were interpretive gestures. The kind institutions call discretion so that nobody has to call it power.

Discretion is the vanilla scent of law: it makes the machinery feel human. And like vanilla, it can be more counterfeit than anyone wants to admit.

There is a story most people don't know about the sweetness they inhale. People sometimes produce "vanilla" flavour from beaver castoreum, an extract from glands near the animal's tail. The romance of the label hides a harsher truth: an industry built on taking what is convenient, selling it as natural, and letting consumers stay blissfully uncurious about the cost. The fragrance is comforting; the origin is not.

Leclerk's courtroom ran the same way.

He discovered-slowly, then greedily-that the robe and jabot made requests feel like rules. That his preferences could be mistaken for law. That he could harvest fear without ever raising his voice.

The first "gift" arrived as gratitude: a bottle of wine sent to chambers, accompanied by a note that never explicitly asked for anything. It didn't need to. Brussels understood the exchange through its own contradictions: politeness allows you to ignore the reality of the situation.

Then came the favors with teeth.

A clerk asked for help to secure a transfer-Leclerk made a call. A lawyer wanted access to a discretionary motion slot-Leclerk made room. A defendant wanted leniency-Leclerk "considered the circumstances." And the price, quietly, formed.

Sometimes it was money: conference fees, "honoraria," "consulting" offered by people with no reason to require his expertise. Sometimes it was obedience: a file moved here, a transcript delayed there. Sometimes it was the more corrosive currency: sex, demanded not with threats but with implication, the way pressure builds inside sealed glass.

The situation was never framed as coercion. The framing presented it as reality.

Leclerk's genius-if you can call it that-was that he did not need to be crude. He only needed the system's allergy to scandal and the human tendency to confuse politeness with morality.

He kept a ledger.

Not a cartoon villain's book of bribes, but a neat record-names, initials, dates, coded marks beside outcomes. A double underline meant useful. A dot meant pliant. A tiny cross meant problematic-watch. The ledger was the opposite of the public record. It was the truth of what the institution could not admit: that human beings, when given unchecked discretion, will build private economies inside public roles.

The victims were not always dramatic.

Many were ordinary professionals trying not to drown.

Élise Martens, a defence attorney, learned this when someone invited her to chambers "to discuss procedural clarifications." She left, understanding it was a negotiation she had not agreed to join.

Leclerk didn't say, "Sleep with me." He didn't need to.

He asked about her career. He praised her "potential." He noted, with a calmness that felt like weather, how quickly reputations form in small circles. He said lightly, as if it were just a professional observation:

"You don't want to be difficult in your first years." Then silence.

In that silence Élise heard what he wanted her to hear: Your clients, your cases, your future-these are threads I can knot or cut.

She went home and washed her hands until the skin stung, as if shame were a substance you could rinse away. But shame doesn't live on the skin. It settles deeper: in the belief that your consent is negotiable when authority is in the room.

Around her, Brussels continued performing itself. The waffle stands worked. The tourist crowds clustered around the peeing statue and laughed. The city's sweetness drifted into alleys where the truth of institutions was far less charming.

How did Leclerk last?

Because a courthouse is an organism designed to protect itself.

Clerks noticed patterns but called them "quirks." Colleagues heard rumours but called them "jealousy." Supervisors saw anomalies but called them "not enough evidence."

In any institution, there are three moral categories:

The believers: those who need the system to be clean because their identity depends on it. The neutrals: those who don't want trouble and mistake quiet for safety.

The cynics: those who assume corruption is normal and therefore treat it as inevitable.

Leclerk fed on all three.

Believers defended him because they couldn't bear the alternative. Neutrals avoided him and told themselves avoidance was righteousness. Cynics complied and called it pragmatism.

Then an investigative journalist received an envelope-no return address, no signature, only photocopies and a timeline. A handwriting sample on one sticky note: Follow the dates. The ledger isn't metaphorical.

That's the thing about systems that rely on perfume: eventually someone follows the scent back to its source. The inquiry that followed was not cinematic. It was administrative and suffocating-the slow grinding of oversight against reputation. Interviews were conducted with clerks. Phone records examined. Financial trails mapped. The ledger, when recovered, did what no speech could: it turned the intangible into proof.

Leclerk stood before a tribunal still dressed like justice. Robe immaculate. Jabot pristine. His mouth offered all the expected words: misunderstanding, misinterpretation, enemies, exaggeration. He spoke of "ethics" as if it were a concept he had invented.

But the institution, after finally deciding that sacrificing him was safer than protecting him, acted with sudden speed-much like some churches, which collapse and then builders quickly reconstruct them, while others disappear forever into grit and memory.

The public saw the headline and felt relief: It's handled. The victims felt something else: it happened. Those are not the same emotions.

Reforms followed, including committees, reporting lines, training modules, and new protocols. These new protocols promised transparency, much like waffle stands promise "real whipped cream" from the bottle. The deeper damage-the erosion of faith in neutrality-would take longer, if it healed at all.

And here, near the end of my book, the conclusion cannot stay polite. The justice apparatus is not a temple. It is a marketplace wearing a robe.

Sometimes it sells the truth. Sometimes it sells the appearance of truth. And too often it sells whatever the powerful can afford, while the vulnerable pay in shame.

Manneken Pis keeps peeing, day after day, because the sculptor built him to do that.

Leclerk's tragedy-his crime-was that he also built a stream and convinced himself it was tradition.

If the reader feels disbelief, let it not be disbelief at his existence. Let it be disbelief at how easily we accept butter as proof of purity-how willingly we let symbolism do the work of conscience-how often we applaud the statue while ignoring who gets drenched.

Because in the end, the question isn't whether the institution has ceremonies. The question is whether it has the courage to smell itself honestly.

PRGR END-CAP - AUTHORED HARM TEST

(for "THE ORDINARY PROFESSIONALS" - case-specific, not boilerplate)

This chapter is dangerous precisely because it isn't gothic. No collars, no robes with theatrical weight. No single villain with a signature sneer. Instead, it shows the mechanism you've been building toward all along: **harm produced by normal people doing normal tasks inside a system that rewards quiet compliance.**

So PRGR here must not chase a "perpetrator." It must name the distinctive hinge of the case: **micro-decisions made by ordinary professionals that cumulatively create irreversible harm while nobody feels like the author.**

PRGR would attach authorship at the step where "I was just doing my job" becomes a moral exemption.

The hinge-steps where PRGR would force the author to exist (ordinary-professional edition)

The first "rubber-stamp" decision

A form is approved. A file is routed. A box is ticked. The professional knows the record feels thin-but it's "within process." PRGR triggers when a decision is made on **known insufficient basis** (missing corroboration, vague justifications, unexplained exceptions). The author must write: what is missing,

why they are proceeding anyway,

what harm is foreseeable if the missing piece matters,

and what stop-gap action they could have taken (request info, escalate, delay with reason). In this chapter, the first harm is usually not an act; it's a *permission granted by default.*

The translation step - turning a warning into a "tone problem"

An employee raises a concern and gets reclassified: "difficult," "anxious," "not a team player."

PRGR triggers at the moment a manager or colleague converts a factual alert into a personality narrative.

They must author:

what factual claim was made,

what evidence contradicts it (if any),

and why "tone" is being treated as more relevant than content.

PRGR makes this move auditable because it's one of the most common ways institutions suppress early signals without appearing to.

The deferral move - "not the right time" as harm

Ordinary professionals love deferral because it feels safe: it postpones conflict and preserves collegiality.
PRGR triggers when someone defers a known risk without setting a deadline and safeguard.

They must author:

why deferral is chosen,

what harm is foreseeable during the delay (continued exposure, evidence loss, retaliation),

and what immediate containment steps are activated. This prevents the slow drift from becoming nobody's fault.

The "I followed policy" substitution

This chapter likely shows policy being used as a shield: "We complied," "It's above my pay grade," "That's the procedure."
PRGR triggers when policy compliance is used to justify a decision that has **foreseeable irreversible harm**.

The author must write:

what the policy allows,

why the allowed action is still ethically acceptable here,

and what alternative policy route exists (exception request, escalation lane).
PRGR turns "policy" back into a reasoned choice instead of a moral anesthetic.

The access-change step - quiet punishment administered through opportunity
Ordinary professionals rarely "punish" openly. They remove oxygen: fewer assignments, less visibility, slower replies, a door that stops opening.
PRGR triggers at any decision that reduces a person's access after they raised concern or refused complicity.

The author must write:

objective criteria for the access change,

evidence supporting it,

foreseeable harm (career impact, silence climate),

and appeal options.
Because retaliation in ordinary settings is often administered through absence.

The record-thinning step - choosing not to write what you know
This chapter's signature harm is likely documentary: notes softened, minutes vague, emails avoided, "let's not put that in writing."
PRGR triggers at the choice to keep the record clean of discomfort.

The author must write:

what is being omitted and why,

what harm is foreseeable from omission (future denial, repeated harm),

and where the complete account will be preserved.
In ordinary-professional harm, the record becomes the crime scene.

What PRGR would force in this case (matched to "ordinary" reality)

1. **A "micro-decision log" for irreversible harm zone**

PRGR would require a lightweight log for specific contexts where normal acts have outsized consequences: safeguarding, finance approvals, disciplinary decisions, complaint intake, evidence handling. Not bureaucracy everywhere-only where harm becomes hard to undo.

2. **A "deferral with timer" rule**
   No deferral without: a named owner, a date, and interim safeguards. This stops the drift where everyone assumes someone else is holding it.

3. **A "content-over-tone" safeguard**
   PRGR requires that any complaint/alert is first recorded as a factual claim before any discussion of "communication style." Tone can be coached; content can prevent harm.

4. **An "author must exist" requirement for policy-based harms**
   If policy is used to justify harmful outcomes, PRGR forces the individual to sign: *I am choosing this policy route knowing X harm is foreseeable.* The signature is the point: it pulls ethics back down to the human level.

The questions that keep this End-Cap true to "ordinary professionals"

Which sentence do you rely on when you don't want to own the outcome-"I followed procedure," "I'm not the decision-maker," or "it's not proven"? Write that sentence down and ask: *who benefits from my non-authorship?*

What is your first hinge-step of courage in an ordinary setting: refusing to thin the record, refusing to reframe content as tone, or refusing to defer without safeguards?

If PRGR were mandatory in your workplace, which of your daily "small" decisions would suddenly feel heavier because you'd have to sign the harm forecast?

PRGR is most necessary in this chapter because ordinariness is the disguise. It makes harm feel like weather. The point of PRGR here is simple and brutal: **if your signature would embarrass you later, the decision is already asking to be examined now.**

75

"THE COURTROOM MAESTRO"

PROCEDURE CAN BECOME A BLADE WHEN HELD WITH A SMILE.

Judicial misconduct investigations, Belgium, 2005-2013 (composite case)

Judge Éric Delorme was a commanding presence in the courtroom, exuding an aura of authority that resonated even in silence. His strikingly pale complexion framed a visage that conveyed both coldness and control, instantly altering the atmosphere upon his arrival. The moment he stepped into the chambers, a palpable shift occurred; lawyers instinctively straightened their postures, clerks quickened their pace, and interns instinctively recoiled, all acutely aware of the formidable power he possessed.

Even the building seemed to respond to him. On damp Brussels mornings, when rain polished the cobblestones outside into dark mirrors, the Palais de Justice held the smell of wet wool and old paper. Voices in the corridor were always a little softer near his door. Footsteps, always a little faster. The court had the rhythm of a place used to being watched, and Delorme understood rhythm the way musicians understand tempo: it could be sped up or slowed, not with force, but with expectation.

Éric was not merely a figure of legal expertise; he was a maestro orchestrating the dynamics of the courtroom, where every glance and gesture served as a cue in the grand performance of justice. His true genius lay in his ability to wield influence with a deft touch, manipulating the courtroom's intricate dance without overt displays of authority. His approach to procedural decisions and courtroom interactions was a finely tuned art, where private discussions and subtle cues became instruments for shaping the behavior of those around him.

He did not shout. He didn't need to. He could fracture confidence with a single pause, a slight tilt of the head, an eyebrow raised at the wrong moment. He could reward loyalty with a compliment said in a hallway-quiet enough to feel personal, public enough to be noticed. For Delorme, power was best when it felt consensual. If others believed they were choosing obedience, he could remain, technically, innocent.

The process of manipulation was gradual, almost imperceptible, as he praised clerks for their initiative while subtly steering them toward errors that allowed him to assert his dominance. This delicate balance left them feeling both grateful for his guidance and insecure in their own capabilities. He would say, "Excellent, you're learning," after a clerk corrected a file that Delorme himself had "overlooked"-an omission so conveniently placed it felt like a test. He would congratulate an intern on "sharp instincts," then ask the same intern to prepare an urgent memo without disclosing the most relevant precedent, so that the final work would be flawed. He would then "rescue" the intern with a patient correction, saving the day and tightening the tether.

Apprentices, drawn into his orbit through mentorship, found themselves ensnared in a web of coercion, their loyalty and judgment tested through framed inquiries that blurred the lines between guidance and manipulation. "If you were advising the prosecutor," Delorme might ask, leaning back as if merely curious, "what weakness would you exploit in the defense's argument?" The question sounded pedagogical. It also trained interns to think in terms of loyalty to him rather than fidelity to fairness. Those who answered with too much independence received the same smile, but colder. Those who agreed with him received praise, coffee invitations, and "opportunities."

In the winter, when the Brussels wind pressed itself against the courthouse windows and the bare trees outside scratched thin lines across the grey sky, the staff spoke in weather metaphors. "It's a storm day," a clerk would murmur when Delorme was in a particular mood. "Keep your head down." "The air is heavy," another would say, as if humidity could predict a summons. They laughed about it, but the laughter carried the taste of caution. As the board chair, Sophie Davondre Lisac noticed troubling patterns emerging within the court's staff dynamics, prompted by whispers of discontent and unease. Sophie had the practical temperament of someone who trusted documentation over impression. She did not dislike Delorme; she distrusted the way the institution rearranged itself around him. When she walked through chambers, she saw junior staff flinch in subtle ways-hesitation before answering, eyes flicking toward doors, the strange politeness of fear.

Éric's selective attention created a hierarchy of dependence. Those who struggled under pressure became increasingly reliant on his direction. He subtly undermined others, diminishing their contributions. Praise and criticism morphed into tools of control, transforming compliance into a perceived achievement and dissent into a mark of failure. The "favored" interns were those who stayed late without complaint, who offered to draft orders without being asked, who learned to follow his preferences so perfectly it looked like talent. The judge rotated out the ones who questioned too clearly, assigned them to duller tasks, or described them as "not ready for the demands of this court."

Colleagues dismissed Sophie's unease at first. "Éric is exacting," one senior judge told her. "That's not a crime." Another shrugged. "He's difficult, but fair." It was always the same defense: a man's rigor should be confused with his virtue. Sophie listened, then began-quietly-to document.

She noted the turnover. She noted which interns asked to be reassigned. She noted the pattern of complaints that never became official because staff feared the stigma of being "too sensitive." She gathered anonymized statements: not accusations of bribery or sexual misconduct or overt illegality, but descriptions of something more insidious-pressure that hid behind professionalism. "He makes you doubt your memory," one clerk wrote. "He praises you, then punishes you for trusting the praise," wrote another. "He enjoys being the one who fixes what he quietly breaks."

The investigation was silent, following a troubling convergence of internal uncertainties, procedural discrepancies, and grievances voiced by staff members. It began, as these things often do, not with a single explosive event but with a convergence: a grievance filed in the wrong tone by a shaken intern; a procedural mistake that appeared repeatedly in cases Delorme oversaw; a senior clerk taking stress leave and leaving behind notes that read like a slow confession.

A thorough examination unveiled a troubling pattern of manipulation directed at junior staff, a selective focus on particular cases, and the exploitation of psychological tactics to exert influence. The panel found Delorme favored certain counsel, not through direct corruption, but through scheduling decisions, through subtle leniency in deadlines, through the "procedural generosity" that looks neutral until you compare its distribution. Nothing violated the letter of the law. That was Delorme's craft: he built his power in the space between rules.

Nature, indifferent, mirrored the institutional mood. One morning, a thin mist rose from the city streets and wrapped the courthouse in a pale veil. Sophie stood at a window and watched pedestrians blur into silhouettes. It reminded her of how Delorme worked: he kept intentions foggy enough that accountability slid off him.

Dismissing the harm as emotion was possible if no one could clearly describe it.

At the tribunal, Éric presented himself with an air of composed authority; his demeanor was calm, his articulation precise, and his robes impeccably arranged, complete with a staged jabot and épitoge. The fabric sat at his throat like a deliberate signal: I belong here. He did not appear defensive. He appeared instructional, as if the tribunal were another classroom.

He spearheaded mentorship and guidance as cornerstones of judicial integrity, vehemently denying any allegations of misconduct. He spoke about "high standards," "professional growth," "the weight of responsibility." He insisted staff were fragile in a modern era and needed firmness. "We cannot permit mediocrity," he said, and some in the room nodded, relieved to interpret cruelty as excellence.

The silent findings highlighted a troubling consistency in his methods, pointing to patterns of subtle coercion and emotional manipulation that undermined the very principles he claimed to uphold. They presented emails that first praised the recipient and then immediately made impossible demands. They presented testimonies that described the same cycle: Delorme induced errors through omission, then rewarded himself for correcting them. They showed patterns of selective mentoring that created factions among interns, ensuring loyalty through competition. The ethical breach was unmistakable: he had made the court's vulnerable members instruments for his private sense of mastery.

The sanctions imposed were procedural, encompassing restrictions on his ability to supervise interns, increased scrutiny of his courtroom conduct, and mandatory ethics training. The institution, careful not to admit it had enabled him, framed the outcome as "improvement" rather than condemnation. Delorme kept his position of authority at another department because systems often prefer to change a powerful figure rather than confront what made him possible.

Yet the atmosphere within the chambers shifted. Staff members asserted their confidence and established clearer boundaries that previously had been blurred. Clerks started requesting written instructions instead of relying on hallway cues. Interns began working in pairs. An almost unnoticeable change, but significant: where Delorme once operated in private, they began insisting on visibility.

The once-dominant sense of invulnerability that surrounded him waned, supplanted by a newfound respect that was cautious rather than fear-driven. Even the building felt different. On the day he returned to his courtroom after the ruling, sunlight broke briefly through cloud and struck the marble floor in a bright square. It looked like a spotlight. Delorme crossed it without slowing, but the symbolism was hard to miss: light makes performance harder.

As Éric returned to his chambers, his appearance remained impeccable, yet the thrill of wielding invisible power had diminished. The dynamics he once navigated with ease now resisted his subtle manipulations. Staff no longer moved like dancers awaiting his cues; they moved like professionals who had learned the cost of deference. He still had authority, but it now had edges-conditions, oversight, witnesses.

In Brussels, whispers persisted of the "Courtroom Maestro," not in admiration but as a warning: that procedure can become a blade when held with a smile, and that legality is not the same as integrity. The larger moral was uncomfortable and therefore useful. It was not enough for a system to rescue its people after harm with investigations and training. If it wanted to deserve the word justice, it had to protect them earlier-by refusing to confuse charisma with competence, strictness with morality, and ceremonial dignity with ethical safety.

Outside, rain began again, soft and steady, tapping the courthouse windows like patient questions. The city would dry up. The building would remain. But in the corridors where interns once recoiled, something had changed: a small, stubborn insistence that power must be seen, named, and limited-before it becomes the weather everyone learns to endure.

76

"THE RECTOR'S SHADOW NETWORK"

A UNIVERSITY IS AN ECOSYSTEM. NETWORKS GROW WHERE OVERSIGHT CAN'T SEE.

Academic misconduct and Criminal/Corporate exploitation, Italy, 2014 (composite case)

By the time the auditors arrived, Rector Alessandro Vitale had already rehearsed his smile.

It was a small meeting room-glass walls, polished table, water bottles aligned as if symmetry could be innocence. Outside, the campus moved with ordinary purpose: students on bicycles, a line at the espresso bar, professors drifting between buildings with folders tucked against their ribs. Life on the surface always looks healthy, like skin that hides inflammation beneath.

The auditors asked for grant documentation, donor disclosures, partner agreements-routine requests that become dangerous only when someone has treated routine as camouflage.

Vitale wore his academic regalia with an ease that felt hereditary. The robe, the trim, the insignia-each piece designed to signal that he was not merely a man, but an institution rendered human. His voice was controlled; his gestures modest. He spoke about "research excellence," "community impact," "international partnerships." All true. Just incomplete.

The university had needed money. Universities always do. Funding is the oxygen of modern research, and oxygen is a quiet tyrant: you can't boycott it without suffocating.

Vitale began by courting respectable benefactors-industry sponsors, development funds, foundations eager to attach their names to prestige. Then, as budgets tightened, he broadened the pool. Construction companies with opaque ownership structures. Biomedical startups with unusually aggressive timelines. Consulting firms that existed mainly as addresses and invoices.

The donors arrived like rainwater into a complex drainage system: at first; it looked like nourishment; later; it carried contaminants.

Vitale's genius was organizational. He didn't simply accept questionable money; he built a network around it-layered, compartmentalized, legally defensible in fragments. Shell entities became "strategic partners." Donations became "service agreements." Sponsorship became "joint innovation initiatives." Each term had the softness of bureaucracy, the ability to absorb moral shock.

In ecology, invasive species rarely announce themselves as invaders. They arrive as something that looks merely adaptable. Then they spread through the root system.

Vitale's office became a control room, lined with plaques and books and ceremonial artifacts that suggested scholarship while functioning as a shield. Meetings happened there that never appeared on public calendars. Intermediaries handled contract routing. Certain faculty promotions accelerated while others stalled-not randomly, but in alignment with cooperation.

The network relied on compliance-quiet, plausible, career-minded compliance. People told themselves they were serving the institution. They told themselves the rector must know what he was doing. They told themselves the money was necessary.

And in that way, moral responsibility diffused like dye in water until no one could point to a single drop and claim, That's where it started.

Clara Moretti did not fit comfortably into that diffusion.

Clara was a lecturer-smart, cautious, not politically ambitious. She liked research, not power. She had the mind that noticed mismatch: a report that didn't align with a budget, a donation that arrived under a corporate name that didn't exist in any registry she could find, a publication pushed out at a pace that suggested marketing rather than science.

She kept notes.

At first it was simply self-protection-documentation in case her questions made her look "difficult." But as she traced projects across departments, the pattern became undeniable. Some outcomes were being steered. Others quietly deprioritized certain negative findings, burying them under "ongoing review" and "reassessment".

It reminded Clara of electrical systems: if you route current through enough junctions, the source becomes harder to locate and the shock becomes harder to prove. Yet the damage still happens.

The turning point came from outside the university.

National authorities had examined organized crime infiltration into public procurement and research funding-an old problem, newly visible. The auditors' questions sharpened. They inquired about both the funded projects and their beneficiaries. They asked about subcontractors. About consulting fees. About why certain vendors kept recurring under slightly different names.

Vitale remained calm. Calm is a useful chemical in these settings; it slows the reaction. He spoke about "complexity" and "misinterpretation." He offered binders of documentation-so much paper that any single inconsistency could drown.

But Clara's notes did something the binders couldn't: they connected the fragments.

She provided timelines. Correspondence. Approval chains. The evidence revealed intentional obscuring of certain financial flows, the shaping of certain research outputs to satisfy sponsor expectations, and the linkage of those expectations, through intermediaries, to interests well outside legitimate academia.

The investigators didn't need melodrama. They needed structure.

Once the structure was visible, the institution moved with the grim efficiency of self-preservation, early enough to prevent full institutional capture. Vitale was removed from administrative control pending review.

Committees formed, and the institution built the wall. Policies tightened. New transparency protocols, announced with the optimistic language institutions use when trying to overwrite memory, were put in place. What the paper accomplished was not clear from the transparency. It absorbs the ink, not the words.

Vitale's defenders framed him as pragmatic-someone who "kept the university alive." His critics called him compromised. The truth, in such composite cases, is often both: he believed he was managing necessity, and he also enjoyed the private satisfaction of being the man who could move money, influence, and outcomes without obvious resistance.

Greed is not the sole builder of a shadow network. It's built from the pleasure of control.

Clara's career did not become triumphant. Critics praised her in careful terms, and people privately thanked and publicly handled her. That is how universities often treat internal disruptors: as necessary instruments rather than moral examples.

But the reforms that followed were real: stricter disclosure requirements, independent review of donor agreements, separation of funding decisions from promotional pathways, and external audits with teeth. None of it guaranteed purity.

It merely reduced the blind spots.

And in institutions built on prestige, blind spots are where damage breeds best-quietly, patiently-until someone like Clara looks.

77

"THE PROFESSOR'S CORRUPTED LAB"

DO YOU WANT SCIENCE, OR DO YOU WANT THEATRE?

Academic misconduct and Corporate/Criminal complicity, Italy, 2011 (composite case)

A publicly renowned authority at a leading Italian university, Professor Marco Bellini-Head of the Faculty of Scienze Matematiche, Fisiche, Naturali-commanded respect in lecture halls and conferences alike. His amaranth toga and silk, neatly embroidered hood weren't merely ceremonial fabric; they were visual proof of belonging to a lineage. In the old halls, where stone held a permanent coolness and dust drifted in sunbeams like slow-moving stars, students watched him with the instinctive deference people reserve for men who seem carved out of the institution itself.

Bellini knew the effect. He cultivated it.

He wore dignity the way certain predators wear camouflage: not to hide entirely, but to ensure no one expects the strike. At academic dinners, he spoke about scientific rigor and public trust with the calm cadence of a priest at the altar. He invoked ethics as a principle-clean, abstract, safely distant. And the more he spoke that language, the more the room relaxed. People like believing in good men. It saves energy. It keeps the climate stable.

Yet beneath this veneer of scholarly gravity, Bellini cultivated covert relationships with corporate sponsors whose operations were ethically dubious and, sometimes, linked to organized crime.

The collaboration began with money, as it so often does, and with a certain institutional hunger. Labs required equipment. Grants were competitive. Rankings were a weather system of their own-pressure rising, pressure falling, everyone adjusting. Sponsors offered private donations for "partnership," "innovation," "impact." Bellini accepted with pragmatic confidence and told colleagues it was the new reality.

"We live in ecosystems," he would remark, smiling faintly, as if he were describing biology rather than compromise. "Survival favors adaptation."

At first, he convinced himself he could steer research toward legitimate outcomes while accommodating sponsor interests. Then accommodation turned into alignment. Alignment turned into obedience. Obedience turned into a quiet craft.

Over time, Bellini became deeply involved in manipulating research outputs: selective publication, tailored experimental designs, and administrative decisions calibrated to corporate objectives. Nothing crude-no obvious falsification shouted across a page. It was more elegant than that, which made it more dangerous. He understood institutions forgive what looks sophisticated.

His lab became a hub of quiet manipulation. Publicly, experiments proceeded according to protocol, results were peer-reviewed, and lectures emphasized rigor. Privately, he adjusted funding allocations, data interpretations, and project assignments in ways that always bent in the same direction: toward sponsor comfort. Like a gardener pruning a tree to force a certain shape, Bellini trimmed away inconvenient branches. Negative findings became "preliminary" indefinitely. Bellini classified unfavorable datasets as "contaminated." He didn't need to invent. He needed only to choose. In statistics, selection is engineering; you can manufacture certainty simply by deciding what counts.

Each change brought Bellini private satisfaction: the sense of control, the thrill of influence, and the reassurance that his outward authority remained untarnished. His personality darkened not with rage, but with contempt. He treated junior researchers as raw material-useful hands, interchangeable, easily corrected. When a doctoral student hesitated about excluding an inconvenient run, Bellini didn't shout. He smiled, indulgently.

"You're confusing purity with intelligence," he said. "Science is for people who can tolerate complexity." Complexity. His favorite shelter. It made deception sound like sophistication and made doubt sound like ignorance.

Parallel studies began showing irregularities, and the discrepancies caught the attention of researchers from a collaborating university in the Netherlands. They were not hunting scandal; they were doing what science demands: replication. But replication is merciless. The natural world doesn't care about reputations, and phenomena don't reproduce themselves out of respect for a professor's toga. The Dutch team found that certain "robust" results dissolved when tested independently, like salt crystals in water-solid confidence turning instantly to solution.

Some experiments yielded results inconvenient to sponsors that were radically suppressed. Student assistants adjusted how they presented data, encouraged-never ordered, always guided-by supervisors. Over several months, the researchers documented dates, funding records, correspondence, and project outcomes. They mapped the pattern the way an ecologist maps a contamination event: follow the flow, trace upstream, note where life fails.

The turning point came when the Directorate-General for Research and Innovation (DG RTD)-a major funder connected to Horizon 2020-began probing corporate influence in European scientific research. The timing felt coincidental, but institutions often fall the way forests burn: not because one match is special, but because everything has been dry for too long.

Head of Research at the Dutch university, Sofia 't Hart-Esposito-coincidentally a former student of Bellini in the early 1990s-provided detailed documentation: version histories, funding conditions, emails where "commercial sensitivity" translated into pressure. What made it lethal wasn't a single message; it was the accumulation. Evidence has weight. Over time, it pulls the truth downward through denial like gravity.

Auditors confirmed that Bellini's ceremonial garments-the toga and hood-had helped to project legitimacy while enabling covert manipulation. That wasn't a metaphor. It was sociology. People had trusted the costume. They had assumed that a man so decorated could not be ethically small.

Public reaction was immediate. Faculty debated oversight reforms with the anxious energy of people realizing they had been living beside rot. Students expressed outrage in plain language administrators couldn't sanitize. The administration intervened quickly-not nobly, but efficiently-acting as systems do when they threaten the brand: they isolate, contain, and reassure.

Review suspended Bellini. Institutional reforms followed: strengthened transparency, not full transparency; independent auditing, not fully independent; separation of fundraising from research decisions, sometimes when doable, and stricter oversight of sponsor influence, until the wind took the worst to the ocean. The announcements were bright, like fresh paint. But paint does not replace wood.

Interlude: When technical truth got a veto.

Elsewhere, in another kind of laboratory - one built from aluminum, vacuum seals, and equations - technical truth did not merely get invited into the room after disaster. Technical truth received authority in the laboratory. A flashback to the chapter "WHEN TECHNICAL TRUTH GETS A CHAIR AT THE TABLE". In 2003, after the Space Shuttle Columbia broke apart during re-entry, the public story could have stayed technical: foam, heat shield, physics. But the investigation refused to let the institution hide behind materials science. The Columbia Accident Investigation Board insisted the failure was also organisational - a system that had learned to normalise anomaly, to treat warning as noise, and to let schedule pressure reframe risk as acceptable.

NASA's most instructive response was not a slogan about culture. It was a rearrangement of power. The agency built a technical veto lane: an Independent Technical Authority with responsibility for engineering requirements and, crucially, the ability to control waivers. The agency insulated the people tasked with protecting reality from the people tasked with meeting milestones-at least on paper and in procedure.

That is what serious reform looks like. It does not ask leaders to be better people. It assumes leaders will remain human. It changes what can be done, by whom, and how easily.

And because institutions forget, NASA also kept a witness in the room. The Aerospace Safety Advisory Panel, an oversight body, positioned itself to speak beyond internal hierarchy and report outward as well as upward. The point was not punishment. It was to make quiet drift harder.

There is no purity in this story, no guarantee. But there is a design principle: when technical truth can stop the launch, it stops being decoration. It becomes governance.

Universities often respond to misconduct by adding posters, committees, and workshops - chairs at the table, without a veto. NASA, after the fire, built gates. It treated safety not as a strong suit but as an architecture.

Bellini defended himself with the calm arrogance of someone used to being believed.

"You cannot expect cleanliness in a dirty world," he said. "Do you want science, or do you want theatre?"

It was a clever inversion: accusing critics of performance while he hid behind ceremony. He spoke as if ethics were a luxury item for those who didn't understand funding-another way to turn moral clarity into naivete. He implied that only the less educated demanded purity, that real intellectuals knew how to "navigate."

But navigation, in his hands, had become surrender.

Bellini's story highlights a brutal lesson: ceremonial authority cannot safeguard ethical standards on its own. Robes, jabots, hoods, and tams enhance perception and credibility, but they do not guarantee integrity. Authority without transparency becomes a greenhouse for misconduct-warm, sheltered, optimized for growth. And what grows in the dark is rarely healthy.

Sofia 't Hart-Esposito's courage mattered because she refused the peaceful refuge of institutional loyalty. Her records and willingness to speak reinforced the principle that scholars must continuously scrutinize and hold scholarly authority accountable, regardless of ceremonial symbols or reputation.

Bellini kept elements of his title for a time in the gray administrative zone where institutions store embarrassment, but he lost credibility, influence, and moral authority. His ceremonial attire, once a mark of prestige, became a warning: a bright, amaranth banner above a compromised structure.

Authority-academic, legal, or ecclesiastical-can be corrupted when oversight is weak and human desire, discretion, and complicity intervene. Clothing may project respect, but it cannot conceal ethical decay indefinitely. Like fungus in a damp wall, the damage spreads quietly until a surface finally collapses, and everyone pretends they didn't smell it coming.

78

"THE JUDGE'S SHADOW"

THE DANGER IN A DISCIPLINED INTELLECT IS NOT THAT IT COMMITS OBVIOUS CRIMES.

Judicial misconduct, Sweden-Scandinavia, 2010s (composite case)

Judge Erik Lindström's courtroom in Stockholm was austere yet imposing. Pale Nordic light filtered through tall windows, falling in clean rectangles across polished cherry-wood benches and the matte black of his robe. The room looked designed to remove drama-no gilding, no flourish, only proportion and restraint. Even the silence felt engineered: a silence that suggested impartiality, a silence that encouraged people to tell the truth because there was nowhere for lies to hide.

Erik's conduct matched the architecture. Calm. Precise. Incorruptible. He spoke with the clipped patience of a man who believed clarity was a moral duty. When he lifted his eyes from the file, counsel felt their own arguments tighten, as if language itself became accountable under his gaze. Across Sweden, colleagues admired his analytical rigor and his mastery of procedural law. His judgments served as a basis for citations because of their logic.; his lectures were admired for their purity of method. People used words like disciplined and principled and assumed those were synonyms for safe.

Yet behind the veneer of disciplined professionalism lay a structured, hidden network of influence cultivated over years of quiet manipulation. Unlike overt misconduct, Erik's misdeeds did not look like greed or rage. They looked like management. He never demanded envelopes. He never raised his voice. He simply learned where discretion lived-in adjournments, in scheduling, in the ordering of witnesses, in what the court asked and what it let pass without insistence. He found the seams in the system and discovered he could pull on them without tearing the cloth.

It began innocuously, as these things often do: a minor change to a hearing schedule so an old colleague wouldn't lose a contract while waiting for resolution; discreet "advice" to an attorney in chambers about how to avoid a procedural misstep; a lenient interpretation of a deadline to prevent what he framed as unnecessary hardship. To the casual observer, it appeared as thoughtful judicial management. Erik even convinced himself it was. He told himself he was keeping the machine smooth, preventing avoidable harm, correcting the bluntness of rules with intelligence.

Over time, a pattern formed. Certain defendants-often those connected socially or professionally to Erik-benefited from invisible nudges, while others faced the full rigor of the law. Nothing was dramatic enough to create a scandal. That was the point. Erik was a man who prized control, and control is best maintained when it doesn't announce itself.

Stockholm's winter helped him. The city's cold has a particular discipline. Water becomes ice; streets become quiet; everything seems cleaner than it is. Snowfall softens edges and makes ordinary surfaces look newly honest. Erik enjoyed walking to the courthouse through that white hush. It felt like entering a world where everyone had to be composed.

But human motives don't freeze just because the weather does.

Lina Hansen, a judge in training, began noticing anomalies while assisting him with complex case files. Lina was not naive, but she still held a person's faith that institutions mean what they say. She admired Erik's intellect-she had underlined passages of his published opinions like scripture. Sitting behind him in court, watching him steer proceedings with minimal effort, she felt the admiration that becomes dangerous: the admiration that makes you want to imitate without examining.

The first crack appeared in a minor commercial dispute. Lina saw a key document filed late-late enough that, in a comparable case, Erik had once excluded similar evidence without hesitation. This time he accepted it with a brief remark about "the interests of completeness." The late filing benefited a defendant whose name triggered a memory: Erik had mentioned him once at a faculty dinner, in the casual tone used for acquaintances. Lina told herself it was a coincidence.

Then, a criminal appeal occurred, and someone glossed over certain witness inconsistencies with unusual speed. Erik moved the hearing along as if the inconsistencies were beneath the court's attention. Another judge might have pressed. Erik did not. The defendant's counsel thanked him afterward with a familiarity that felt too relaxed for a courtroom corridor.

Lina kept notes-not accusatory, just precise. Dates. Case numbers. What was emphasized and what was bypassed. She did it at first to reassure herself that she was imagining patterns. But the notes accumulated, and accumulation changes the nature of doubt. One strange event is a shrug. Ten strange events are a climate.

Erik maintained a private record as well: a parchment-bound notebook coded with shorthand only he understood. It looked archaic, almost romantic-leather, thick paper, a kind of object one might associate with scholarship. Lina noticed it once when she delivered files to his chambers. It lay half-open on his desk, filled with tight lines of symbols and abbreviated Swedish, more like a mathematician's scratchpad than a diary.

When Erik noticed her glance, he closed it calmly.

"Personal notes," he said, neither defensive nor friendly. Lina nodded, but the moment lodged in her mind like grit.

Erik's motivations were a complex mixture of idealism and personal gratification. He believed he was subtly correcting imperfections in the judicial system, balancing strict legality with human judgment. And in a sense he was-just not equally. The ability to bend procedure without being caught gave him a private thrill, like a pianist playing wrong notes in a piece no one else knew well enough to challenge. He enjoyed seeing attorneys adjust themselves around him, sensing his preferences and trying to please them. He enjoyed knowing he could nudge outcomes while maintaining the appearance of neutrality. Above all, he enjoyed the hidden mastery: the sensation that he alone knew how to tighten the strings of the system, which was an instrument.

Here was the contradiction at the heart of him: he preached impartiality as principle while practicing discretion as privilege. He taught that law should protect the weak from the strong, but he repeatedly softened the law for those who already had networks, money, or social proximity. He rationalized it as refinement, yet the refinements always flowed in the same direction.

Lina's own contradiction grew beside his. She respected him and feared him. She wanted to learn from him and escape his orbit. She felt loyalty to the institution and loyalty to the idea of justice, and she realized those loyalties were not always the same. Doubt became a character in her life, a shadow, because it stretched longer the closer she got to the truth. The shadow asked relentless questions while she brushed her teeth, while she stared at case notes on the tram, while she tried to sleep: Are you misreading competence as manipulation? Are you jealous? Are you too to judge the judge? Will noticing lead to punishment?

The turning point came not with a bribe or a dramatic confession, but with a small procedural choice that Lina could not excuse. A case involving an assault had a vulnerable witness whose testimony was critical. Erik, unexpectedly, limited the scope of questioning in a way that reduced the witness's credibility without openly saying so. He framed it as "keeping the hearing efficient." Lina read the transcript twice and felt her stomach tighten. Efficiency had become a weapon.

After that, the shadow's questions changed tone. They stopped asking if she was imagining and began asking how long she would tolerate it.

Lina reported her findings to the Swedish Judicial Oversight Board. She did it with careful Swedish restraint-documentation, chronology, comparison against precedent. Not outrage. Facts. She understood her opponents would use emotion against her. She filed quietly and then returned to work as if nothing had happened, though her body behaved differently in Erik's presence: shoulders slightly tight, breath slightly shallow.

Investigators analyzed the notebook and cross-referenced it with court records. What had looked like scattered anomalies aligned? The shorthand entries corresponded to cases, and the cases corresponded to outcomes. The notebook did not say "corruption" in plain language, but it functioned like a map of intent: reminders about which arguments to favor, which motions to delay, which counsel to "guide," which procedural gates to open for some and keep closed for others. New patterns emerged people could no longer dismiss as coincidence.

The investigation was discreet but thorough. Erik continued to preside publicly with calm authority, robe immaculate, gestures precise, voice steady. Colleagues still treated him with respect; attorneys still angled for his approval. Yet behind closed doors the scrutiny tightened. Requests arrived for records. Informal interviews multiplied. The air in the courthouse grew thin, as if everyone was breathing a little more carefully. People spoke in shorter sentences. Jokes died halfway through.

Erik sensed it, of course. He was too observant not to. He began meeting colleagues in hallways rather than in his chambers. He stopped leaving the notebook on his desk. He watched Lina with a new attention that was almost clinical.

One afternoon, after a hearing, he spoke to her in a corridor where their footsteps echoed off pale stone. "You've been distracted," he said.

"I've been learning," Lina replied, keeping her tone neutral. Erik's eyes stayed calm. "Learning requires trust."

Lina held his gaze. "So does the public."

For a moment something flickered in him-annoyance, respect, calculation-then it vanished behind professional smoothness.

The tribunal concluded Erik had violated judicial ethics. No criminal charges resulted. But an ethical breach does not require a gunshot. It requires a deviation from duty, and someone documented the deviation.

They formally reprimanded him, restricted his discretionary decisions in high-profile cases, and initiated oversight for his future interventions. The measures were procedural, which suited Sweden: discipline as structure rather than spectacle. Yet the consequences for Erik were intimate. The private thrill of invisible control was gone. His discretion-once a secret instrument-was now monitored. Every adjournment, every scheduling choice, every small "managerial" adjustment had to survive scrutiny.

When he returned to court after the ruling, nothing looked different to a casual visitor. The same pale light. The same cherry-wood benches. The same black robe. But those who worked in the building felt the shift. Lawyers no longer treated his pauses as benign. Prosecutors no longer accepted his "suggestions" as wisdom. Clerks documented more. Lina, now more confident, asked sharper questions and insisted on written rationales.

Erik maintained dignity outwardly, but inwardly he confronted a bleak truth about human weakness: he had enjoyed being necessary. Not merely respected-necessary. He had liked the sense that outcomes depended on his private intelligence. The oversight did not merely limit his power; it exposed what his power had been feeding.

Lina's standing strengthened, though not without cost. Some colleagues praised her quietly and avoided her publicly. Others treated her as if she had broken a spell and therefore invited cold weather. But she had learned something essential: the danger in a disciplined intellect is not that it commits obvious crimes; it is that it can justify small distortions until distortion becomes method.

The narrative endured not as a tale of spectacular criminality, but of psychological nuance: a judge whose composure concealed preference, whose procedural elegance hid favoritism, whose private notebook captured the thrill of steering without leaving fingerprints. In Stockholm, where winter light is honest and thin, the story carried a final, bracing implication: authority is never safest when it looks most perfect. Authority is safest when people can question it without fear-when the shadow has nowhere left to stand.

79

"THE JUDGE'S SILENCE"

SILENCE CAN BE AN ACTION-SOMETIMES THE MOST POWERFUL ONE.

Judicial corruption and misconduct, Spain, 2000s-2010s (composite case), PRGR

Judge Alejandro Castillo's misconduct was not overt. He never solicited bribes, nor did he issue public threats. Instead, he mastered the art of selective silence. Key evidence would disappear, the court would overlook witness testimony, and procedural delays would benefit preferred parties. His discretion was subtle, almost invisible-a whisper of influence that guided outcomes without ever breaking the letter of the law.

Valencia has a particular light. Even in winter it arrives bright, angled, and confident, turning stone facades pale gold and making the city feel older than its own troubles. In the mornings, sea air drifts inland, carrying salt and the faint bitterness of orange peel from the markets. On those days, the courthouse seemed washed clean by atmosphere alone-high ceilings, cooled marble, polished olive-wood benches worn smooth by generations of restless hands. The room had the feeling of permanence, as if justice itself were a kind of architecture.

Alejandro fit that permanence. His robes were immaculate; his authoritarian ceremonial collar framed a face that conveyed both intellect and moral certainty. When he entered, conversation flattened into murmurs. Lawyers changed posture without thinking. Defendants stared at the floor as if the floor could absorb shame. To the outside world he was a model of judicial integrity-fair, precise, incorruptible. He presided over high-profile fraud cases, organised legal seminars, and contributed to national discussions on judicial reform. He spoke of public trust with the calm confidence of a man who appeared to embody it.the conversation

Yet behind the curtain of incorruptibility lay a careful and secret network of influence that tilted justice in subtle, often invisible ways. He did not need to tell anyone what to do. He simply decided which matters he would hear, which he would delay, and which he would treat as irrelevant. In court, attention is oxygen. Remove it, and even the strongest claim suffocates.

Evidence from certain defendants repeatedly disappeared, while other evidence miraculously remained. The timing of rulings seemed inconsistent, often benefitting clients with connections to Alejandro's social and political circles. A motion that should have been urgent drifted for weeks; a filing that should have failed on technical grounds would be accepted "in the interests of completeness." No single incident was explosive enough to provoke scandal. But patterns are storms built from slight changes in pressure.

Marta Rodríguez, a clerk with a reputation for diligence, felt admiration for his intellect rise alongside a creeping unease. The contradiction began affecting her like vertigo. In public, Alejandro was all symmetry: reason, composure, restraint. In the file room, the symmetry didn't hold. She felt her own competence shrinking under the weight of what she couldn't name. When you work near an authority figure who never looks uncertain, your uncertainty feels like personal failure.

The earliest thing she noticed was a gap in a case file that shouldn't have been possible. A key email chain referenced repeatedly by prosecutors was missing from the court's record. Marta checked the archive, then the digital register. The entry existed. The document did not. She assumed clerical error-hers, someone else's, the system's. She requested a re-upload.

The re-upload arrived... incomplete.

Then the court treated a witness statement in a fraud case as if it had never been filed.

Marta knew she had filed it;she had stamped it herself. When she mentioned it gently after the session, Alejandro didn't look surprised. "Ah," he said, almost kindly. "There are many papers. We cannot inflate every detail."

"It wasn't detail," Marta said carefully. "It affects the chain of knowledge."

Alejandro's expression remained smooth. "Marta, we are here to find the truth, not drown in paperwork." That sentence lodged in her mind because it contained a quiet reversal. Paperwork-evidence, record, trace- was the means by which truth survived personalities. To dismiss it was to elevate the judge above the file. Marta went home that evening and stood on her balcony, listening to the wind move through palm fronds along the avenue. The leaves sounded like whispered warnings.

Human weakness entered the story in small places first, as it always does. Marta wanted to believe in him because belief made her life easier. Belief meant the system was coherent, and coherence is a kind of psychological shelter. She also feared being wrong. She feared being seen as paranoid or incompetent. She feared the consequences of asking questions in a building designed to reward silence. Those fears didn't make her weak; they made her human. And Alejandro's genius was that he could use human instincts as levers without ever touching them.

One evening, after reviewing a convoluted corporate fraud case, Marta discovered Alejandro had annotated files in a personal ledger. It was a slim volume, worn at the edges, kept in a drawer that was never locked yet always felt off-limits-like a boundary enforced by habit rather than metal. Coded shorthand and dates filled the pages. She read only a little before her throat tightened.

Notations: aplazar-delay. A name. A case number. A reminder: "ignorar testigo 3." Another line: "evitar pericial; enfocar en restitución." The ledger was methodical, obsessive, chilling in its precision. It didn't describe bribes or threats; it described choreography. It showed a mind treating justice as something you could tune-lowering certain voices, raising others, shaping what the room would hear.

Marta felt a strange dual reaction: disgust and awe. Disgust at the manipulation; awe at the discipline required to maintain it for years without visible rupture. That awe frightened her because awe is one step away from surrender.

For days she lived with the ledger in her mind like a second heartbeat. Reporting a judge of such stature carried enormous risk; ignoring the evidence felt like complicity. Alejandro wielded power outside the courtroom. It extended through political connections, social networks, and legal prestige. Challenging him could end her career-or at least freeze it, quietly, in the way institutions can. Marta saw herself as a point on a map during a weather system: if she moved, the whole air could change.

She developed her own companion: a character of doubt she called La Bruma-the sea mist that rolls in early and makes familiar streets look ambiguous. La Bruma whispered excuses: You don't know the full context. He might protect someone. The code could mean something else. You'll be alone. The system will close around him. It also whispered the opposite: If you stay silent, you become part of the ledger.

Alejandro's motivations were complex. He believed he was protecting societal stability, guiding justice toward outcomes he considered "right" in a larger sense. He spoke privately-when he spoke at all-of preventing chaos, of managing reputational harm to institutions, of keeping "the economy" calm. He told himself he was steering away from outcomes that could inflame politics or damage influential families whose collapse would "hurt many." That was his most seductive self-justification: harm minimized through control. Yet beneath the ideology was a simpler appetite: the private thrill of shaping lives without being seen shaping them. It made him feel like an architect of reality rather than a servant of procedure.

The turning point arrived when Marta, after weeks of internal deliberation, reported her findings to the Consejo General del Poder Judicial. She did it carefully, not as an accusation but as documentation: copies of docket inconsistencies, timestamps, comparison of filings, and finally the ledger itself. She felt her hands shake as she assembled the packet, furious at her own body for betraying fear. But fear, she learned, doesn't negate courage; it defines it.

Investigators cross-referenced the ledger with case files, timelines, and procedural anomalies. Patterns emerged the investigators could no longer explain as coincidence. The same names appeared again and again-connected defendants, favored counsel, businesses that contributed to the social ecosystem around Alejandro. Missing evidence aligned with ledger entries. Delays aligned. Over the years, Alejandro had systematically altered outcomes to aid specific individuals and entities through an almost elegant restraint:

influence exercised by omission.

The investigation was tense. Alejandro remained composed, presiding over sessions with his signature calm authority. His black robes and ceremonial collar stayed flawless, voice steady, gestures measured. Yet internally he recognized the encroaching threat. His web-precise, quiet, built from small choices-was unraveling under ethical scrutiny. He sensed, in the way people sense a change in pressure before rain, that the building no longer belonged solely to his mood.

Witnesses were cautious. Some attorneys claimed forgetfulness. Others insisted the judge's "management style" was simply efficient. Few wanted to admit they had benefited. Human weakness again: people will defend the system that fed them, even if it fed them unfairly. And Alejandro had counted on that. He had relied on gratitude and fear in equal measure.

The tribunal's findings were damning: Alejandro had violated judicial ethics, exerting impermissible influence through selective silence and covert manipulation. They decided against pursuing criminal charges. Yet the moral breach was unmistakable. The Minister of Justice removed him from sensitive cases, reprimanded him publicly, and placed him under monitoring-an institutional way of saying: your discretion is no longer yours alone.

For Alejandro, the consequences were profound precisely because they were not dramatic. He did not lose his robe. He did not vanish in disgrace. Instead, he lost the private room inside the system where he had lived-where his silence had been sovereign. The courtroom, once a stage for invisible mastery, now operated under scrutiny. Lawyers watched him differently, not openly hostile but cautiously alert. Prosecutors arrived prepared to make records of everything. Clerks documented more aggressively. Every omission now looked like potential intention.

Marta's standing strengthened, though not without social cost. Some colleagues praised her quietly and avoided her publicly. Others treated her like someone who had broken a fragile peace. She understood then another contradiction: institutions claim to love integrity, but they often prefer comfort until integrity becomes unavoidable.

Even after the reprimand, Alejandro maintained appearances with dignity. He sat straighter. He spoke with the same controlled cadence. But the thrill of covert control-the private satisfaction of steering outcomes unseen-had drained away. Each ruling now carried the weight of oversight and accountability, a restraint he had never experienced. The ledger, once his secret instrument, became evidence of his own need to play god with a system built to resist gods.

And in Valencia, where the sea keeps moving whether people behave, the story lingered in professional memory as a reminder that silence is not neutral. Silence can be an action-sometimes the most powerful one. And like sea mist, it hides a coastline until the sun suddenly burns through, revealing what was always there: not a single dramatic crime, but the slow, deliberate shaping of justice by what remained unsaid.

PRGR END-CAP - AUTHORED HARM TEST

(for "THE JUDGE'S SILENCE" - case-specific, non-boilerplate)

This case isn't about what the judge did in open court. It's about what the judge **refused to do** when action was still possible. Silence here is not the absence of speech; it is an institutional act: the decision to let harm proceed because intervention would be costly-socially, professionally, reputationally.

PRGR would attach authorship at the hinge-step where the judge observes a risk and chooses "not my role" as a shield. Because in a courtroom, silence has force. It becomes a precedent for everyone watching.

The hinge-steps where PRGR would force the author to exist

The first observed irregularity - and the choice to let it pass
When the judge notices a procedural distortion (late disclosure that cripples defense use, a witness incentive hinted but not explored, counsel visibly under-resourced, a defendant not understanding the process) and chooses not to intervene, PRGR triggers.

The judge must author:

what was observed,

what intervention options existed (continuance, disclosure order, voir dire inquiry, limiting instruction, sealed inquiry),

why no intervention was chosen,

and what harm is foreseeable from letting it pass (coerced plea, unfair trial, wrongful conviction).
In this story, the first silence is usually the one that makes later silences feel "consistent."

The "tone of restraint" step - civility used to avoid responsibility
Judicial restraint can be a virtue. Here, restraint is a cover for avoidance.

PRGR triggers when the judge invokes neutrality ("I can't appear biased," "that's for the parties") to justify inaction in the face of known imbalance or rights risk.

He must author:

what neutrality is protecting (fairness vs. appearance),

why intervention would be improper,

and what alternate safeguard will protect the vulnerable party.
PRGR forces the judge to separate *neutrality as principle* from *neutrality as refuge.*

The record-closure step - declining to build a record when harm is foreseeable
Silence becomes durable when the record stays thin: no inquiry, no reasons, no note that an issue was raised.
PRGR triggers when the judge declines to require the parties to put key issues on the record (witness benefits, disclosure timing, comprehension checks).

He must author:

why a fuller record was rejected,

what foreseeable harm arises from an unreviewable record (appeal barriers, repeated misconduct), and

what minimal documentation could have been required without prejudicing the case.
A silent record is not neutral; it is future-proofing.

The misconduct deferral - "take it up later" as denial
If a complaint about an advocate/prosecutor emerges and the judge postpones it to a future forum that is unlikely to act, PRGR triggers at the deferral.

He must author:

where the complaint is being routed,

why that forum is competent and likely to respond,

what interim protections exist in the current proceeding.
PRGR prevents "later" from becoming the institutional trash chute.

The sentencing / remedy hinge - refusing to use discretion to correct imbalance
If the judge has discretion (sentencing, evidentiary rulings, continuances, suppression determinations, jury instructions) and declines to use it despite recognizing imbalance, PRGR triggers at the decision.

He must author:

what corrective options existed,

why they were rejected,

what harm is foreseeable from maintaining the imbalance.
Here, silence isn't passive; it is exercised discretion disguised as inevitability.

The post-case silence - seeing a pattern and choosing non-escalation
Often judges learn later: a prosecutor's pattern, a lab's unreliability, a defense funding crisis, a witness incentive practice.
PRGR triggers when the judge chooses not to escalate pattern knowledge to oversight mechanisms (chief judge, ethics body, administrative reform).

He must author:

what pattern was recognized,

why escalation was rejected,

and what foreseeable harm follows from non-escalation (future wrongful cases, repeated rights violations).
This is where silence becomes complicity.

What PRGR would force in this case (matched to judicial power)

1. **A "silence-as-decision" record**
   PRGR requires that when a judge explicitly chooses not to intervene in the face

of identified risk, the choice is recorded: observation → options → reason → harm forecast. Not for spectacle-so silence can't masquerade as inevitability.

2. **A "record integrity" safeguard**
   PRGR would require minimal record-building on known risk points: disclosure timing, witness benefits, comprehension checks, resource denials. Because a thin record is how injustice survives review.

3. **A pattern-escalation trigger**
   If the judge sees repeated irregularities across cases (late discovery, incentivized witnesses, defense underfunding), PRGR demands an automatic internal escalation pathway. Not public grandstanding-formal institutional notice with accountability.

4. **A neutrality clarification rule**
   If the judge invokes neutrality to avoid action, PRGR forces a written explanation distinguishing: neutrality that protects fairness, from neutrality that protects the judge.

Questions that keep this End-Cap specific to "the judge's silence"

If you were the judge: what exactly did you see and choose not to touch-late disclosure, coercive plea leverage, a defendant's confusion, counsel's visible incapacity? Would you sign the harm forecast of your non-intervention?

If you were counsel/defendant: which single moment would you want forced into record-the court's awareness of imbalance, or the court's reasons for letting it stand?

If you were court leadership: how many silent judges does it take before silence becomes policy?

PRGR fits this chapter because it treats silence as what it is here: **an authored choice with foreseeable consequences.** It forces a name at the exact hinge where the judge's inaction stops being restraint and becomes the quiet permission that lets harm continue.

80

"THE MONK'S HIDDEN ICON"

AN IMAGE KEPT IN DARKNESS STILL SHAPES THE ONE WHO HIDES IT.

Recurring real-world patterns of illicit antiquities trafficking and the quiet disappearance of icons / relics from monasteries (composite).

The monastery of Panagia Lithari clung to the hillside like a thought that refused to leave. Pines leaned over its walls, and in summer the cicadas sang as if they were counting time. In winter, fog rolled down from the ridge and filled the courtyard, turning monks into moving shadows.

Brother Stephanos had taken vows. His hands learned the rhythms-prayer, work, silence-until his body moved through them without resistance. The monastery assigned him to the old storage room: a stone chamber beneath the chapel where they kept candles, oils, and broken furniture. The room smelled of wax and damp rock, and in its back corner, wrapped in cloth like a sleeping child, lay an icon few visitors ever saw.

It was ancient-gold leaf dulled, faces softened by centuries of kissing. The Theotokos held the Child with a tenderness that seemed to oppose the world's brutality. When Stephanos unwrapped it to check for mold, he felt the familiar ache: beauty that survives ruin.

He brought it out at night.

Not for worship alone-though he told himself that. He brought it out to sit with it, to let its gaze steady him. Plotinus wrote that the soul, seeing beauty, remembers what it once knew; Stephanos felt that remembrance like thirst. The icon became his private consolation.

Then a visitor came-a scholar from Athens, Dr. Charalambos Leontis-who spoke of icons as "cultural treasures." He walked through the monastery with reverent eyes and asked careful questions.

"There are rumors," Leontis said, voice low, "that you have a pre-Iconoclast piece here. If true, it would be... extraordinary."

The abbot denied politely. Stephanos stood behind him, silent, and felt the icon's presence in the cellar like a heartbeat.

Weeks later, a storm tore through the hillside. Rain hammered the roofs, and water seeped into the cellar. Stephanos found the cloth-wrapped icon damp at the edges. Panic rose. He dried it with trembling hands, whispering prayers that sounded like apologies. In that panic, Leontis's earlier words returned: extraordinary. Extraordinary things attract extraordinary predators.

Leontis returned with an "offer," disguised as help. He knew a conservator. He knew donors. He knew museums that would "protect" such a piece better than a damp cellar could. He spoke like a physician offering surgery. "It's safer with professionals," he said.

Stephanos replied, "Safer for whom?"

Leontis smiled. "For the icon. And for you. The world is changing. Robbers raid monasteries. Fires happen." That night, fog pressed against the windows, and Stephanos remembered a lesser-known Roman moralist, Sallustius, who wrote about the decay that comes when private gain replaces public virtue. Stephanos felt that decay tempted him: to accept "protection" that was really removal.

He didn't take money. That was how he kept the story clean in his own mind. He agreed solely to "let the icon be examined." He carried it out, wrapped, beneath his cloak like contraband. Pines dripped rain onto the path, and the monastery bell sounded once behind him-lonely, accusing.

The examination happened in a city apartment. Bright lamps. White gloves. Cameras. Leontis's hands hovered as if he were already the owner.

"It's worth a fortune," Leontis whispered. Stephanos flinched. "It's not for sale."

Leontis's gaze stayed calm. "Everything is for sale. The question is whether you admit it."

Stephanos returned to the monastery without the icon. He told himself it was temporary-restoration, protection. But days became weeks, and the icon did not return. Leontis stopped answering calls. The abbot asked why Stephanos looked hollow. Stephanos lied with a monk's soft voice.

Then the news arrived: a museum abroad added an "anonymous" icon matching the description to their collection. Photographs circulated online. The faces on the icon looked the same-Mary's tired tenderness, the Child's solemn gaze-now displayed under glass, labeled, priced by silence.

When the abbot confronted Stephanos, his voice was not angry. It was worse-broken. "Why?" the abbot asked.

Stephanos's throat tightened. "I thought I was saving it." The abbot replied, "You saved it from us."

Outside, spring arrived. Snowmelt ran down the hillside in thin streams, carving channels through the soil. Stephanos watched those streams and understood the parable: one slight cut becomes a path; then the water keeps going there because it's easier.

He had cut the path.

The monastery filed reports. Authorities asked questions. Leontis vanished into the world of intermediaries and paperwork.

The icon remained displayed in a place that called itself safe, while the monastery carried the absence like a wound.

Rescue-investigations, petitions, statements-came after the loss, because prevention would have required something unromantic: seals, inventories, audits, and the humility to admit even monks can be tempted.

Stephanos returned to the cellar.

The cloth lay empty.

The stone room smelled of damp and regret. An icon can be hidden.

But it still shapes the one who hides it.

81

"THE MAGISTRATE'S MOSAIC"

A PERFECTLY DESIGNED FACADE CAN HIDE A ROOM WHERE SOMEONE IS QUIETLY TEACHING OTHERS TO OBEY.

Recurring Spanish judicial-corruption and abuse-of-office cases, and the way prestige-legal or artistic-can be used as a shield, Spain, 2014 (composite case)

Barcelona makes you argue with yourself even before you enter a courtroom.

On one corner, a Gaudí facade rises like a fever dream in stone-bone curves, scaled tiles, balconies shaped like masks that grin at the street. Tourists stop and gape as if they're at a shrine. Locals pass with two different pride: the pride of ownership and the pride of tolerance.

For some, Gaudí is untouchable-genius made architecture. For others, he's the city's most expensive argument: an ornament pretending to be meaning, an overgrown vine choking honest lines.

Both reactions can be true at once. Barcelona thrives on contradictions.

Magistrate Javier Molina understood that. He lived on contradictions the way certain buildings live on scaffolding: you stop seeing the supports and start believing the shape is natural.

In Courtroom Three, he was ceremony incarnate-flowing black robe, jabot folded to the crisp geometry of legitimacy, voice calm enough to make obedience feel voluntary. He had the look of a man whose decisions came from principle rather than appetite. Attorneys lowered their tone when he entered. Defendants straightened as if posture could influence fate. Clerks moved papers with the reverence of acolytes handling relics.

The public loved him. Newspapers described him as "rigorous." Legal conferences invited him to speak about ethics with the smug assurance of institutions that enjoy quoting rectitude. In corridors, lawyers spoke his name the way architecture students speak Gaudí's: as if it were proof that a craft could still produce greatness.

And yet-outside, on the Ramblas-street artists painted portraits in minutes. They knew the trick that Molina also knew: if you can make it look convincing fast enough, people stop asking what's underneath.

His first abuses weren't dramatic. They were aesthetic.

A case delayed by a week-"for clarity." A motion granted with a raised eyebrow that said, remember this. A gentle suggestion, delivered in chambers, that certain paths "lead to smoother outcomes."

Procedure, in Molina's hands, became design. He didn't break the law; he arranged it. Like mosaic tiles: each piece small, harmless alone. Together, they formed an image you couldn't unsee.

He collected "considerations" the way collectors gain art: not always for the money, but for the feeling that the world offered itself to him.

A financier's "donation" to a cultural foundation he patronized. A watch offered after a hearing, presented as gratitude rather than payment. A weekend invitation disguised as networking, the price of access wrapped in charm.

He told himself it was normal. Barcelona ran on gifts and favors, didn't it? A city of patrons, benefactors, sponsors. Even Gaudí had patrons-Eusebi Güell, the wealthy hand behind the impossible curves. Without money, art collapses into sketches. Without influence, justice collapses into backlog.

That was Molina's private sermon: I'm only oiling a rigid machine. But oil can also be a lubricant for sliding downhill.

Clara Ortega met him first as a defense attorney with too much talent and not enough insulation. She entered his courtroom with clean arguments and the naive belief that the law-like mathematics-rewarded correctness.

She argued a bail application with precision, cited precedent, and kept her voice level.

Molina granted the bail. Not because her reasoning compelled him, but because he wanted her to understand the power dynamic early: I can give. I can take.

A week later, his clerk delivered a message: the magistrate would like a "private procedural discussion" in chambers.

Clara arrived in a tailored suit that felt suddenly like a costume. Molina's chambers were orderly, tasteful-books aligned, desk immaculate, a framed print of Barcelona's skyline on the wall. He offered her coffee. He complimented her clarity. He spoke about her "future."

Then he tilted the conversation, gently, as if moving a chess piece.

"You're gifted," he said. "But talent needs protection. Some judges are... less reasonable than I am." It sounded like mentorship until it didn't.

His hand hovered near hers on the desk-no grab, no force, only the implication of force. His gaze held hers long enough to be a test. He spoke about "trust" and "discretion," as if those words were incense that made misconduct sacred.

Clara understood the invitation: not to a drink, but to an arrangement.

She declined politely, the way women often decline danger-softly, so the danger doesn't wake up.

Molina smiled as if he admired her principles. Then, with the gentlest shift, he punished her without ever appearing to do so: a hearing scheduled at an impossible time; a motion questioned with sudden skepticism; her credibility chipped at through small, legalistic irritations that left no bruise a committee could photograph.

Her doubt grew like mold: slow, persistent, hard to prove until it's everywhere.

Raúl Fernández learned Molina's other appetite-money-when his civil dispute landed in Courtroom Three. Raúl owned a logistics company, the kind that lived on thin margins and paperwork. The dispute was significant but not glamorous. He expected the usual: arguments, delays, stress.

What he didn't expect was the intermediary.

A man in a neat suit approached him outside the courthouse, smiled with the warmth of a stranger who already knows your schedule, and said: "The magistrate values efficiency. There are ways to avoid... complications." The offer wasn't explicit. It didn't need to be. Barcelona's air is full of implication; even Gaudí's chimneys look like they're whispering secrets to the sky.

Raúl refused at first. Then his case rotted.

Documents were "missing." A key witness's availability suddenly "changed." A procedural clarification he needed was delayed, then delayed again, until his lawyers looked at him as if he were the problem.

He paid-not as a bribe, he told himself, but as a fee for survival.

That's how institutional harm works when it's refined: you don't feel like a victim. You feel like a participant in your own compromise.

Meanwhile, court staff watched and said nothing. Not because they were stupid, but because they were human. People protect themselves first. They protect their pension, their mortgage, their children's stability. And the robe, the jabot, the title-those things make the predator look like the building itself. You don't accuse a building.

You navigate it.

But Barcelona has another truth: even stone wears down. Sea air erodes iron. Tourists rub the same spot on a statue until the bronze turns shiny. A city's beauty is also its decay.

The case broke because of details-always the details.

An accounting irregularity in a judge's declared assets. A clerk who noticed a pattern in scheduling. A journalist with a taste for numbers rather than gossip.

They pulled threads. Donations connected to rulings. Gifts linked to outcomes. Private meetings that correlated too neatly with courtroom decisions. And-most damning-the human constellation of fear: lawyers who grew pale when they heard Molina's name; defendants who changed their story mid-sentence; clerks who avoided eye contact like people walking past a crime scene.

The city's ancient cynicism seemed like a second language when Barcelona reacted with half outrage and half shrug to the first report, just as it does to every scandal. Some people said, "Of course." Others said, "Not him." Many said nothing at all, choosing the safer role of spectator.

Molina appeared in court during the initial scrutiny with impeccable composure. His robe hung perfectly. His jabot looked ironed by ritual itself. He spoke calmly about "misunderstandings," about "professional jealousy," about the dangers of "undermining public confidence."

He sounded like a museum curator defending a famous painting: You simply don't understand what you're seeing.

But art can't save a man when the evidence forms its own picture.

Under inquiry, the mosaic of his behaviour became visible. Not one incident, but an architecture of abuse: the way he positioned people, cornered them with procedure, converted fear into compliance, and called it "discretion." The investigation uncovered enough to suspend him, then prosecute him, and the spectacle of a magistrate on the receiving end of the system he had manipulated was almost too perfect-like a morality play staged in a city obsessed with design.

Still, the most violent part wasn't the verdict. It was the aftertaste.

Clara, even after the exposure, felt contaminated-by the meetings, by the doubt, by the instinct to question her own memory. She had not been "assaulted" in a way the public could easily dramatize. An authority reshaped her, making her choices feel smaller than they were. That kind of injury survives headlines.

Raúl didn't feel vindicated so much as exhausted. He had paid to avoid ruin; he had paid because the alternative was collapse. The system's collapse had simply revealed that he'd been living in one already.

And you, the reader, face the uncomfortable reflection that Barcelona so readily presents.

We worship institutions the way we worship landmarks. We photograph the facade. We argue over whether the style is genius or grotesque. Meanwhile, inside, ordinary human desires-sex, money, dominance-walk the corridors wearing respectable cloth.

People rebuild beloved buildings with lightning speed after they shattered. Some buildings burn, others collapse, and people abandon the rest to time, letting them vanish. And some don't at all-they rot quietly from the inside while tourists keep admiring the roofline.

Molina's robe and jabot did not create his corruption. They merely made it look like tradition.

That is the harsh lesson Barcelona teaches with every mosaic and every cracked tile: beauty can distract, ceremony can seduce, and a perfectly designed facade can hide a room where someone is quietly teaching others to obey.

82

"THE BISHOP'S SHADOW"

HOLY WATER CAN WASH HANDS. IT CANNOT DISINFECT A SYSTEM THAT REFUSES TO NAME ITS INFECTION.

Clerical boundary violations and institutional silence (composite case).

The Church outlasts weather, wars, governments, scandals. The Church remains. Bishop Henri Delacroix walked the long corridors of Saint-Pierre Cathedral with the measured calm of a man who had learned to move like a verdict. His polished shoes tapped against stone that had absorbed centuries of footfall-pilgrims, penitents, tourists, priests. In that sound there was always a suggestion: continuity.

To the faithful, Delacroix was an image of authority made flesh: ceremonial black, collar crisp, jabot white as an altar cloth. He knew exactly how the cloth worked on the mind. It softened questions. It lengthened silences. It made people interpret discomfort as their own moral weakness. A bishop didn't need to raise his voice; the institution had been raising it for him since childhood, through catechisms and candles, through the choreography of kneeling and blessing. He inherited an instrument that predated any man.

He had also inherited the Church's favorite public myth: ritual can wash away wrongdoing. Holy water. Confession. A penance like a small toll. The soul scrubbed clean; the account balanced. For ordinary human failings-petty cruelty, jealousy, negligence-perhaps these gestures can be honest attempts at repair. But Delacroix learned something darker: rituals can also be used as detergents for appearances, not for the rot underneath. A confession can be theatre. A blessing can be camouflage.

And institutions-especially ones that rely on sacred mystery-can become baskets of disease. Not because faith is sickness, but because power without sunlight always grows mold. The Church teaches its people to come for healing. It does not always notice when the building itself is the source of infection.

The first misstep appeared harmless. During a routine visitation, a seminarian approached him with a question-nervous, eager, reverent. Delacroix placed a hand on his shoulder. Mentorship, he told himself. A reassurance. The seminarian stiffened as if a cold current had passed through him.

Delacroix felt it too: the tiny shiver of influence. Not sexual yet, not explicitly. More primitive. The thrill of discovering how easily the body becomes compliant when the mind believes it must obey. He withdrew his hand, smiled, and offered a mild word about humility. He watched the seminarian swallow his confusion, just as believers often swallow doubt quickly so they cannot taste it.

That was how it began. Not with a crime in the dramatic sense, but with a discovery.

Delacroix progressively developed scenarios where he could mask intimacy as attentiveness. Private meetings in the bishop's residence. "Spiritual direction" sessions scheduled after hours. Trips framed as pilgrimages, but structured so a priest found himself alone in a car with a man whose authority had no equal in his life.

Delacroix did not pounce; he arranged. He let the institution do the heavy lifting. The seminary was already an architecture of obedience. The only thing he added was intent.

Confession became his most efficient laboratory. The confessional invites disclosure. It trains the penitent to deliver their shame into the hands of a representative of God. Delacroix listened the way all confessors listen-patient, still, receptive-but he also stored what he heard. He catalogued vulnerabilities: a priest's loneliness, a parishioner's guilt, a family's fear of scandal. The secrets became less like stories and more like keys. He didn't use them overtly. He didn't have to. The knowledge itself changed the balance of every future conversation.

A person who has confessed to you rarely feels free around you again. Even if you never mention what they said, the confession becomes a shadow in their mind. Delacroix learned to exploit that shadow with elegance. His violations were often so subtle that victims struggled to describe them. A touch that lasted one second too long. A compliment framed as spiritual discernment that suddenly felt like appraisal. A question asked with "pastoral concern" that was really a probe: Are you alone? Do you struggle with temptation? Do you ever think of me? The brilliance of such abuse is that it forces the victim to do the self-doubt for the abuser. The faithful learn to examine themselves first. To suspect their own motives. To interpret discomfort as sin.

And whenever anyone flinched, Delacroix had a ready remedy: ritual.

"Let us pray," he would whisper, as if prayer were a disinfectant. He offered confession like an eraser. He spoke of grace like a solvent. He encouraged people to "leave it at the altar," which sounded merciful but functioned like disposal. If the Church can persuade you that cleansing is always available, it can also persuade you that reporting is unnecessary.

As years passed, Delacroix's appetite widened. One domain rarely satisfies influence. He exerted pressure in financial matters, too, because money-like sex-tests obedience. Wealthy families approached him for counsel on trusts and donations. He suggested endowments "for the cathedral's future." He encouraged gifts for youth programs and restoration projects. Holy language wrapped the requests, but the pattern was familiar: devotion turned into leverage.

Some families complied out of faith. Others complied because they feared being seen as insufficiently committed. That is another disease institutions can spread: that belonging must be purchased. Delacroix did not have to demand. He merely hinted, and the machinery of guilt did the rest.

Meanwhile, the Church, as an institution, behaved like many institutions: it protected its continuity first. Scandal threatens donations, attendance, influence, and the fragile belief that the Church is morally distinct from ordinary power structures. Abundant credibility allows to conceal excess. When credibility is thin, excess becomes fatal. Delacroix understood this and played accordingly. He did not create chaos. He maintained order. He kept the cathedral looking serene. He ensured the candles stayed lit.

The first cracks appeared not from a single accusation but from accumulation, like mold finally visible on a wall that has been damp for years. Seminarians began avoiding private encounters. One priest asked for a transfer with no logical explanation. Another developed insomnia, then panic, then a sudden decision to leave the vocation. Initially, they attributed these events to personal fragility. "They are sensitive," someone said. "Seminary is demanding." The institution prefers psychological explanations when moral ones are dangerous. But then a small group of seminarians confided in the cathedral administrator. Their accounts were different but identical in texture: the sense of being cornered without a corner; pressured without an explicit threat; made to feel that holiness required compliance. They spoke of shame that felt foreign, shame that came not from their own actions but from being turned into objects in a sacred place. They spoke of confusion that made prayer taste like ash.

At first, the internal review moved at the Church's natural speed: cautious, procedural, protective. The team gathered documents, anonymized testimonies, and reviewed letters. Each step aimed not only to discover truth but to control it. The institution behaved like a body trying to contain infection by sealing off the limb-quiet quarantine, minimal exposure, preserve the whole.

But patterns do not stay sealed forever. The more evidence gathered, the clearer the shape became: repeated misconduct-sexual, financial, psychological-hidden behind the same sacred instruments that were supposed to prevent it.

Delacroix's removal from active duties was quiet, almost polite. No dramatic arrest at the cathedral door. No public confession to the chandeliers. Absence. A chair was empty at Mass. A name omitted from announcements. The Church has long practiced disappearance as a method of containment: remove the carrier, preserve the host.

Yet the damage remained because disease is not only an event; it is a system of transmission.

Parishioners who had trusted him felt their faith destabilize. Some found that fear intertwined with what they called "God's presence" in the cathedral. Some found they could no longer kneel without remembering hands that were not holy. The scars were not only on bodies or reputations, but on belief itself-on the inner place where the faithful once expected shelter.

Spiritual authority's abuse particularly colonizes the soul, which is its cruelty. It teaches the believer to doubt their own perception of good and evil. It makes prayer feel unsafe. It makes the very idea of God sound like the voice of an institution that failed you.

And the cathedral-ancient, imposing-continued to stand, as cathedrals do. Chandeliers still shimmered. Choirs still sang. Stone arches still held. Continuity persisted.

But credibility does not rebuild as easily as architecture. Architecture replaces the old with the new. Same foundation, same materials. Only another look.

The lesson Delacroix left behind was not that confession is meaningless, or that ritual is fraud. The lesson was harsher: cleansing is not the same as accountability, and institutions that claim to heal can also carry disease. Prioritizing organizational survival over safeguarding the vulnerable turns it into a beautiful but internally corrupt entity.

Holy water can wash hands. It cannot disinfect a system that refuses to name its infection.

83

"THE MAGISTRATE OF QUIET STREETS"

PATTERN IS EVIDENCE'S COUSIN. IT DOESN'T CONVICT BY ITSELF, BUT IT POINTS.

Judicial conduct Commissioner investigations, Australia, 2012-2018 (composite case)

Priya Dawson wrote the complaint at her kitchen table with the blinds down.

Outside, the town's main street lay quiet in the way certain places go quiet after dusk-not peaceful, just held. The streetlights hummed. A moth battered itself against the glass of the porch lamp, repeating the same collision as if repetition could become a solution. In the distance, a magpie gave one sharp call and then fell silent, as though it had remembered where it lived.

Priya had been in the job for eight months. She still believed, as rookies often do, that if you did the work cleanly, the system would respond cleanly. That belief had cracked the first time she watched Magistrate Leonard Hale. The case was easy on paper: a local councilor's son, drunk, clipping a curb at speed outside the hotel and missing two pedestrians by a margin no one should have to measure. The arrest was solid-bodycam, witnesses, test results, chain of custody. Priya had written the brief with the care of someone placing evidence into a sealed bag: neat, complete, ready to withstand scrutiny.

Hale dismissed it within ten minutes.

No speech. No anger. Just a mild, practiced irritation about "overzealous policing," a few questions asked as if he were educating the room, and then a decision so lenient it felt less like discretion and more like a signal. The councilor's son walked out smiling. Outside the court, he lit a cigarette as if consequences were a myth told to keep other people obedient.

Priya's sergeant had breathed it-almost kindly-like an older officer handing down weather wisdom. "That's Hale. Don't make yourself a target."

But Priya couldn't stop thinking about the pedestrians: the physics of the near miss, the simple reality that two bodies and a bumper had nearly met. When a magistrate treats that as minor, it does something to you. It changes your perspective on how force travels through the world; privilege, rather than justice, can prevent an impact.

So Priya filed the complaint.

What she didn't know was that Hale had been a low-grade rumor for years-always present, never quite solid enough to grasp. In small towns, reputations function like temperature: they influence everything while remaining hard to point at directly. Hale had cultivated a public image of calm decency. "The gentleman on the bench." He spoke softly, rarely raised his voice, and wore his robe and jabot as if they were part of his body.

The lace at his throat framed his face with a kind of ceremonial innocence. People saw the costume and filled in the moral blank.

A blind spot you don't notice becomes a feature you rely on.

The oversight office took Priya's report seriously, but cautiously. They began by examining patterns: dismissals that favored certain surnames, inexplicable harshness toward defendants with no local standing, a curious consistency in who received mercy and who received the full weight of the law.

Pattern is evidence's cousin. It doesn't convict by itself, but it points. The first tangible crack came from Hale's chambers.

A court officer, acting under formal authority, opened a locked drawer in an antique desk. Inside was a leather-bound notebook-thin, tidy, almost elegant. The handwriting was precise. The entries were not financial accounts in any official sense, yet it was unmistakably a ledger:

Names. Dates. Small annotations. "Cooperative." "Reliable." "Slow pay. Pressure needed." "Remains fearful." "Favors earned."

It wasn't a ledger of money.

It was a ledger of people.

In biology, predators do not always hunt by speed. Some hunt by learning. They map habits, weaknesses, and routes. Hale's ledger read like this: a private ecology of vulnerability. It categorized individuals who could be leaned on, who could be soothed, who could be frightened, and who could be made to owe.

Then came the harder part-the part that never looks clean on paper.

A former court clerk described how Hale summoned vulnerable defendants to chambers after hearings under the guise of "private cautioning." These meetings weren't violent. They didn't need to be. Hale's method was atmospheric: close the door, lower the voice, create the sense that something intimate is happening, and then let fear do the work.

People described the same sensation in different words: being pinned without being touched, reduced without being shouted at, watched in a way that made their own skin feel untrustworthy. One woman said she felt as though his attention had "taken something" even though nothing visible happened.

The inquiry still needed a spine-something the institution couldn't shrug off as personality or misunderstanding. That spine arrived as Desmond Frost.

Frost was a mechanic with a record-petty theft, drugs, a few fights, the file the system reads quickly and dismisses. He had always pled guilty, always received strangely soft outcomes from Hale, and always left court shaken in a way that didn't match the verdict.

When investigators approached him, he refused at first.

"You don't go against a bloke like that," he said. "He reads you like a diary." But fear has limits, and so does silence.

Frost described the chamber meetings: Hale's gentle tone, the way he asked questions that weren't about law but about shame-family, sex, addiction, the private humiliations that turn a person pliable. Hale didn't need to threaten. Through implication and timing, he let Frost understand he could tighten or soften outcomes depending on compliance.

It was coercion refined into etiquette.

The oversight team began reconstructing cases with unaccustomed eyes, much like a scientist re-checks data after realizing the instrument has been biased. Files that once looked like harmless discretion now looked like managed outcomes. Each small anomaly-each postponement, each unexplained adjustment-added up, like tiny stresses accumulating along a fault line.

Hale responded the way such men often do: with composure that doubles as contempt. He dismissed allegations as misunderstandings, "vendettas," the oversensitivity of those who "misread mentorship." His robe remained immaculate. His jabot remained centered. He behaved as if calm proved virtue.

But then the atmosphere changed.

Institutions respond to liability the way the body responds to infection: they contain it. The Council of Magistrates demanded his suspension pending review. On the day they delivered the notice, Hale stood in chambers and smoothed the lace at his throat as though preparing for a photograph.

His hands trembled only once-an involuntary tremor, like a needle jumping when voltage shifts.

He resigned two days later.

There was no grand moral ending. No single moment where the town collectively understood what had happened. Instead, there was the slow social drift of recalibration: people lowering their voices, re-reading old decisions, remembering discomforts they'd once explained away.

Priya did not feel triumphant. She felt older.

She had learned something that training doesn't put into manuals: corruption isn't always cash in an envelope.

Sometimes it's the quiet conversion of authority into psychological leverage-pressure applied so steadily that people stop trusting their own interpretation of events.

And in a town of quiet streets, that kind of harm travels far-because silence, too, carries sound.

84

"THE FALLEN MAGISTRATE"

IT WAS THE INSTINCT TO PROTECT REPUTATION FIRST, TO TREAT TRUTH AS A CONTAMINANT RATHER THAN A NECESSITY.

Magistrate's alleged child pornography scandal, Netherlands, early 2000s, PRGR

The floorboard didn't squeal. It sighed.

Kneeling in the attic of the canal house belonging to the magistrate, Jeroen, the maintenance worker, used a pry bar in his gloved hand, working by the meager winter light that entered through the dormer window. The renovation was ordinary-replace rotten joists, insulate, tidy the mess left by decades of damp. In old Dutch houses, moisture behaves like a slow animal: it finds the softest wood, the smallest crack, the place where no one looks, and then it stays.

Jeroen lifted the board and found something that didn't belong to rot: a plastic-wrapped bundle wedged between beams, hidden with deliberate care. Not tools. Not cash. Storage media and printed material that strongly suggested illegal content involving minors.

He re-wrapped it, hands suddenly clumsy. For a moment he just sat there, listening to the house settle. Somewhere below, a radiator clicked as it cooled. Outside, gulls cried over the canal, sharp and indifferent. Jeroen went straight to the authorities.

By the time police arrived with warrants, Magistrate Hendrik van Loenen was at work, wearing his robe and bef with the precise care of someone who believed appearance was a form of moral proof. His chambers smelled of paper and coffee. His desk was orderly. His handwriting in the docket was neat-small, educated, controlled.

Van Loenen's composure was well known. He spoke to defendants with a calm that often sounded like kindness, and to lawyers with a mild superiority that suggested he was doing them a favor by tolerating argument. He had the manner of a man convinced the system's dignity lived in him.

That conviction was his arrogance-and his camouflage.

Earlier that day he had scolded a defendant for "poor choices," the tone paternal and faintly contemptuous. He liked the difference between them: educated restraint on top, "impulse" below. The less polished you were, the less he treated your words as real.

When investigators entered his chambers and presented the warrant, Van Loenen didn't shout. He adjusted his cuffs, asked to read the document, and said-coolly-that this was absurd.

The search was careful, exhaustive. The police seized devices. They cataloged the hidden storage. The searchers discovered a second concealed compartment, built into a cabinet with a craftsmanship that suggested planning, not panic. The evidence did not rely on rumor. It relied on objects.

Van Loenen's face remained controlled, but the skin around his eyes tightened, as if his body were trying to keep a secret from escaping.

The news broke anyway.

A judge's scandal travels fast because it doesn't merely offend; it destabilizes. It turns the court itself into a suspect. Photographs appeared: the canal house, the courthouse entrance, Van Loenen in his robe.

Commentators reached for words like "unthinkable," as if naming the act could keep it distant. Inside the courthouse, the reaction was less dramatic and more revealing.

Administrators immediately worried about "public confidence." Colleagues asked whether cases he had handled might need review. Meetings convened not to understand how such a failure had been possible, but to contain what might spread. The institution moved like a body trying to isolate infection-tighten boundaries, minimize exposure, protect the appearance of health.

Some staff admitted, in private, that Van Loenen had long shown a particular disdain for others. He treated clerks like furniture. He spoke about "simple people" as if they were unreliable narrators of their own lives. That kind of superiority doesn't prove hidden crimes, but it creates silence: people stop challenging a man who radiates inevitability.

Van Loenen resigned almost immediately, framing it as respect for the judiciary rather than necessity. He described his departure as "stepping aside" to let the institution carry on its "vital work." He did not apologize to anyone who had believed the robe meant safety. He fought. He wanted to beat the system he once served, instead of bowing to it and taking responsibility. Something he always demanded through his toga and bef.

The legal process moved forward with restraint. Public speculation outpaced actual knowledge. The institution emphasized safeguards, promised review, and spoke in a procedural language that sounded like disinfectant. Technicalities spared Van Loenen the worst. The court accepted an argument and dismissed the case: the argument stated that the images could not reliably establish that the subjects were minors, and he claimed that what appeared to be evidence was illusion-alteration, ambiguity, uncertainty. The judges accepted the framing. Public outrage did not end there. To many, it looked less like justice than self-protection-one man shielded by others who wore the robe themselves. The decision echoed like shockwaves after a lightning strike: first deafening, then thinning out, fading into silence as if the sound had simply left the world.

Jeroen watched the coverage and felt something like nausea. Alongside praise, he heard whispers-predictable, ugly-accusing him of snooping, suggesting he craved attention, and implying that a working man couldn't be trusted to interpret what he saw. Class prejudice surfaced quickly: educated people defending educated people, even in disgrace.

But the evidence was what it was. It didn't depend on Jeroen's vocabulary.

Months later, the judiciary announced policy updates and training sessions, as if posters and procedures could restore what had fractured. Perhaps they helped. Perhaps they were necessary. But none of it answered the question that hung in the building like damp air:

How did a man so compromised rise so high with no one wanting to look too closely?

Maybe the answer was structural. When an institution treats titles as proof of character, it outsources judgment. People see the robe and assume there is nothing beneath it that could rot.

Yet rot does not need permission. It needs darkness and time. Jeroen disappeared from public view.

The canal kept flowing. Winter turned to spring, and the trees budded as if renewal were automatic.

Van Loenen returned to his work, not at the court, but at a university with the same architectural structure-basements, attics, stairwells-places where hidden damp reveals itself in soft wood and stained plaster. He would later say that the worst part wasn't the discovery. It was the instinct to protect reputation first, to treat truth as a contaminant rather than a necessity.

But trust-once cracked-doesn't bud on schedule.

It behaves more like old timber: it can look solid for years, and then one day, under ordinary weight, it gives way with a quiet, devastating sigh.

PRGR END-CAP - AUTHORED HARM TEST

(for "THE FALLEN MAGISTRATE")

Primary mechanism: PROCEDURE - evidentiary standards become a shield, and the institution treats reputation as the patient.

Sector: LAW (with spillover into PUBLIC TRUST)

PRGR trigger: any step that (a) ends or effectively neutralises a criminal accountability pathway, or (b) manages institutional exposure in a way that predictably harms public safety, trust, or a witness/whistleblower.

Decision-points in this case where PRGR would bite:

The dismissal hinge: the court accepts the argument that the images cannot reliably establish the subjects are minors - and the case is dismissed.

The containment hinge: internal leadership meetings prioritise "public confidence" language and risk-management over truth-telling and victim-safety.

The re-entry hinge: the disgraced magistrate quietly returns to adjacent authority (university work) without a transparent risk rationale.

Required signatories (case-specific):

The presiding judge / panel chair who signed the dismissal judgment **and** each judge concurring in it.

The prosecutorial authority responsible for appeal posture (appeal / no appeal) and for explaining the downstream risk of closure.

The court's administrative head (or equivalent) who chose the public narrative and internal safeguarding steps.

Any hiring authority that later restores the individual to trust-adjacent work (screening, disclosure rationale, safeguards).

PRGR record must state (in plain language, not doctrine):

Action: what exactly was done (dismissal, non-appeal, containment strategy, re-entry decision).

Reason: why this action, now - and why the alternative was rejected.

Foreseeable harm:

the predictable public inference of **robe-protects-robe** (institution shields its own),

the chilling effect on ordinary witnesses like **Jeroen** (the "snooping" smear becomes part of the deterrent system),

the risk of **future access** to vulnerable people if reputation management outruns safeguarding,

the corrosive effect on legitimacy: the court becomes "a suspect" in the public mind, not an arbiter.

Remedy trigger: what would automatically reopen a review if later facts emerge (new forensic capability, corroborating material, pattern evidence, later admissions, linked allegations).

What the institution tries to keep unowned in this chapter:

the moment *legal ambiguity* is used as a **moral exit**,

the moment "public confidence" becomes code for **containment**,

the moment an ordinary worker is reframed as the risk because the credentialed man cannot be.

Counterfactual (the PRGR pressure-test):

PRGR would not force a different verdict by magic. It would force a different *ownership structure*: the dismissal would have an author in ink, the containment strategy would have a name attached, and the decision to let the story "fade into silence" would no longer be an unowned institutional reflex.

Pause: In this story, the floorboard "sighs," not squeals. That is the warning: harm can surface quietly and still be catastrophic.

Ask yourself (case-specific):

Which signature would you demand first: the judge who dismisses, the prosecutor who declines appeal, or the administrator who chooses containment language?

Where does your own organisation hide behind "we can't prove it" while still knowing what it is protecting?

If you were Jeroen, what would you need, structurally, to keep you from becoming the problem for reporting the truth?

If you were inside the institution, what is the single safeguard you'd require before any "return to work" in another trust-adjacent role is allowed?

85

"THE JUDGE'S VENDETTA"

SEX AND MONEY DON'T MAKE CHOICES. THEY ARE INSTRUMENTS.

Judicial misconduct, Russia, 2021 (composite case)

In St. Petersburg, winter doesn't simply arrive-it occupies. The Neva hardens into a slate of ice. Breath becomes visible truth. Streetlamps cast halos in the snow as if the city itself is trying to sanctify its own endurance. Everything looks clean when it's frozen. That's the illusion cold provides: it makes disorder appear paused, as though corruption cannot move in sub-zero air.

But corruption doesn't need warmth. It needs people.

Judge Alexei Petrov presided over a prominent courthouse with the air of unassailable authority. His ceremonial black robe and crisply tied jabot signalled centuries of judicial tradition, the impartiality expected of Russian courts. Lawyers, clerks, defendants-everyone met him with a kind of controlled posture, as if the room had agreed on a single rule: do not provoke the man behind the bench. Petrov cultivated that posture carefully. He spoke about order. He invoked the dignity of the law. He wore the costume so convincingly that people did what institutions always hope they'll do: they confused the uniform with the moral body inside it.

Behind the facade, he kept a ledger.

Not just money, but a record of compliance: who yielded, who paid, who obeyed. The ledger did what ledgers always do-it made human life reducible to entries. It removed tone and left only notes. And Petrov, like a conductor who mistakes volume for music, learned how to cue people into fear.

His misconduct was systematic and deliberate. Junior attorneys seeking promotion, court clerks seeking advancement, defendants seeking favorable rulings-each encountered the same quiet mechanism. Sexual exploitation arrived under the language of mentorship. Financial extortion arrived as "administrative fees," "donations," contributions to projects that were never truly public. The robe and jabot amplified everything, turning implicit threats into something that felt official. Victims didn't experience him as one man asking too much; they experienced him as the system itself leaning closer.

Ekaterina Morozova, a defence attorney, first encountered Petrov's coercion during her second year in practice. Her superiors assigned her a high-profile case and summoned her to his chambers "to discuss procedure." Her superiors assigned her a high-profile case and summoned her to his chambers "to discuss procedure." Because in a courthouse, procedure is not neutral. Procedure is power with grammar.

The meeting was not dramatic. Petrov didn't shout. He didn't corner her with melodrama. He simply spoke, presenting certain assumptions as already agreed upon: her future could be smooth or jagged. His tone implied inevitability. He didn't say, give me something. He said: "You know how this works."

This is where disaster begins: not with the product-sex or money-but with the story someone tells themselves about choice.

Sex and money pull people into disaster because they are easy to justify. One can frame sex as affection, "mutual," and an inevitable human appetite.One can frame sex as affection, "mutual," and an inevitable human appetite. Money can be framed as a necessity, a reward, or an efficiency. But what else pulls people in? The things that are harder to name: vanity, hunger for control, resentment, boredom, the desire to feel above ordinary rules. The craving to be the exception. The wish to conduct the world like an orchestra.

Petrov craved not only sex or money. He found addiction in the sensation of deciding.

That's why the metaphor matters: sex and money are not authors of catastrophe. They are instruments. They do not choose to be played. They do not choose the tune. A person chooses. A person reads the notes and still misses the tone. The tragedy is not in desire or currency; it is in the musician who uses them to turn other people into sound.

Financial extortion ran alongside sexual coercion. Discretionary case fees, administrative funds, fines-money moved like meltwater under ice, redirected into Petrov's ventures or distributed to allies who reinforced his reach. Refusal carried consequences that were rarely explicit but always felt: stalled promotions, lost client opportunities, sudden procedural strictness that seemed to appear only when someone displeased him. The courtroom, which should protect the vulnerable, became a stage where vulnerability was harvested.

And yet the system helped him.

Administrators saw irregularities and called them "style." Senior colleagues sensed patterns and called them "eccentricity." Oversight committees, where they existed, lingered, as if speed itself would be a scandal.

Reporting mechanisms existed in the way fire extinguishers exist: present in theory, hard to access when the smoke is already thick.

Here is the other thing that pulls people into disaster: silence-and the minor comforts silence buys. Silence buys stability. Silence buys reputation. Silence buys the illusion that you can outrun moral accounting. It turns a courthouse into a frozen river: everyone knows the ice is thin, but everyone keeps walking because stopping would mean admitting danger.

Ekaterina lived inside that contradiction. She carried the moral conflict like a second coat. Each time she told herself she was "enduring" for her clients, she wondered whether endurance was just another form of complicity. Some nights she imagined filing a report. Then she imagined the report disappearing. She imagined her cases becoming impossible, her name becoming a warning. In such places, courage is not only hard-it is expensive.

Eventually, investigative journalism and whistleblower accounts forced the matter into the light. The investigative journalism and whistleblower accounts corroborated the patterns. Petrov faced suspension and a criminal investigation. Reforms followed: monitoring, more transparent reporting, audits of discretionary funds. The institution, as institutions do, spoke in the language of prevention after years of permitting harm.

Yet for those harmed, "reform" is a word that arrives too late. What lingers is the internal damage: the way authority sounds afterward, the way a closed door feels, the way the jabot-once a symbol of justice-becomes a trigger. Careers bent. Some promising attorneys left the profession rather than keep paying the hidden fees of survival.

And Petrov? The ledger that once gave him mastery became evidence. The robe and jabot still existed, still carried their historical meaning, but the meaning had shifted. Symbols don't die; they tarnish. They mean two things at once: the ideal and the betrayal.

That is the ultimate point framing insists on: choices must be made. A priest makes a choice. A judge makes a choice. Sex and money don't make choices. They are instruments. The disaster begins when a person plays them in the wrong orchestra-when they read the notes of tradition, procedure, moral language, and still miss the tone of humanity.

Because the tone is this: power protects. When power uses human desire as leverage, it turns the law into acting without mercy-perfectly performed, technically correct, and spiritually false. And the curtains of the theatre have two sides. Both visible. Both are telling or hiding stories. Which one only depends on what side one is standing.

APPENDIX B - PRGR TOOLKIT (DETAILS, TRIGGERS, IMPLEMENTATION)

MORAL AUTHORSHIP IS NOT A WEAPON TO DISCIPLINE STAFF. IT IS A MIRROR HELD TO POWER.

This appendix collects the instrument chapters and implementation notes so the main narrative can move without repeating the technical scaffolding.

Moral authorship is not a weapon to discipline staff. It is a mirror held to power.

This appendix collects the instrument chapters and implementation notes so the main narrative can move without repeating the technical scaffolding.

THE ENGINE OF IRREVERSIBILITY

> The appeals process did not function like a rescue mission. It functioned like a funnel.

Procedural deadlines. Standards of review. Harmless error. Waiver. Deference. The vocabulary of not reopening what has already been closed.

Fresh evidence surfaced like bones after rain.

Someone pressured a witness. A report had been "misplaced." A forensic claim had been overstated with the confidence of a salesman. A timeline had been "interpreted." Each revelation was treated not as a moral emergency but as an administrative inconvenience.

The state did not argue, "He is guilty." It argued, "It is too late."

Time is the institution's favorite weapon because it looks neutral while doing violence. Time makes outrage tiring. Time makes families go broke. Time makes attorneys burn out. Time makes the public forget the details and remember only the label: convicted.

Time is mist.

And mist is useful because it blurs the line between events and their records.

Joshua sat in a cell and learned the real curriculum of a failed system: you can be correct and still lose. You can be innocent and still die. You can show the cracks and still be told the wall is sound because the wall has certified the wall.

Execution day arrived the way execution days always arrive: with normal weather, normal traffic, normal lunch breaks. Institutions don't tremble when they kill. They schedule.

Joshua's last hours were a procession of formality. Forms, signatures, witnesses behind glass. A chaplain offering words that sounded like mercy and felt like procedure.

When the needle entered his vein, no truth entered with it. Only the state.

His death did not prove guilt. It proved only that the system has a lever it refuses to admit is irreversible. This is the worst thing a system can do: convert uncertainty into death and call it order.

THE LIE OF THE "RIGHT PEOPLE"

The jury or kitchen table is a sacred cow.

Heresy is how people treat questioning it. But this book has lived too long in the rooms where people die from politeness.

A courtroom is not a town hall. It is a machine that processes evidence into irreversible outcomes.

And we keep feeding it ordinary human beings-good people, decent people, people who mean well-then pretending their decency qualifies them to interpret complex forensic science, assess coerced testimony, understand cognitive bias, recognize narrative manipulation, and resist the gravitational pull of authority. We seat them beneath the robe and tell them to be fearless.

But fear is contagious in court. Fear moves faster than logic.

We pretend emotions do not belong in a courtroom while building a courtroom that weaponized them: photographs, grieving families, prosecutorial outrage, a defendant's "demeanor," a judge's tone, a lawyer's polish, an accent, a pause, a stutter, a tear.

The system says it runs on facts.

In reality, it runs on human susceptibility.

And the most dangerous susceptibility of all lies in the desire to believe that the institution cannot be wrong, because if it can be wrong, then any of us can be consumed.

THE ARCHITECTURE OF HUMAN FAILURE

From individual error to systemic pattern.

"The Robe and The Ledger" reads less like a catalogue of separate miscarriages of justice and more like a single, repeating pattern, where institutions produce harm by doing what they are built to do. Taken together, the cases suggest that the central problem is not a few poor actors departing from the norm, but the norm itself-authoritative systems that can generate injury through routine, defensible, and even "proper" functioning.

What emerges is a quiet but devastating logic. When authority organizes itself around roles, rules, and procedures, it often treats moral judgment as a contaminant. The visible task becomes compliance: follow the process, satisfy the formal requirements, stay within the lane. The invisible cost is that responsibility migrates. It moves away from the person and into the office, away from conscience and into protocol. The robe and jabot are not just garments; they are instruments that help this migration feel natural. They mark a transformation in how the wearer sees themselves: not as an author of consequences, but as an agent of an authorised sequence.

This is how harm becomes possible without anyone needing to intend it. The person inside the role can sincerely believe they are acting correctly, even virtuously, while they treat the human impact as incidental-an externality that belongs to someone else, or to the system as a whole, or to "the way things work." It doesn't erase empathy outright; it narrows perception. Only what counts procedurally remains sharply in view.

Everything else-the lived reality of the people affected-fades into the background as noise.

The cases also show why this narrowing persists. Institutions train members to treat dissent as danger. The great existential risk is not injustice, but deviation: being seen as difficult, unprofessional, disloyal, naive, or unstable. In that economy of obedience, silence earns rewards, and they pathologize discomfort. Even when someone senses something is wrong, the system offers many ways to interpret that feeling as a personal failing rather than a signal: you're emotional; you don't understand the constraints; you're overreacting; you're not being objective. In this environment, "objectivity" becomes a rhetorical shelter for avoidance.

And once harm has occurred, the institution's priorities often shift from adjudication to self-protection. The institution treats legitimacy as survival, which makes error existential. The institution reframes accountability as an attack. The question stops being "What happened?" and becomes "What must we say, do, or withhold to preserve confidence?" That shift does not require conspiracy; it requires only a structure that equates admitting fault with losing authority.

One of the most corrosive features of the pattern is fragmentation. Responsibility is not merely shared; it is engineered into pieces small enough for everyone to deny ownership. Each participant can accurately claim, "I didn't make this decision." The result, at the level where outcomes are experienced, is catastrophe without authorship-harm that arrives fully formed while no one can be located as morally accountable. The procedure becomes a conveyor belt: many hands touch the object, and therefore no hand is responsible for what it becomes.

With repetition, moral attrition sets in. What once felt intolerable becomes manageable, then normal, then invisible. At that stage, observers no longer perceive injustice as a malfunction but accept it as proof that the system is stable. The machinery is working: complaints are absorbed, anomalies are neutralised, reputations are contained, and the institution continues uninterrupted. The cost is paid elsewhere-in the lives that are altered, diminished, or broken by outcomes that arrive stamped with legitimacy.

Therefore, the book's cases, read as a unified corpus, do more than critique individual decisions. They expose a structural conflict between legality and justice when authority is permitted to operate without ownership. Law becomes a ritual of correctness rather than a practice of responsibility. Decisions can be "sound" while being morally hollow. The symbols of justice remain in place, but their meaning drains away.

The damage does not end with the initial injury. There is a second layer of harm that comes from being injured by a system that one is told to trust, and then being met with procedural indifference, minimisation, or silence. The betrayal lies not only in the outcome, but in the institution's refusal to recognise the human reality of what it has done. That refusal deepens trauma because it denies the victim the basic acknowledgement that suffering is real and morally relevant.

Another consequence exists, less discussed but equally bleak: avoiding responsibility also diminishes those individuals. To act repeatedly under authority while refusing moral authorship is to gradually surrender ethical selfhood. The robe protects, but it hollows. The role offers safety at the price of agency, and eventually even the capacity to feel the loss may erode.

Seen this way, "The Robe and The Ledger - Robes, Jabots and Human Failure" does not argue that injustice requires malice. It argues something more unsettling: injustice can be the natural output of systems that make it easy to act without owning consequences. No grand plot is required-only design. Human vulnerabilities like fear, conformity, fatigue, and careerism do the rest, not as anomalies but as reliable inputs.

The missing condition of justice, across the unified pattern, is responsibility-personal, irreducible, and morally answerable responsibility inside formal authority. Procedural refinement may reduce some errors, but it cannot restore meaning if the system remains structured to disperse ownership and punish dissent. What is required is precisely what institutions resist: the reintroduction of moral accountability where it is most uncomfortable, even when it threatens hierarchy, convenience, and the institution's preferred self-image.

Without that, robes and jabots-and whatever other symbols authority adopts-will continue to function less than emblems of justice than as its camouflage.

ANTICIPATED INSTITUTIONAL COUNTER-ARGUMENTS - AND RESPONSES

Institutions confronted with critiques such as those advanced in this book respond in predictable ways. These responses are not signs of bad faith; they are part of the defensive logic the book analyses. Addressing them directly strengthens both the argument and its ethical seriousness.

> Counter-Argument 1:
> "These cases are exceptional, not representative."

This objection relies on statistical logic, where structural analysis is required. The argument is not that all institutional action is unjust, but that the mechanisms enabling injustice are recurrent and normalised. The similarity lies not in outcomes, but in processes: role absorption, responsibility diffusion, procedural defensiveness.

Exceptional harm does not disprove systemic vulnerability. It reveals it.

> Counter-Argument 2:
> "Institutions must follow rules; discretion would create chaos."

This is a false dichotomy. The book does not argue against rules, but against rule-following without moral ownership. Bureaucratic and legal theorists have long recognised that discretion is unavoidable. The debate centers on whether discretion exists and whether it receives ethical acknowledgment or institutional denial. A system that claims to eliminate discretion merely conceals it-often in ways that evade accountability.

Counter-Argument 3:
"We cannot hold individuals responsible for systemic outcomes."

The book does not argue for individual blame in isolation. It argues for moral responsibility without scapegoating. Responsibility is not synonymous with punishment. It is the acknowledgment that one's actions take part in outcomes that affect human lives.

To deny all individual responsibility is to accept a system where harm has no moral owner-an ethically untenable position.

Counter-Argument 4:
"Retrospective moral judgment is unfair."

This objection misunderstands ethical evaluation. Moral responsibility is not a matter of hindsight perfection but of contemporaneous awareness. Many cases show that warnings were available, people raised concerns, and alternatives existed-but the institution discouraged these alternatives.

The issue is not failure to foresee everything, but refusal to see what was already visible.

Counter-Argument 5:
"Critique undermines public trust in institutions."

The opposite is more plausible. Critique undermined public trust not, but by unacknowledged harm and defensive silence. Trust depends on the belief that institutions can recognise and correct their own failures. A system that demands trust while resisting responsibility erodes its own legitimacy.

Closing reflection

Institutions often respond to critique by asking: "Where does this end?"

The answer offered by this book is simple and demanding: ***it ends where responsibility begins.***

"The Robe and the Ledger - Robes, Jabots and Human Failure" does not call for moral heroism. It calls for moral presence-the willingness of individuals within institutions to remain human, answerable, and ethically awake, even when procedure invites silence.

Without that presence, justice becomes a performance. With it, institutions may once again deserve the authority they claim.

THE LINE THAT CANNOT BE CROSSED

A non-negotiable mechanism
for institutional accountability

This book has shown the problem repeatedly. It now ends the indulgence.

If an institution claims legitimacy while refusing the mechanism below, that refusal is no longer defensible as prudence, complexity, or risk management. It becomes evidence.

What follows is not a proposal among many. It is the minimum condition under which authority may still plausibly claim moral standing.

The mechanism:
Mandatory Personal Reason-Giving Record
(PRGR)

For every institutional decision that foreseeably causes serious harm, one named individual must justify the harm in writing, in their own words, to the person harmed-and sign it.

No delegation. No collective authorship. No procedural substitution. No anonymity. Hard conditions (this is where institutions flinch)

Trigger is objective, not discretionary

PRGR is mandatory when a decision foreseeably affects:

- liberty
- livelihood
- legal standing

- professional exclusion
- long-term reputational harm
- physical or psychological safety

If harm is foreseeable, the record is required. There is no exemption for urgency, hierarchy, or tradition.

Authorship is forced

The institution must designate one Responsible Signatory. Not: the committee; the department; the chair; the office. One human being.

This does not assign sole liability. It assigns undeniable moral authorship.

If no one will sign, the institution has already admitted the decision is unjustifiable.

Justification is substantive,not procedural

The justification must explicitly answer:

- What harm will this decision cause to you?
- Why is causing this harm acceptable rather than preventing it?
- What less harmful alternative did I reject-and why?

The following phrases invalidate the record if used as justification:

- "Policy requires..."
- "Procedure dictates..."
- "I lacked discretion..."
- "This was not my decision..."

They may be mentioned. They may not be the reason.

If the harm cannot be justified without hiding behind structure, the decision fails.

The audience is the harmed person

This is not intended for supervisors, legal counsel, courts and archives. It is written to the person harmed.

This single feature collapses moral distance more effectively than any training, code, or audit ever devised.

Irreversibility

Once issued, the PRGR cannot be edited, anonymised, or withdrawn.

It becomes part of the permanent institutional record, reviewable in any later proceeding. Institutions may explain. They may not erase.

Why this is unavoidable

All cases prove three things beyond dispute:

- Harm persists because no one has to say: "I chose this."
- Institutions survive because they spread responsibility too thinly, causing it to disappear.
- Ethical failure is structural, not attitudinal.

PRGR attacks all three simultaneously. It does not rely on virtue, courage, empathy, training, or culture change. It relies on exposure.

Why institutions will fight this (and why that matters)

Institutions will claim: legal risk, chilling effects, operational paralysis, unfair personal burden.

These objections are revealing. Institutions already tolerate audits, compliance documentation, internal reviews, external oversight, and endless reporting.

They object only when the cost is moral ownership. That is the point.

An institution that cannot survive requiring one person to say "I believe this harm is justified" does not deserve the authority to cause harm at all.

THE RED LINE

From this point forward, the moral test is simple:

No inquiry into intent is required. No one needs to speculate about the complexity. The refusal itself is the finding.

This is not idealism. It is a boundary.

The PRGR does not promise justice. It promises no more unowned injustice.

It will not eliminate harm. It will eliminate harmless harm-harm no one admits to causing. And that alone would have prevented or altered most cases in this book.

Ultimate word to institutions

You may retain hierarchy, procedure, discretion, authority. You may not retain harm without authorship.

If you refuse this mechanism, you are no longer managing risk or preserving order. You are protecting a system that depends on human disappearance.

From here on, silence is no longer neutrality. It is a choice.

And choice, at last, has a name.

THE PRGR MANUAL (IMPLEMENTATION GUARDRAILS)

Institutions will try to turn PRGR into a form. They will automate it, template it, dilute it, and call the dilution "implementation." This manual exists to prevent that.

PRGR is not transparency, training, or compliance. It is a structural constraint: if you will cause foreseeable serious harm, you own that harm in writing, to the person harmed, under your name.

A. The minimum moral standard

A PRGR exists only if all the following remain true-no matter the institution, no matter the jurisdiction:

- **Trigger is objective:** PRGR is mandatory when a decision foreseeably affects liberty, livelihood, legal standing, professional exclusion, long-term reputational harm, or physical/psychological safety.
- **One Responsible Signatory:** one human being is designated as the author. Not "the committee." Not "the department." Not "the office."
- **Substantive justification:** the signatory answers three questions:
  (1) what harm will this cause you?
  (2) why is causing it acceptable rather than preventing it?
  (3) what less harmful alternative did I reject-and why?
- **Audience is the harmed person:** written to the person harmed, not to counsel, not to supervisors, not to the archive.
- **Irreversibility:** it cannot be edited, anonymised, or withdrawn. Corrections happen as dated addenda, never as quiet replacements.

B. A system, not a document

PRGR fails when it is issued after the harm is already locked in. It must be embedded as a pipeline with gates-points where the institution cannot proceed without authorship:

- Gate A - **Triage:** Does the decision meet the trigger threshold?
- Gate B - **Ownership:** who has real stop-power here (and therefore must sign)?
- Gate C - **Alternatives:** what less harmful option was considered and rejected?
- Gate D - **Delivery:** how is the PRGR delivered in a comprehensible way to the person harmed?
- Gate E - **Permanence:** where is it stored, who can audit it, and how are addenda handled?

C. Role design: authorship without scapegoating

PRGR dies if you force a powerless person to sign on behalf of a system. The Responsible Signatory should be the smallest role that stops, modifies, or delays the decision, or forces a higher review. If no such role exists, the institution has built harm into the architecture.

D. The veto lane

Every PRGR system requires at least one veto lane: a step where the decision cannot proceed until the signatory has named the harm, named the less harmful alternative, and written why it is rejected. This is where "technical truth" stops being mere input and becomes a moral choice.

E. Records architecture: permanence without reckless exposure

Permanence is non-negotiable. Public broadcast is not. Use two-layer permanence:

- **Delivered PRGR:** addressed to the harmed person, in plain language, without legal fog.
- **Sealed institutional PRGR file:** kept for appeal/oversight/audit; access-logged; append-only.

Irreversibility means you cannot erase. It does not mean you cannot clarify. You may add. You may not rewrite history.

F. Anti-boilerplate controls

Copying can complete if PRGR last week's phrasing, it has already failed. Build resistance into the system:

- **Plain-language rule:** cross-references and policy citations are not reasons.
- **Alternative-analysis rule: at least one rejected less harmful alternative must be specific, plausible, and operational.**
- **Repetition audits**: oversight flags identical phrasing across PRGRs as evidence of procedural laundering.

G. Due process and workforce protections

PRGR must not replace due process; it must expose the human choice inside it. Where hearings exist, PRGR is issued after the person has responded-except for interim emergency measures (which require an interim PRGR and a later final PRGR).

PRGR also requires protections:

- Good-faith signatories are indemnified.
- Refusal-to-sign when honest justification is impossible is protected.
- PRGR is resourced as governance work, not treated as an extra punishment. Moral authorship is not a weapon to discipline staff. It is a mirror held to power.

APPENDIX C - READER INDEXES (CHAPTERS 1-52, CASEFILES 53-85)

INDEX BY COUNTRY - INDEX BY SUBJECT

Index by Country

Country - Chapters 1-52; Case files 53-85. Entry numbers (Part in brackets).

Index by Subject

Subject - Chapters 1-52; Case files 53-85. Entry numbers (Part in brackets).

APPENDIX D - PRGR END-CAP

INDEX CORE OF THE CASE.

Chapters

Chapter 2 - THE PROSECUTOR'S SHADOW

- Core: A prosecutor weaponizes "ordinary management" (assignments, evaluations, access) to convert mentorship into career control and quietly throttle a junior's future.

Chapter 6 - THE GABBAI'S KITTEL

- Core: A charity gatekeeper uses sanctity and "dignity" framing to block oversight, turning donation handling into untraceable discretionary power over money and people.

Chapter 11 - THE IMAM AND THE DONATION LIST

- Core: A donation list becomes a lever: publicised giving is used to allocate status and pressure, converting generosity into governance and coercion.

Chapter 12 - THE ARCHBISHOP'S SILENT DEAL

- Core: A church leader's 'quiet deal' trades truth for institutional protection, normalising off-record bargaining with external power to keep scandal and accountability sealed.

Chapter 16 - THE MONSIGNOR'S HIDDEN DESIRE

- Core: A senior cleric uses closeness and spiritual framing to erode boundaries, tying opportunities and reputation to compliance while keeping the risk deniable.

Chapter 21 - THE DEAN'S COMPROMISED AGENDA

- Core: A university dean manages the record-minutes, wording, and internal 'resolution'-so harm becomes procedural vapour and the institution can pretend nothing substantive happened.

Chapter 26 - THE ADVOCATE'S DARK DEAL

- Core: An advocate's back-channel bargain with organised crime bends advocacy into collusion, using courtroom legitimacy to launder outcomes while keeping hands 'clean.'

Chapter 31 - THE WARNING LETTER of THE QUIET ERASURE

- Core: This case turns on the warning letter and its procedural framing: the author is 'quietly erased' through administrative language that avoids naming a decision-maker or acknowledging foreseeable harm.

Chapter 32 - THE LAWYER WHO SENT THE INNOCENT TO DEATH

- Core: A defence lawyer's strategic choices and silence steer an innocent client toward death; the system then redistributes blame through procedure and finality.

Chapter 37 - THE MAGISTRATE'S SHADOW

- Core: A magistrate is pressured into 'survival for an institutional decision that can cause irreversible harm' compromises under criminal influence; small procedural choices become the shadow mechanism that reshapes justice.

Chapter 43 - THE RECEIVER'S INVOICE AND THE COURT'S SILENCE

- Core: A case to serve as a warning rather than an example of how to do things differently, the courts sacrificed a lawyer after needing an example.

Chapter 44 - THE PROSECUTOR'S GAME

- Core: A prosecutor treats cases like a game of emphasis and timing-perfect punctuation, selective action-so the worst harm arrives packaged as routine process.

Chapter 48 - THE BARRISTER'S GLIDE

- Core: A high-profile barrister 'glides' through accountability by rearranging blame and narrative until it looks like responsibility, while the substantive wrongdoing stays untouched.

Chapter 50 - THE VERDICT THAT OUTLIVED THE TRUTH

- Core: A wrongful-execution pathway persists because the system refuses the exact moment correction is possible; procedure protects finality over truth.

CASE FILES

case file 55 - THE BISHOP'S COMPLICITY

- Core: A bishop enables and shields wrongdoing through office and discretion, turning pastoral authority into institutional cover for irreversible harm.

case file 59 - THE ABBÉ WHO COUNTED COINS

- Core: An abbé treats coins and accounts as a private instrument, using religious trust to justify opacity while money becomes a control surface.

case file 65 - THE BISHOP'S LEDGER

- Core: A bishop's ledger becomes the centre of power: records are curated, access is managed, and accountability is displaced into paperwork and silence.

case file 69 - THE PROFESSOR WHO CLAIMED OTHERS' GENIUS

- Core: A professor captures credit and authorship, claiming others' genius and using status to make exploitation of work feel 'normal' and unchallengeable.

case file 74 - THE ORDINARY PROFESSIONALS

- Core: Ordinary professionals-no villains, just role-players-keep harm moving by doing "their part," letting procedure substitute for conscience.

case file 79 - THE JUDGE'S SILENCE

- Core: A judge's silence-at the moment speech matters-functions as the decision; the record stays clean while the harm becomes permanent.

case file 84 - THE FALLEN MAGISTRATE

- Core: A judge's defence - instead of admitting when needed to take responsibility - evidentiary standards become a shield.

APPENDIX E (SUPPLEMENT)-PRGR PILOT:

"IRREVERSIBLE DECISION PATHWAY" (12 WEEKS)

IMPLEMENTATION MODEL

Hard-nosed scaffolding: governance, budget, audit trail, and failure modes

PURPOSE AND POISTURE

This appendix treats PRGR as a test condition, not a moral slogan: harm must be authored; the forecast must be written; and repair must be pre-committed. The implementation stance is deliberately non-romantic: it does not assume angels. It assumes ordinary humans in robes will drift toward convenience unless the drift has a cost.

PRGR exists to stop institutions from converting harm into weather - something that 'happened,' rather than something someone did - by forcing authorship: a system must name an author, not a process.

PILOT OVERVIEW

A. PILOT LANE

The PRGR pilot should run on a single, high-stakes pathway where irreversible harm is common and deniable. The goal is to choose a lane that regularly produces irreversible outcomes, and where procedural ambiguity can be used as a shield.

Recommended pilot lane: employment termination / credential removal / expulsion / disbarment / dismissal (select one institutional variant).

B. PILOT RULE

PRGR is mandatory at two gated moments only:

1. Pre-action gate: immediately before the last reversible step (e.g., before issuing a termination letter; before publishing a reputational label; before sealing or withholding evidence).

2. Post-action gate: on a fixed review date (mandatory reopen even if nobody complains).

C. PILOT DURATION AND VOLUME

1. Duration: 12 weeks (long enough for drift, short enough to hold attention).

2. Expected volume: 50-150 decisions (depending on lane).

3. Goal: measure whether PRGR reduces preventable harm and procedural manipulation, rather than argue about intentions.

D. THE LINE PRGR DRAWS

PRGR is not 'extra paperwork.' It is a workflow lock: a decision cannot proceed past the last reversible step until the PRGR exists and is stored in a place that can be audited.

E. DEFINITIONS

LAST REVERSIBLE STEP

The last action point before the institution triggers a consequence that cannot be cleanly undone (or whose reversal becomes theoretical rather than real). Examples: issuing formal notice; publishing a reputation label; disabling access credentials; closing a file that forecloses appeal.

IRREVERSIBLE HARM (pilot-relevant)

Harm is treated as foreseeable and actionable when it affects liberty, livelihood, reputation, safety, or access - especially when the institution can later hide behind procedure.

REMEDY TRIGGER

A remedy trigger is not a punishment. It is a pre-agreed repair path that activates without begging.

THE PRGR RECORD

One page, maximum plus anchors.

PRGR is constrained to one page, but it is not allowed to be vague. The record must contain the core fields below, and it must attach verifiable anchors that make claims auditable.

DECISION BEING TAKEN

Plain-language description of the action.

DECISION-AUTHOR AND REVIEWER

Names and roles; the reviewer is empowered to reject/return the record.

FACTS RELIED ON

What you believe is true; and explicitly, what you have not checked.

FORSEEABLE HARM

What could happen to a person if you are wrong.

Why proceeding is justified given the forecast harm.

DISCLOSURE STATEMENT

What was shared; what was withheld; and why.

REMEDY TRIGGER

What automatically happens if later evidence shows you were wrong.

REVIEW DATE

When the decision must be reopened, even if nobody complains.

ANCHOR REQUIREMENT (ANTI-THEATRE)

Every PRGR must attach at least two verifiable anchors:

- One primary document (notes, report, signed statement, assessment).
- One system extract (email thread, access log, version history, case timeline).

F. COUNTER-BOILERPLATE RULES

The PRGR is rejected if any of the following are true:

- 'What you have not checked' is empty.

- Foreseeable harm is generic ('impact to stakeholders') rather than person-legible.
- Remedy trigger is absent, discretionary, or framed as 'may consider.'
- Disclosure statement is replaced with 'confidential' without an explanation.
- Required anchors are missing or non-verifiable.

G. THE PEOPLE

Decision-Author (DA)

The person with ultimate authority. The DA cannot disappear into 'committee,' 'policy,' or 'the office.'

Reviewer (RV)

Peer senior enough to block progression; outside the DA's direct reporting line; empowered to reject/return PRGRs.

Custodian (CU)

Maintains the PRGR register and permissions; enforces workflow locks; runs audit sampling; escalates discrepancies.

Independent Review Pool (IRP)

Panel convened when remedy triggers fire or audits flag material issues; outside the chain of command that benefited.

Executing Office (EO)

Implements the decision; countersigns where execution can be used as a shield.

H. AUTHORITY TO STOP THE LINE

1. RV can reject and return PRGRs.
2. CU can block progression if the record is missing, incomplete, or non-auditable.
3. IRP can trigger stays, reopenings, and referrals when defined thresholds are met.

For the pilot lane, PRGR is required whenever the institution is about to do something that cannot be cleanly undone, or that predictably silences challenge.

- Irreversible steps: dismissal/expulsion/credential removal.
- Reputation locks: labels like 'vexatious,' 'unreliable,' or 'non-compliant' that become fate.
- Secrecy walls: redactions, sealed files, privilege claims, 'handled internally.'

A PRGR is only as real as its audit trail. The register must be tamper-evident and maintained by CU.

- PRGR ID; case ID (or pseudonymous hash); timestamps (created/reviewed/executed).
- DA and RV identities; EO identity where applicable.
- Trigger type (irreversible step / reputation lock / secrecy wall).
- Remedy trigger(s) selected.
- Review date.
- Attachment list with integrity hashes or immutable version references.

When a signatory lies, the system must not respond with 'training.' It must respond with cost. Detection controls:

- Mandatory 'what you have not checked' field; cannot be blank.
- Anchor verification (document + system extract).

- Text similarity checks (boilerplate detection).
- Discrepancy flags when later evidence conflicts with the PRGR record. Enforcement response (ladder):

Perverse incentives include risk dumping, scapegoating, and over-caution. The pilot must treat these as measurable failure conditions.

Controls:

- Dual accountability: DA signs for decision; EO countersigns for execution where execution can be used as a shield.
- Disclosure discipline: if information is withheld, the PRGR must state why.
- Alternative rejected requirement: state the alternative considered and rejected.
- Mandatory review-date reopen prevents permanent freezes and forces learning loops.

Boilerplate is an attempt to resurrect 'process as alibi.'

- Automatic similarity detection and rejection thresholds.
- Rejection triggers: generic harm language; missing 'not checked'; missing anchors; vague remedy triggers.
- Internal metrics: boilerplate rate by unit (pressure upward).

The pilot binds remedy triggers to measurable conditions so repair is automatic rather than begged for.

I. DEFAULT REMEDY TRIGGER PACK

1. Immediate preservation order (no disposal; no 'lost files').
2. Temporary stay while review is pending.

3. Automatic reopen/rehearing when defined doubt threshold is met.

4. Independent review outside the benefiting chain of command.

5. Restitution pathway (correction of record; reinstatement where applicable).

6. Referral trigger where fabrication or conflict is suspected.

J. DEFINED DOUBT TRESHOLD

Define doubt in a way that cannot be dissolved into vibes. Example definitions:

- New evidence contradicts a core asserted fact relied on in PRGR.
- Anchor verification fails (missing, altered, or incompatible record).
- A procedural irregularity is discovered that materially affected the decision pathway.

PRGR without an audit is ceremonial. This budget assumes reuse of existing case systems and the smallest viable lock + register.

K. (indicative) PEOPLE

1. 0.5 FTE Custodian / Program Manager (register, permissions, reporting).

2. 0.2 FTE Legal/Policy (privacy, HR/industrial constraints, disclosure rules).

3. 0.5 FTE Workflow/Systems engineer (workflow locks, versioning, logging).

4. 0.4 FTE Audit Analyst (sampling, anchor verification, escalation).

5. Independent Review Pool (sitting fees, as-needed).

L. TOOLS AND OPERATIONS

1. Tamper-evident storage and logging (prefer existing platforms with immutable history).

2. Training sessions and internal communications.

3. Simple analytics (sampling, boilerplate detection, trigger tracking).

M. BUDGET PRINCIPLES

The non-negotiable spend is audit. Without it, PRGR becomes costume: passive voice returns, secrecy becomes virtue again, and process resumes its role as alibi.

N. METRICS (how the pilot is judged)

Core outcome measures

1. Preventable harm indicators: reversals, successful appeals, reinstatements, proven factual errors, verified procedural manipulation events.

2. Time-to-resolution versus quality: whether PRGR slows decisions without improving correctness.

3. Disclosure quality: meaningful disclosure statements versus blanket confidentiality.

4. Remedy activation rate: how often triggers fire; what outcomes result.

5. Integrity measures(anti-theatre)

- Boilerplate rate (text similarity).
- Anchor verification pass rate.
- Completeness rate for 'what you have not checked.'
- Audit discrepancy rate and severity.

O. CULTURAL SIGNAL

Evidence that decisions previously described as 'system outcomes' are now authored, named, and revisitable.

P. IMPLEMENTATION TIME LINE(12-week plan)

Week 0-1: Build the lock

- Define pilot lane and trigger moments.
- Configure workflow gating: no PRGR ID, no irreversible step.
- Create register and immutable storage.

Week 2: Train for specificity

- Train authors and reviewers on 'not checked,' foreseeable harm, disclosure writing, and remedy triggers.
- Train auditors on anchor verification and discrepancy escalation.

Weeks 3-10: Run and audit

- Run the lane; enforce Gate 1 and Gate 2.
- Audit weekly; apply the enforcement ladder when discrepancies appear.

Weeks 11-12: Close out and publish findings

- Publish results against critique criteria: harm reduction, fairness impacts, perverse incentive evidence, cost/benefit.
- Decide: scale, modify, or terminate.

TEMPLATES

PRGR form-(one page)

Copy/paste template (complete all fields; attach anchors):

PRGR ID

- Case / Matter ID Trigger type
- Irreversible step / reputation lock / secrecy wall / other
- Decision being taken (plain language)
- Decision-Author (name, role)
- Reviewer (name, role)
- Executing office (if applicable)
- Facts relied on - what I believe to be true
- Facts relied on - what I have not checked
- Foreseeable harm if I am wrong
- Why I proceed despite that risk
- Disclosure statement - shared
- Disclosure statement - withheld and why
- Remedy trigger(s) and thresholds
- Review date
- Anchors attached - document
- Anchors attached - system extract

- Integrity references (hash/version IDs)
- Signatures–Decision Author
- Signatures–Reviewer
- Signatures–Executing office (if applicable)

Audit checklist (weekly sampling)

1. ◻ PRGR exists prior to the last reversible step.
2. ◻ All required fields are present and specific.
3. ◻ Anchors exist and match the claims.
4. ◻ Disclosure statement includes reasons for withholding (if any).
5. ◻ Remedy trigger is concrete (automatic, threshold-based).
6. ◻ Review date is set and tracked.
7. ◻ Boilerplate similarity flagged and handled.
8. ◻ If discrepancies exist: stay/reopen/referral actions taken as required.

This appendix exists to prevent the institutional reflex of minimization - truth invited in, thanked for attending, then seated where it cannot touch consequence. The pilot model above corners the institution into a measurable choice: if the decision cannot survive a signature, it should not survive at all.

GLOSSARY

A

Abaya - a loose outer cloak worn in some Muslim communities.

Acta - official records; "the paperwork that proves what happened."

Affidavit - a written statement sworn to be true.

Altar - the main table/holy focus point in a church.

Appeal - asking a higher authority/court to review a decision.

Arbitration - a private decision process outside a public court.

B

Bands / Neckbands - the white strips worn at the neck by some judges/barristers.

Beit din - a Jewish religious court.

Bimah - the raised platform in a synagogue where readings/prayers happen.

Bisht - a formal cloak of status in some Arab contexts.

Bribery - trading money/favors for decisions.

C

Cassock - a long clerical robe worn by some priests.

Censure / Reprimand - an official scolding by a professional body.

Chain of custody - the documented path showing who handled evidence.

Chambers - a judge's private office.

Charism(a) - personal magnetism that makes people follow without thinking.

Compliance - "rule-following"; sometimes used as a mask for ethics.

Composite story - a story built from several real patterns, not one person.

Countersignature - a required second sign-off by an independent role to reduce lone-author abuse.

D

Dayan - a judge in a Jewish religious court.

Deference - automatic respect that discourages questions.

Defendant - the person accused in court.

Discovery - the process of sharing evidence/documents in a case.

Due process - basic fairness rules: notice, a chance to respond, impartial decision-maker.

E

Eid - major Muslim religious festival days.

Eminence / Excellency - formal titles for senior clergy.

Enkolpion - a pectoral (chest-worn) religious medallion/icon (often for bishops).

Entropy - the natural drift toward disorder; "things fall apart unless maintained."

Epitrachelion - an Orthodox stole worn around the neck by priests.

Ethics body - a professional authority that investigates misconduct.

F

Facade - the "official face" that hides what's inside.

FOI (Freedom of Information) - laws that let the public request government records.

Forensic - technical evidence work (documents, DNA, data, etc.).

Foundation (legal) - an organization used to hold/manage money or assets.

G

Gabbai - a synagogue administrator/organizer; often handles logistics and funds.

Governance - how an organization is run: who decides, who checks, who reports.

Grant - funding given for research or projects.

Grey zone - not clearly illegal, but ethically rotten.

H

Habeas corpus - a legal demand that a detained person be brought before a court.

Harassment - repeated unwanted behavior that intimidates or pressures someone.

Hierarchy - rank order; "who is above whom."

Hillul Hashem - "desecration of God's name"; often invoked to avoid scandal.

I

Ikhlas - sincerity; doing good without seeking praise (Islamic concept).

Imam - a Muslim prayer leader.

Imamah - a turban-style wrap (varies by region).

Impartial - not taking sides; fair.

Incense - aromatic smoke used in some worship.

Institutional capture - when outsiders/insiders bend an institution to serve them.

Irreversible harm - harm that cannot realistically be undone (e.g., execution, deportation, permanent reputational or liberty loss).

J

Jabot - a decorative white neckpiece worn with robes in some legal/ceremonial dress.

Judicial review - a court checking whether official decisions followed the law.

Jurisdiction - the area/authority where a law or court has power.

Jubbah / Thawb - long robe-like garments worn in some Muslim cultures.

K

Keffiyeh / Shemagh - a headscarf worn in parts of the Middle East.

Kippah - a Jewish skullcap.

Kittel - a white robe worn by some Jews on holy days.

Khutbah - a sermon (often the Friday sermon in a mosque).

L

Lashon hara - "harmful speech" (gossip/slander) in Jewish ethics; sometimes misused to silence criticism.

Ledger - a record of money in/out; an account book.

Legitimacy - the public belief that an authority "has the right" to decide.

Liability - legal responsibility for harm or loss.

M

Magistrate - a judge (often for lower-level matters; varies by country).

Ma'at - ancient Egyptian idea of truth/balance/order.

Mantle - a ceremonial cloak (religious or academic).

Mentorship - guidance from a senior person; can be used as cover for control.

Moral authorship - a named person taking responsibility for the reasons, foreseeable harms, and repair commitments of a decision.

Minbar - the pulpit in a mosque where sermons are delivered.

Misconduct - serious bad behavior in a professional role.

N

Narrative management - shaping the story so the institution looks "clean."

Nave - the main central space of a church.

NMR - Nuclear Magnetic Resonance

Nuremberg - post-WWII trials emphasizing personal responsibility for atrocities.

O

Ombudsman - an independent complaints investigator.

Opaque - hard to see through; unclear; secretive.

Oversight - independent checking power; "who watches the watchers."

P

Patronage - favors/jobs/resources given for loyalty, not merit.

Pectoral - worn on the chest.

Plea bargain - a deal: plead guilty for a reduced charge/sentence.

Procedure - the official steps; sometimes used as a shield against truth.

PRGR (Personal Reason-Giving Record) - a signed written record of reasons for an institutional decision that can cause irreversible harm.

PRGR END-CAP - the structured end-of-case prompt that identifies the mechanism, decision-point, trigger, and repair pathway.

Proportionality - "not excessive"; a response that fits the issue.

Prosecutor - the lawyer representing the state/government in criminal cases.

Public record - information officially available to the public.

Q

Qabba - a garment collar or neckband (term varies by region).

Quorum - the minimum number needed to make a decision official.

R

Reassignment - moving a person to another role/location instead of confronting the harm.

Recusal - stepping aside because of conflict of interest.

Red line - a non-negotiable threshold where PRGR is triggered because foreseeable harm is irreversible or severe.

Remedy trigger - a pre-committed repair action that activates if the forecasted harm occurs (or if key safeguards fail).

Regulator - an authority that enforces rules.

Retaliation - punishing someone for complaining or reporting.

S

Sacristy - a room where church items/vestments are kept.

Sadaqah - voluntary charity (Islam).

Sanction - a penalty imposed by an authority.

Sealed record - information kept private by rule or order.

Separation of powers - splitting power so one group can't control everything.

Shell company - a company used mainly to hide ownership/money movement.

Stole - a long scarf-like vestment worn by clergy.

Sublease - when a tenant rents the space to someone else.

T

Tallit - Jewish prayer shawl.

Thawb - see Jubbah

Tzitzit - the fringes on a tallit (ritual reminders).

Tzedakah - charity/justice-giving in Jewish tradition.

Trust (legal) - a structure that holds assets for someone else under rules.

Tribunal - a formal decision panel (often professional discipline).

U

Undertow - a hidden current; metaphor for unseen institutional force.

V

Vestments - religious ceremonial clothing.

Vicar / Parish priest - a local church priest (terms vary).

Whistleblower - someone who reports wrongdoing inside an institution.

W

Waqf - an Islamic charitable endowment (property held for religious/public benefit).

Writ - a formal court order/document.

Z

Zakat - obligatory charity (Islam).

SYNONYMS

Understanding Robes and Jabots from around the World

In the world of legal and ceremonial attire, terms for robes and jabots often vary depending on the country and tradition. These garments, while serving similar functions, may go by different names depending on cultural context, profession, and historical influence.

Robes

- **Capes**–sometimes used in a ceremonial context in some European courts -
- **Cassocks**–typical clerical robes, used by religious figures like priests and bishops -
- **Exorason/anteri** (outer), cassock (inner), monastic black robe, **mantya/cloak** are Coptic / Greek / Orthodox equivalents -
- **Gowns**–usually used in the UK, the United States, and Canada -
- **Judicial robes**–a more generic term used worldwide to describe the formal attire of judges -
- **Kapoteh/bekishe**–Rabbinic frock/long coat - black suit, **kittel** (high holy days), dayanim's formal attire (varies by community). Jewish robes equivalents -

- **Mantles**–often used in religious or academic contexts, such as in Catholic Church settings -
- **Thawb/jubbah, bisht** (cloak of status), **abaya** (regional), judge's robe in civil systems. Muslim robes equivalents-
- **Togas**–used in Brazil, Italy, the Netherlands, and some other civil law countries.

Jabots and Similar Neckpieces

- **Bands**–a common term in the UK, New Zealand, and some Commonwealth countries for the white neckpieces worn by barristers and judges -
- **Bef**–mostly a V-shaped neckpiece with folds, used in the Netherlands and Belgium -
- **Collars**–used in many European jurisdictions, such as France and Italy, as a less ornate alternative to jabots -
- **Cravats**–a type of cloth tie or neckpiece historically worn by aristocrats, similar in function to modern jabots in some European legal traditions -
- **Epitoga**–dressed over the left shoulder, a decoration made of white fur, to display academic achievement -
- **Epitrachelion**–stole-literally "around the neck", plus enkolpion medallion as "office made metal." Coptic / Greek / Orthodox equivalents -
- **Imamah–turban** wrap and tail, **keffiyeh/shemagh** folded at the collar, formal scarf/stole-like wraps used in some regions; also the microphone and minbar function as "neckpiece" equivalents jabots in Muslim symbolism (the voice made official) -
- **Neckbands**–often synonymous with bands, seen in countries like South Africa and Australia -

- **Ruffs**–elaborate neckpieces worn in early European courts, somewhat related to the jabot's function as a formal neckpiece -
- **Stoles**–used in religious contexts, such as by priests, or in academic regalia, similar to a ceremonial jabot -
- **Tallit**–draped at the shoulders/neck (with tzitzit visible), a **gartel** (belt) as ritual "binding," the **kippah** as constant public sign of role/obedience. Jewish jabot equivalents (neck/authority marker) -

While the terminology may vary, the purpose of these garments remains consistent across different countries and professions. They serve not only to signify professionalism, authority, and respect for tradition but also to reinforce the solemnity and dignity of the roles they represent-whether in a courtroom, a church, or a scientific institution.

DEDICATION

To my wife, and to our two beautiful daughters- who endured my long absences during the years I lived as a business director, and then endured a different absence when I became a father fighting a premature end of life. You swallowed what you should never have had to swallow: an institution that could not bend, could not see, could not make room for a human story. This book carries what I couldn't carry home. Love, regret, and gratitude for the life you kept holding together when mine was being rearranged infuse this writing.

And to Roger L.-lawyer, colleague, and friend- who cannot read these pages. Although he passed naturally, the system that brought me down also defeated him with its ignominy. A great man with a soft heart, deeply engaged with the personal problems of his clients, he never received a fair chance. I represented him through over 135 cases brought against him-nothing grand, nothing cinematic: minor disputes, arguable issues, matters that could have turned differently if the eyes reading them were willing to use minus instead of plus. Maybe he deserved scrutiny -but also proportion, dignity, and a hearing that was not already decided.

Roger, this is for you too.

And for all the victims of any system, alive or deceased.

ABOUT THE AUTHOR

Born in the Netherlands, Alex Matthews began his working life in the classroom-as a primary school teacher-before turning to economics and later teaching at high school level, preparing adolescents for university and other higher education. He eventually left education to become a director of several companies. At forty, a serious car accident changed everything. Told he would never return to work, he refused to accept a protocol that didn't match his ambitions. He enrolled in law and tax law, completing both within two and a half years. He practised as a lawyer and became a solicitor/barrister, tax lawyer, certified court mediator, chartered tax accountant, and arbitrator, moving within a highly engaged professional community in the legal world.

Then his story turned. The comfortable assumptions behind institutions, such as how authority speaks, how harm hides, and how reputations are managed, became personal. This book begins at that hinge: where a life built on competence and trust meets the machinery that can undo both.

Today, settled in Australia, Matthews is a well-known collector and photographer of minerals and runs a food business with his wife. Writing a book was never on his horizon. But horizons move-sometimes quietly, sometimes all at once-and this is the one he found himself compelled to cross.

www.ingramcontent.com/pod-product-compliance
Lightning Source LLC
LaVergne TN
LVHW100245210926
848480LV00003B/831